P9-BTY-455

Belles Lettres

Manuscripts by the Masters of French Literature

Acknowledgments

We would like to thank the following individuals and estates for their kind assistance, both in allowing us to examine the manuscripts published here, and for granting us permission to reproduce the works in this book: Frédéric d'Agay, Annie Angremy, J. Arbier, Françoise Arnaud, Jean-Claude Barat, Pierre Bergé, Jean-Loup Bernanos, Mauricette Berne, Ella Bienenfeld, Thierry Bodin, Gilbert Boudar, Eugénie de Brancovan, Marc Brossollet, Michel Butor, Hélène Cadou, Catherine Camus, Myriam Cendrars, Marie-Claude Char, Andrée Chedid, Bernard and Stéphane Clavreuil, Jean Dérens, Albert Dichy, Brigitte Drieu La Rochelle, Sylvie Durbet-Giono, A. Elkaïm-Sartre, Cécile Éluard-Boaretto, Aube Elléouet-Breton, Odile Faliu, Hélène Favard, Jacques Fraenkel, Marie-Odile Germain, Catherine Gide, Jean-Pierre Giraudoux, Yannick Guillou, Marie-France Ionesco, François Labadens, Sylvia Lorant, Florence de Lussy, Colette Magne, Florence Malraux, Dominique Marny, Jean Mauriac, Jacqueline Pagnol, Mireille Pastoureau, Yves Peyré, Armande Ponge-de Trentinian, Claire Poumès, Maxime Rebière, Dominique Remande, Jean Ristat, Alain Rivière, Olivier Rony, Dominique Roussel, Béatrice Saalburg, André Schmidt, Ursula Vian-Kübler, Sylvie Weil, the Estate of Paul Claudel, the Estate of Marguerite Duras, the Estate of Charles Péguy, the Estate of Saint-John Perse, and the Estate of Georges Schehadé.

We would also like to express our gratitude to the authors of the commentaries: Dominique Marny, Professor Claude Mignot, Alain Brunet, Pierre Chalmin, Paul Desalmand, Professor Bernard Magné, Pierre-Emmanuel Prouvost d'Agostino, Professor Michel Simonin, and Yves Stalloni. We are also most grateful to the publishing houses that have authorized publication of various texts included in the book: © Denoël: Blaise Cendrars (p. 162), Louis Aragon (p. 182). © Éditions de Fallois: Marcel Pagnol (p. 220). © Fayard: Boris Vian (p. 202). © Flammarion: Colette (p. 142), Andrée Chedid (p. 228). © Gallimard: Guillaume Apollinaire (p. 152), Jacques Audiberti (p. 204), Marcel Aymé (p. 178), Albert Camus (p. 198), René Char (p. 200), E. M. Cioran (p. 206), Paul Claudel (p. 140), Jean Cocteau (p. 158), Robert Desnos (p. 166), Pierre Drieu La Rochelle (p. 172), Paul Éluard (p. 214), Eugène Ionesco (p. 208), Max Jacob (p. 162), André Malraux (p. 176), Henry de Montherlant (p. 194), Charles Péguy (p. 148), Francis Ponge (p. 210), Jules Romains (p. 170), Saint-John Perse (p. 190), Antoine de Saint-Exupéry (p. 192), Jean-Paul Sartre (p. 188), Georges Schehadé (p. 218), Simone Weil (p. 186), Marguerite Yourcenar (p. 222). © Grasset: Anna de Noailles (p. 134), François Mauriac (p. 174), Jean Giono (p. 180). © Hachette: Georges Perec (p. 224). © Lachenal and Ritter: André Breton and Philippe Soupault (p. 164). © Mercure de France: André Gide (p. 144). © Éditions de Minuit: Michel Butor (p. 216), Marguerite Duras (p. 226). © Plon: Georges Bernanos (p. 184). © Seghers: René-Guy Cadou (p. 212).

Finally, we would like to thank Jeanne Castoriano and Lucile Jouret of Éditions de La Martinière, who designed and edited the French edition of the book; and in addition, Renaud Bezombes and Sylvie Garrec.

Roselyne de Ayala
Jean-Pierre Guéno

Editor, English-language edition: Elaine Stainton
Design Coordinator, English-language edition: Tina Thompson

Library of Congress Cataloguing-in-Publication Data

Plus beaux manuscrits de la littérature française. English.
Belles lettres : original manuscripts by the masters of French literature / Roselyne de Ayala and Jean-Pierre Guéno ; translated from the French by John Goodman.
p. cm.
Includes bibliographical references and index.
ISBN 0-8109-0617-1 (alk. paper)
1. French literature—Manuscripts—Facsimiles. 2. Manuscripts, French—Facsimiles. I. Ayala, Roselyne de. II. Guéno, Jean-Pierre. III. Goodman, John, 1952 Sept. 19- IV. Title.
PQ1109 .P58513 2001
840.8—dc21 2001002310

Printed and bound in Spain by Artes Gráficas Toledo S.A.U.
D.L. TO: 787 - 2001

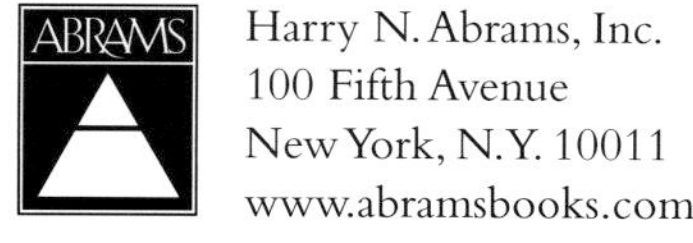

Harry N. Abrams, Inc.
100 Fifth Avenue
New York, N.Y. 10011
www.abramsbooks.com

Belles Lettres

Manuscripts by the Masters of French Literature

ROSELYNE DE AYALA
JEAN-PIERRE GUÉNO

Translated from the French
by John Goodman

Harry N. Abrams., Inc., Publishers

CONTENTS

PREFACE

There is something magical, mysterious, almost sacred about an original manuscript. To touch the very paper that a writer long ago touched, to see the marks of the very pen he or she held—this is a wonderful thing indeed. Sometimes a manuscript is of astonishing antiquity. It seems almost miraculous to see the very parchment on which the poet Charles d'Orléans wrote in the fifteenth century. Can it be possible, today, to recognize a handwriting so ancient? Yes, it is; and the very possibility of that recognition makes the experience of it all the most wonderful. The manuscripts shown in this book—these parchments, these papers, these relics of moments now long gone—still speak to us across the years, as one spirit speaks to another, in any time or place.

In every manuscript that we have chosen to illustrate in this book, we can see the traces of a distinct and noble hand, sense the presence of a now-lost humanity, almost hear the voice of its writer. Thus it is in artefacts like these that the past comes alive once again. For us, searching for these fragments in the libraries and archives of today has been a work of love, like seeking a Holy Grail of the imagination, a Golden Fleece of the heart and mind. In these fragments we can sense the presence of the heroes of our childhood, a glittering treasure of sensation as powerful as knowledge itself. Their goal in writing is much the same as ours in reading: adventure, visions, and dreams. All of us, following in their footsteps, have traveled the world in search of a meaning that is revealed in bits and pieces, but is never whole. For us, the Grail is nothing more than writing itself, fragments that represent humanity's eternal quest for sustenance and meaning.

In the beginning, meaning in words was transmitted invisibly. It was limited to the magic of speech, without which it went unexpressed. Then, some 5,000 years ago, in Mesopotamia, Egypt, and China, people began to combine words and images in an effort to translate the meaning of their divinations, to indicate to posterity that they could communicate with the gods.

Seers and magi became readers, then writers, transmitting memories and traces of the messages and language of the stars. Incised on rocks, inscribed in clay, transcribed onto velum or written with ink on paper, writing was present when humanity first translated the language of the gods into symbols. It was a transcription of sound, an image of words and music. With the advent of ink and graphite, of pen and pencil, writing became a manuscript expression of human knowledge and memory, of the writers' laws, fantasies, and inventions, of their dreams, suffering, and ecstacy. Written texts were copied, elaborated into rich calligraphy, and recopied, with marks responsive to the subtlest inflections of human feeling.

The present book is a celebration of such markings. At a time when writing seems utterly domesticated, and is generally laid out in neat columns by computer, handwritten documents still convey something of the vicissitudes that shape the particulars of human life, love, and creation, shaping in turn the confidences that men and women variously commit to blank pages— their hesitations, revisions, and fits of enthusiasm, their pleasure and sadness—in short, the fitful music of the human soul. These documents tell us that only writing makes us privy to the successive stages of an author's thought and invention, to the gesture of his hand, to his vacillations and second thoughts.

Almost everyone has received and kept handwritten letters, their paper slightly crumpled, their creases becoming more compliant with every successive reading, making it easier to replace them in the envelope on which some loved soul has inscribed an address. Some of these manuscripts that we all cherish are notes from children, written in halting strokes that recall countless penmanship exercises on ruled paper. Others are missives from a dearly loved mother, whose hands prompt countless intimate memories, perhaps with the faint scent of her perfume, or a mannerism of writing redolent of so much about her—the color of her eyes, her profile, her gestures—all suggested by the curving lines of her vowels.

Medieval literary manuscripts speak of the incredible finesse of illuminators of their period, who managed to render complex compositions in minuscule dimensions, and with such control that they survive enlargement to the scale of billboards on the street. Images such as these speak to us all of how writers in the age of doublet and hose drew upon the animal, vegetable, and mineral kingdoms to produce inks and dyes. In them we can see colors made from ground stone, crushed plants, and macerated leather.

The manuscripts in this book will speak of many things. One will recall Blaise Pascal's feverish night of religious mysticism, when, after dating the testimonial account known as the *Mémorial* (which he would carry next to his heart, sewn into his clothing, until the end of his life), the only word he could think of to describe the force of the revelation he had experienced was "Fire." Another, written in tight handwriting, the manuscript of *Dangerous Liaisons*, is terrifying with the force of its vision of depravity. Still another will whisper of the torment of Victor Hugo mourning the death of his daughter "at the hour when the countryside turned white," in a realm where loss imbues the dawn with infinite pain.

Other documents will speak in George Sand's impassioned sentences, lay out Proust's scroll-like addenda, and recall Apollinaire's walks along the Seine. They will reveal the writings of Verlaine, of Zola, of Saint-Exupéry, of Sartre, and Marguerite Yourcenar, and teach us all about the carnal dimension of writing, an electrocardiogram that registers thought in rhythm with the pulse in the writer's fingertips.

These documents will reveal the flash of inspiration in manuscript, a talisman that captures the instant of creation forever. They will also illustrate manuscripts of works in progress, with their successive revisions; final versions; fine copies destined for the printer; autograph copies; rough drafts; notes; hand-corrected proofs.

Texts are rooted in their original manuscripts. This book is not meant to promulgate a literary canon or an academic pantheon, but rather to spur reflection on the following: that, if humanity has spent nearly five million years learning to write, unfurling from remote antiquity to the present day a long scroll of script, these original manuscripts, touched by stardust and Grail-dust that tint its inks and the words that they trace, call forth once more the vibrations, the emotions of human life, language, and culture.

Jean-Pierre Guéno
Roselyne de Ayala

The Romance of the Rose

Guillaume de Lorris, early thirteenth century

A monumental work of more than 28,000 octosyllabic lines, *Le Roman de la Rose* (*The Romance of the Rose*) required two authors and almost a century to complete. A coded narrative of amatory initiation "encompassing the whole of the art of love," it was begun early in the thirteenth century by Guillaume de Lorris. In first adolescence, the narrator dreams that he has entered the Garden of Pleasure and become enamored of a rosebud. Transgressing the counsel of Reason, he resolves to conquer the young Rose, combating Hatred and Jealousy and allying himself with Fair-Welcome. We are here in the realm of full-blown allegory.

The first part of the poem adheres to the conventions of courtly romance: the Rose represents the love of the ideal woman, inaccessible in her garden of frigid allegories; Danger, Wicked-Tongue, and Shame defend Fair-Welcome from the assaults of the lover, who must win the prize he covets through refined strategies. However, in the second part, written by Jean de Meun around 1275, the Rose represents only physical voluptuousness. Lorris's preciosity gives way to a franker realism, idealism to sensuality, exaltation to cynicism. The Rose (whose function as a sexual metaphor could hardly be more explicit) is conquered as Nature triumphs over Spirit, passion over reason.

The Romance of the Rose, which was immensely popular in the Middle Ages, is interesting on two counts that make it unique in French literature: its composition was interrupted by a hiatus of at least fifty years, and it records a significant shift in French mores. Nonetheless, it must be admitted that a contemporary of Guillaume de Lorris, Chrétien de Troyes (see p. 14), wrote more vigorously than he, and that it is Jean de Meun's contribution that guaranteed *The Romance of the Rose* its continuing fame.

Pierre Chalmin

Many a man has wept bitterly
Because dreams and visions are
But vain imaginings and lies,
But I believe that they may truthfully
Forecast the future. And this seems
Clearly and plainly to be so,
Judging by the famous of Scipio,
Of which Macrobius long ago
Wrote the story, and thus affirmed
That dreams may indeed be truthful.
Moreover, if someone thinks
That it is foolish to pay respect to
Visions, since they cannot be proven
True, that man dares to call
Me fool; for I insist that
I fully trust the shadowy warnings
Of night-time, and I believe that dreams
Can tell men of coming good or ill,
Their shadows showing, in darkness
Everything that shall occur
In the clear light of day.

It was in my twentieth year,
When Love demands that all hearts
Pay her what she is due,
That on my bed I lay one night,
Asleep, as was my custom,
When over my spirit fell
A wonderful and pleasant dream,
That filled me with delight.
And nothing that took place in it
Failed to come to pass.
And so now, I, in this my verse
Will tell the story to pass your time,
And cheer your hearts, by Love's command.
Should either man or maid demand
The name of what I write, I say
"It is called—written as it is for lovers—
The Romance of the Rose,
A romance that discloses all of Love's gentle arts.
The subject is good, and fair, and true,
May God grant that is graceful, too.
And as for her for whom it was written,
She is worthy, before all others, I swear
The fragrant name of Rose to bear.

The suns of five years have rolled past,
Since that love-filled month of May
in which I dreamed this dream.
O joyful month, that draws all
Nature to happiness and pleasure;
Bush and tree put on the dress of spring
A dress of leaves that have so long in buds
Reposed, covered from the light of day,
While woods and thickets don their
Splendid coats of green

Translation by E. M. Banks

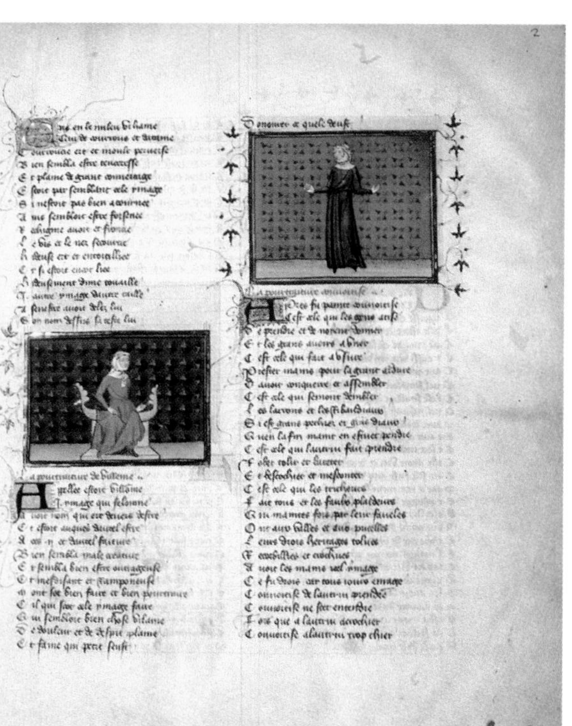

There are some 250 extant manuscripts of *The Romance of the Rose,* more than survive of any other French medieval text, but none of these is an actual work of Guillaume de Lorris's hand. Both of the illustrated examples (left and opposite) are in the Bibliothèque Nationale de France, Paris. Above, a translation of the opening lines.

Dela Mare . 270 . Reg. 6988.2.2.

1.

Lancelot

Ca. 1225

In the borderland between Gaul and Brittany, there were once two kings, who were brothers and had two sisters. One of the two kings was named Ban de Benoic and the other king was named Bohort de Gaunes. King Ban was an old man, and his wife was young and exceedingly beautiful. She was a surpassingly good woman and beloved of all people. She had had but a single child by him, a boy who bore the surname Lancelot, although his baptismal name was Galahad. Further along, the tale will explain the reason why he was called Lancelot, for indeed this is not the place, nor is it the proper time. Instead, the tale will hold to the straight and narrow path and tell that King Ban had a neighbor whose lands bordered on his in the direction of Berry, which at that time was called the Deserted Land.

Around 1180, at the request of his patroness the countess Marie de Champagne, the French poet Chrétien de Troyes wrote a novel in octosyllabic verse, *Le Chevalier à la charrette* (*The Knight of the Cart*). This extended poem devoted to the legend of King Arthur and the knight Lancelot has established Chrétien as the first French novelist. Roughly half a century later, this work inspired another writer, now unknown to us, to write a prose novel entitled *Lancelot du Lac* (*Lancelot of the Lake*). In *The Knight of the Cart,* Lancelot comes to the aid of Queen Guinevere, with whom he has fallen deeply in love, after her abduction by one Méléagant. In order to save Guinevere, whom he has sworn to protect, he must withstand a thousand trials, notably a humiliating ride in a wretched cart set aside for the transport of criminals and driven by a dwarf, the episode that gives the work its title.

The prose novel *Lancelot of the Lake* begins in Lancelot's infancy, with his abduction from the cradle by the Lady of the Lake, who raises him in her underwater castle. It goes on to tell of his arrival at the court of King Arthur, of his being smitten for life—at first sight—with Queen Guinevere, and of his many subsequent adventures and amours. These overlap with those of the other knights of the Round Table, and include Lancelot's quest for the Holy Grail, for which he proves unworthy because of his adulterous love. Eventually, this affair triggers a calamitous series of events that lead to the death of King Arthur and the destruction of his kingdom. The central theme of *Lancelot,* which left its mark on the imagination of the entire late Middle Ages, is the transgression of the code of courtly love by Lancelot's physical consummation of his passion for the queen. Because of this sin, Lancelot can never find the Holy Grail and is humiliated a hundred times during his wanderings in search of it. In choosing the earthly reward of carnality, he betrays the higher love represented by the Grail, and thus loses the personal purity required to find it. Since Lancelot's travels and ordeals were particularly well suited to colorful description in prose, his story played a key role in the crucial transition in French literature from verse to prose narration.

Pierre Chalmin

Opposite: Lancelot manuscript, ca. 1450–1475. Paris, Bibliothèque Nationale de France. Typically, medieval manuscripts of *Lancelot of the Lake* are in a large format with two text columns per page. Above, a translation of the first lines of text on the illustrated page (beginning after the four lines in red).
Right: Illumination (from a different manuscript) picturing the knights of the Round Table.

The Book of the City of Ladies

Christine de Pizan, 1405

Christine de Pizan's career demonstrates that even in periods highly unsympathetic to the achievement of women, a woman of great talent may nonetheless make a name for herself. Left a widow with three young children at twenty-five, Christine is probably the first woman since antiquity to make her living as a professional writer and scholar. In the early years of the fifteenth century, during the bloody civil war between the Armagnacs and the Burgundians, Christine was an international celebrity—which is to say, a European celebrity, for such, in the view of the period, was the extent of the civilized world. Her reputation for learning grew to the point that the Duke of Milan, Galleazzo Sforza, offered her a generous stipend to place her talent at his disposal. However, she refused, preferring to remain in France, where courtly protocols allotted women a high position. There she wrote a noteworthy biography of the late king, Charles V, known as Charles the Wise.

Christine's prose was vigorous and passionate. A satirist, novelist, and gifted with such intelligence that she was fully capable of holding her ground in debate with the most brilliant clerics of her day, she wrote two famous treatises defending women against the accusations leveled against them in *The Romance of the Rose*. Her opponent, Jean de Meun, who had finished that poem, was one of many men who have shown their disdain for women of intellect over the centuries. Jean regarded Christine with frank hostility, writing of her: "[She is] cunning and deceitful . . . because she is a woman"—a strangely one-dimensional reaction to this extraordinary woman.

Pierre-Emmanuel Prouvost d'Agostino

Here begins *The Book of the City of Ladies*, whose first chapter tells why and for what purpose this book was written.

According to my habit and the discipline that rules the course of my life, that is to say, the tireless study of the liberal arts, I sat one day in my study, surrounded by books on many different subjects. My spirit somewhat weary from applying myself in absorbing the learning so many authors, that I looked up from my book, deciding then to leave weighty questions for a moment and to read some poetry for pleasure. In this frame of mind, there fell into my hands a certain small book that did not belong to me, but which had been given to me for safekeeping for a time. When I opened it I saw that its title was *The Lamentations of Mathéole*. I smiled, for I had never seen it before, but I knew that this book had the reputation of saying very good things about women! . . . I thought, therefore, to amuse myself a little by browsing in it. But I had not been reading for very long when my good mother called me to the table, it being already time for supper. Intending to take the book up again the next day, I put it down for the moment. The next morning, returning to my study as was my custom, I did not forget to pursue my decision to read again in the book by Mathéole.

Translation by E. M. Banks

The Book of the City of Ladies was widely read and copied in its day, and indeed, twenty-seven manuscripts survive. The pictured example, which dates from the author's lifetime, boasts three miniatures by a Parisian artist. It belonged to the Duc de Berry, whose signature it bears. Paris, Bibliothèque Nationale de France.

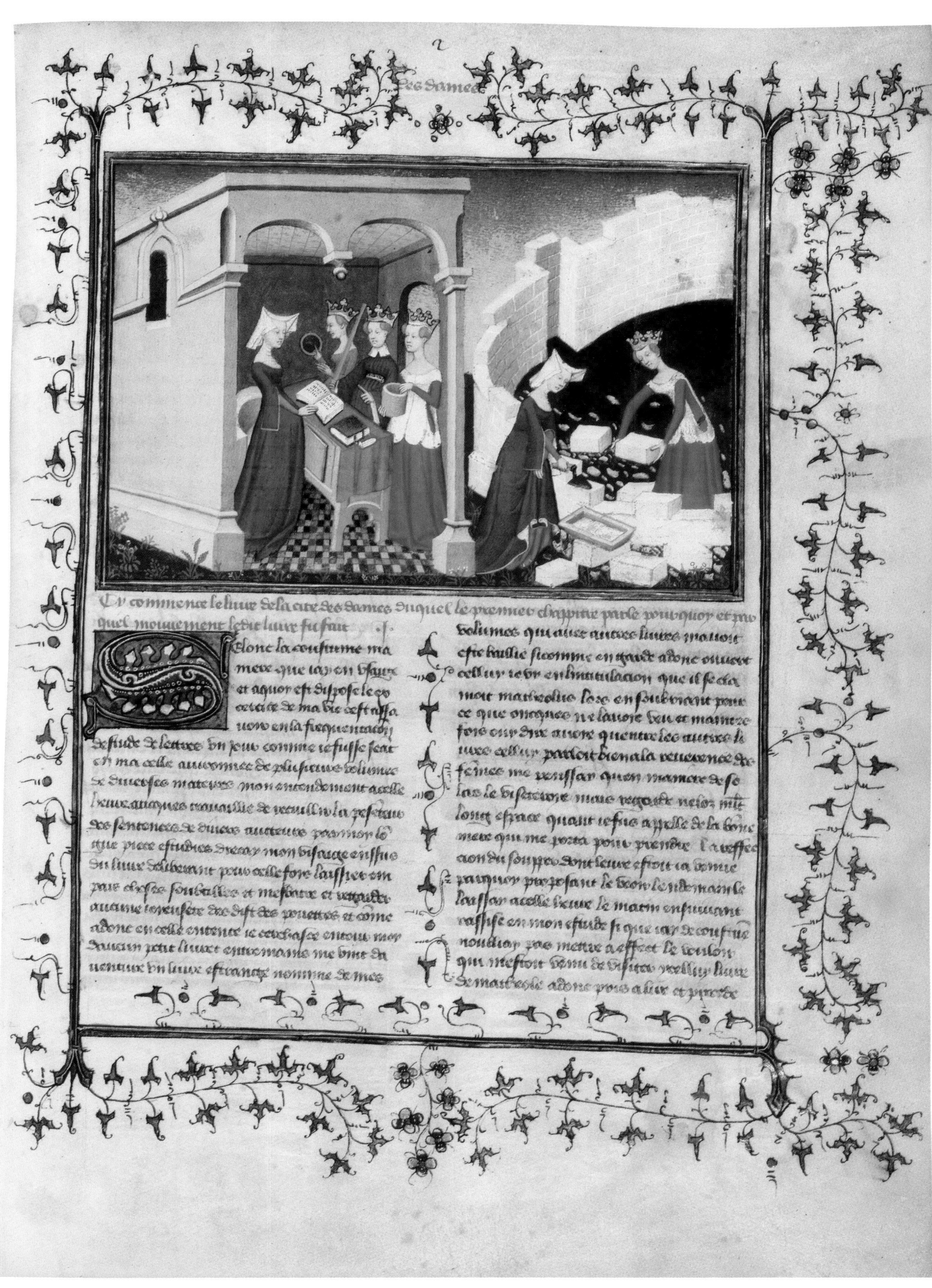

Rondels

Charles d'Orléans, early fifteenth century

The uncle of Charles VI, king of France, Charles d'Orléans at age twenty was taken prisoner at the Battle of Agincourt (1415) by the English, who held him captive for twenty-five years. This was more than enough to incline him toward melancholy. A prince of letters as well as of the blood, he wrote fine poetry even before his exile. During his captivity he continued to write, understandably cultivating an attitude of *nonchaloir,* that is to say, indifference.

In place safe and sound
My heart orders me to stay
And by indifference—
My doctor—be governed.

After returning to France, Charles d'Orléans—whose quarter-century of imprisonment had ruined his life twice-over, both personally and politically—was interested only in women and poetry, which in his case amounted to much the same thing. He spent his remaining twenty-five years composing the *Rondels* that would make him immortal. He gave voice both to the last murmurs of courtly love and to the first clamors of amorous lyricism. Acutely aware of our ultimate subjection to death, and of the consequent vanity of all earthly accomplishment, Charles d'Orléans was attached above all to the fragile instant, to fleeting beauty, to transient impressions. He was that rare creature, a poet simultaneously clear-sighted and cheerful:

First here, then there
Both high and low
More and more
Things come and go.

Five centuries later, the poet Jean Tardieu aptly remarked of him: "I see a man of another age suddenly become young as the day. He consumed, dreamed his life so that he could extract from it a few essential sounds, in other words redirect the course of reason in the world. . . . He was among the first to use the words of the French language to magical ends."

Pierre Chalmin

Rondel 221

Because pleasure is dead
This May I wear black
It is most piteous to see
My heart so ill at ease.

I dress in the only way
That seems fitting
    Because pleasure is dead . . .

The weather brings news
That it shouldn't have
But with its driving rain
Closes the door to the fields.
    Because pleasure is dead . . .

Rondel 222

Heart, who can advise you?
To no one can you reveal
The agonizing displeasure
That keeps you in pain and sorrow.

I hold that nowhere under the sun
Is there more perfect martyr than you.
    Heart, who can advise you? . . .

At least give the appearance
Of burying [your sorrow]
It is but death to languish so
In such unequaled martyrdom!
    Heart, who can advise you? . . .

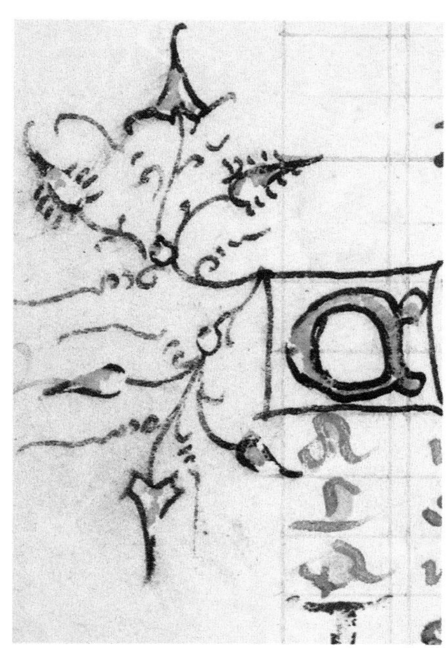

The manuscript of the *Rondels* of which a page is illustrated here—the "album of the court at Blois," a thick, small-format volume whose pages have been cropped—contains, in addition to a core of texts predating 1450, the later poetic production of Charles d'Orléans and his circle. Several additions are due to copyists, but most pages are in a hand clearly recognizable as that of Charles himself. Paris, Bibliothèque Nationale de France.

016.
66

Rondel. 221

Pour ce que Plaisance est morte
Ce may suis vestu de noir
C'est grant pitié de veoir
Mon cueur qui s'en desconforte
Je m'abille de la sorte
Que doy pour faire devoir
Pour ce que &c.
Le temps ces nouvelles porte
Qui ne veult deduit avoir
Mais par force de plouvoir
Fait des champs clore la porte
Pour ce que &c.

Rondel. 222

Avisez a qui prendrez vostre conseil
Quant nul ne povez destourner
Le chaugoisseux desplaisir
Qui vous tient en peine et travail
Le tiers quil na soubz le soleil
Le vostre plus parfait vray martire
Avisez &c.
Au meins faictes vostre appareil
De bien vous faire ensevelir
Ce n'est que mort d'ainsi languir
En tel martire nonpareil
Avisez &c.

Discourse on Joy and Sadness

Pierre de Ronsard, 1576

Pierre de Ronsard made part of his living from the royal purse, in exchange for duties that were not always agreeable to him. Although he was more comfortable writing than speaking, when Henry III asked him to participate in philosophical debates that he was organizing, Ronsard nevertheless acquitted himself well. The result was his *Discourses,* devoted to the relative merits of various intellectual and moral qualities—desire, joy, and sadness. These are certainly not his best work, and we know that he did not take great pride in them, for when he prepared, with considerable care, an edition of his own works, he left these discourses out.

Since he lived in the sixteenth century, Ronsard saw at close hand the fierce and sometimes bloody conflicts between Catholic and Protestant that so strongly marked his time. Having a distinct deference for power, he remained firmly within the Catholic camp, and sometimes scored his points in the battle with considerable spirit. Once, when he learned that his deafness had been attributed by a certain Protestant to his having had syphilis, he responded as follows:

You accuse me, you cockroach, of having had syphilis:
A chaste preacher of deeds and words
Should never make so villainous a remark;
But what does he draw from his sack? What it is full of.
Thieves always think about their plunder,
And libertines talk always of libertinage.
Quiet, impudent runt, [talk about] the Gospel.

But taking part in these conflicts weighed heavily on Ronsard. He excelled at satire, and knew how to write "with a pen of fire on paper of steel," but writing of this sort was not in his true nature, and he said as much after having fulfilled his obligations: "And shall I tell you what I found most tiresome about the unrest? I could not allow my mind free play, nor could I study freely, as I did before."

His real calling, as evidenced by his copious verse production and the meticulous care with which he edited his collected works, was what one critic aptly called his "relentless, hand-to-hand combat with the word."

Paul Desalmand

Sire, this learned company, which it pleases you to honor with your presence, resembles a feast boasting all manner of exquisite and well prepared meats. Arriving last, at the end of the banquet, I can offer you nothing new, unless it be a small sweet by way of dessert. Your ears are sated, dizzied and distracted by so many spiritual meats that offering you more would only bore and irritate you. Thus I will have my say on the matter in a hundred words, seeking only the truth.

Philosophers disagree about the passions, notably about whether they come from the body or from the soul. Pythagorians and Platonists maintain that the soul is itself free of disturbance, but that it is sullied by the contagion of matter and corporeal nature, just as a good man taken in by a wicked host is tainted, shamed, and dirtied by the stains and excrement and vice that he finds in the bad lodging. Of the stain and taint produced in the soul by its proximity to the body, our theologians complain vigorously, saying that the corporeal mass compromises and binds the soul to matter, so much so that the soul can neither contemplate nor return through meditation to its first origin, and even the great Saint Paul says: "I would like to be above these material agitations and disturbances, which are of the body, so as to contemplate God perfectly." Now such questions belong to theologians. . . .

Top left: Anonymous, *Portrait of Pierre de Ronsard,* seventeenth-century (after a bust on the poet's tomb in the church of Saint-Cosme, near Tours). Blois, Musée de Beaux-Arts.
Opposite: Pierre de Ronsard, *Discourse on Joy and Sadness,* page of autograph manuscript. Paris, Bibliothèque Nationale de France.
Below: Portion of a musical setting for Psalm 113, thought to have been translated by Ronsard.

Sire cette docte compaignie qu'il vous plaist
honorer de vostre presence ressemble un festin
garny de toutes sortes de viandes exquises
et bien apprestees mais qui viens le dernier
sur la fin du banquet je ne vous puis apporter
qu'un peu de dragee que je vous presente pour
le dessert [illegible] aux oreilles plaines
[illegible] de tant de viandes
spirituelles que vous en a presté [illegible]
Je prie vos oreilles en faste pour en
peu parler je diray ce qu'il me semble
sans rechercher autre chose que la verité

Les filosofes ne s'accordent pas touchant
les passions si elles procedent sinon du
corps ou de l'ame. Les pytagoriciens et
platoniques [illegible]
asseurent que l'ame n'a point de
perturbations d'elle mesme mais que par
la contagion de la matiere et de la nature
corporee comme du [illegible]
qui est [illegible] homme [illegible] ne se
salit [illegible] et souille par les taches
et ordures qu'il traine de dans le
mauvais logis [illegible]

Les stoiciens au contraire disent que les
perturbations [illegible] de l'opinion et estimation
du bien et du mal present et
de la quelle tache et souillure que l'ame
prend par le voisinage du corps [illegible]

45

Essays

Michel de Montaigne, 1588

"I have taken a road along which I shall continue . . . as long as there is ink and paper in the world" (*Essays*, III, 9). Montaigne, who was born in 1533 and made himself the subject of his writing, from which he has become virtually indistinguishable, could not imagine finishing his *Essays.* Indeed, their creation would be interrupted only by death, which arrived in the autumn of 1592. The day before, he was still making corrections and additions, organizing and reconsidering, in some cases, passages that he had already changed several times. The results sometimes flooded the margins of his copy of the 1588 edition of his work, which he was carefully revising for a new edition. Thanks to the efforts of his friend and adopted daughter, Marie de Gournay, this was published in 1595.

The first edition of the *Essays* had appeared in 1580, issuing from the presses of the provincial publisher Simon Millanges. This small-format, two-volume book—which begins with the lines "Reader, this is a book of good faith"—was intended for his family and personal friends. In it, he offered a written portrait of himself, so that he might continue to live in the memories of those who had known him—and to make it possible for them to compare their view of him with his own. A book of this sort was a complete novelty, and one that soon sparked the interest of a surprisingly wide audience; its readers included not only lovers of literature, but courtiers and military men as well, for the *Essays,* thoughtful as they are, bear the traces of an active and vital public life. Montaigne had served in the army, had been a magistrate in Bordeaux, and at the king's command had twice been mayor of the city.

Montaigne was motivated by two opposing aspirations, one for an active life, the other for a contemplative one. He wisely opted to give each its due according to his humor, and to satisfy what he regarded as his obligations as a gentleman. In the end, however, what most attracted him—more than the sword (which he had wielded during the Wars of Religion)—was diplomacy, the role of negotiator. Montaigne endeavored to broker an agreement that would bring peace in the troubled years at the end of the sixteenth century. The countless hours he spent in pursuit of this goal were not wasted, although their issue was in his writing rather than in the political world. In 1582, newly returned from a trip to Switzerland, Germany, and Italy, after having met the Pope himself (and having been awarded the coveted title "Roman citizen"), he published a second edition of the *Essays.* There remained to him ten years of life, which he divided between service to the king and sporadic writing.

"I want to be seen here in my simple, natural, ordinary fashion," he wrote, and indeed, every line of the *Essays* was an attempt to honor this promise, made by the author in his foreword. Every day, however, Montaigne became more aware of the difficulty of presenting himself "entire and wholly naked." Two obstacles blocked his way: the language he had at his disposal, which was ill suited to his novel enterprise, and the search for his self, his "I." For, while "it is very easy, on solid foundations, to build what one wants" (*Essays,* II, 12), here everything is changeable, "the world is nothing but perpetual motion," including writing, as inconstant as Circe. Everything about it is formidable, like his own thoughts, which Montaigne comes to regard as the "droppings of an old mind."

The result was a many-sided, profoundly human, forever modern book perpetually moving toward truth. As Montaigne wrote: "I don't paint being. I paint transition."

Michel Simonin

Top left: Portrait of Michel de Montaigne, French school, sixteenth century. *Opposite:* A page from "De l'amitié" ("Of Friendship") in the 1588 edition of Montaigne's *Essays,* with extensive additions and revisions in the author's hand. Bordeaux, Bibliothèque Municipal.

If you press me to tell why I loved him, I feel that this cannot be expressed, unless I answer: Because he was he, because I was I.

Beyond all my understanding, beyond what I can say about this in particular, there was I do not know what inexplicable and fateful force that was the mediator of this friendship. We sought each other even before we met, because of the reports we heard of each other, which had more effect on our affection than such reports would reasonably have; I think it was by some ordinance from heaven. We embraced each other when all we were to each other was our names, and at our first meeting, which by chance came at a public celebration and a great gathering of people in the city, we found ourselves so taken with each other, and already so well acquainted, so bound together, that from that time on nothing was so close to us as each other. He wrote an excellent Latin satire, which is published, in which he excuses and explains the precipitancy of our mutual understanding, so quickly grown to its perfection. Having so little time to last, and having begun so late, for we were both grown men, and he a few years older than I, our friendship could not waste time in conforming to the pattern of ordinary friendships, which need so many precautions in the form of long preliminary association. Our friendship has no other model than itself, and can only be compared with itself. It is not one special consideration, nor two, nor three, nor four, nor a thousand; it is I do not know what quintessence of all we bring to it, which, having seized my whole will, led it to plunge and lose itself in his; and which, having seized his whole will, led it to plunge and lose itself in mine, with a kind of hunger, equal on both sides. I say lose, in truth, for neither of us reserved anything for himself, nor was anything either his or mine.

When Laelius, in the presence of the Roman consuls—who, after condemning Tiberius Gracchus, prosecuted all those who had been in his confidence—came to ask Caius Blossius, who was Gracchus's best friend, how much he would have been willing to do for him, he answered: "Everything." "What, everything?" pursued Laelius. "And what if he had commanded you to set fire to our temples?" "He would never have commanded me to do that," replied Blossius. "But what if he had?" Laelius insisted. "I would have obeyed," he replied. If he was such a perfect friend to Gracchus as the histories say, he did not need to offend the consuls by this last bold confession, and he should not have backed away from his own belief in what Gracchus would have truly wanted. But nevertheless, those who say that his answer was seditious do not fully understand, and fail to assume first what is true, that he knew exactly what Gracchus would have wanted, both by his power over him, and by his knowledge of him. These two were friends before they were citizens, friends more than merely friends or enemies of their country or friends of ambition and disturbance. Having committed themselves absolutely to each other, they held completely the reins of each other's inclination; and if you assume that this team was guided by the strength and leadership of reason, as indeed it is quite impossible to harness it without that, Blossius's answer is as it should have been. If their actions went astray, they were to my mind neither friends to each other, nor friends to themselves.

l'autre, d'vn melange si vniuersel, qu'elles effacẽt, & ne retrouuent plus la couture qui les à iointes. Si on me presse de dire pourquoy ie l'aymois, ie sens que cela ne se peut exprimer. Il y à ce semble au delà de tout mõ discours, & de ce que i'en puis dire, ne sçay qu'elle force diuine & fatale mediatrice de cette vnion. Ce n'est pas vne particuliere consideration, ny deux, ny trois, ny quatre, ny mille : c'est ie ne sçay quelle quinte essence de tout ce meslange, qui ayant saisi toute ma volonté, l'amena se plonger & se perdre dans la sienne. Ie dis perdre à la verité, ne luy reseruant rien qui luy fut propre, ny qui fut sien. Quand Lælius en presence des Cõsuls Romains, lesquels apres la condemnation de Tiberius Gracchus, poursuiuoyẽt tous ceux, qui auoyent esté de son intelligẽce, vint à s'enquerir de Caius Blosius (qui estoit le principal de ses amis) cõbien il eut voulu faire pour luy: & qu'il eut respondu, toutes choses. Comment toutes choses, suiuit-il, & quoy s'il t'eut commandé de mettre le feu en nos temples? Il ne me l'eut iamais commandé, replica Blosius. Mais s'il l'eut fait? adiouta Lælius: I'y eusse obey, respondit-il. S'il estoit si parfaictement amy de Gracchus, comme disent les histoires, il n'auoit que faire d'offenser les consuls par cette derniere & hardie confession : & ne se deuoit départir de l'asseurance qu'il auoit de la volonté de Gracchus, de laquelle il se pouuoit respondre, cõme de la sienne. Mais toutefois ceux, qui accusent cette responce comme seditieuse, n'entendent pas bien ce mystere: & ne presupposent pas, comme il est, qu'il tenoit la volonté de Gracchus en sa manche, & par puissance & par connoissance: & qu'ainsi sa respõce ne sonne nõ plus que feroit la miẽne, à qui s'enquerroit à moy de cette façon: si vostre volonté vous commãdoit de tuer vostre fille, la tueriez vous? & que ie l'accordasse: car cela ne porte aucũ tesmoignage de consentemẽt à ce faire, par ce que ie ne suis point en doute de ma volõté, & tout aussi peu

Sonnets

François de Malherbe, 1608

The seventeenth-century poet and critic Nicholas Boileau has left us the following lines:

Finally came Malherbe, who first in France
Gave verse the savor of right cadence:
Taught the power of a word in its place
And compelled the Muse to honor rules.

Introduced to the court of Henry IV by Cardinal Perron, Malherbe was so well liked that he remained in favor after the king's death, when he placed his considerable gifts at the service of the new king, Louis XIII, who made him something approximating an official poet. Producing laudatory verse to mark the reign's great moments, he praised the monarchy for keeping would-be rebels at bay and preserving a glorious peace:

Our families will be showered with every good,
Our harvests will exhaust the sickle
And our fruits surpass the promise of their flowers.

Malherbe's love poetry and didactic verse are quite conventional; his true originality lay precisely in his having renounced inspiration and invention in favor of craftsmanship and formal purity. Dismissing Ronsard's view that "prosaic style is the capital enemy of poetic eloquence," Malherbe cultivated elegance and simplicity, rejecting such artifices as archaisms, inversions, dropped words, newly coined words, hiatuses, and soft rhymes. In their place he introduced a classical rigor and a taste for rules for inspiration to work within. Suspicious of the suave authority and sweet music of his stanzas, posterity has tended to belittle Malherbe's lofty self-regard, so brazenly proclaimed in his "Sonnet for the King":

You can all praise, but not to like degree
Ordinary works last a few years:
Those by Malherbe for eternity.

Pierre Chalmin

Sonnet for the Dauphin and
the Prince d'Orléans

Destiny, I know that you have decreed
The earth's division among my King's two sons
And that after death this miraculous war
Will still be admired by posterity.

That their courage, great like their prosperity,
Will shatter all proud miens like glass:
And that anyone confronting the thunder of
their combat
Will be punished for their temerity.

That an imaginary circle equidistant
From North and South
Will limit their power to like extent.

But being sons of so glorious a father
Pardon me, Destiny, whatever their lot might be
It would be too little, even if each had a world.

Another on a Mistress's Absence

Large and beautiful buildings that will last forever
Superb in their materials, and variously worked
In which the most worthy king in the universe
Makes nature succumb to the miracles of art.
Beautiful park and handsome gardens that,
within your walls
Always offer flowers and verdant shadows,
If not without some demon to prevent winter
From ever erasing the agreeable picture.

Places that instill in hearts so many agreeable
desires,
Woods, fountains, canals, if among your pleasures,
My mood is dour and my face sad.

It is not because you lack charms,
But whatever you have, you do not have Calista
And myself, when I see not her, I see nothing.

Top left: Briot and Jollain, François de Malherbe, Gentleman of the King's Chamber, 1658.
Right: Giovanni Battista di Jacopo, View of the Château de Fontainebleau, fresco, c. 1540. Château de Fontainebleau.
Opposite: Autograph manuscript of two sonnets by Malherbe. Paris, Bibliothèque Nationale de France.

Sonnet Pour mess.rs le Daufin & D'orleans.

Destins, je le cognoys, vous avez arresté
Qu'aux deux fils de mon roy se partage la terre
Et qu'apres le trepas ce miracle de guerre
Soit encor adorable en sa posterité.
Leur courage aussy grand que leur prosperité
Tous les fronts orgueilleux brisera comme verre
Et qui de leurs combats attendra le tonnerre
Aura le chastiment de sa temerité.
Le Cercle imaginé qui de mesme interuale
Du Nort et du Midy les distances egale
De pareille grandeur bornera leur pouuoir
Mais estans fils d'un pere ou tant de gloire abonde
Pardonnez moy Destins, quoy qu'ils puissent auoir
Ce leur sera trop peu, s'ils n'ont chacun vn monde.

Autre sur l'absence d'une maitresse

[illegible] et grands bastimens d'eternelle structure
Superbes de matiere & d'ouurage divers
Ou le plus digne Roy qui soit en l'Vniuers
Aux miracles de l'art fait ceder la nature.
Beau parc & beaux Jardins qui dans vostre closture
Avez tousiours des fleurs & des ombrages vers
Non sans quelque demon qui deffend aux Hyuers
D'en effacer iamais l'agreable peinture.
Lieux qui donnez aux coeurs tant d'aimables desirs
Bois, fontaines, canaux, si parmy vos plaisirs
Mon humeur est chagrine & mon visage triste
Ce n'est pas qu'en effet vous n'ayez des appas
Mais quoy que vous ayez, vous n'avez point Caliste
Et moy je ne voy rien quand je ne la voy pas.

Memoirs

Cardinal de Retz, 1636

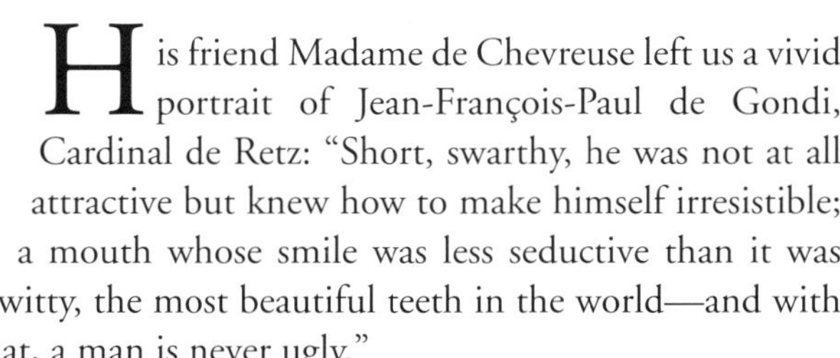

His friend Madame de Chevreuse left us a vivid portrait of Jean-François-Paul de Gondi, Cardinal de Retz: "Short, swarthy, he was not at all attractive but knew how to make himself irresistible; a mouth whose smile was less seductive than it was witty, the most beautiful teeth in the world—and with that, a man is never ugly."

In the civil war of 1648–52 known as the *Fronde* (the sling), the French monarchy was forced to defend its way of life. In Paris, barricades were built in the street by the citizens in a battle against, not the king—Louis XIV, who was still a boy—but his government. A man of the cloth, Retz hitched up his robes and entered the fray, allying himself with the fledgling republican party that went down to glorious defeat. Later, he summed up the adventure in a remark that bespeaks his youth and ambition: "Until then, I had only made small talk with the violins in the pit; finally, I was to assume my role on the stage." Although his grand gamble failed, his memoirs—which are utterly free of resentment—are a dazzling literary testament to a waning glory reluctant to surrender its fire and momentum. Long before Alexandre Dumas made him a central character in *The Three Musketeers,* he described his own actions with sovereign brio. Although this vigorous defender of a lost cause was denied the destiny he so ruthlessly sought to secure, he won a measure of posthumous revenge through his *Memoirs,* which have won him literary immortality.

Pierre-Emmanuel Prouvost d'Agostino

I had blamed, perhaps, a hundred times, speaking with la Rochepot, the Inaction of the Duke of Orléans, and of the Count de Soissons at Amiens. Yet I must own that I found my self just in the same Case; that is, that upon the Point of executing a thing which I had myself renewed the thoughts of in la Rochepot, I felt something within me that might be taken for Fear, tho' I took it only for a Scruple. I am not positive which of the two it was, but 'tis certain that my Imagination brought into my Mind an unpleasant view of the Assassination of a Priest and of a Cardinal. La Rochepot laughed at me for it, saying, "When you are in the Army, you will beat up no Enemy's Quarters, for fear of killing People in their Sleep." This shamed me out of my Reflection: I embraced the Crime which appeared to me consecrated by great Examples, and made justifiable and honorable by the Danger. We concerted our matters together, and came to a Resolution. I engaged in our Enterprise that same Evening Launoy, whom you see now at Court under the Name of Marquis de Piennes. La Rochepot made sure of la Frette, of the Marquis de Boisi, and of l'Etourville, whom he [knew to be in the Duke of Orlean's interest, and incens'd to the last degree at the Cardinal. We prepared all our Matters, and look'd on the Execution as sure. The Danger indeed was great, but we might reasonably enough expect to overcome it, because the Duke's Guards which were within the Place, had certainly taken our part against the Cardinal's, which could be but at the Gate. But Fortune, stronger than his Guards, sav'd him from our Attempt. . . .

Memoirs of the Cardinal de Retz, translated by P. Davall, 4 vols. (London: Jacob Tonson, 1723), vol. 1, pp. 30–31.

Top left: Portrait of Jean-François-Paul de Gondi, Cardinal de Retz (detail), French school, seventeenth century. Blois, Musée des Beaux-Arts.
Right: Episode from the Fronde *(1648–52): Two Knights on Horseback Engage below the Fortifications of the Bastille,* French school, seventeenth century. Châteaux de Versailles et de Trianon.
Opposite: A page from the autograph manuscript of Cardinal de Retz, *Memoirs.* Paris, Bibliothèque Nationale de France.

trompai Mais en fin l'imagination d'un attachat d'un
prebtre d'un Cardinal me
vint a l'esprit, La Rochepot
se moqua de moi et il me
dit ces propres paroles, quand
vous serés a la guerre vous
ne leverés point de quartier
de peur de assasiner des
gents endormis. Cette pensée de
ma reflexion l'embrassai le
crime qui me parut consacré
par de grands exemples justifié
et honnoré par le grand peuple
nous jurames, et nous confir-
masmes notre resolution, l'engageai
dés le soir Sannois qui devoit
venir a la cour sous le
nom de Marquis de Bièvre,
La Rochepot s'asseura de la
frere du Marquis de Boisi
de Sebouville qu'il sça-

Letter to Constantijn Huygens

René Descartes, 1642

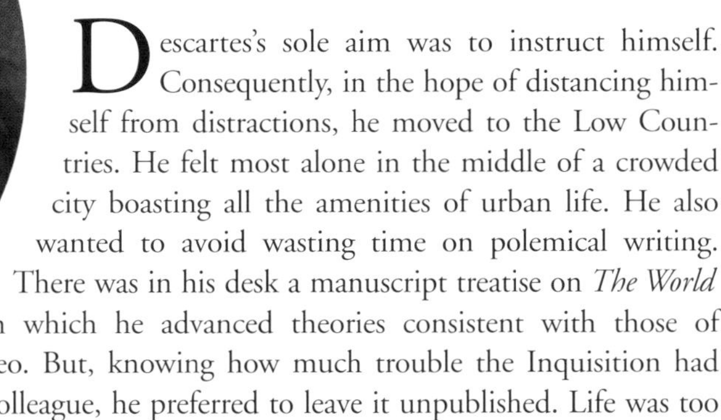

Descartes's sole aim was to instruct himself. Consequently, in the hope of distancing himself from distractions, he moved to the Low Countries. He felt most alone in the middle of a crowded city boasting all the amenities of urban life. He also wanted to avoid wasting time on polemical writing. There was in his desk a manuscript treatise on *The World* in which he advanced theories consistent with those of Galileo. But, knowing how much trouble the Inquisition had caused his colleague, he preferred to leave it unpublished. Life was too short to waste time arguing—to no avail—with ignorant theologians.

Even in his solitude, however, Descartes was not alone, for he maintained a vigorous correspondence. His views were sought on every conceivable subject: the possibility of a universal language, the sound of the flute, mirrors, the weight of metals, beauty, infinity, glass-cutting, echos, ghosts, the fall of bodies, the nature of the soul and of the gland that houses it, the relationship between intelligence and happiness, how fireplaces might be prevented from smoking, etc. He always responded, calmly and politely.

His letters, like those of his eminent contemporaries, were not private documents. They were read in public, copied, discussed, functioning much like today's magazines. Nonetheless, Descartes expressed himself in them more freely than in his published texts. He whose motto was *Larvatus prodeo* ("I advance masked") revealed himself in them. For example, in this letter to Constantijn Huygens (father of Christiaan Huygens, the great natural philosopher and mathematician), in which he admits to a shortcoming that he holds to be widespread: a tendency to believe more readily something that has been proven rationally than a dogmatic position that must be accepted on faith—a view that, to his mind, presented no threat to religion. He regarded natural laws, the rules of mathematical reasoning, and even the operations of human intelligence as divine creations. From which it followed that there was no better way to honor God than to make free use of one's mind.

Paul Desalmand

Monsieur,
I am doubly obliged to you, insofar as neither your affliction, nor the many obligations which I am sure it entails prevented you from thinking of me, or from taking the trouble to send me this book, for I know that you are very fond of those close to you, and that you cannot help but be greatly affected by their loss. I also know that you have a very strong spirit, and that you are familiar with all the remedies that might lessen your pain, but, even so, I cannot prevent myself from telling you about one that I have found to be quite effective, not only in helping me to bear patiently the deaths of those I love, but also in preventing me from fearing my own, despite my being one of those who most love life. It consists in considering the nature of our souls, which I think I know quite clearly must last longer than our bodies, and be born for pleasures and felicities much greater than those available to us in this world, that I cannot conceive anything about those who die, unless it be that they pass to a life that is sweeter and calmer than ours, and that one day we will rejoin them, even with recollection of things past; for I discern in us an intellectual memory that assuredly is independent of the body. And while religion teaches us many things on this subject, nonetheless I admit to a weakness that, it seems to me, is common to most men, namely that, although we may strive to believe, and even think we believe strongly, in everything that religion teaches us, we nonetheless tend to be less convinced of these things than we are of those that we have been persuaded to accept by manifest natural reasons. I am

Monsieur,
Your very humble
and most obedient servant
Descartes
Endegeest, October 10, 1642

Top left: Anonymous, *Portrait of Descartes* (detail), seventeenth century. Toulouse, Musée des Augustins.
Left: Thomas de Keyser, *Portrait of Constantijn Huygens and His Clerk,* 1627. London, The National Gallery.
Opposite: Letter from René Descartes to Constantjin Huygens, October 10, 1642, autograph manuscript. Paris, Bibliothèque Nationale de France.

152

Monsieur

J'ay employay la iournee d'hyer a lire les Dialogues de Mundo que vous m'avez fait la faueur de m'envoyer, mais ie n'y ay remarqué aucun lieu ou ie pense apercevoir que l'autheur eust envie de me contredire, car pour celuy ou il dit qu'on ne sçauroit faire de lunetes d'approche plus parfaites que celles qu'on a desia, il y parle si avantageusement de moy que ie serois de mauuaise humeur si ie le prenois en mauuaise part. Il est vray qu'en plusieurs autres endroits il a des opinions fort differentes des miennes, mais il ne tesmoigne pas qu'il pense a moy, non plus qu'en quelques autres ou il en a aussy qui s'accordent avec ce que i'ay escrit, et ie laisse fort volontiers a vn chascun la liberté que ie desire pour moy, qui est qu'on puisse escrire ingenuement ce qu'on croit estre le plus vray, sans se soucier s'il est conforme ou different des sentimens d'un autre. Je trouue plusieurs choses fort bonnes en son troisiesme Dialogue, mais pour le second ou il a voulu imiter Galilee ie iuge que tout ce qu'il contient est trop subtil pour estre vray, car la nature ne se sert que de moyens qui sont fort simples. Je voudrois qu'il se fist quantité d'ouvrages de cete sorte, car ie croy qu'ils pourroient preparer les esprits a receuoir d'autres opinions que celles de l'Eschole, et ie ne croy pas qu'ils nuisissent aux miennes.

Au reste Monsieur, ie vous suis doublement obligé de ce que, ny vostre affliction, ny la multitude des occupations qui, comme ie voy, l'accompagnent, ne vous ont point empesché de penser a moy, et prendre la peine de m'envoyer ce liure, car ie sçay que vous avez beaucoup d'affection pour vos proches, et que leur perte ne peut manquer de vous estre extremement sensible. Je sçay bien aussy que vous avez l'esprit tres fort, et que vous n'ignorez aucun des remedes qui peuuent servir pour adoucir vostre douleur, mais ie ne sçaurois neanmoins m'abstenir de vous en dire vn que i'ay trouvé tres puissant, non seulement pour me faire supporter patiemment la mort de ceux que i'aymois, mais aussy pour m'empescher de craindre la miene, nonobstant que ie sois du nombre de ceux qui ayment le plus la vie. Il consiste en la consideration de la nature de nos ames, que ie pense connoistre si clairement deuoir durer plus que les cors, et estre nées pour des plaisirs et des felicitez beaucoup plus grandes que celles dont nous iouissons en ce monde, que ie ne puis conceuoir autre chose de ceux qui meurent, sinon qu'ils passent a une vie plus douce et plus tranquille que la nostre, et que nous les irons trouuer quelque iour, mesme avec souuenance du passé, car ie reconnois en nous vne memoire intellectuelle qui est assurement independante du cors. Et quoy que la religion nous enseigne beaucoup de choses sur ce suiet, i'auoue neanmoins en moy vne infirmité qui est ce me semble commune a la plus part des hommes, a sçauoir que quoy que nous vueillions croyre et mesme que nous pensions croyre fort fermement tout ce que la religion nous apprend, nous n'avons pas toutesfois coustume d'en estre si touchez que de ce qui nous est persuadé par des raisons naturelles fort euidentes. Je suis

Monsieur

Vostre treshumble et tresobeissant serviteur
Descartes

D'Endegeest le 10 Oct. 1642

Mémorial

Blaise Pascal, 1654

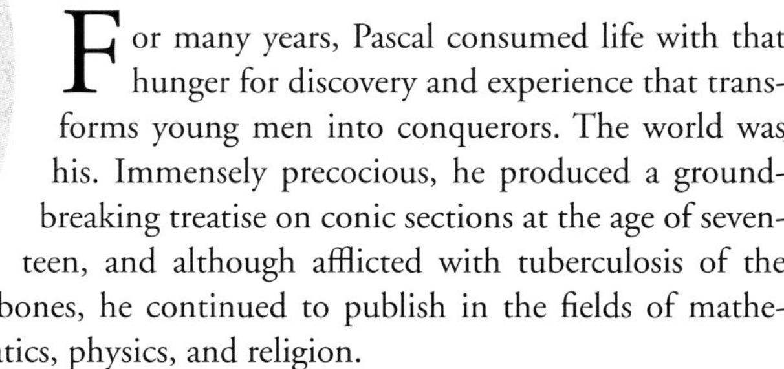

For many years, Pascal consumed life with that hunger for discovery and experience that transforms young men into conquerors. The world was his. Immensely precocious, he produced a groundbreaking treatise on conic sections at the age of seventeen, and although afflicted with tuberculosis of the bones, he continued to publish in the fields of mathematics, physics, and religion.

Between the ages of twenty-eight and thirty-one, perhaps to forget the pain of his father's death, and possibly also to escape his intellectual exertions, he gave himself over to the artificial but immediate pleasures of salon life, to fashionable society and games of chance. Gradually, however, he and his family were drawn to an austere form of Catholicism known as Jansenism. On the night of November 23, 1654, a Monday, he found himself in the grip of a mystic fervor. In less than two hours, the religious conviction that had begun to affect Pascal's thinking invaded his soul with the force of a conflagration and the suddenness of an explosion. So great was the intensity of this experience that he was only able to describe in disjointed sentences.

For the first time in his life, Pascal no longer felt like a conqueror: he gave himself, surrendered himself. Instead of being a source of light, he was now its receptacle. The faith that penetrated him was no longer a matter of hypothesis or hope, something about which one could make a wager. It was a matter of pure certainty.

He had just discovered that God was not the culmination of life but its point of departure. He had, in fact, been reborn. He had but eight years to live. Eight years during which he would write the *Provincial Letters* and *Pensées* (*Thoughts*).

Until his death (August 19, 1662), he kept a copy of this scribbled piece of parchment sewn into the lining of his doublet, as if he needed to keep this precious token of the existence of grace next to his earthly body.

Jean-Pierre Guéno

†
Year of Grace 1654

Monday, November 23, day of Saint Clement, pope and martyr, and of others of the martyrology
Eve of the [day of] Saint Chrysogonus, martyr, and others.
From about ten-thirty in the evening until about twelve-thirty,
Fire.
God of Abraham, God of Isaac, God of Jacob
not that of philosophers and scientists
Certainty. Certainty. Feeling. Joy. Peace.
God of Jesus Christ.
Deum verum et Deum vestrum.
Your God will be my God.
Obliviousness to the world and everything, save God.
He can be found only along the ways taught by the Gospels.
Grandeur of the human soul.
Just father, the world did not know you but I knew you.
Joy, joy, joy, tears of joy.
I was separated from him.
Dereliquerunt me fontem aquae vivae.
My God, will you leave me?
May I not be separated from him for eternity.
For this is eternal life, which can become known to you only through the true God and through he who was sent by you, Jesus Christ.
Jesus Christ.
Jesus Christ.
I have been separated from him. I fled him, renounced him, crucified him.
May I never be separated from him.
He can be retained only by the ways taught by the Gospels:
Total and sweet renunciation.
Total submission to Jesus Christ and to my [spiritual] director.
Eternal joy for one day's exercises on earth.
Non obliviscar sermones tuos. Amen.

Top left: Jean Domat, *Blaise Pascal* (detail), drawing in red chalk fixed to the front cover of a 1583 edition of Justinian's *Corpus Juris Civilis*. Paris, Bibliothèque Nationale de France.
Right and Opposite: Autograph of Pascal's *Mémorial,* which he had sewn into his clothing. Paris, Bibliothèque Nationale de France.

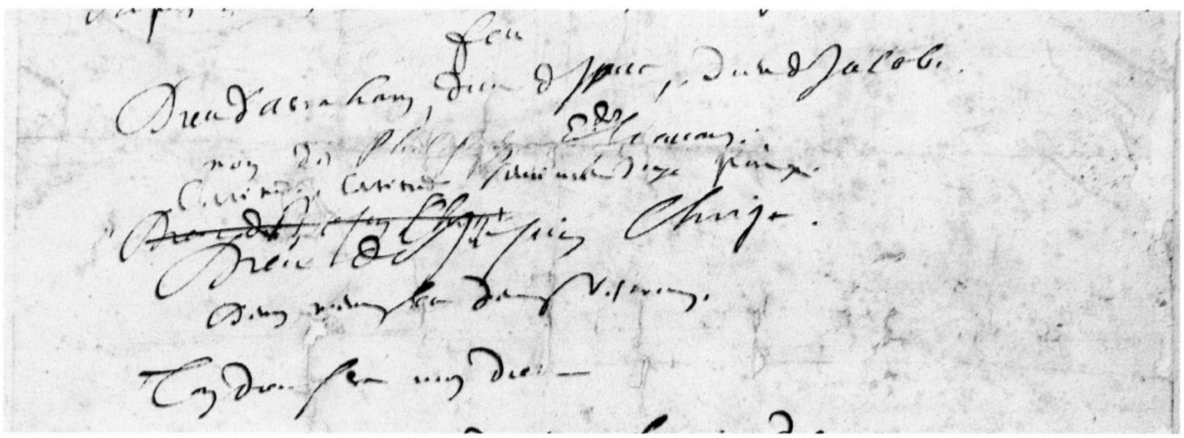

1

D

+

L'an de grace 1654

Lundy 23 novembre jour de St Clement pape et martir et autres au martirologe.

veille de St Chrysogone martir et autres.

Depuis environ dix heures et demi du soir jusques environ minuit et demi

Feu

Dieu d'Abraham, Dieu d'Isaac, Dieu de Jacob.

non des philosophes et des savans.

Certitude certitude sentiment joye paix.

Dieu de Jesus Christ.

Deum meum et Deum vestrum.

Ton Dieu sera mon Dieu.

Oubly du monde et de tout hormis Dieu.

Il ne se trouve que par les voyes enseignées dans l'Evangile.

Grandeur de l'ame humaine.

Pere juste le monde ne t'a point connu, mais je t'ay connu.

Joye joye joye pleurs de joye.

Je m'en suis separé.

Dereliquerunt me fontem aquae vivae

Mon Dieu me quitterez vous

Que je n'en sois pas separé eternellement.

Cette est la vie eternelle qu'ils te connoissent seul vray Dieu et celuy que tu as envoyé J.C.

Jesus Christ.

Jesus Christ.

Je m'en suis separé je l'ay fuy renoncé crucifié

Que je n'en sois jamais separé.

Il ne se conserve que par les voyes enseignées dans l'Evangile.

Renonciation totale et douce.

3

The Little Billiards Table

Jean de La Fontaine, 1660

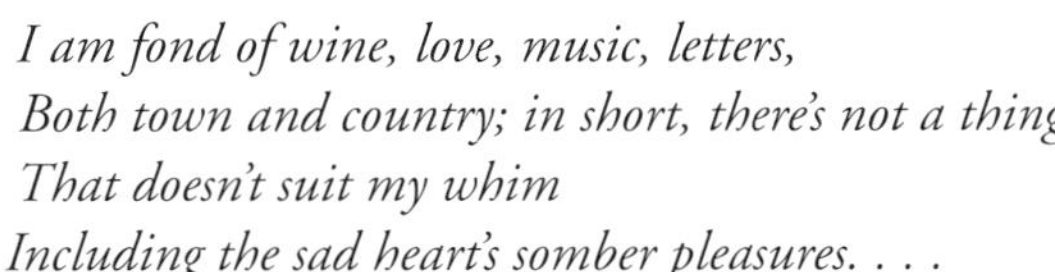

I am fond of wine, love, music, letters,
Both town and country; in short, there's not a thing
That doesn't suit my whim
Including the sad heart's somber pleasures. . . .

In these words La Fontaine, known best as a writer of fables, described himself. This Molière of the barnyard, who cast his shrewd observations of human affairs as a carnival of animals, wrote poetry that flows as smoothly as a natural spring. His seemingly artless words, however, were in fact carefully contrived and meticulously worked. Jean de La Fontaine was a perfectionist, an author determined to mask the immense effort he lavished on his productions behind a surface of nonchalant elegance.

An ambiguous figure, this very official Overseer of Forests and Waterways studied nature without feeling obliged to impose on it the geometric regularity so admired in his day. A friend of the landscape architect André Le Nôtre, he loved the baroque paradise of Le Nôtre's early garden at the château of Vaux-le-Vicomte, but had reservations about the horticultural absolutism that his friend later designed for Versailles. La Fontaine was a libertine, and thus wary of controlled pleasures and official festivities. He was a key member of the brilliant creative team assembled by Nicolas Fouquet, Louis XIV's ambitious treasury minister who was imprisoned for embezzlement. After Fouquet's disgrace and the king's appropriation of the group's services for himself and his own self-aggrandizing purposes, La Fontaine assumed a more marginal role. His discomfort with this turn of events can be seen in *Psyche,* a libretto commissioned to celebrate the beauty of Versailles' gardens and park. A digressive verdant labyrinth, it offers not the expected panegyrics but rather a text more consistent with La Fontaine's own predilections: an erotic mythological narrative punctuated by philosophical debates.

Possessed of a fantastical imagination, a cultivator of friendship and the muses who preferred solitude to the intrigues of the court, La Fontaine was, notwithstanding his ties to classical literature, a harbinger of the pre-romantic voluptuary excesses of the late eighteenth century; neither melancholy, nor misanthropy, nor revery were unfamiliar to him. A moralist, he was also a subtle analyst of the soul. An Epicurean, he perhaps loved love more than he did women, and knew and gave voice to the bittersweet regrets of a sensitive heart.

Pierre-Emmanuel Prouvost d'Agostino

For Madame de Coulanges:
To Madame de La Fayette,
On Sending Her a Small Billiards Table

This billiards table is small: don't value it any the less.
I have it by reliable witnesses
That Venus had such a one
Made for her son.
This pleasure occupied the Cupids and Laughs
Indeed the whole population of Cythera.
I can easily compare this distraction
To the pretty game of love,
And give billiards an allegorical meaning:
The goal is a proud heart, the balls are poor lovers;
The wicket and cues are the means whereby
To attain with despatch the object of one's love.
The pockets are so many perilous detours
Into which we fall, due to
Dangerous moves or, often, of our own will.
And sometimes, through cleverness or stratagem,
A rival manages to throw us there.
But the comparison "clangs," as they say:
It is but a conceit
Unworthy of your genius.
What then can I say to please you, Urania?
Pomp and Friendship are, as we know,
Divinities inclined to liberality;
It is no small matter to distinguish between their gifts:
Friendship gives few, Pomp many more,
Especially in the eyes of the vulgar.
You assess such superfluous gifts differently;
My billiards table is succinct, my note hardly.
So I will add to my long discourse
Only this, which comes from a sincere heart:
I love you, love me always.

De la fontaine

Left: Anonymous, *Portrait of the Comtesse de La Fayette,* French school, seventeenth century. Private collection. *Right:* Antoine Trouvain, *Louis XIV Playing Billiards.* The game was quite popular in the seventeenth century. Châteaux de Versailles et de Trianon. *Top left:* Hyacinth Rigaud, *Portrait of Jean de La Fontaine* (detail). Paris, Musée Carnavalet. *Opposite:* Opening lines of "To Madame de La Fayette, On Sending Her a Small Billiards Table," as copied by La Fontaine for Madame de Coulanges. A rare document, for few of La Fontaine's autograph manuscripts survive.

Pour Madame de Coulanges,
A Madame de la Fayete,
En luy envoyant un petit billard.

Ce billard est petit, ne l'en prisez pas moins.
Je prouveray par bons témoins
qu'autrefois Vénus en fit faire
Un tout semblable pour son fils.
Ce plaisir occupoit les Amours, et les Ris,
Tout le peuple enfin de Cythere.
Au joli jeu d'aymer je pourrois aisément
Comparer apres tout ce divertissement;
Et donner au billard un sens allégorique.
Le but est un coeur fier; la bille un pauvre amant;
La passe et les billards c'est ce que l'on pratique
Pour toucher au plustost l'objet de son amour;
Les belouzes ce sont maint périlleux détour,
Force pas dangereux ou souvent de soy mesme
On s'en va le précipiter;
Et souvent un rival s'en vient nous y jetter
Par adresse et par stratageme.
Toute comparaison cloche ~~en~~ ce que l'on dit.
Celle cy n'est qu'un jeu d'esprit
Au dessous de vostre génie:

Letter to the Abbé de Pure

Pierre Corneille, 1660

On August 25, 1660, when Pierre Corneille wrote this letter to the Abbé de Pure, he was fifty-four. Nearing the end of work on the first complete edition of his plays, he told his correspondent about the three discourses on poetic drama that he had just written for it. One of them is a consideration of the theory of the three dramatic unities first expounded by Aristotle (unity of time, place, and action), a subject of intense interest at the time, and one about which he held controversial views. He respected these Aristotelian rules "in his fashion," an approach that sometimes got him into trouble with the Académie Française, guardian of French traditional culture. Indeed, he himself described his opinions "about the principal points of the art" as "heretical." Despite the Baroque trappings of Corneille's theater, the central themes of his work are the tragic dilemmas of human life, rather than the pedantic theories expounded by critics in his century. Despite its archaic language, his work remains surprisingly contemporary.

This ostensibly "level-headed bourgeois" was in fact something of a subversive. And he remained astonishingly prolific; during the last twenty years of his life he wrote eleven plays, notably *Agésilas* and *Suréna.* The first of these heralds the triumph of the mercantile over the aristocratic ethos; the latter is a virtual staging of the defeat of Corneille's characteristic hero.

Corneille's prototypical hero—often mistakenly reduced to a stiff classical stereotype—is, first of all, Corneille himself: a torn figure who was simultaneously honored as the prince of contemporary dramatists, but one who was nevertheless regarded in the aristocratic society of his day as a pariah. He was also a rebel in search of power, if one who invariably ended by admitting his own powerlessness: he sometimes prevailed over others, even over himself, but he never managed to tame his nature, which even the imposition of extreme rigor proved unable to transform. Like Icarus, Corneille's archetypal hero seeks first to escape the limits of the human condition, then to dominate the world. We know how this old story is always fated to end. . . .

Jean-Pierre Guéno

To Monsieur the Abbé de Pure
Rouen, August 25, 1660

[. . . I am coming to the end of a demanding task concerning a delicate subject. In three discourses, I consider the principal] questions of the art of poetry for the three volumes of my plays. I propose some new readings of Aristotle and advance a few ideas and maxims unknown to our ancients. I refute those on which the Académie based its condemnation of *Le Cid* and I differ with Monsieur d'Aubignac, despite the good things he says about me. When they appear, I have no doubt they will occasion criticism; defend me a little. My first discourse considers whether the aim of dramatic poetry is utility or pleasure, the uses to which it can properly be put and their parts, whether integral, like subject matter and mores, or quantitative, for example prologue, episode, and exode. In the second, I discuss the conditions that determine whether a subject is fit for tragedy, the qualities that its constituent incidents and its characters must have to excite pity and fear, how this pity and fear can purge the passions, and how to treat things so they seem credible and inevitable. In the third I talk about the three unities, those of action, time, and place, and of how, after them, there is little of real importance to mull over, that what's left is mere embellishment such as can be added by rhetoric, morality, and politics. Thinking I would do nothing but thank you, I find I have given you an account of my intentions. They took me longer to write than I could have managed in my spare time. You will find they contain little in the way of lofty elocution or high doctrine, but, even so, I confess that these three discourses cost me more dearly than three plays would have. I forgot to tell you that all of my modern examples come from my own work, and that, although I indeed sometimes take issue with Monsieur d'Aubignac and the members of the Académie, I never name them and always discuss them as if they had never had anything to say about me. I also examine each of my plays, and do not spare myself. So prepare yourself to be one of my protectors, and know that I will always be

Monsieur
Your very humble and very obedient servant
Corneille

Top left: After Charles Le Brun, *Portrait of Pierre Corneille* (detail). Châteaux de Versailles et de Trianon. *Right:* Abraham Bosse, *A Tennis Court Used as a Theater,* 1630. Paris, Bibliothèque Nationale de France. *Opposite:* Letter from Pierre de Corneille to the Abbé de Pure (end), autograph manuscript. Paris, Bibliothèque Nationale de France.

158

questions de l'art poetique sur mes trois volumes de comedies. J'y ay fait quelques explications nouvelles d'Aristote, et avancé quelques propositions, et quelques maximes inconnues a nos anciens. J'y refute celles sur lesquelles l'Academie a fondé la condamnation du Cid, et ne suis pas d'accord avec Mr d'Aubignac de tout le bien mesme qu'il a dit de moy. Quand cela paroistra, ie ne doute point qu'il ne donne matiere aux critiques, prenez un peu ma protection. Ma premiere preface examine si l'utilité ou le plaisir est le but de la poesie dramatique, de quelles utilités elle est capable, et quelles sont les parties, tant integrales comme le sujet et les moeurs, que de quantité comme le prologue, l'episode et l'exode. Dans la seconde ie traite des conditions du sujet de la belle tragedie, de quelles qualités doivent estre les incidents qui la composent et les personnes qu'on y introduit afin d'exciter la pitié et la crainte, comment se fait la purgation des passions par cette pitié et cette crainte, et des moyens de traiter les choses selon le vraysemblable ou le necessaire. Je parle en la troisiesme des trois unités, d'action, de iour et de lieu. Et je croy qu'apres cela, il n'y a plus guere de questions d'importance a remuer et que ce qui reste n'est que la broderie qu'y peuvent adiouster la rhetorique, la morale et la politique. En me pensant vous faire qu'un remerciment, ie vous ay insensiblement conté mes desseins. L'execution en demandoit un plus long estude que mon loisir ne m'a permis, vous n'y trouverez pas grande erudition ni grande doctrine, mais avec tout cela, i'advoue que ces trois prefaces m'ont plus cousté que n'auroient fait trois pieces de theatre. J'oubliois a vous dire que ie ne prens d'exemples modernes que de moy, et bien que ie contredise quelquefois Mr d'Aubignac et Mrs de l'Academie ie ne les nomme iamais, et ne parle non plus d'eux que s'ils n'avoient point parlé de moy. J'y fais aussi un examen de chacun de mes poemes en particulier, ou ie ne m'espargne pas. Derechef preparez vous a estre mon protecteur et croyez que ie suis tousjours

Monsieur

vostre tres humble et tres obeissant serviteur

Corneille

Iphigenia in Taurus

Jean Racine, 1674

The purest verse in all of French literature issued from prose sketches such as this one. They resemble Versailles under construction, an architect's working drawings: songs still being hammered out, but whose grand lines, perspective views, and axial compositions can already be discerned. Racine had little interest in contriving *coups de théâtre,* nor did he use the baroque *deus ex machina,* with its magical resolution of all earthly problems. Strict moralist that he was, he let crime be crime and wickedness retain its darkness, making them burn in the hell of the footlights. He abandoned man to his nature, and nature to its disorder. The order that triumphs is that of destiny: Racine is the man of the elided anecdote, of action unfolding as slowly as the passage of the royal train. The bloodstains of passion, the shadows of shame, despair, and crime remain buried in his characters' souls, finding expression only through carefully wrought verse. Passion is made as rigorously geometrical as a French classical garden. Here, the protocols of shattered hearts resemble those of the court whose treacherous undercurrents are revealed to us by Saint-Simon.

"After Racine, nothing," asserted the twentieth-century writer Georges Bernanos. Yet how unorthodox is the religion of this theater! Racine, alert to sensuality and violence, found it difficult to believe in the exemplarity of Man. In one of Nero's speeches in *Britannicus,* the tragic monsters of Sade seem to stir; and in his unfinished *Iphigenia in Taurus* we see the emergence of a new anti-heroine. In his earlier play, *Iphigenia,* which deals with the Mycenaean princess's escape from being sacrificed by her father's hand through the intervention of the goddess Artemis, she was only a near-victim. In this work, Racine would have given us a more compelling figure: a haughty, solitary priestess with few illusions.

Pierre-Emmanuel Prouvost d'Agostino

Act I, scene I

Iphigenia enters with a captive Greek woman, who is astonished by her distress. She asks if it is caused by the Festival of Diana's taking place with the sacrifice of a male foreigner. "Ask yourself," says Iphigenia, "whether that is a sentiment worthy of Agamemnon's daughter. You know with what loathing I prepared the miserable creatures that have been sacrificed since I have presided over these cruel ceremonies. I was overjoyed that Fortune had sent me no Greek for this day, and I alone gloated over the pain common to the rest of the island, where the lack of victims for this feast is held to be a bad omen. But I cannot resist the secret sadness that has preoccupied me since the dream I had last night. I thought I was in my father's house at Mycenae, my father and mother seemed to be swimming in blood, and I myself held a dagger in my hand to cut the throat of my brother Orestes. Alas, my dear Orestes!"

Top left: Posthumous portrait of Jean Racine (detail) by his eldest son, Jean-Baptiste Racine, ink, after 1714. Private collection.
Right: Jean Jouvenet, *The Sacrifice of Iphigenia,* 1685. Troyes, Musée des Beaux-Arts.
Far right: Jean-Auguste Dominique Ingres, *Studies for the Apotheosis of Homer: Profile of Raphael; Hands of Apelles, Raphael, and Racine.* c. 1827. Paris, Musée du Louvre.

Acte 1.er Scene 1. 95.

Iphigenie vient auec vne captiue Grecque, qui s'estonne de sa tristesse. Elle demande si c'est qu'elle est affligée de ce que la feste de Diane se passera sans qu'on luy immole aucun estranger. Tu peus croire dit Iphigenie si c'est la vn sentiment digne de la fille d'Agamemnon. Tu sçais auec quelle repugnance j'ay preparé les miserables que l'on a sacrifiez depuis que je preside a ces cruelles ceremonies. Je me faisois vne joye de ce que la Fortune n'auoit amené aucun Grec pour cette journeé, et je triomphois seule de la douleur commune qui est respandüe dans cette Isle, ou l'on conte pour vn presage funeste de ce que nous manquons de victimes pour cette feste. Mais je ne puis resister a la secrette tristesse dont je suis occupée depuis le songe que j'ay fait cette nuit. J'ay crû que j'estois a Mycene dans la Maison de mon Pere, il m'a semblé que mon Pere et ma Mere nageoient dans le sang, et que moy mesme je tenois vn poignard a la main pour en esgorger mon frere Oreste. Helas mon cher Oreste! Mais Madame vous estes trop esloignez l'vn de l'autre pour craindre.

Letter to Madame de Grignan

Marquise de Sévigné, 1684

Marie de Rabutin-Chantal, marquise de Sévigné, loved her daughter Madame de Grignan with an affection that, if encountered in life rather than literature, would strike us as among the worst examples of sentimental cannibalism. She had given birth to this child, and, being a devoted mother, showered the girl with kisses, made her afraid of solitude, fed her natural sense of disquietude, and yet reassured her affectionately, all to make sure that her daughter would always return to her.

The marquise, an intellectual lady, was beautiful enough to have dreamed, at one point, of supplanting the mistress of the king. Her youth was carefree, but when the civil war known as the Fronde erupted in 1648, striking a blow at the foundations of French absolutism, the refined world to which she belonged did not know how to react. Snubbing Versailles, this highly ambitious married woman resolved that, instead of risking the Sun King's displeasure, she would confine her literary efforts to correspondence, to distinctly private letters in which she would track closely the climactic changes in her own heart.

A keen observer of herself, she possessed sufficient inner nobility to transcend her time; heedless of the failing light, she revealed herself candidly in her prose. Proust would adore this worldly woman who made a work of futility, of insouciance, with a seriousness that initially is difficult to discern, and whose elegant tone is that of a lost era, one in which everything could be expressed, thanks to the paradoxical freedom afforded by the constraining, innately pure French of her day.

Pierre-Emmanuel Prouvost d'Agostino

Saumur, Monday evening, September 18 [1684]

Ever an adverse wind, my sweet one, since I left you; so strong does it blow against me that everything must be done with oars. It obliged me to remain a day longer than I had planned, and I won't arrive in Angers until tomorrow, which will be exactly eight days after my departure; I think that I'll find my son there. I will write to you from that fine city. Tomorrow, before I leave, I will see my niece de Bussy, whose convent supervisors barked at me for not yet having visited her. The beauty of the countryside has been my sole amusement. We spent fourteen or fifteen hours, our good friend and I, in this carriage, which amused us; my carriage is fitted out differently than it was the last time. We look forward to our dinner as something important in our day. We have warm meals; our terrines cede nothing to those of Monsieur de Coulanges. I did some reading but was distracted, and studied the decor instead of continuing to apply myself to stories about others; that will right itself, if it please God. Imagine, my darling, that I am always writing to you; surely I bore you with this boring account of my sad trip, and it has been eight days since I received word from you. Every day our schedule has been disturbed, but I hope to receive something tomorrow in Angers. I look forward to it very much; you can well imagine this, my dearest, and how, having been obliged to think of you constantly, I couldn't help revisiting all my reasons for loving you, and your own tenderness, and likewise how my own is ever warm and constantly renewed. Providence has ordained it so: we have had no society. There is much that one could say about the pleasures and hindrances that it would bring. Our very good friend is content and in perfect health, as am I; he embraces you. Remember me to all your family. And your health, my dear, is it good? Tomorrow I will learn all about that, and about your trip to Versailles. We both embrace you.

Top left: Claude Lefèbvre, *Portrait of Madame de Sévigné* (detail). Paris, Musée Carnavalet.
Left: Madame de Sévigné's desk. Private collection.
Right: Pierre Mignard (after), *Portrait of the Comtesse de Grignan.* Private collection.
Opposite: Letter from Madame de Sévigné to the Marquise de Grignan, autograph manuscript. Paris, Bibliothèque Nationale de France.

Le Lenvoyeur recit de mon triste voyage et
depuis huit jours je nay pu recevoir un seul
mot de vous, toutes nos sources ont esté
derangees, mais jespere den recevoir demain
a angers, jen ay une extreme envie vous le
croyes bien ma tres chere bonne, et nayant
esté contrainte de penser sans lettre a vous, je
nay pas manqué de repasser sur tous les sujets
que jay de vous aymer, et des preuves de
votre tendresse, et quoique la mienne est
toute chaude, et toute renouvelee, la providence
la ainsy ordonné, toutefois cela nous a manqué
il y aurait bien des choses a dire sur le plaisir, ou
la contrainte quon en recevroit, notre tres bon
bon est content de sa parfaite santé, et moy aussy
et vous embrasse, parles de moy a toute votre famille

The Adventures of Telemachus

Fénelon, ca. 1694

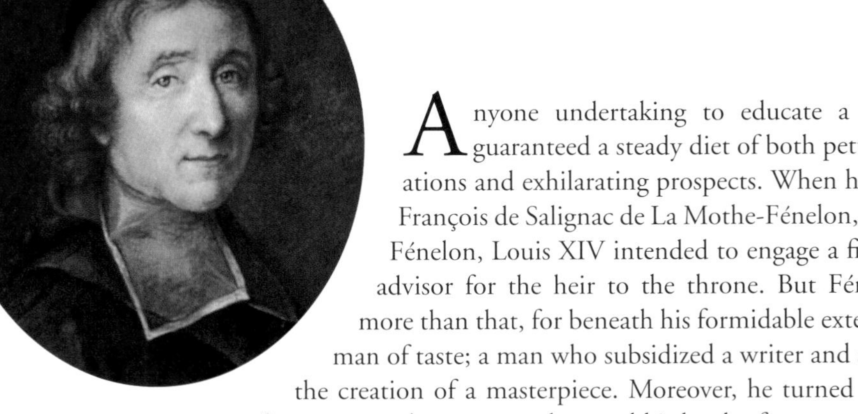

Anyone undertaking to educate a prince is guaranteed a steady diet of both petty humiliations and exhilarating prospects. When he engaged François de Salignac de La Mothe-Fénelon, known as Fénelon, Louis XIV intended to engage a fit spiritual advisor for the heir to the throne. But Fénelon was more than that, for beneath his formidable exterior was a man of taste; a man who subsidized a writer and sponsored the creation of a masterpiece. Moreover, he turned out to be as fine a poet as he was a teacher, and his book of poetry won him a place in posterity. Versailles was an academy of courtly strategy whose protocols would have been as inscrutable to a novice as advanced algebra. Thanks to two great diarists, Saint-Simon and the Princess Palatine, we are reasonably well-informed about what was happening behind the scenes: these two had their biases, to be sure, but their frank, front-line accounts of court intrigue are all the more valuable for that, and are far more revealing than the stilted productions of the reign's official historians.

The court at which Fénelon, known as the "swan of Cambrai," taught the dauphin was not characterized by the *politesse* and exquisite delights later celebrated by Talleyrand. But the swan knew how to bite: below his graceful exterior, which fooled only dreamers and innocents, there resided a man of forceful character. While the celebrated preacher Bossuet spoke from the pulpit, Fénelon contented himself with giving astute lessons in good sense to a boy whose future responsibilities were likely to be burdensome. Such straightforward lessons may seem amusingly obvious, but they are among the strong points of a classicism whose aims La Fontaine expressed succinctly at the beginning of his *Fables*:

To instruct without displeasing
And while instructing, entertain.

Pierre-Emmanuel Prouvost d'Agostino

He applied himself, with great diligence, to revive commerce, which had long languished by a gradual decline: in matters of great importance, he took the advice of Narbal, yet did not submit implicitly to his direction; in every instance, he made the administration of government his own act, and took cognizance of all things with his own eye: he heard every one's opinion, and then determined according to his own; he is, consequently, the idol of his people; and, by possessing their affections, he is master of more wealth than the cruel avarice of his father could ever hoard; for there is not a man in his dominions that would not freely part with his whole property, if, upon a pressing necessity, he should require it of him: what he leaves his people, therefore, is more effectually his own, than it would be if he took it away. All precautions for the security of his person are unnecessary; for he is continually surrounded by the surest guard, the affections of his subjects: there is not a subject in his kingdom who does not dread the loss of his prince as a calamity to himself....

Translation by John Hawkesworth, as revised by G. Gregory: Fénelon, *The Adventures of Telemachus, the Son of Ulysses*, 2 volumes (London: John Manson, 1797), vol. 1, pp. 137–38.

L'Abbé de Fenelon

Top left: Anonymous, *Portrait of François de Salignac de La Mothe-Fénelon* (detail), painted on vellum and placed at the head of the autograph manuscript of *Les Aventures de Télémaque*. Paris, Bibliothèque Nationale de France.
Right: Jean Raoux, *Telemachus Recounting His Adventures to Calypso*, oil on canvas. Paris, Musée du Louvre.
Opposite: Page from the autograph manuscript of *Les Aventures de Télémaque*. Paris, Bibliothèque Nationale de France.

faire refleurir le commerce qui languissoit tous les jours de plus en plus. il a pris les conseils de Narbal pour les principales affaires. ^et n'est pourtant point gouverné par lui, car il veut tout voir par lui même, il écoute tous les differents avis qu'on veut lui donner, et decide ensuitte sur ce qui lui paroît le meilleur il est aimé des peuples. en possedant les coeurs il possede plus de thresors que son pere n'en avoit amassé par son avarice cruelle, car il n'y a aucune famille qui ne lui donnât tout ce qu'elle a de bien, s'il se trouvoit dans une pressante necessité. ~~il n'a~~ aussi ce qu'il leur laisse est plus a lui, que s'il le leur otoit. il n'a pas besoin de se precautionner pour la sureté de sa vie, car ~~il n'y a aucun~~ il ~~est~~ toujours autour de lui ~~garde de~~ la plus sure garde qui est l'amour des peuples. il n'y a aucun de ses sujets qui ne craigne de le perdre, et qui ne hazardât sa propre vie pour conserver celle d'un si bon Roi. il vit heureux, et tout son peuple est heureux avec lui. il craint de charger trop ses peuples. ses peuples craignent de ne lui offrir pas ~~une~~ une assez ~~de~~ grande partie de leurs biens. il les laisse dans l'abondance, et cette abondance [...] rend ni indociles ni insolents. [...] sont laborieux, addonnez au commerce

Memoirs

The Duc de Saint-Simon, 1697

Louis de Roucroy, duc de Saint-Simon was born into privilege, and after having seen his cherished ambition for a position at court frustrated, awoke one morning more embittered than a discharged valet. Saint-Simon wrote with a poison pen. This noble of Old France, piqued at seeing the old virtues woven into coarse fabric and—with the power of royal mistresses—the scepter become a distaff, decided to vindicate his name through writing; if he could not have the honor he coveted, then he would vent his indignation on the page. Powerless to effect reform, he bore witness to the things that filled him with contempt.

Saint-Simon was a lay preacher who ascended the pulpit, took aim at the meanness of the "Great Century," and decades before the Revolution, stigmatized the aristocracy whose heads would one day roll. He railed against a Versailles that, like Babylon, was doomed to crumble into dust. In a sense, reactionaries always fix their sights on the future, seeing in the present only the seeds of impending decline, firmly believing that the worst will surely come to pass. Saint-Simon does not predict; he laments and accuses.

He takes sad stock of the imminent demise of his own class; if he exaggerates, that is because he must do so in order to reveal the truth. In his *Memoirs*, the duke, a modern student of Suetonius, delivers the goods on the great; it's as if he were observing them through the lorgnette of the *oeil-de-boeuf* (bull's eye), the small round window in the coving of the anteroom of the king's ceremonial bedchamber. One imagines him offering beautiful marquises sugared almonds laced with pepper. Every star has its hidden side, about which astronomers can only speculate. Saint-Simon actually visited that of the Sun King, from whose overweening magnificence he was able to extract some dark lessons.

Pierre-Emmanuel Prouvost d'Agostino

But as regards the place of lady-in-waiting to Madame la Duchesse de Chartres, little sought, and by people with whom Monsieur le Duc had no reason to wish to burden himself, he could not refuse Madame de Montespan, however ill disposed they might be towards one another, nor Madame la Duchesse de Chartres, with whom he was then living on intimate terms, nor disregard his own concern for people whose marriage he had arranged, and who found in it only what he had made of it, and had avoided taking an interest in something of such concern to them and which cost him nothing. Thus he obtained this place from the king and Madame de Maintenon, without whose support such posts were unobtainable, and was so good as to send for him in Languedoc, where Monsieur and Madame de Castries and Cardinal Bonsy then were, before they can have known that the post was open. They remained in their residence a bit longer to conclude their affairs, then came to settle permanently at the Court.

Madame de Castries was a diminutive woman, a kind of botched porcelain figurine, extremely short but quite solid, and could have passed through a middling ring, having neither behind, nor breast, nor chin; quite ugly, always seeming in pain and startled; and withal, features bursting with spirit and that were even more articulate. She knew everything: history, philosophy, mathematics, ancient languages, but it always seemed as though she knew nothing save how to speak French; but she spoke it with precision, energy, eloquence, and grace, even about the most ordinary things; with that turn of phrase unique to Mortemart. Amiable, amusing, gay, serious, all things to all people, charming when she wanted to please, droll, but naturally and with great finesse, without trying to be, and striking blows against the ridiculous such as they could never forget; vainglorious, shocked by a thousand things with a plaintive tone that captured the attention, cruelly vicious when it suited her, and a very good friend, usually polite, gracious, and obliging, without gallantry, but delicate of mind and generous of spirit when it pleased her; withal, a gift for storytelling that charmed, and, when she wanted to improvise a story on-the-spot, an astonishing source of production, variety, and delight. With her vainglory, she thought she had married well because of her friendly regard for her husband; she made allowances whenever his interests were in question, and she was just as vain of him as she was of herself. In return, she received the like from him, and all manner of consideration and respect . . .

Top left: Perrine Viger Durigneau, *Portrait of Saint-Simon* (detail), second half of the nineteenth century. Châteaux de Versailles et de Trianon.
Left: Arnoult, details of three eighteenth-century prints, from the series *Life at Versailles under Louis XIV*, illustrating games popular at Court: *dames*, billiards, and dice.
Opposite: A page from the autograph manuscript of Saint-Simon's *Mémoirs*. Paris, Bibliothèque Nationale de France.

n'avoit aucune raison de s'embarrasser, il ne put refuser a Me de Montespan quoyque peu cordialem^t qu'ils fussent ensemble, a
Me la Duch. de Chartres avec qui il vivoit alors intimem^t, et sa propre pudeur pour des gens dont il avoit fait le mariage,
et qui n'avoient trouvé en luy rien moins de ce qu'il l'avoit fait faire, de s'interesser pour eux en chose si fort a leur convenance
et qui ne luy coustoit rien. il obtint donc cette place du Roy et de Me de Maintenon, sans laquelle ces sortes d'emplois ne se
~~donnoient~~ s'accordoient point, et se donna le merite de la mander en Languedoc a M. et Me de Castries et le Card. Bonzi, avant
qu'ils pussent scavoir que ce poste estoit a remplir. ils demeurerent encore quelque temps chez eux a achever leurs affaires,
et puis vinrent s'establir pour toujours a la Cour. Me de Castries estoit un quart de femme, une espece de biscuit manqué,
extremem^t petitte mais bien prise, et auroit passé dans un mediocre anneau. ny derriere ny gorge ny menton, fort
laide, l'air toujours en peine et estonné, avec cela une phisionomie qui eclattoit d'esprit et qui tenoit encore plus
parole. elle scavoit tout. histoire philosophie mathematiques langues scavantes, et jamais il ne paroissoit
qu'elle sceut mieux que parler françois, mais son parler avoit une justesse une energie une eloquence une grace
jusques dans les choses les plus communes, avec ce tour unique qui n'est propre qu'aux Mortemarts. aimable amusante
gaye serieuse toutte a tous charmante quand elle vouloit plaire, plaisante naturellem^t avec la d^re finesse
sans la vouloir estre, et assenant aussy les ridicules a ne les jamais oublier. glorieuse, choquée de mil choses avec
un ton plaintif qui emportoit la piece, cruellem^t meschante quand il luy plaisoit, et fort bonne amie. polie
gracieuse obligeante en g^l sans aucune galanterie, mais delicate sur l'esprit amoureuse de l'esprit ou elle le
trouvoit a son gré. avec cela un talent de raconter qui charmoit, et quand elle vouloit faire un roman sur le
champ, une source de production de varieté et d'agrement qui estonnoit. avec sa gloire elle se croyoit bien mariée
par l'amitié qu'elle eut pour son mari. elle l'estendit sur tout ce qui luy apartenoit, et elle estoit aussy glorieuse pour luy que pour elle
elle en receut le reciproque en toutes sortes d'egards et de respects

1697

Me de Jussac auprés de Me la Duch. de Chartres

On ajousta bientost apres une nouvelle ~~personne~~ a la suitte mais interieure de Me la Duch. de Chartres, mais
sans aller a Marly ny paroistre avec elle en public hors de son apartem^t, sinon en des voyages, ou en des choses
familieres. ce fut Me de Jussac qui avoit esté sa gouvernante, et qui s'en attira la plus constante confiance.
elle s'appelloit St Just, et avoit esté longtemps aupres de Me de Montespan avec l'estime de Me de Maintenon.
... les ... de la p^re feme de mon pere, qui par confiance la donnerent a ma soeur quand elle espousa le Duc de Brissac
... elle entra chez Me de Montespan qui aprés les brouilleries domestiques qui ne tarderent pas, l'en detacherent ... jusqu'a son mariage avec M le Duc de Chartres. son
mari aupres de Mlle de Blois dont elle fut gouvernante jusqu'a son mariage ... de Fleurus en 1690. c'estoit une g^de feme de bonne mine
mari fut tué escuyer de M le Duc du Maine a la bat. de Fleurus en 1690. ... elle estoit d'une mediocre bonne, mais sage avisée,
et qui avoit esté fort agreable, toujours parf^t vertueuse. elle estoit d'une ... toujours en sa place, et qui avec la
qui connoissoit fort le monde et les gens, vraye et droitte, polie respectueuse, toujours en sa place, et qui avec la
confiance et l'amitié intime de Me la Duch. de Chartres et de Me de Montespan, et depuis avec assez de confiance
de Me de Maintenon, ne voyoit rien a l'aveugle, discernoit tout, et scavoit toujours se bien demesler sans flatterie et
sans fausseté, et sans rien perdre avec elles. elle s'estoit aussy attiré une vraye consideration et des amis ~~considerables~~ distingués
a la Cour quand elle y fut mise, et toujours sans sortir de son estat, ny oublier avec eux ce qu'elle y avoit esté. il est
tres singulier qu'avec tres peu de bien, elle maria ses deux filles a deux freres, Mrs d'Armentieres et de Conflans
qui n'avoient rien, et que ce soit ces deux mariages qui les ayent remis au monde et le ch. de Conflans leur 3e
frere, et qui les aient tiré de la poussiere ou l'indigence faisoit languir cette ancienne Maison depuis si longtemps

Mort de Bignon Cons^r d'Estat et de son frere Pr Presid. du grand Conseil dont Vertamont son gendre a la place

Je perdis au com^t de cette année M Bignon Cons^r d'Estat si ami de mon pere qu'il voulut bien estre mon
tuteur, quoyque sans aucune parenté, lorsqu'a la mort de Me la Duch. de Brissac en 1684 elle me fit son legataire
universel. c'estoit un Magistrat de l'ancienne roche pour le scavoir l'integrité la vertu la modestie, digne du
nom qu'il portoit si connu dans la robe et dans la Republique des lettres, et qui en ses peres avoit esté Avocat G^l.
il avoit esté beaucoup ... de Pontchartrain qu'il avoit toujours extremem^t aimée,
avec g^de reputation. il estoit veuf de la soeur unique de Pontchartrain ... et avoit 80 ans ... a qui je
et qui fit de ses enfans ... des siens. Bignon n'estoit point riche, et avoit ... son frere qui estoit P^r P^t du g^d
le regrettay beaucoup, et je ne faisois rien dans mes affaires qu'avec son conseil. son frere ... celuy la estoit riche par un mariage. il n'avoit
Conseil et qui en avoit fermé cette charge, le suivit 8 jours apres. celuy la estoit riche par un mariage. il n'avoit
qu'une fille mariée a Vertamont Me des Req^tes fils du p^re de la Mse d'Estrades, qui eut sa charge. la place
de ~~...~~ l'autre dans le Conseil des parties fut donnée a Caumartin proche parent et ami particulier de

Caumartin Cons^r d'Estat

Pontchartrain, qui s'en servoit tres principalem^t dans l'administration des finances dont il estoit l'un
des Intendants. c'estoit un g^d hom beau tres bien fait, fort capable dans son mestier de robe et de finances,
qui scavoit tout en histoires, en genealogies, en anecdottes de cour, avec une memoire qui n'oublioit rien
de ce qu'il avoit veu ou leu jusqu'a en citer les pages sur le champ dans la conversation. il estoit fort du
g^d monde avec beaucoup d'esprit, et il estoit obligeant et au fond honneste hom. mais sa figure la
confiance de Pontchartrain et la cour l'avoient gasté, il estoit glorieux quoyque respectueux, avoit
tous les g^ds airs qu'ils faisoient ouvriquer, et haïr outre de ceux qui ne le connoissoient pas, et un
... il portoit sous son manteau ... la fatuité que le Mal de Villeroy estalloit sous son baudrier.
* ... on s'en moqua ... une singularité de personne ... Les Intend. des finances qui

Gaigne sa pretension de sa datte d'Intendant des Finances sur les Cons^rs d'Estat posterieurs

il pretendit une seance qui forma un procés que je raporteray tout de suitte. Les Intend. des finances qui
ne sont pas Cons^rs d'Estat entrent en manteau court au Conseil des parties, et ont seance du jour de
leurs provisions d'Intend^ts des finances, et la conservent au dessus des Cons^rs d'Estat qui ne le deviennent
que depuis que les Intend^ts des finances ont achepté leurs charges. sur ce fondem^t Caumartin devenu Cons^r
d'Estat pretendit preceder ceux la par ce qu'il les avoit toujours precedés. Eux pretendoient que les Intend^ts
des finances qui n'estoient point Cons^rs d'Estat n'estoient point du Conseil quoyqu'avec seance et voix, a
en donnoient pour preuve qu'ils n'y estoient ny cou Me des Req^tes, ny cou Cons^r d'Estat, dont ils ne portoient pas
ny l'une ny l'autre robe, et concluoient que leur seance et voix n'estant que d'honneur pour decorer leurs charges,
et ne les incorporant point dans le Conseil, ils en devoient prendre la queue quand a proprem^t parler ils
venoient a y entrer cou membres, en estre faits Cons^r d'Estat, dont alors seulem^t ils revestoient la robe
et quittoient le manteau. la chose portoit directem^t sur Phelypeaux frere de Pontchartrain, qui se trouvoit
le p^r et le plus ancien des Cons^rs d'Estat faits depuis que Caumartin estoit Int. des finances. Pontchartrain

The Inheritance

Marivaux, 1736

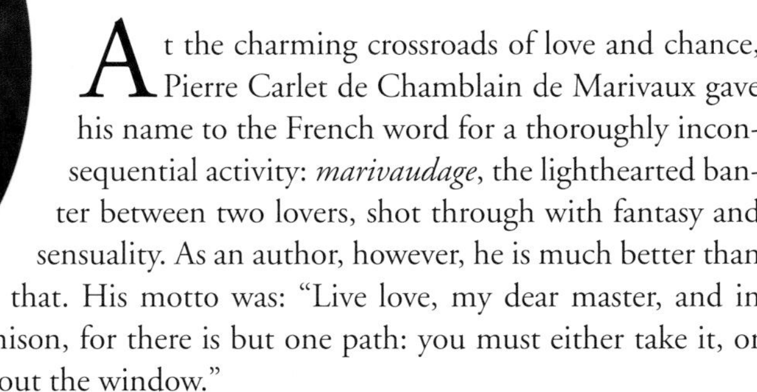

At the charming crossroads of love and chance, Pierre Carlet de Chamblain de Marivaux gave his name to the French word for a thoroughly inconsequential activity: *marivaudage*, the lighthearted banter between two lovers, shot through with fantasy and sensuality. As an author, however, he is much better than that. His motto was: "Live love, my dear master, and in unison, for there is but one path: you must either take it, or jump out the window."

Jules Renard remarked: "In any play by Marivaux, there are only about fifty words that don't seem to have been written in our own time." It is the principal subject of his theater that gives it its contemporaneity: the story of instantaneous passion; of the struggle to overcome all obstacles blocking its consummation; of false confidences and surprise developments—narrative devices martialed to confirm the fundamental truth that "all pleasures are diminished by their gratification."

Marivaux was a Romantic before Romanticism. He tells us that when he was seventeen and smitten, he saw something that made a great impression on him: the young woman who was the object of his desire standing in front of a mirror, testing the expressions she intended to use on him. Marivaux staged his beautiful amorous epiphanies as a means of cultivating his nostalgia for a world prior to such studied manipulation. In his hands, we embark for Cythera as in a painting by Watteau. All the soaring lightness of a century in which revolution was unimaginable is present in his work. The masters love their wives, and the valets the chambermaids; the erotic audacity ceases when it brushes up against hallowed social conventions. Marivaux was trying to determine whether "men or women offered the best example of infidelity," surely an exercise doomed to delicious failure.

Pierre Chalmin

Top left: Louis-Michel Van Loo, *Portrait of Marivaux* (detail), 1753. Paris, Comédie Française.
Right: Characters from Marivaux's plays, original watercolor by Maxime Rebière.
Opposite: Page from a manuscript of Marivaux' *Le Legs* (The Inheritance): not an autograph but a copy made ca. 1750, with many cuts indicated for a performance at the private theater of the Comte de Clermont at Berny. Paris, Bibliothèque de l'Arsenal.

COUNTESS: Me, have contempt for the most natural thing in the world? That would not be reasonable: I have nothing against love. What I object to is the general run of lovers, not the feeling itself, which is quite respectable, permissible, and involuntary. It's the sweetest feeling there is; how could I hate it? Not at all; and there are certain men I would forgive for loving me, if they admitted it to me with the candor that I just praised in you.

MARQUIS: You mean, when one says it openly, as one feels it. . . .

COUNTESS: Then there's no problem; one hasn't done anything wrong. There: that's what I think. I don't have the soul of a savage.

MARQUIS: It would be a great pity if you did. You're in such wonderful health!

COUNTESS: (aside) As if he were thinking about my health! (out loud) It's the fresh country air.

MARQUIS: City air affects you the same way: the most vivacious eyes, the freshest of complexions!

COUNTESS: I feel quite well, thank you; but do you know you're complimenting me without realizing it?

MARQUIS: Why, I'm quite aware of it.

COUNTESS: Keep your compliments for the one you love.

MARQUIS: Ah! And if you were that person, I'd have no reason to hold them back.

COUNTESS: What if it were me? Am I the one? Are you declaring your love to me?

MARQUIS: Oh! Not at all!

COUNTESS: Ah! Then why this talk of my complexion, my health? Who's fooling who?

MARQUIS: It's only a manner of speaking: I'm just saying that it's a shame you don't want to love anyone, or remarry, that I'm mortified by it, because I don't know of any woman who'd be better suited to it than you are. But I won't say anything more about it, for fear of annoying you.

COUNTESS: Yet again, you speak to me of love, without a doubt. You're in love with me; you've just said so expressly.

MARQUIS: Well, yes, if you were the one, you needn't get angry about it. Now surely everything's lost! Calm down, pretend I didn't say anything.

pas une ame sauvage.

vous avés la plus belle santé.

(a part)
il est bien question de ma santé. (haut) c'est l'air de la campagne.

le teint le plus frais!

je me porte assés bien. mais savés vous bien que vous me dites des douceurs sans y penser?

moy, j'y pense.

gardés les pour la personne que vous aimés

il n'y auroit que faire de les garder.

comment! si c'etoit moy? est ce de moy dont il s'agit? est ce une declaration d'amour que vous me faites?

~~oh! point du tout~~. ~~mais quand ce seroit vous~~?
rien dit.

eh! de quoy vous avisés vous donc de m'entretenir de mon teint, de ma santé? qui est ce qui ne s'y tromperoit pas?

de peur de vous deplaire.

mais, encore une fois, vous me parles d'amour je ne me trompe pas: c'est moy que vous aimés; vous me le dites en termes exprès.

The Spirit of Laws

Montesquieu, 1748

Montesquieu seems like a Renaissance flower blossoming in the eighteenth century: a ferocious appetite for knowledge, admiration for the ancients, skepticism about dogma, critical spirit replacing the principle of authority, love for life, a refusal of transcendence, and thus a secularized approach to explaining the world. He is the very model of a humanist for whom man is the measure of all things.

In *The Spirit of Laws*, Montesquieu laid the groundwork for sociology, applying rational explanation to a domain that even Descartes had forbidden himself. He did not invent this approach; he was preceded by a number of thinkers, including Aristotle. Nonetheless, his book was indeed a new beginning.

Our democracies, which are based, to the extent possible, on the separation and balance of powers, are children of his thought. He understood very early that ideas can kill, and that good government requires a sense of relativism.

Like Montaigne, a kindred spirit, he had a sense of humor, as well as its inevitable companion, a subversive mind. His prose was meant for those able to read between the lines. The great principle is that of eliding intermediary ideas. This can lead to wonderfully incisive formulations, for example: "The lovers of the woman one loves are always idiots."

The author of *The Spirit of Laws* was also a thinker of singular pertinence to one of the great problems of our own time: how to reconcile a commitment to human rights with a respect for other cultures. In effect, he holds that there are a few universal principles that transcend cultural difference.

Montesquieu is an archetypal humanist because of his inflexible rejection of the superhuman and his conviction that, in the political realm, everything must be based on an inviolable respect for the individual.

Paul Desalmand

Chapter I
Of laws in their relation to various beings

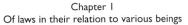

Laws, in the broadest sense, are necessary relations that derive from the nature of things, and in this sense all beings have their laws: divinity has its laws ("The law," says Plutarch in *On the Moral Education of Princes*, "is queen of all, mortal and immortal"), the material world has its laws, animals have their laws, man has his laws.

Those who have said that blind fate produces all the efforts we see in the world have uttered a great absurdity; for what could be more absurd than a blind fate producing intelligent beings?

There is, then, a primitive reason, and laws are both the relations that exist between it and different beings, and the relations of different beings amongst themselves.

Secondat de Montesquieu

Top left: Anonymous, *Portrait of Montesquieu*, eighteenth century. Versailles, Musée National du Château.
Left: Red leather writing case, eighteenth century. Bayonne, Musée Bonnat.
Opposite: Two pages from a copy of an early draft of *The Spirit of Laws*, with autograph additions. Paris, Bibliothèque Nationale de France.

2

Chapitre 1.

Des Loix dans le raport qu'elles ont avec les divers êtres.

Les Loix dans leur Signification la plus étendue Sont les raports necessaires qui derivent de la nature des choses, et dans ce Sens tous les êtres ont leurs Loix, la Divinité + a ses Loix, le monde materiel a ses Loix, les Intelligences Superieures

+ la loy, dit Plutarque, est la Reine de tous mortels et immortels au traité qu'il est requis qu'un prince soit Scavant

a l'homme ont leurs Loix, les bêtes ont leurs loix, l'homme a ses loix.

Ceux qui ont dit qu'une fatalité aveugle a produit tous les effets que nous voions dans le monde, ont dit une grande absurdité, car quelle plus grande absurdité qu'une fatalité aveugle qui auroit produit des êtres intelligens.

Il y a donc une raison primitive et les Loix Sont les raports qui se trouvent entre elle, et les differens êtres et les raports de ces divers êtres entre eux.

The Nun

Denis Diderot, 1760

Diderot took his pleasures very seriously. Blessed with many gifts, he was supremely equipped to savor the social and intellectual delights of pre-Revolutionary Paris. But behind the disguises needed to flourish in this redoubt of pleasure and wit, he always remained himself, holding forth, joking, and making love without ulterior motives, as if dusting off his collar.

Atheism suited him very well, for it allowed him to adore the daughters of Eve without accountability to God the Father. He was a libertine, but only insofar as it allowed him to enjoy women without loving them. He was a moralist, but not to an extent that would limit his sex life. Less ideological than Rousseau, more epicurean than Voltaire, he bedded philosophy, bringing it down from the pedestal on which it was dying of stony boredom. He never wrote a line whose hook failed to catch an idea. An angler for sin, he expected vices to nibble at his bait.

Nonetheless, he died working. There wasn't a lazy bone in his body. Curious about everything and fooled by nothing, an agreeable voyeur, he exposed the indiscreet jewels of a period in which the rustle of crumpled silk, the tinkling ivories of a harpsichord, obscured dark currents that would issue in the work of de Sade. Diderot was too much the hedonist to become a martyr, too obliging a confessor to seem altogether Catholic.

Pierre-Emmanuel Prouvost d'Agostino

Top left: Louis-Michel Van Loo, *Portrait of Diderot* (detail), 1767. Paris, Musée du Louvre.
Right: Fleury-François Richard, *Gallery in a Convent.* Lyon, Musée des Beaux-Arts.
Opposite: Page from the autograph manuscript of *La Religieuse* (*The Nun*). Paris, Bibliothèque Nationale de France.

I order you to flee your mother superior, to refuse her caresses vigorously, to never find yourself alone in her rooms, to close your door to her, especially at night, to leave your bed, if she enters your room despite you, to go into the hall, to call out if need be, to go completely nude as far as the altar, to fill the house with your cries, to do everything that a love of God, a fear of crime, the holiness of your state, and interest in your health might inspire in you, if Satan himself appeared to you and pursued you. Yes, my child: Satan. It is from this angle that I must make you see your mother superior. She is deep in the abyss of crime; she is trying to draw you into it, and you might already be there with her, if your very innocence had not terrified her and stopped her." Then, raising his eyes heavenwards, he cried: "My god! Continue to protect this child . . . Repeat with me: *Satana, vade retro, apage, Satana,* If this unfortunate woman interrogates you, tell her everything. Repeat to her what I've said. Tell her that it would have been better if she had never been born, or for her to cast herself alone into hell by a violent death."

—"But, my father," I answered him, "you just heard her confession yourself."

He said nothing in reply; but heaving a deep sigh, he placed his hands against the walls of the confessional and rested his head on his arms like a man in great pain. For a time he remained thus. I didn't know what to think. My knees were shaking. I was in such distress, such turmoil, as can scarcely be conceived: like a traveler walking in the dark between cliffs that he cannot see, and who hears voices calling out to him on all sides: "You're done for!" Then, looking at me calmly but tenderly, he said to me: "Are you in good health?"

—"Yes, my father."

—"You wouldn't be too inconvenienced by passing a night without sleeping?"

—"No, my father."

—"Well then!" he said to me. "You won't sleep tonight. Immediately after the evening meal, you will enter the church. You will prostrate yourself before the altar; you will pray all night. You don't realize what danger you were in. You will thank God for having kept you safe; and tomorrow you will take communion with all the nuns. As penance, I ask only that you avoid your mother superior and reject her poisoned caresses. Go. Myself, I will join my prayers to yours. How concerned I will be for you! I realize all the consequences of the advice I give you; but I must counsel you thus, for both our sakes. God is master and there is but one law."

My memory of what he said, Monsieur, is very unclear. Now, comparing his words as I have just recounted them to you and the terrifying impression he made on me, I find they don't match; but that's because it is rambling and disjointed, lacking many things [that I don't remember, as I didn't associate them with any distinct ideas.]

et l'ennemi de votre salut, vous inspiroit; c'est satan en personne qui
parloit à vous et vous poursuivoit. oui, mon enfant, satan. c'est sous cet
aspect que je suis contraint de vous montrer votre supérieure. elle est enfoncée
dans l'abîme du crime; elle cherche à vous y plonger, et vous y seriez déjà
peut-être avec elle, si votre innocence même ne l'avoit remplie de terreur et
ne l'avoit arrêtée. puis levant les yeux au ciel, il s'écria, mon dieu continuez
de protéger cet enfant. dites avec moi, satana, vade retro; apage, satana.
si cette malheureuse vous interroge, dites-lui tout. répétez-lui mon discours.
dites-lui qu'il vaudroit mieux qu'elle ne fût pas née, ou qu'elle se précipitât seule
aux enfers, par une mort violente... mais, mon père, lui répliquai-je, vous
l'avez entendue elle-même tout à l'heure. il ne me répondit rien; mais
poussant un soupir profond, il posa ses bras contre une des parois du confessionnal
et appuya sa tête dessus comme un homme pénétré de
douleur. il demeura quelque temps dans cet état. je ne savois que penser.
les genoux me trembloient. j'étois dans un trouble, un désordre qui ne se
conçoit pas; tel seroit un voyageur qui marcheroit dans les ténèbres entre des précipices qu'il
ne verroit pas, et qui seroit frappé de tous côtés par des voix qui lui crieroient : c'en est fait de vous.
me regardant ensuite avec un air tranquille, mais attendri; il me dit, avez-
vous de la santé... oui, mon père. ne seriez-vous point trop incommodée d'une
nuit que vous passeriez sans dormir... non, mon père. eh bien, me dit-il,
vous ne vous coucherez point celle-ci. aussitôt après votre collation, vous
irez dans l'église, vous vous prosternerez aux pieds des autels; vous y
passerez la nuit en prière. vous ne savez pas le danger que vous avez
couru. vous remercierez dieu de vous en avoir garantie; et demain
vous approcherez de la sainte table avec toutes les religieuses. je ne vous
donne pour pénitence que de tenir loin de vous votre supérieure
et de repousser ses caresses empoisonnées. allez. je vais de mon côté
joindre mes prières aux vôtres. combien vous m'allez causer d'inquiétudes!
je sens toutes les suites du conseil que je vous donne; mais je vous
le dois et je me le dois à moi-même. dieu est le maître, et nous n'avons
qu'une loi.

je me rappelle, monsieur, que très imparfaitement tout ce qu'il me dit.
quand je compare son discours tel que je viens de vous le rapporter avec
l'impression terrible qu'il me fit, je n'y trouve pas de comparaison; mais
cela vient de ce qu'il est brisé, décousu, qu'il y manque beaucoup de choses,

Letter to d'Alembert concerning Rousseau

Voltaire, 1762 or 1763

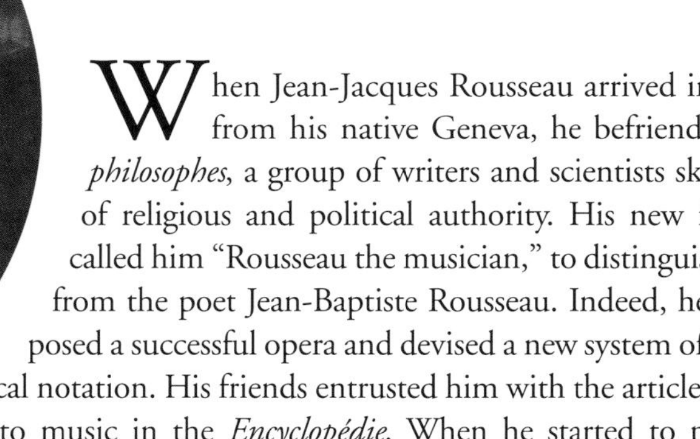

When Jean-Jacques Rousseau arrived in Paris from his native Geneva, he befriended the *philosophes*, a group of writers and scientists skeptical of religious and political authority. His new friends called him "Rousseau the musician," to distinguish him from the poet Jean-Baptiste Rousseau. Indeed, he composed a successful opera and devised a new system of musical notation. His friends entrusted him with the articles relating to music in the *Encyclopédie.* When he started to publish polemical work, however, everything was ruined. Both his first discourse (on the impact of what we would call technical progress) and his second (on social inequality), published respectively in 1750 and 1755, proved incendiary.

The *philosophes,* whose leader was Voltaire, maintained that advances in science and the arts benefited humanity. For faith in a beneficent and protective God, they had substituted faith in progress. Rousseau challenged this credo. All of his work followed from a single premise: that man is born good, but society corrupts him. Consistent with this view, he attacked the theater as antithetical to good morals.

Voltaire regretted losing a soldier who, he realized, "could have served well" in the army of Enlightenment. But for Voltaire, those who were not with him were against him, and, when it came to attacking them, he felt few scruples. Thus he informed all Europe that this hack who was meddling in matters of public morals had abandoned his five children.

Rousseau's diatribe against the theater particularly angered Voltaire. It was virtually a personal attack, for Voltaire had had his plays performed in Geneva before mounting them at his estate in Ferney. In effect, Rousseau was, like some eighteenth-century Ayatollah, asking the city's Calvinist ministers to condemn Voltaire. To Voltaire, Rousseau's contention that theater inevitably fostered the corruption of morals was aberrant. In his view, only instruction could facilitate humanity's emergence from ignorance. Accordingly, Voltaire sought to discredit Rousseau's heresies against the religion of progress, maintaining that, when a good cause was in question, the ends justify the means.

Paul Desalmand

June 1, 1762 or 1763

An excess of pride and envy has undone Jean-Jacques, my illustrious philosopher. This monster daring to speak about education! He who could not be bothered to raise any of his sons, and who left them at the foundling hospital! He abandoned his children as well as the wretch on whom he fathered them. He did everything but attack this wretch in print, as he did his friends. I'd feel sorry for him if he were hung, but only on humanitarian grounds, for personally I look upon him as Diogenes' dog, or rather as a dog descended from that dog's bastard.

I don't know if he is as detested in Paris as he is by all decent people in Geneva. Rest assured that anyone who abandons the philosophes will come to a bad end.

Did you attend the meetings where they read my insolent remarks about *Radugune?* I speak the truth and will continue to do so, but always with a certain politeness. I defy anyone itching to disagree with me, to produce a solid objection to even one of my observations. I know a bit about the theater, having, unfortunately, fifty years' experience behind me. Should you want to laugh, go to meetings where they are reading Caldéron's *Heraclius,* or Shakespeare's *Julius Caesar* translated word-for-word in blank verse.

Brother Thierot says that Father Bite–Them (abbé *Mords-les*)* has written a fine book. Crush the infamy without its being able to bite you on the heel. If this monstrous Rousseau had wanted, he could have served well as a light infantryman. Decent officers are being trained everywhere, but I find the French generals a bit half-hearted.

I embrace you warmly,

V.

Voltaire

* a pun on the name of abbé André Morellet, a free-thinking Jesuit who contributed articles to Diderot's *Encyclopédie.*

Top left: Anonymous, *Portrait of Voltaire at His Desk* (detail), 1775. Paris, Musée Carnavalet.
Left: Gabriel de Saint-Aubin, *The Crowning of Voltaire at the Théâtre Français* (detail). Paris, Bibliothèque Nationale de France.
Opposite: First page of letter from Voltaire to the mathematician Jean d'Alembert, June 17, 1762 (or 1763), autograph manuscript. Paris, Bibliothèque Nationale de France.

A M. d'Alembert

47

Nota Bene
cette lettre n'est point dans l'édit. de Beaumarchais.

17 juin 1762, ou 1763

l'excez de l'orgueuil et de l'envie a perdu jean jaques, mon illustre philosophe. ce monstre ose parler d'éducation! luy qui n'a voulu elever aucun de ses fils, et qui les a mis tous aux enfans trouvez. il a abandonné ses enfans et la gueuse a qui il les avait faits. il ne luy a manqué que d'écrire contre sa gueuse, comme il a écrit contre ses amis. je le plaindrai s'il est pendu, mais par pure humanité, car je ne le regarde personellement que comme le chien de Diogene, ou plutot que comme un chien descendu d'un batard de ce chien. je ne sçais pas s'il est abhorré a paris comme il l'est par tous les honnetes gens de geneve. soyez sur que quiconque

Dangerous Liaisons

Choderlos de Laclos, 1778

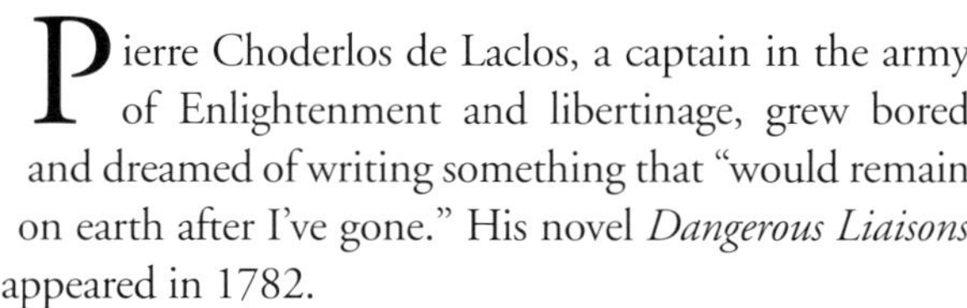

Pierre Choderlos de Laclos, a captain in the army of Enlightenment and libertinage, grew bored and dreamed of writing something that "would remain on earth after I've gone." His novel *Dangerous Liaisons* appeared in 1782.

A "Warning from the Publisher," in fact written by Laclos, advised readers that there were no real-life models for the book's protagonists, whose morals are so debased that it is difficult to imagine their living in a "century in which philosophy or Enlightenment, widely dispersed, rendered, as everyone knows, all men respectable and all women so modest and reserved."

Six centuries after the advent of courtly love, Laclos invented love-as-war, which in eighteenth-century France succeeded the love of war. A precursor of the modern battle of the sexes, such engagements, in which the participants' sights remain squarely focused on the bed, have perhaps lost some of their charm.

There remain the sumptuous language, supreme intelligence, and utter originality of *Dangerous Liaisons*, a story of vicious libertinage inspired by Racinean models and the ethos of courtly love: a startling blend of sources, genres, and tones that never escapes the author's control. A marvel of insolent equipoise, it made him a virtual meteor in the heavens of French literature.

Laclos never finished another book. Severely reprimanded for this one by his military superiors, he renounced literature. After an eventful career, he died in September 1803, by which time he was a general in Murat's army. He left behind an incomplete work entitled *Of Women and Their Education*, in which he argues that the finer sex should be taught "reason, so as to know good; kindness, so that they will want to act accordingly; and amiability, so that they will have the means to do so."

Pierre Chalmin

Cécile Volanges to Sophie Carnay at the Ursuline Convent of—
Paris, August 3, 17—

You see, my dear friend, that I keep my word, and that I don't devote all of my time to hats and frills; there will always be some left over for you. I have, however, seen more finery on this single day than in our four years together; and I think that the superb Tanville will be made even more miserable by my first visit, when I certainly intend to ask for her, than she thought she was making us every time she came to see us all decked out. Mama has consulted me about everything; she treats me much less like a schoolgirl than she used to. I have my own chambermaid; I have a bedroom and a closet to myself, and I am writing to you on a very pretty desk whose key I've been given, so I can lock anything in it I choose. Mama told me that I am to see her when she gets up every morning; that I need only worry about my hair when we dine, as we will always be alone, and that then she will tell me when I am to join her each afternoon. The rest of my time is my own, and I have my harp, my drawing, and my books, as at the convent; only Mother Perpétue isn't there to scold me, and if I choose to remain idle, it's my own affair: but as my Sophie isn't here to talk and laugh with me, I'd just as soon keep busy.

Top left: Joseph Ducreux (?), *Choderlos de Laclos* (detail), pastel. Châteaux de Versailles et de Trianon.
Opposite and below: Page from the autograph manuscript of *Dangerous Liaisons*. Paris, Bibliothèque Nationale de France.

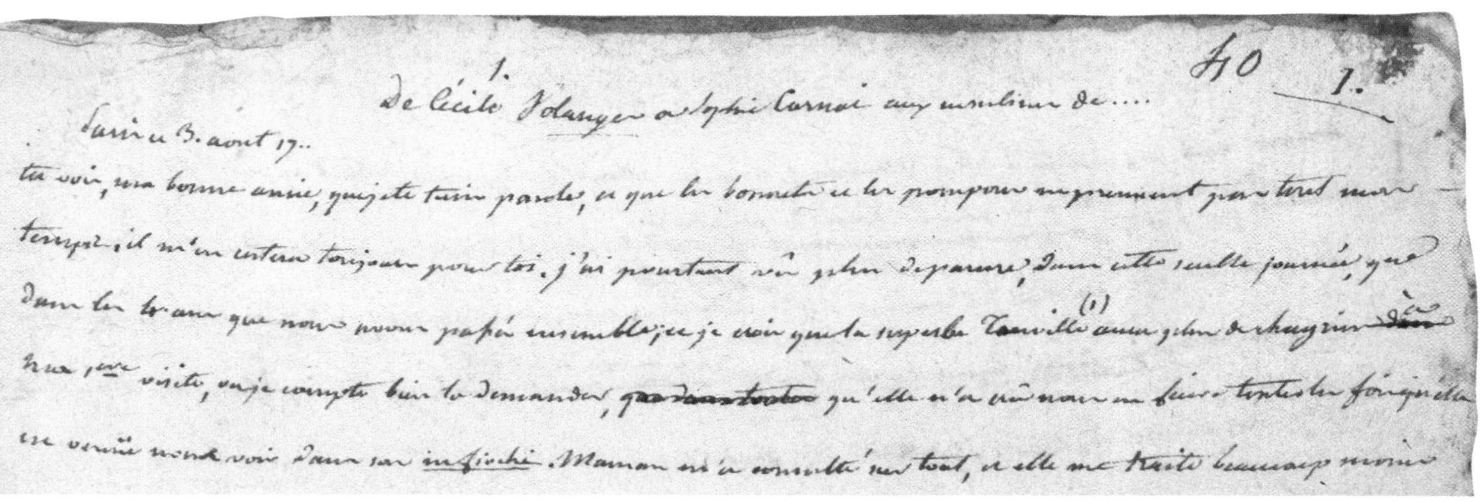

1. 40 1.

De Cécile Volanges à Sophie Carnay aux ursulines de ....

Paris ce 3. aout 17..

tu vois, ma bonne amie, que je te tiens parole, et que les bonnets et les pompons ne prennent pas tout mon
temps; il m'en restera toujours pour toi. j'ai pourtant vû plus de parure, dans cette seule journée, que
dans les trois ans que nous avons passé ensemble; et je crois que la superbe Tanville[1] aura plus de chagrin
à ma première visite, où je compte bien la demander, qu'elle n'a crû nous en faire toutes les fois qu'elle
est venüe nous voir dans ses in fiocchi. Maman m'a consultée sur tout, et elle me traite beaucoup moins
en pensionnaire que par le passé. j'ai une femme de chambre à moi. ~~qui me paroit fort bien venir~~ j'ai une
chambre et un cabinet dont je dispose, et je t'écris à un secrétaire très joli dont on m'a remis la clef, et
où je peux renfermer tout ce que je veux.
maman m'a dit que je la verrois tous les jours à son lever; qu'il suffiroit que je fusse coiffée pour dîner, parce que
nous serions toujours seules, et qu'alors elle me diroit, chaque jour, l'heure où je devrois l'aller joindre l'après-midi.
le reste du temps est à ma disposition, et j'ai ma harpe, mon dessein et des livres comme au couvent: si ce n'est que
la mère perpétue n'est pas là pour me gronder, et qu'il ne tiendroit qu'à moi d'être toujours sans rien faire: mais
comme je n'ai pas ma sophie pour causer ou pour rire, j'aime autant m'occuper. il n'est pas
encore 5. heures et je ne dois aller retrouver maman qu'à 7. voila bien du temps si j'avois quelque chose à te
dire: mais on ne m'a encore parlé de rien; et sans les apprêts que je vois faire et la quantité d'ouvrières qui
viennent toutes pour moi, je croirois qu'on ne songe pas à me marier, et que c'est un radotage de plus
de la bonne joséphine[2]. cependant maman m'a dit si souvent qu'une demoiselle devoit rester au couvent
jusqu'à ce qu'elle se mariât, que puisqu'elle m'en fait sortir, il faut bien que joséphine ait raison.
il vient d'arrêter un carosse à la porte, et maman me fait dire de passer chez elle, tout de suite.
si c'étoit le Monsieur? je ne suis pas habillée. la main me tremble et le cœur me bat. j'ai demandé à ma
femme de chambre si elle savoit qui étoit chez ma mère: vraiment, m'a-t-elle dit, c'est M.r
C*** et elle rioit. oh! je crois que c'est lui. je reviendrai surement te raconter ce qui se sera passé.
voila toujours son nom.
il ne faut pas se faire attendre. adieu jusqu'à un petit moment.

comme tu vas te moquer de la pauvre Cécile! oh! j'ai été bien honteuse: mais tu y aurois été attrapée

Confessions

Jean-Jacques Rousseau, 1782

Many famous authors are widely misunderstood. Rousseau challenged the notion, taken for granted in his day, that technical progress made men better and happier. But he never recommended that the clock be turned back. On the contrary, he insisted on the irreversibility of history and even went so far as to affirm that whatever disadvantages this entailed, Man could realize his full potential only by becoming a social animal.

The wheel of History, then, cannot be reversed, and all attempts to revert to a lost age are doomed to fail. The only thing to do is to search for palliatives. Human beings can be improved through education (the subject of *Émile*), and the organization of human society can be transformed by political reflection (the aim of the *Social Contract*).

Rousseau is also, mistakenly, considered the spiritual father of the Reign of Terror. It is true that his texts galvanized many of the men who fomented the Revolution. But there was nothing sanguinary about Rousseau. He says as much in a letter to the Countess of Wartensleben: "The blood of a single man is worth more than the liberty of the entire human race."

Perhaps because he was self-taught, Rousseau transformed every field that he broached. Others had written their autobiographies before him, but in his *Confessions* he reinvented the genre, effectively inaugurating a rich tradition of world literature. In the view of Stendhal, who was greatly influenced by him, if he had not had so pronounced a taste for emphatic declamation, he would have been the Mozart of the French language.

Paul Desalmand

The road passes the foot of the finest waterfall I have seen in all my days. The side of the mountain is so sheer that the water leaps away from it and falls in an arc wide enough to allow one to pass between it and the rock, sometimes without even getting wet. But unless you take special care, you can easily fool yourself about this, as I did. For, because of the cascade's great height, the sheet of water breaks into a mist of droplets. If you pass too near this cloudlike spray without noticing that you may get wet, you are drenched in an instant.

Finally I arrived, and I saw her again. She was not alone. The Intendant General was with her when I came in. Without speaking to me, she took my hand and introduced me to him with that graciousness that opened all hearts to her: "Here he is, sir, the poor young man. If you will be so good as to give him your protection as long as he deserves it, I shall not worry about him for the rest of his life." Then, she addressed me: "My child, you are the King's man; thank Monsieur l'Intendant, who offers you a livelihood." My eyes opened wide, but I said nothing, not knowing how to take so much in. My head was full of nascent ambition; in my mind I was already a younger version of the Intendant. As it turned out, my fortune proved less brilliant than this beginning led me to imagine. But, for the moment, I had enough to live on, and that for me was a great deal. This was where things were.

Judging by the state they were in after the wars he had waged, King Victor Amadeus had done everything he could to exhaust his ancestral lands, which would one day slip from his grasp. A few years earlier, he had resolved to tax the nobility, and so had ordered a general tax on the entire country, with the object that the revenue might be gathered more fairly. This project, which he began, was later completed by his son. Two or three hundred men, some of them surveyors, who were called geometricians, and some of them writers, who were called secretaries, were engaged in this task, and it was in this latter group that my mother had found me a place. Although the post was not particularly well paid, at least it gave me enough to live on comfortably in that country. The problem was that it was only temporary employment, but it did put me in a position to wait and seek other work, and thinking ahead, my mother had tried to ingratiate me with the Intendant, so that when this project was finished, I might move on to more stable employment.

I took up my duties a few days after my arrival. There was nothing difficult about the work, and I was doing it easily. And so it was that after four or five years of moving about, of folly, and of hardship, I began for the first time to make an honest living.

Translation by E. M. Banks

Top left: Charron, *Jean-Jacques Rousseau in Switzerland, Persecuted and Without Refuge* (detail). Paris, Musée Carnavalet.
Left: John-Claude Nattes, *View of the Park at Montmorency, with Lodging of Jean-Jacques Rousseau.* Châteaux de Versailles et de Trianon.
Opposite: Page from the autograph manuscript of Rousseau's *Confessions* (Book Four), begun in 1762 and published in 1782, four years after the author's death. Paris, Bibliothèque de l'Assemblée Nationale.

Le chemin passe au pied de la plus belle cascade que je vis de mes jours. La montagne est tellement escarpée que l'eau se détache net et tombe en arcade assez loin pour qu'on puisse passer entre la cascade et la roche, quelque fois sans être mouillé. Mais si l'on ne prend bien ses mesures on y est aisément trompé comme je le fus: car à cause de l'extrême hauteur l'eau se divise et tombe en poussière, et lorsqu'on approche un peu trop de ce nuage, sans s'appercevoir d'abord qu'on se mouille bientôt on est tout trempé. 89.

J'arrive enfin, je la revois. Elle n'étoit pas seule. M. l'Intendant general étoit chez elle au moment que j'entrai. Sans me parler elle me prend par la main et me présente à lui avec cette grace qui lui ouvroit tous les coeurs; le voila, Monsieur, ce pauvre jeune homme, daignez le protéger aussi longtems qu'il le méritera, je ne suis plus en peine de lui pour le reste de sa vie. Puis m'addressant la parole; mon enfant, me dit-elle, vous appartenez au Roi: remerciez M. l'Intendant qui vous donne du pain. J'ouvrois de grands yeux sans rien dire, sans trop savoir qu'imaginer. Il s'en fallut peu que l'ambition naissante ne me tournât la tête, et que je ne fisse déja le petit Intendant. Ma fortune se trouva moins brillante que sur ce début je ne l'avois imaginée; mais quant-à présent c'étoit assez pour vivre, et pour moi c'étoit beaucoup. voici dequoi il s'agissoit.

Le Roi Victor Amedée jugeant par le sort des guerres précedentes, et par la position de l'ancien patrimoine de ses peres qu'il lui échaperoit quelque jour, ne cherchoit qu'à l'épuiser. Il y avoit peu d'années qu'ayant resolu d'en mettre la noblesse à la taille il avoit ordonné un cadastre général de tout le pays, afin que rendant l'imposition réelle on put la repartir avec plus d'égalité. Le travail commencé sous le pére fut achevé sous le fils. Deux ou trois cents hommes, tant arpenteurs qu'on appelloit Geometres, qu'écrivains qu'on appelloit Secretaires, furent employés à cet ouvrage, et c'étoit parmi ces derniers que maman m'avoit fait inscrire. Le poste, sans être fort lucratif, donnoit dequoi vivre au large dans ce pays-là. Le mal étoit que cet emploi n'étoit qu'à tems, mais il mettoit en état de chercher et d'attendre, et c'étoit par prevoyance qu'elle tâchoit de m'obtenir de l'Intendant une protection particuliére pour pouvoir passer à quelque emploi plus solide, quand le tems de celui-là seroit fini.

J'entrai en fonction peu de jours après mon arrivée. Il n'y avoit à ce travail rien de difficile, et je fus bientot au fait. C'est ainsi qu'après quatre ou cinq ans de courses, de folies et de souffrances depuis ma sortie de Geneve, je commencai pour la prémiére fois de gagner mon pain avec honneur.

Ces longs détails de ma prémiére jeunesse auront paru bien pueriles, et j'en suis fâché: quoique né homme à certains égards j'ai été longtems enfant, et je le suis encore à beaucoup d'autres. Je n'ai pas promis d'offrir au lecteur un grand personnage; j'ai promis de me peindre tel que je suis, et pour me connoitre dans mon age avancé, il faut m'avoir bien connu dans ma jeunesse. Comme en général les objets font moins d'impression sur moi que leurs souvenirs, et que toutes mes idées sont en images, les prémiers traits qui se sont gravez dans ma tête y sont demeurés, et ceux qui s'y sont empreints dans la suite se sont plustôt combinés avec eux qu'ils ne les ont effacés. Il y a une certaine succession d'affections et d'idées qui modifient celles qui les suivent et qu'il faut connoitre pour en bien juger. Je m'applique à bien developper par tout les prémiéres causes pour faire sentir l'enchainement des effets. Je voudrois pouvoir rendre mon ame transparente aux yeux du lecteur, et pour cela je cherche à la lui montrer sous tous les points de vue, à l'éclairer par tous les jours, à faire en sorte qu'il ne s'y passe pas un mouve=

The Marriage of Figaro

Beaumarchais, 1784

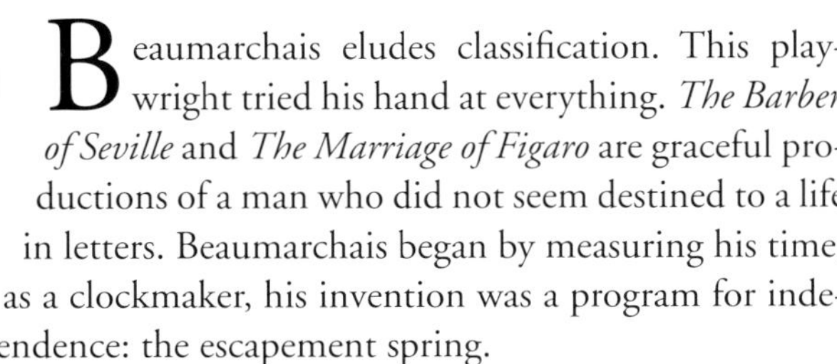

Beaumarchais eludes classification. This playwright tried his hand at everything. *The Barber of Seville* and *The Marriage of Figaro* are graceful productions of a man who did not seem destined to a life in letters. Beaumarchais began by measuring his time; as a clockmaker, his invention was a program for independence: the escapement spring.

His life amounted to performances of various roles in a play he never found the time to write. Harp teacher to the daughters of Louis XV, secret agent, arms trafficker to the American insurgents. Imprisoned in the Bastille, he had his butler deliver his meals. The French Revolution bored him; this refined gourmet refused to taste the coarse red wine of anarchism. A libertine, he annoyed Robespierre but survived the Terror. Oblivious when this was expedient, he nonetheless understood perfectly what was happening. His only sin was "indifference to the world, when he wasn't contemptuous of it."

At the first performance of the *Barber* at the residence of the Prince de Conti, the nobility of France laughed at its own requiem. The Marie Antoinette who played Rosine at the Trianon would later lose her head; scatterbrained, glibly delivering Beaumarchais's witty retorts to the powdered audience, she was playing with fashionable matches that would ignite a general conflagration.

Pierre-Emmanuel Prouvost d'Agostino

Act II

The scene is a superb bedroom with a large alcove bed on a dais. Backstage right, the entry door. Forestage left, a closet door. To the rear, door to the maids' rooms. On the other side, a window.

Scene I
The countess and Suzanne enter through the door at right.

COUNTESS (throwing herself into an armchair): Close the door, Suzanne, and tell me everything in great detail.

SUZANNE: I haven't hidden anything from madame.

COUNTESS: What, Suzanne, he tried to seduce you?

SUZANNE: Certainly not! My lord isn't as particular as that with his servants. He wanted to buy me.

COUNTESS: And the little page was there?

SUZANNE: He was hiding behind the big armchair. He'd come to ask me to intervene with you on his behalf.

COUNTESS: Why didn't he come to me directly? Could I have refused him, Suzanne?

SUZANNE: That's what I told him, but he is so sad about leaving, and especially about leaving madame! "Ah! Suzanne, how noble and beautiful she is! How imposing! But she's as proud as the sun and doesn't let anyone look her directly in the face."

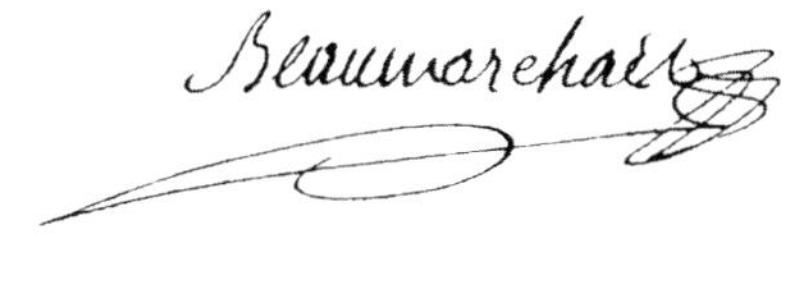

Top left: Jean-Marc Nattier (copy after), *Portrait of Beaumarchais* (detail). Paris, Comédie Française.
Left: Scene from *The Marriage of Figaro*, watercolor by Maxime Rebière.
Opposite: Page from a manuscript copy of *The Marriage of Figaro*. Paris, Bibliothèque Nationale de France.

33.

Acte Second

Le Théâtre représente une chambre à Coucher Superbe. Un Grand Lit en alcove. Une Estrade au devant. La porte pour entrer s'ouvrant et se fermant à la 1re Coulisse à droite. Celle d'un Cabinet à la 1re coulisse à Gauche. Une porte dans le fond qui va chez les Femmes. Une Fenêtre qui s'ouvre de l'autre côté.

Scene Premiere

La Comtesse Suzanne entrent par la Porte Fermante.

La Comtesse se Jette sur une Bergère.

Ferme la Porte Suzanne et Conte moi tout dans le plus grand detail.

Suzanne

Je n'ai rien caché à Madame

La Comtesse

Quoy Suzon il voulait te séduire ?

Suzanne

Oh que non. Monseigneur n'y met pas tant de façon avec sa servante. Il voulait m'acheter.

La Comtesse

Et le Petit Page était Présent ?

Suzanne

C'est à dire caché derriere le grand Fauteuil des Malades. Il venait vous prier de demander sa Grace.

La Comtesse

hé Pourquoi ne pas s'adresser à moi même ? est-ce que je l'aurais refusé ? Suzon.

Suzanne

C'est ce que j'ai dit, Mais ses regrets de Partir, et surtout de Quitter Madame ! " ah Suzon qu'elle est noble et Belle ! " Mais qu'elle est imposante ! aussi Fière que le Soleil, elle ne souffre point qu'on la " regarde en Face .

Paul and Virginia

Bernardin de Saint-Pierre, 1785

Throughout his life, Bernardin de Saint-Pierre was an impressionable sort. Greatly affected by *The Lives of the Saints* and *Robinson Crusoe* in his youth, he would always oscillate between mystic exaltation and fantastic revery. An undisciplined loner, his adventurous spirit took him from Martinique to the Ile-de-France by way of Malta, Amsterdam, Moscow, St. Petersburg, Warsaw, Dresden, Vienna, and Berlin. Fleeing people who "plotted to make him happy," he caused problems and squabbles everywhere he went and wearied a series of protectors. After some years, however, he developed a sense of compromise. A fervent royalist until 1791 and a patriot until 1802, he then, by force of circumstance, became an ardent Bonapartist—and a contented one: he was elected to the Académie Française, of which he soon became president.

An awkward and vexing work that was revised over twenty years before finally appearing in 1788 (in volume four of *Études de la nature*), *Paul and Virginia* was, with Rousseau's *New Héloise* and Laclos's *Dangerous Liaisons*, one of the final triumphs of pre-Revolutionary French fiction, and it won its author immortality. Rejecting verism, Bernardin contrived a myth in which he identified virtue with nature, losing himself in the byways of Rousseauist doctrine. Carried away by his ardor, he accentuated the naïveté of this children's tale by adding liberal doses of sentimentality.

There remain, however, his touching evocation of a bounteous nature in harmony with the angelic charm of his young lovers—"I find mysterious traces of you in the air through which you've passed, on the grass where you've sat"—and his dramatic account of the shipwreck of the *Saint-Géran,* in which Virginia perishes. It is probably to these features that *Paul and Virginia* owes its lasting fame, for it is essentially an exercise in "women's" fiction, a book that delights the imagination but requires that its readers suspend their critical faculties.

Pierre Chalmin

Mademoiselle, they tell me you are leaving in three days. Aren't you afraid of exposing yourself to the dangers . . . of the sea, which so frighten you?—I must, answered Virginia, obey my parents, honor my obligations.—You leave us, responded Paul, for a distant relation whom you have never seen!—Alas, said Virginia, I wanted to remain here all my life; my mother doesn't want me to. My confessor tells me that it is God's will that I leave, that life is a trial . . . Oh! It is a very difficult one!—What, answered Paul, you have so many reasons to go, and none to stay? Ah! There are others that you don't mention. Wealth is very attractive. You will soon find, in a new world, someone to call brother, which you no longer call me. You will choose him, this brother, from among those worthy of you by birth and fortune, things that I cannot give you. But, to be happier, where do you want to go? What land could be dearer to you than the one in which you were born? Where will you find society more agreeable than that of your loved ones? How will you do without your mother's caresses, which you've gotten so used to? What will become of her, already getting on, when she no longer sees you beside her at the table, in the house, on her walks, when she used to lean on you? What will become of my own mother, who loves you as much as she does? What will I say to them when I see them crying over your absence? You are cruel! I haven't said anything about myself; but what will become of me when I no longer see you with us in the morning, and when night falls without bringing us together; when I see the two palm trees that were planted when we were born, witness to our mutual friendship for so long! Ah! When a new fate beckons you to seek out a country other than your native land, and goods other than those I can make for you, let me accompany you on the ship that takes you away. I will comfort you during storms, which so frighten you on land. I will place your head on my breast, warm your heart against my heart; and in France, where you go to seek wealth and grandeur, I will be your slave. Happy merely because of your happiness, in those townhouses where I will see you waited upon and adored, I will find riches and nobility enough by making the greatest sacrifice for you, by dying at your feet.

Top left: Paul Carpentier (after Elisabeth Hervey), *Portrait of Jacques-Henri Bernardin de Saint-Pierre.* Châteaux de Versailles et de Trianon.
Left: Scene from *Paul and Virginia,* watercolor by Maxime Rebière.
Right: Binding of the autograph manuscript of *Paul and Virginia.* Paris, Bibliothèque de la Sorbonne.
Opposite: Page from the autograph manuscript of *Paul and Virginia.* Paris, Bibliothèque de la Sorbonne.

paul lui dit. Mademoiselle vous partez dans trois jours vous ne craignez
de vous exposer aux
pas les dangers de la mer. de la mer dont vous etes si effrayée.

il faut que j'obeisse a mes parens, a mon devoir.

vous quitter [illegible] pour une parente eloignée, qui vous hait
est ma mere qui le veut

j'ai vu que Dominque etoit vieux mais enfin ma mere toujours malade

helas je voulois travailler pour eux toute ma vie [illegible] ne la pas voulu.

mon confesseur m'a dit que c'etoit la volonté de dieu que je partisse que la vie etoit
une epreuve.. oh c'est une epreuve bien dure.

tant de raison vous [illegible] a retenir [illegible] ah il en est encore que vous
ne me dites pas. [illegible] la richesse a de grands attraits. vous
trouverez bientost dans ce nouveau monde a qui donner le nom
de frere que vous ne me donnez plus. ce seront de gens [illegible]
dignes de vous [illegible] bien que
je ne puis [illegible]. mais pour etre plus heureuse ou voulez vous
aller, [illegible] plus chere que celle ou vous etes
née. [illegible] une societé plus aimable que celle qui
vous aime. que deviendrez vous sans les caresses de votre mere et de la mienne
auxquelles vous etes accoutumée. que deviendra t elle elle meme [illegible]
lorsqu'elle ne vous aura plus [illegible] a la table, au bain, au promenade [illegible]
[illegible] sa fille [illegible]
[illegible] que deviendrai je moi [illegible]
[illegible] quand [illegible]
quand le matin je ne vous verrai plus, lorsque la nuit viendra, [illegible]
dans la montagne, je verrai [illegible] mais ciel
[illegible] que ta chere [illegible] pays natal.
[illegible] nouveau sort te touche [illegible] pays natal [illegible]
bien que [illegible]
[illegible]
[illegible] je te suivrai [illegible] je te rassurerai dans les tempetes
qui te donnent tant d'effroy sur la terre [illegible] je reposerai ta tete [illegible] sur mon sein je rechaufferai
ton coeur contre mon coeur, et [illegible]
en france ou tu vas chercher de la grandeur je te [illegible]
[illegible] dans ces hotels [illegible] je te [illegible]
[illegible] de mon indigence [illegible]
[illegible] de ton bonheur, je serai encore au milieu de mon indigence assez
noble assez riche pour te faire [illegible] le plus
grand des sacrifices en mourant a tes pieds.
comment [illegible] de votre mere [illegible]
que deviendra t elle lorsqu'elle ne vous verra plus a la table [illegible] que deviendrai je
que deviendra la mienne [illegible]
[illegible] quand je ne verrai plus de votre absence

The Misfortunes of Virtue

Marquis de Sade, 1787

The Revolution was a factory of slaves to conformity, but no one was less pliant than the Marquis de Sade, who proudly traced his lineage back to Laura, Petrarch's muse. Sade was not about to be drawn in by the Rights of Man; for him, liberty was totalitarian, without limits. His version of the Terror paid no obeisance to the collective good, being an entirely individual affair. He was disgusted by the guillotine of 1793, a mere machine for equality; he saw himself as a superior being, a sad and lonely demiurge on the brink of his abyss, contemplating the boiling of bad desires in the caldron of the world.

This libertine, given to paroxysm and paradox, was "master of himself as of the universe"; he elevated the bestial to the level of a martyr's epiphany. A philanthrope after the manner of Rousseau, longing for a nature from which humanity had been removed, Sade was something of a conservationist *avant la lettre*. With him, blasphemy, licence, and obscenity are no mere grace notes; they are key constituents of an ideology pushed to its limits, to the point where flesh succumbs to the lash, where it bleeds and sweats. His prisons were flesh and physical pleasure (an amusing physics of love made white-hot, even molten). In his world, Piranesi's etchings run with blood. The divine marquis was no more infernal than he was celestial: he was all too human. A great lord because it suited him, a wicked man because human nature is intractable. His dark work suggested that the Enlightenment would have disquieting consequences: that, liberated of all constraints, Man would be frightened to see, looking at himself in the mirror, instead of "borrowed" angelic qualities, his beast's muzzle and his grimace of the damned.

Pierre-Emmanuel Prouvost d'Agostino

—I was not born for so much bliss, she said to Madame de Lorsange. . . . Oh! My dear sister, surely it can't last long.

We assured her that all her problems were over, that there was no further cause for concern, but nothing could calm her; one would have said that this sad creature, destined solely for misfortune, whose hand she always sensed suspended above her, already foresaw the final blows that would crush her.

Monsieur de Corville was still living in the country. It was towards the end of summer; a planned walk seemed likely to be undone by the approach of a frightful storm; due to the extreme heat, everything had been left open. Lightning flashed, hail fell, the wind blew, the fire in the heavens agitated the clouds, making them shake horribly; it was as though nature, bored with its work, was about to mix everything together to give them new forms. Madame de Lorsange, frightened, begged her sister to close everything, as quickly as possible; Thérèse, anxious to calm her sister, flew to the windows, which were already breaking; she fought against the wind for a full minute, then a bolt of lightning struck her down in the middle of the salon.

Madame de Lorsange uttered a frightful scream and fainted; Monsieur de Corville called for help; there was concern for both women. Madame de Lorsange recovered consciousness, but the unfortunate Thérèse had been struck so violently that there was little hope for her; the lightning had entered through her right breast, and, after consuming her chest and her face, had exited through her stomach. This miserable creature was dreadful to behold: Monsieur de Corville ordered her carried away. . . . No, said Madame de Lorsange, rising with great calm; no, leave her so I can see her, monsieur; I need to contemplate her to strengthen my resolve. Listen to me, Corville, and above all don't try to prevent me from doing as I've decided; now, nothing in the world can distract me from the plan I've adopted. The unprecedented misfortunes suffered by this unlucky woman, despite her having always done as she should have, are too extraordinary not to have made me look at myself clearly; don't imagine that I've been blinded by the false allure of bliss enjoyed, in the course of the adventures of Thérèse, by the villains who corrupted her. These whims of the heavens are enigmas that it is not our place to solve, but that must never seduce us. Oh my friend! Prosperity won by crime is but a trial put in the way of virtue by Providence; it is like the lightning flashes used by the fires of deceit to illuminate the atmosphere for an instant, only to precipitate those unfortunate enough to be dazzled by them into the abyss of death.

Top Left: Man Ray, *Imaginary Portrait of the Marquis de Sade*. Houston, De Ménil Museum.
Left: Léopold Boilly (or Marguerite Gérard), *The Hasty Departure*. Paris, Musée Cognac-Jay.
Opposite: Page from the autograph manuscript of *The Misfortunes of Virtue* (later transformed into *Justine, or Good Conduct Well Chastised*), 1787–88. Paris, Bibliothèque Nationale de France.

136 Sans pouvoir elle même expliquer le sujet de ses larmes

si les siens jamais pour ~~un tel~~ comble de ~~bonheur~~ félicité disait-elle 249

quelque fois Mlle de Lorange ... oh ma chère soeur

il est impossible qu'il puisse durer on avoit beau lui dire

~~représenter~~ que toutes ses affaires étoient finies elle ne devoit

plus avoir aucune sorte d'inquiétude l'attention qu'on avoit

eu de ne point parler dans le mémoire qui avoit été fait en sa faveur

~~[illegible]~~ d'aucun de personnage avec lesquels elle avoit

été compromise et dont le crédit pouvoit être redoutable, ne

pouvoit que la calmer ~~encore~~ cependant rien n'y parvenait,

on eut dit que cette ~~malheureuse~~ femme triste créature étoit uniquement destinée

au malheur et sentant la main de l'infortune toujours

suspendue sur sa tête prévoit déjà le dernier coup dont

elle alloit être écrasée

Mlle de Lorange habitait encore la campagne on était

sur la fin de l'été on projettait une promenade que cet affreux orage du 13 juillet 1788

~~orage~~ ~~affreux~~ menaçant ~~qui [illegible]~~ paraissoit devoir déranger

l'excès de la chaleur avoit contraint de laisser tout ouvert

~~dans le sallon~~ le clair brillé la grêle tombe les vents sifflent avec

impétuosité ~~de~~ le fracas agitant les arbres ~~[illegible]~~ d'une manière horrible

Mlle de Lorange effrayée ... Mlle de Lorange qui avoient

~~[illegible]~~ le tonnerre supplie ses soeurs de fermer

tout le plus promptement qu'il ~~[illegible]~~ Mlle de Corville

venoit en ce moment ~~[illegible]~~ empressée de calmer

se voir volée au fenêtre elle veut l'atteindre une minute

contre le vent qui la repoussoit à l'instant un éclat de foudre

se renverse au milieu du sallon ~~et la laisse [illegible]~~

~~[illegible]~~

Mlle de Lorange jette un cri épouvantable et ~~elle~~ s'évanouit,

Mlle de Corville appelle au secours les siens de ville, on

rappelle Mlle de Lorange à la lumière, mais la malheureuse

Julie étoit frappée de façon à ce qu'il lui soit même

la pouvoit plus se rétablir, ~~reposé~~ la foudre étoit entrée

par la ~~[illegible]~~ droit et avoit brulé sa poitrine, elle étoit renversée

la bouche se défigurant tellement son visage que elle

faisoit horreur à regarder. Mlle de Corville voulut emporter

à l'instant. Mlle de Lorange se leve avec l'air du plus grand

calme et s'y oppose, non dit elle à ~~Mlle de~~ Corville non

son amant

Memoirs of My Life

René de Chateaubriand, 1809

Rare are the mythic literary couples who, in lieu of china, don't hurl unflattering epithets at one another. In the presence of Chateaubriand, his mistress Madame Récamier had the good sense to be beautiful and remain silent. But it was with a steady hand that the aging lady copied, at her retreat at La Vallée-au-Loups, in 1826, long passages from her former lover's *Mémoires de ma vie* (*Memoirs of My Life*)—as, in the evening twilight, one caresses the indistinct features of a beloved face as it vanishes into darkness. And indeed, Chateaubriand's life was altogether extraordinary.

Like his cherished enemy Bonaparte, Chateaubriand cut a striking figure; as it happens, the withering gazes and romantic locks of both men were captured by leading painters of the day. Bonaparte subdued much of Europe, while Chateaubriand's struggles, less momentous but just as heated, found issue in prose of captivating lyricism. Rebellious children of the Enlightenment, both men had an impact on their time. After fifteen years of military exertion, Napoleon left it to others to fashion his legend for posterity. Chateaubriand managed to compose his own literary memorial. An extended aria sung by a disabused enchanter, it is addressed to the only worthy reader its author could imagine: himself. This requiem, composed in some of the most beautiful prose in the whole of French literature, marks the beginning of the age in which we now live. In a flattering twilight, a new Juliette and her graying Romeo, ghosts from their own past, sing an elegy for a love that now burns with the colors of the setting sun, sumptuous, sad, and beautiful like the end of an Empire.

Pierre-Emmanuel Prouvost d'Agostino

Another time I accompanied my mother to Combourg; she wanted to furnish the château because she was expecting my brother, who was to bring his wife; my brother never came to Brittany, and soon after he mounted the scaffold with the young wife for whom my mother had prepared the nuptial bed. Finally, I went to Combourg a third time on my way to set sail for America: the chateau was abandoned. I was obliged to have the caretaker accompany me. While wandering in the great wood, I glimpsed at the end of a dark allée the deserted steps, the door, and the closed windows. I began to feel ill, returned to the village with difficulty, and left in the middle of the night.

After an absence of twenty-six years, before leaving France again for the Holy Land, I went to Fougères to embrace what remained of my family. I lacked the courage to undertake the pilgrimage to the paternal fields to which the greater part of my existence seemed attached. It was in the wood at Combourg that I became what I am, that I first began to feel the sickness that I have carried with me the rest of my life, the vague sadness that has been both my torment and my happiness. It was here that I looked for a heart that might understand my own, it was here that I saw my family come together and then disperse; here my father dreamed of having his name cleared and the fortune of his house restored, another chimera that was swept away by time and the Revolution. Of the six children that we once were, only three remain; my brother, Julie, and Lucile are no more; my mother died from heartbreak; the ashes of my father were wrested from his tomb and thrown to the winds.

If my works survive me, if I should leave a name after myself, perhaps one day a traveler guided by these memoirs will visit the places that I have described; but he will search in vain for the great wood. The cradle of my dreams has disappeared like the dreams themselves; now standing in isolation on its rock, the ancient keep seems to weep for the oaks, old companions that once surrounded and protected it from tempests. Likewise isolated, I, too, have witnessed the fall of the family that made my days beautiful and protected me; happily, my life is not as solidly rooted in the earth as were the days of my youth, and man is less resistant to storms than are the monuments built by his hands.

Chateaubriand

Top left: Anne-Louis Girodet-Trioson, *Portrait of Chateaubriand* (detail), 1811. Versailles, Musée du Château.
Left: Louis-Gabriel-Eugène Isabey, *The Tomb of Chateaubriand.* Paris, Musée du Louvre.
Opposite: Three pages from the manuscript copy of passages from an early draft of Chateaubriand's autobiography made by Madame Récamier, with the assistance of Charles Lenormand, at La Vallée-aux-Loups in 1826. Paris, Bibliothèque Nationale de France.

923

laquelle ma mère avoit vainement préparé le lit nuptial ; enfin je passai une troisième fois à Combourg en allant m'embarquer pour l'amérique ; le château étoit abandonné, je fus obligé de descendre chez le régisseur ; lorsqu'en errant dans le grand bois, j'apperçus du fond d'une allée obscure le Perron désert, la porte et les fenêtres fermées, je me trouvai mal, je regagnai avec peine le village et partis au milieu de la nuit.

après vingt six ans d'absence, avant de quitter de nouveau la France pour passer en terre Sainte, j'allai embrasser le reste de ma famille, à Fougères. je n'eus pas le courage d'entreprendre le pélérinage

924

de ces champs paternels, où la meilleure et la plus grande partie de mon existence, semble attachée ; c'est des bois de Combourg que je suis devenu ce que je suis, que j'ai commencé à sentir la première atteinte de l'ennui que j'ai porté le reste de ma vie, de cette vague tristesse qui a fait à la fois mon tourment et ma félicité, c'est là que j'ai cherché un cœur qui peut entendre le mien, c'est là que j'ai vu se réunir, puis se disperser ma famille ; mon père y rêva son nom rétabli, la fortune de sa maison renouvelée, autre chimère que le temps et la Révolution ont dissipée ; de six enfans que nous étions nous ne restons plus

925

que trois ; mon frère, Julie, et Lucile ne sont plus ; ma mère est morte de douleur ; les cendres de mon père, ont été arrachées de son tombeau et jetées aux vents.

si mes ouvrages me survivent, si je dois laisser un nom après moi, peut être un jour un voyageur guidé par les mémoires, viendra visiter les lieux que j'ai peints, mais il cherchera vainement le grand bois. le berceau de mes songes a disparu comme les songes ; demeuré seul debout sur son rocher, l'antique donjon semble pleurer les chênes vieux compagnons qui l'environnoient et le protégeoient contre les tempêtes. isolé comme lui, j'ai vu comme lui

Meditations

Alphonse de Lamartine, 1816

Romanticism is a venerable—and contagious—disease. The history books date the outbreaks of the great epidemics precisely, like the origins of literary trends. The public, the critics, and poor students need unambiguous chronological benchmarks. From this perspective, Lamartine's timing was impeccable: the publication date of his first *Méditations poètiques* (Poetic meditations), 1820, is absurdly easy to remember. It doesn't hurt that this (hugely successful) collection contains all the clichés of French Romanticism, less febrile and more disembodied than its German counterpart. One poem, "The Lake," became the model elegy for many others. The poet Charles Baudelaire wrote of the difficulty of "inventing an original platitude," but Lamartine managed to achieve this tour-de-force. He found his own voice, which nonetheless echoes that of his predecessors, the English lake poets.

After him, anemic sylphs nestled in small boats would float languorously, by moonlight, over expanses of water seemingly supplied by rivers of tears. Achille Devéria made a lithograph depicting Lamartine's ideal reader: a nymph with curled hair, swan neck, and tiny waist wearing a dress with leg-of-mutton sleeves, a cashmere shawl over her shoulders, a handkerchief at her eye.

Lamartine dallied in politics. First a Catholic royalist (he was an aide to Louis the XVIII during the Bourbon Restoration), then a moderate republican (he served in the legislature under Louis-Philippe and briefly headed the government of the Second Republic), he was one of those blinkered types who imagine that a people's future can be settled by words alone. Thanks to him, good republicans long tended to make excessive use, at the speaker's tribune, of the rhetoric of the 1848 Revolution. As a historian of just causes, he made an unpersuasive attempt to rehabilitate the indecisive actions of the Girondins in 1792–94, arguing extenuating circumstances. His career as a poet ended sadly: having become something of a literary hack, he was always angling for editorial advances and never managed to raise enough funds, through subscription, to finance a complete edition of his work, which had become unfashionable.

Less haughty than Alfred de Vigny but still a bit stiff, this member of the lesser provincial nobility remains the apologist for a love so disembodied as to be bloodless. He bequeathed his lyrical idiom—ultimately, no less consumptive than the pining heroines so fashionable in the nineteenth century—to Victor Hugo, who infused it with new life.

Pierre-Emmanuel Prouvost d'Agostino

First Meditation
to Julie

The sun of our days grows dimmer from its dawn;
O my dear Julie! It will give forth only
A few more feeble rays to combat the night!
Shadows lengthen; the day dies, everything fades
and flees!

How others, before this prospect, either shrink
or shudder!
How they fear to fix the bottom of the precipice;
They cannot hear without growing pale
the sad song of the dead, quite ready to hear
the sounds of the gravedigger, who with a mercenary arm,
digs a hole in the earth for the next coffin,
whistling the while;
nor the moaning bronze whose confused accents
announce to mortals that an unfortunate is no
more!

I salute you, o death! Celestial liberator!
You do not appear to me under that dreadful
aspect
long attributed to you through fear or error;
you are not armed with a destructive sword;
your face is not cruel nor your gaze perfidious;
night is not your sister nor chance your guide.
You do not annihilate! You save! Your hand,
celestial messenger, carries a divine torch!
When my weary eyes close out the light
you come to flood my eyelids with a purer light
and with hope, your intimate, dreaming of a
future tomb
obscured by a curtain that you rip down!

Top left: Madame de Lamartine, *Portrait of Alphonse de Lamartine* (detail). Paris, Musée de la Vie Romantique.
Right: Achille Devéria, *Dozing Young Ladies*, 1827. Paris, Musée du Louvre.

1re Méditation —

a Julie 1

le Soleil de nos jours, pâlit dès son aurore;
ô ma chère Julie! à peine il jette encore
quelques rayons tremblants qui combattent la nuit!
l'ombre croît, le jour meurt, tout s'efface et tout fuit!

qu'un autre à cet aspect, ou recule, ou frémisse!
qu'il craigne de fixer, le fond du précipice!
qu'il ne puisse, de loin entendre sans pâlir,
le triste chant des morts, tout prêt à retentir.
le bruit du fossoyeur, qui d'un bras mercenaire,
pour un prochain cercueil, creuse, en sifflant, la terre,
ou l'airain gémissant dont les accents confus,
annoncent aux mortels, qu'un malheureux n'est plus!

16

je te salüe, ô mort! liberateur céleste!
tu ne m'apparois point, sous cet aspect funeste,
que te prêta longtems, l'épouvante ou l'erreur;
ton bras n'est point armé, d'un glaive destructeur,
ton front n'est point cruel, ~~ni~~ ton regard perfide,
la nuit n'est pas ta sœur, ni le hasard ton guide,
tu n'anéantis pas! tu délivres! ta main
Céleste messager! porte un flambeau divin!
quand mon œil fatigué, se ferme à la lumiere,
tu viens d'un jour plus pur, inonder ma paupière,
et l'espoir, près de toi, rêvant sur un tombeau
de l'avenir caché, déchire le rideau!

Viens donc! Viens détacher, mes chaines corporelles!
Viens! ouvre ma prison! Viens! prête moi tes ailes!

Lorenzaccio

Alfred de Musset, 1834

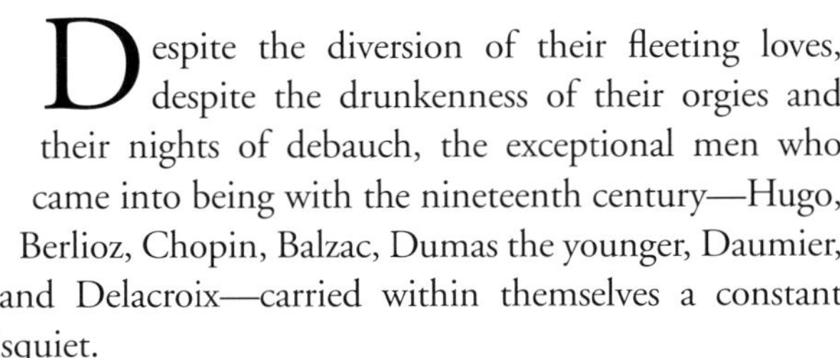

Despite the diversion of their fleeting loves, despite the drunkenness of their orgies and their nights of debauch, the exceptional men who came into being with the nineteenth century—Hugo, Berlioz, Chopin, Balzac, Dumas the younger, Daumier, and Delacroix—carried within themselves a constant disquiet.

They had experienced the ruin of the Napoleonic Empire, itself still smoking from the fires of Revolution. Inculcated in their youth with aristocratic values whose time had passed, they found little to admire in the ascendant bourgeois ethos, from which they distanced themselves.

They had expected the Revolution of 1830 and the fall of Charles X to issue in something quite different from Louis-Philippe and the July Monarchy. They sought to drown in drink their disgust with its sterile materialism and political corruption. Caught in the trap of a society eager to sate its hungers, they were trying to ward off total despair. They were all too aware of the ephemeral nature of all earthly pleasures; in 1832, an outbreak of cholera in Paris claimed more than 18,000 victims.

It is in this context that Romanticism shook Europe with the force of an earthquake. Affecting heart, soul, and spirit, this eruption surely saved this generation from delirium and collective suicide by obliging it to reinvent poetry, painting, literature, music—and love.

In this atmosphere of despair, rebellion, and invention, the love affair of George Sand and Alfred de Musset, who had met some weeks before, gave rise to *Lorenzaccio*. Inspired by one of Sand's first literary efforts, perhaps written with Musset's help, it was given final form by Musset, whose genius unmistakably stamps it.

At age twenty-four, Alfred de Musset was already a schizophrenic genius, a tortured dandy, a brilliant but lazy writer capable of great love and even greater contempt. A divided and paradoxical figure, adorable and maladjusted, he was simultaneously sentimental and cynical, enthusiastic and reserved, smitten with purity and contamination; torn between the ideal and the real, he frequented sleazy bars, opium dens, and bordellos. Like Lorenzaccio, he was above all a disappointed child: humanity had "lifted its skirt" and "shown him its monstrous nudity." It is this that spurred him to write this compelling play, which is nothing less than the first confession of a child of the new century.

Jean-Pierre Guéno

LORENZO: You will paint Florence, its piazzas, houses, and streets?

TEBALDEO: Yes, my lord.

LORENZO: Why couldn't you paint a courtesan, if you can paint such a nasty place?

TEBALDEO: I'm not used to hearing my mother called that.

LORENZO: Who are you calling your mother?

TEBALDEO: Florence, my lord.

LORENZO: Well, then you're nothing but a bastard, for your mother's a whore.

TEBALDEO: A bloody wound can introduce corruption into the healthiest of bodies. But the precious drops of my mother's blood are like a perfumed flower that heals all ills. Art, that divine flower, sometimes has need of manure to enrich the soil and make it fruitful.

LORENZO: How do you mean?

TEBALDEO: Peaceful and happy nations have sometimes shone with a pure light, but a weak one. There are many strings on angels' harps; gentle breezes can set the weakest ones to murmuring, drawing from them a suave and delicious harmony; but the golden string vibrates only when struck by the north wind. It is the noblest and most beautiful one, yet it responds well to the touch of a coarse hand. Enthusiasm is akin to suffering.

LORENZO: You are saying that an unfortunate people produces great artists. I will gladly play chemist to your alambic: it transforms a people's tears into pearls. Perish the devil! I like you. Families can be distraught, nations can die of poverty, and that is fuel for monsieur's brain. A fine poet! How do you reconcile that with your religion?

TEBALDEO: I don't laugh at a family's misfortunes; I say that poetry is the sweetest form of suffering, and that it loves its sisters. I am sorry for unfortunate peoples, but I do think that they produce great artists. Battlefields produce rich harvests, earth that is defiled can grind celestial wheat.

LORENZO: Your doublet is worn. Would you like one of my livery?

TEBALDEO: I belong to no one. For thought to be free, the body must be, too.

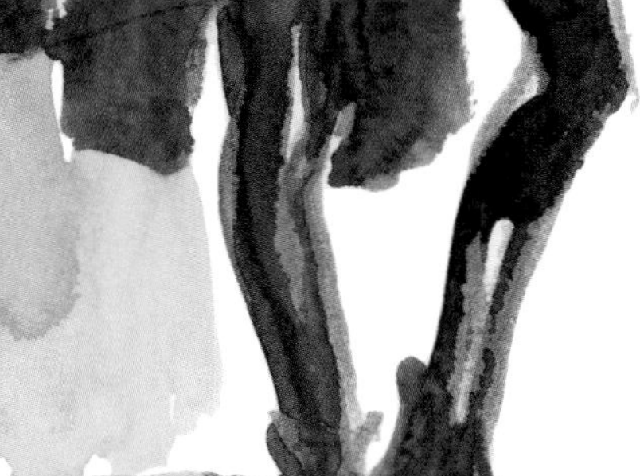

Top left: Pollet (after Charles-Zacharie Landelle), *Portrait of Alfred de Musset*, nineteenth century. Paris, Comédie Française.
Left: Lorenzaccio, watercolor by Maxime Rebière.
Opposite: Page from the autograph manuscript of *Lorenzaccio* (Act II, scene 2) used for the original edition of 1833. The play was first produced in 1896, with Sarah Bernhardt in the title role. Paris, Bibliothèque de la Comédie Française.

Lorenzo

Viens chez moi ; je te ferai peindre La Mazzafirra toute nue.

Tebaldeo

je n'~~ai~~ respecte point mon pinceau, mais je respecte mon art ; je ne puis faire le portrait d'une courtisane.

Lorenzo

Ton Dieu s'est bien donné la peine de la faire ; tu peux bien te donner celle de la peindre. Veux-tu me faire une vue de Florence ?

Tebaldeo

Oui, monseigneur.

Lorenz

Comment t'y prendrais-tu ?

Tebal

Je me placerais à l'Orient, sur la rive gauche de l'arno. C'est de cet endroit que la perspective est la plus large et la plus agréable.

Lorenz

Tu peindrais Florence, les places, les maisons, et les rues ?

Tebal

Oui, monseigneur.

Lorenz

Pourquoi donc, ne peux-tu peindre une courtisane, si tu peux peindre un mauvais lieu ?

Tebal

On ne m'a point encore appris à parler ainsi de ma mère.

Lorenz

Qu'appelles-tu ta mère ?

Tebal

Florence, seigneur.

Lorenzo

alors tu n'es qu'un bâtard ; car ta mère n'est qu'une catin.

Tebal

Une blessure sanglante peut engendrer la corruption dans le corps le plus sain. Mais des gouttes précieuses du sang de ma mère sort une plante odorante qui guérit tous les maux. L'art, cette fleur divine, a quelquefois besoin du fumier pour engraisser le sol qui la porte.

Père Goriot

Honoré de Balzac, 1835

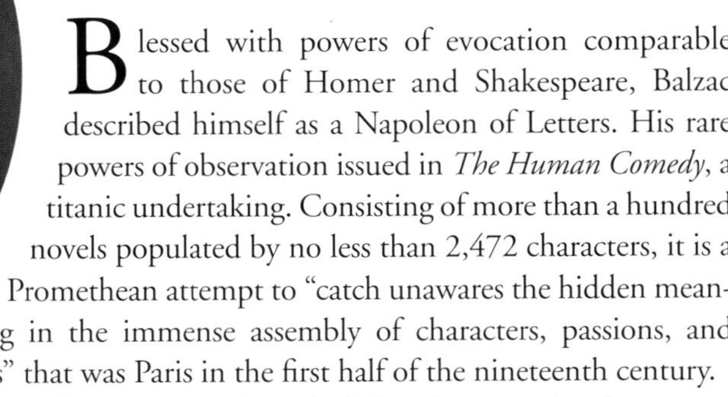

Blessed with powers of evocation comparable to those of Homer and Shakespeare, Balzac described himself as a Napoleon of Letters. His rare powers of observation issued in *The Human Comedy*, a titanic undertaking. Consisting of more than a hundred novels populated by no less than 2,472 characters, it is a Promethean attempt to "catch unawares the hidden meaning in the immense assembly of characters, passions, and events" that was Paris in the first half of the nineteenth century.

Beginning with *Père Goriot* (1835), Balzac began to implement an "idea of genius" (Proust): to have characters from one novel reappear in others. Rastignac is eighteen in *Père Goriot*, where he begins his Parisian career, and twenty-five years old in *The Fatal Skin*. We meet him again in *The Firm of Nucingen*, and in later novels he figures as a government minister. Lucien de Rubempré is a major character in *Lost Illusions* and *A Harlot High and Low*, and like Rastignac, he reappears in other works. Vautrin, an ex-convict become a man of means, then a convict again, a priest, and the chief of police, traverses *The Human Comedy* under various names and in various guises. Doctor Bianchon appears in more than twenty novels. In order "to coordinate [this] tremendous narrative, of which each novel is a chapter," Balzac tried to limit the number of his characters, already sufficiently large "to compete with the Civil Registry."

"Chance is the greatest novelist of all: to be fruitful, one need only study it," Balzac liked to say. But his body of work surpasses mere observation, becoming so visionary as to produce a startling illusion of truth. During the 1848 revolution, Maxime du Camp visited the reclusive novelist and told him about the uprising that was shaking all Paris. "Let's get back to reality!" interrupted an impatient Balzac, who proceeded to recount the latest plot developments in his *Envers de l'histoire contemporaine* (*The Seamy Side of History*). In a like spirit, the dying Balzac, wracked with pain, insisted that his fictional Dr. Bianchon be summoned to his bedside.

Pierre Chalmin

The Death of the Old Man

The next day, Rastignac was awakened at two in the afternoon by Bianchon, who, obliged to go out, asked him to take charge of Goriot, whose condition had grown much worse since morning.

"The good man hasn't three days to live," said the medical student, "but we can't stop fighting the disease—and treatment would be expensive. We can watch over him ourselves, but I haven't a penny; I turned out his pockets and rummaged through his drawers; there's nothing. I questioned him when he had his wits about him; he said he didn't have a dime."

"What do you have?"

"I've got twenty francs left," said Rastignac, "but I'll gamble with them, I'll win."

"If you lose?"

"Then I'll ask his sons-in-law and his daughters for money."

"We'll see about that," retorted Bianchon. "The most pressing thing just now is to wrap his feet and legs in boiling hot mustard plasters. If he screams, there may be hope. Can you see to that? Christophe will help you; me, I'll go to the chemist to get all the medicines we'll need. It's too bad the poor man wasn't taken to our office, he would have been better off ... Come along, I'll set you up, and don't leave him until I return."

The two young men entered the bedroom where the old man was lying. Eugène was startled by the change in Goriot's face, which was contorted, pale, and utterly moronic.

"How are you, papa!" he said to him, leaning over the mattress.

Goriot turned his dull eyes toward Eugène and looked at him attentively. It was more than the student could bear; tears came to his eyes.

"Bianchon, shouldn't there be curtains in the windows?"

"No, atmospheric condition won't affect him; it would be a good thing if he felt hot or cold. Even so, we'll need a fire. I'll send round some wood. I burned yours and what little the poor man had yesterday or last night. It was damp, water was dripping down the walls. I could scarcely dry out the room. Christophe swept the floor, it was really a stable. I burned some juniper, it smelled something awful."

de Balzac

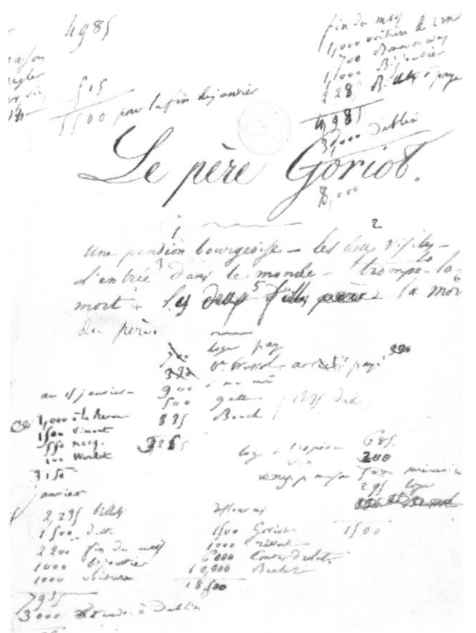

Le père Goriot.

Top left: J.-A.-G. Seguin, *Portrait of Balzac* (detail). Tours, Musée des Beaux-Arts.
Far left: Title page of the autograph manuscript of *Père Goriot*, on which Balzac, obsessed with his financial difficulties, tallied his accounts. Paris, Bibliothèque de l'Institut.
Left: An intimate glimpse of Balzac's house in Paris, now a museum: autograph manuscripts with Balzac's coffee pot.
Opposite: Page from the autograph manuscript of *Père Goriot*. Paris, Bibliothèque de l'Institut.

153.

La mort du Père.

Le lendemain Rastignac, fut
éveillé sur les deux heures après midi par Bianchon qui forcé de
sortir, le pria de garder le père Goriot dont l'état s'était fort
empiré pendant la matinée. — le bonhomme n'a pas trois jours
à vivre dit l'élève en médecine et cependant nous ne pouvons pas
cesser de combattre le mal — il va falloir lui donner des soins coûteux. nous serons bien ses gardes-
malades, mais je n'ai pas le sou moi — j'ai retourné ses
poches, fouillé ses armoires — il n'y a rien — Je l'ai questionné dans
un moment où il avait sa tête, il m'a dit ne pas avoir un
liard à lui — qu'est-ce que tu as? — Il me
reste vingt francs répondit Rastignac, mais j'irai les jouer
je les gagnerai. — si tu les perds... — je demanderai de l'argent à ses gendres et à ses filles — nous verrons, repartit
l'élève Bianchon — le plus pressé dans ce moment est de
l'envelopper d'un sinapisme bouillant
depuis les pieds jusqu'à moitié des cuisses — s'il crie, il y aura
de la ressource... tu sais comment cela s'arrange? Christophe
t'aidera — moi, je passerai chez l'apothicaire répondre de tout
les médicaments que nous y prendrons. il est malheureux que
le pauvre bonhomme n'ait pas été transportable à notre hospice
il y aurait été mieux... allons, viens que je t'installe et ne le quitte pas que je ne sois revenu. les deux jeunes gens
entrèrent dans la chambre où gisait le vieillard. Eugène
fut effrayé du changement de cette face convulsée, blanche et
profondément débile. — Hé bien, papa! lui dit-il
en se penchant sur le grabat. M. Goriot leva sur
Eugène des yeux vernis et le regarda fort
attentivement. — l'étudiant ne soutint pas ce spectacle
sans que des larmes humectassent ses yeux — Bianchon
ne faudrait-il pas des rideaux aux fenêtres — non, les
circonstances atmosphériques ne l'affectent pas — ce serait
trop heureux, s'il avait chaud ou froid — néanmoins
il nous faut du feu — je t'enverrai des falourdes
qui nous serviront jusqu'à ce que nous ayons du bois,
j'ai brûlé le tien et les mottes du pauvre homme
hier et cette nuit — il faisait humide, l'eau dégouttait des
murs — à peine ai-je pu sécher la chambre — Christophe
l'a balayée, c'était une écurie — j'y ai brûlé du genièvre

The Venus of Ille

Prosper Mérimée, 1837

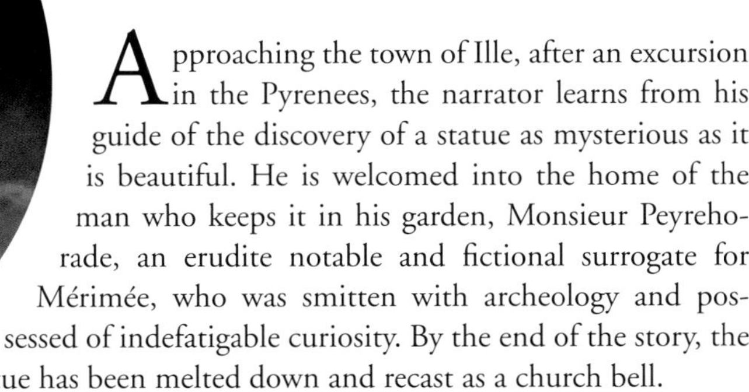

Approaching the town of Ille, after an excursion in the Pyrenees, the narrator learns from his guide of the discovery of a statue as mysterious as it is beautiful. He is welcomed into the home of the man who keeps it in his garden, Monsieur Peyrehorade, an erudite notable and fictional surrogate for Mérimée, who was smitten with archeology and possessed of indefatigable curiosity. By the end of the story, the statue has been melted down and recast as a church bell.

In a tale of crisp, even dry contours and narrated in short, briskly paced sentences, Mérimée spreads, in the words of Baudelaire, an "icy mantle that hides a modest sensibility and an ardent passion for the Good and the Beautiful." A chance encounter with a bronze statue at the foot of a dead olive tree precipitates a return to the past: to a world whose laws are unknown to some of the characters, denied and ridiculed by others, while those least ill-treated by the statue are the ones most afraid of it. In Ille, we anachronistically experience an episode in the struggle between pagan and Christian beliefs, one in which those lacking faith of any kind have no place and are eliminated, one in which the statue stands for Evil and the bell for Goodness.

Mérimée did not want us to read his *Venus of Ille* as if it were a medieval legend. Its fantastic elements sow doubt, but at the same time give some purchase to an alternative reading of reality. Today, we are not necessarily alert to everything that there is in the world, and we should be on our guard, especially where our sensual perceptions are concerned. Ultimately, the story is an indictment—one from which the narrator is not spared—of those who lead complacent lives, who do not question the legitimacy of their certainties. This was Mérimée's way of challenging the positivist, scientific biases so pervasive in the nineteenth century.

Michel Simonin

Top left: Simon Rochard, *Portrait of Prosper Mérimée*, 1852, pastel. Paris, Musée Carnavalet.
Right: Aphrodite, bronze with silver eyes, Hellenistic period (first half of the 3rd century B.C.). Paris, Musée du Louvre.
Opposite: Four pages from the autograph manuscript of *The Venus of Ille*. Paris, Bibliothèque Nationale de France.

It was indeed a Venus, and wondrously beautiful. The entire upper torso was nude, as the ancients usually represented their great deities; the right hand was raised as high as the breast, the palm turned inwards, the thumb and two forefingers extended, the others slightly bent. The other hand, near the hip, held some drapery that covered the lower part of the body. The general posture of the statue was reminiscent of the *Morra Player*, better known, I don't know why, as the *Germanicus*. Perhaps it was meant to represent the goddess playing morra.

In any case, it is impossible to see anything more perfect than the body of this Venus, more suave, more voluptuous than its contours, more elegant and noble than its drapery. I was expecting something from the late Empire; what I saw was a masterpiece of sculpture's finest moment. What most struck me was the exquisite truth of the forms; one would have thought them cast from nature, if nature ever produced such perfect models.

The hair, pulled back from the front, seemed originally to have been gilded. The head, small as in most Greek statues, bent forward slightly. As for the face, I would never manage to describe its strange character, which set it apart from any other ancient statue I could recall. It did not have the calm and severe beauty of the Greek sculptors, who systematically gave all facial features a majestic immobility. Here, by contrast, I noted with surprise the artist's clear intention to render a malice verging on viciousness. All the features were slightly tensed: the gaze a bit oblique, the mouth pinched at the corners, the nostrils a tad dilated. Disdain, irony, and cruelty were legible on this face, which nonetheless was incredibly beautiful. In truth, the more one looked at this admirable statue, the more one sensed, uneasily, that here marvelous beauty was combined with a total absence of feeling.

"If the model ever existed," I said to Monsieur de Peyrehorade, "and I doubt the heavens ever produced such a woman, how I pity her lovers! She must have delighted in making them suffer. There is something ferocious about her expression, yet I've never seen anything so beautiful."

—"It is Venus herself gloating over her prey!"[1]

1. Racine, *Phaedra,* Act I, scene 3 (Phaedra to Oenone)

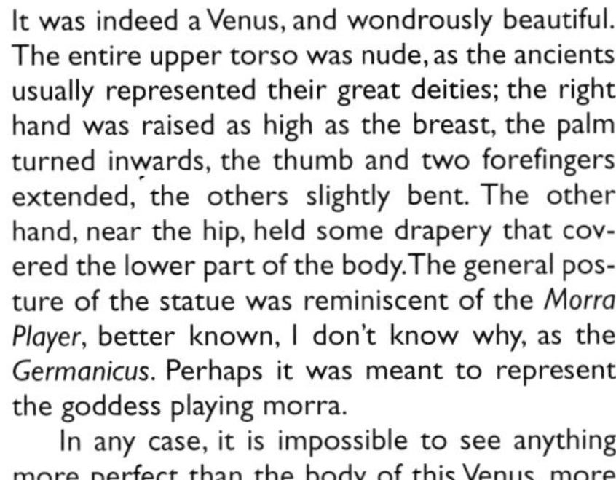

18

en dedans, le pouce et les deux premiers doigts étendus, les deux autres légèrement ployés. L'autre main rapprochée de la hanche soutenait la draperie qui couvrait la partie inférieure du corps. L'attitude de cette statue rappelait celle du joueur de Mourre, qu'on désigne je ne sais trop pourquoi sous le nom du Germanicus. Peut-être avait-on voulu représenter la déesse jouant au jeu de Mourre. Quoiqu'il en soit, il est impossible de voir quelque chose de plus parfait que le corps de cette Vénus; rien de plus suave de plus voluptueux que ses contours; rien de plus élégant et de plus noble que sa draperie. Je m'attendais à quelque ouvrage du bas empire, je voyais un chef d'œuvre du meilleur temps de la statuaire. Ce qui me frappait surtout c'était l'exquise vérité des formes, en sorte qu'on aurait pu les croire moulées sur nature, si la nature produisait d'aussi parfaits modèles.

La chevelure relevée sur le front paraissait avoir été dorée autrefois. La tête petite comme celles de presque toutes les statues grecques était légèrement ~~penchée~~ inclinée en avant. Quant à la figure, jamais je ne parviendrai à exprimer

19

son caractère étrange et dont le type ne se rapprochait de celui d'aucune statue antique dont il me souvienne. Ce n'était point cette beauté calme et sévère des sculpteurs grecs qui par système donnent à tous les traits une majestueuse immobilité. Ici, au contraire, j'observais avec surprise l'intention marquée de l'artiste de rendre la malice arrivant jusqu'à la méchanceté. Tous les traits étaient contractés légèrement: les yeux un peu obliques, la bouche relevée des coins, les narines quelque peu gonflées. Dédain, ironie, cruauté, se lisait sur ce visage d'une incroyable beauté cependant. En vérité plus on regardait cette admirable statue et plus on éprouvait un sentiment pénible, qu'une si merveilleuse beauté pût s'allier à l'absence de toute sensibilité!

— "Si le modèle a jamais existé," dis-je à Mr de Peyrehorade, "et je doute que le ciel ait jamais produit une ~~telle~~ femme, ~~elle a~~ que je plains ses amans. Elle a dû se complaire à faire mourir ~~ses amans~~ de désespoir. Il y a dans son expression quelque chose de féroce, et pourtant je n'ai jamais rien vu de si beau!"

— "C'est Vénus tout entière à sa proie attachée"!

"The Death of the Wolf"

Alfred de Vigny, after 1838

Vigny is the great unknown, the most completely misunderstood member of the Romantic generation. His restrained English gentleman's attire made gaudy waistcoats unfashionable, prompting French youth to rethink their sartorial lexicon. Far from the hubbub, he appeared as his generation's Moses, condemned to a stormy solitude on the heights. He had a knack for giving invective a classical concision: when Marie Dorval cheated on him with George Sand, he made Samson the mouthpiece for his beliefs about the future of love, which resembled those later promulgated by Nietszche:

And, looking askance at one another,
The two sexes will die apart!

What can one say about "The Death of the Wolf," a poem from *Les Destinées* (*Destinies*) seemingly contrived deliberately for inclusion in poetry anthologies? Its interesting anecdote aside, what a bitter lesson about pride! Henri de Montherlant aptly noted the similarity of its most famous line—"Only silence is great, the rest is weakness"—to Sufi wisdom. In his *Journal of a Poet*, Vigny reveals a tortured soul, a sensibility wracked by doubt beneath its defensive armor. His correspondence with Charles Baudelaire evidences a fascination with blood, cruelty, and suffering. The two men shared a violent distaste for all contemporary manifestations of mediocrity. Such affinities are never innocent, and it is time to revisit Vigny, whose universe encompasses, as a complement to its pellucid neoclassical skies, regions that are darker and more equivocal.

Pierre-Emmanuel Prouvost d'Agostino

The Death of the Wolf

I

Clouds sped past the burning moon
Like smoke fleeing a conflagration,
And the woods were dark to the horizon.
We walked in silence through the damp sod,
In the thick fog and the tall heather,
When, under pines like those of the Landes
We glimpsed large paw prints made
By the traveling wolves we had tracked.
We listened, holding our breath, our
Steps suspended. Neither wood nor plain
Uttered even a sigh; only
A mournful weathervane cried to the heavens.
For the wind blowing high above the ground
Skimmed, below, only solitary towers,
While the oaks, inclining toward the rocks,
Seemed to lean on their elbows and sleep,
So nothing rustled when, lowering his head,
The oldest of the hunters in pursuit
Looked at the sand, waiting, on his knees,
For a star to shed some light on us;

Alfred de Vigny

Top left: Alfred de Vigny, *Self-Portrait,* 1825. Paris, Comédie-Française.
Right: Jean-Baptiste Oudry, *Wolf Hunt*, 1725. Chantilly, Musée Condé.

La mort du Loup.

I

Les nuages couraient sur la lune enflammée
comme sur l'incendie on voit fuir la fumée
et les bois étaient noirs jusques à l'horizon.
– Nous marchions sans parler, dans l'humide gazon,
dans la bruyère épaisse et dans les hautes brandes,
lorsque, sous des sapins pareils à ceux des landes
nous avons aperçu les grands ongles marqués
par les Loups voyageurs que nous avions traqués.
Nous avons écouté, retenant notre haleine
et le pas suspendu. – Ni le bois ni la plaine
ne poussaient un soupir dans les airs ; seulement
la girouette en deuil criait au firmament.
Car le vent, élevé bien au-dessus des terres
n'effleurait de ses pieds que les tours solitaires
et les chênes d'en bas, contre les rocs penchés,
sur leurs coudes semblaient endormis et couchés. –
– Rien ne bruissant donc, lorsque, baissant la tête
le plus vieux des chasseurs qui s'étaient mis en quête
a regardé le sable, attendant, à genoux
qu'une étoile jetât quelque lueur sur nous ;

Lucien Leuwen

Stendhal, 1840

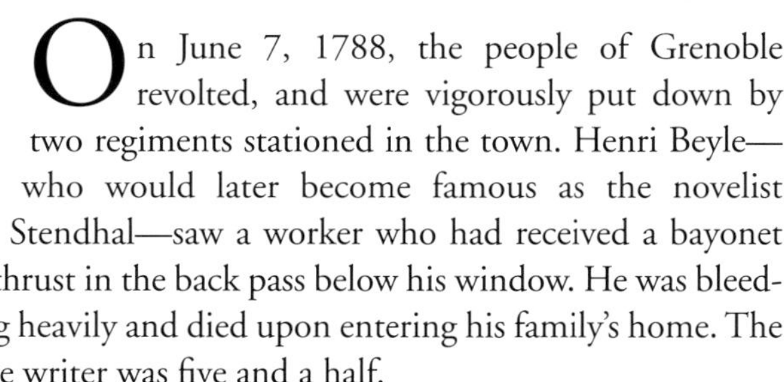

On June 7, 1788, the people of Grenoble revolted, and were vigorously put down by two regiments stationed in the town. Henri Beyle—who would later become famous as the novelist Stendhal—saw a worker who had received a bayonet thrust in the back pass below his window. He was bleeding heavily and died upon entering his family's home. The future writer was five and a half.

In *Lucien Leuwen*, Stendhal's last novel, abandoned unfinished but well advanced, the eponymous hero, who had dreamed of military glory, finds himself reduced to assaulting the barricades and killing workers. The prefect, refusing to negotiate, had insisted they be taught a lesson. A passage not retained in the posthumous edition describes the actions of Lieutenant Leuwen's men without ambiguity: "His eight chasseurs, restless, entered a house and killed a woman and a thirteen-year-old child."

The mere juxtaposition of these two episodes, one real and the other imaginary, suggests the importance of childhood memories for Stendhal—indeed, for all writers. Above all, it makes it easier to understand Stendhal's never having published the book. When one is dependent on the government for one's income, it is better to leave some texts in the drawer.

The tone of *Lucien Leuwen*, which was partly written and partly dictated, is caustic. It shows politics and military life in their true colors, which are not exactly brilliant. But this is not the crucial thing. Through his protagonist, Stendhal poses a question that preoccupied him his entire life: How can we avoid behaving despicably when we find ourselves immersed in a despicable world? In other words, how can we be happy and honorable in a world without God and without morality?

Lucien Leuwen is also a novel in which Stendhal describes the father he would like to have had. Before the fact, he followed Nietzsche's advice: "When one doesn't have a good father, one must create one." Lucien Leuwen's father is rich, intelligent, and Parisian, a bit amoral but generous, and completely devoted to his son. Which is to say the exact opposite of Stendhal's own father, Chérubin Beyle of Grenoble, at least in the eyes of his son.

Paul Desalmand

This pious ceremony took place at the Penitents, a very pretty church, neatly whitewashed, otherwise decorated only with a few highly polished walnut confessionals. "This is a poor house, but one with very pure taste," thought Lucien. He quickly perceived that there was no one there save the best people of the region. (The entire bourgeoisie of eastern France are patriots.)

Lucien saw the beadle give a sou to a rather well-dressed woman of the people, who, seeing the church open, seemed to consider entering.

"Keep going, mother," said the beadle; "this is a private chapel."

Apparently, the offer was insulting; the little bourgeoise blushed to the whites of her eyes and let the sou fall; the beadle made sure no one was watching and returned the sou to his pocket.

"All of the women around me and the few men with them have perfectly agreeable faces," Lucien said to himself. "The doctor doesn't make any more fun of me than he does of everyone else; that's all I could ask for." Having thus assuaged his vanity, Lucien greatly enjoyed himself. "It's just as in Paris," he said to himself. "The nobility thinks that religion makes men easier to govern. And my father says it was hatred of the priests that made Charles X fall! By making a show of being pious, I'll turn myself into a noble."

He saw that everyone had a book. "It isn't enough to be here, one must cut the same figure as everyone else." He turned to the doctor. Immediately, the latter left his place and requested a book from the Countess de Commercy, who had instructed her lady in waiting to bring several in a velvet satchel. The doctor returned with a superb quarto and explained to Lucien the coat of arms decorating its magnificent binding. One corner of the escutcheon was occupied by the eagle of the house of Hapsburg. The Countess de Commercy indeed belonged to the house of Lorraine, but to an old branch of it, unjustly dispossessed; the line having become muddled, it believed itself nobler than the emperor of Austria. Listening to these fine words, Lucien, persuaded that people were looking at him and fearing above all crazy laughter, studied closely the alerions of Lorraine stamped on the cover.

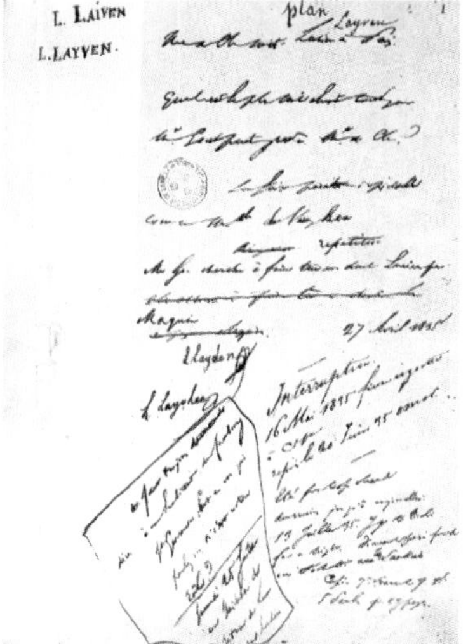

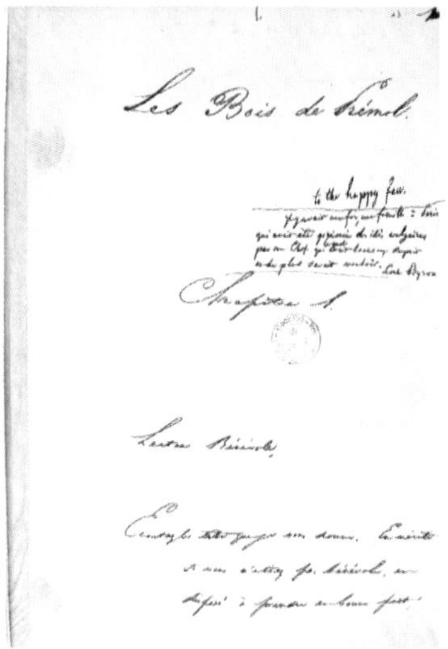

Top left: Henri Lehmann, *Portrait of Stendhal* (detail), graphite, 1841. Grenoble, Bibliothèque Municipal.
Left: Autograph notes relating to *Lucien Leuwen*. Grenoble, Bibliothèque Municipal.
Opposite: Page from the autograph manuscript of *Lucien Leuwen*. Grenoble, Bibliothèque Municipal.

corrigé le 1 mai 35

l'église au bedeau offrit [illegible] à une femme du peuple qui voyait une église ouverte fit mine d'entrer

— Passez la main dit le Bedeau, ceci est une Chapelle particulière. La petite Bourgeoise rougit en laissant tomber le sou que le Bedeau mit dans sa [illegible]

[illegible] beaucoup.

[illegible] celui-ci quitta sa place et alla demander un livre à Mad. Comtesse de Coumercy. Le Docteur revint avec un [illegible] superbe à reliure gothique et expliqua à L. [illegible] Coumercy appartenait à la maison de Lorraine et par conséquent était cousin de l'Empereur d'Autriche. [illegible] de Lorraine frappée sur la couverture avec des fers à froid.

Vers la fin du M' [illegible] dit, [illegible]

The Count of Monte Cristo

Alexandre Dumas, 1844

This man of Gargantuan appetite—an artistic force of nature—was as voracious as his belly was large. A descendant of slaves from the Antilles, he was the most inveterate exploiter of blacks in literature. The inventor of novelistic mass production, he contrived extended adventure fiction for publication, in installments, in the great newspapers of his day. Journalist and essayist, he was a Samson of the column, a boxer of the headlines, an emperor of the phrase "to be continued in the next issue"—which in his case left readers frantic, breathless to know the fate of the handsome Stanislas de la Mole, the outcome of d'Artagnan's secret mission to Buckingham, the dark fate of the flamboyant Milady de Winter.

However, we must not confuse Dumas—who, determined to conquer Romantic Paris, fed a boundless appetite for success, women, and wealth—with those contemporary fabricators of shameless melodrama who churned out text by the inch. Balzac, too, was familiar with the curse of the deadline, of constant demand on his inventive powers. Like him, Dumas belonged to the race of impertinent geniuses indifferent to ridicule and accusations of bad taste. He laughed at them, grabbing the impossible by the hair. Uninterested in pedantic historical accuracy, he re-created historical periods freely, as though he had lived through them himself. We know that, while preparing *The Three Musketeers,* he studied seventeenth-century sources, and that, for *Twenty Years Later* and *Bragelone,* he devoured the memoirs of Cardinal de Retz. But these excellent references only betray his culinary scruples, his aversion to all but the finest victuals, his predilection for writers possessed of natural elegance. In the words of Paul Morand: "He raped history, siring immortal bastards." It is true that, repeatedly and at a frantic pace, French history was impregnated by Dumas's works; but each of them has a legitimate claim to the honors of posterity.

Pierre-Emmanuel Prouvost d'Agostino

The Count of Monte Cristo

Impressions of a trip through Paris
All roads lead to Paris

Early in 1838, I encountered in Florence one of my Parisian friends, Count Albert de Mortcerf, and it was agreed between us that we would spend that year's Carnival in Rome.

As it is no small matter to spend Carnival in Rome, especially when one doesn't care to sleep in the Piazza del Popolo or in the Campo-Vaccino, we quickly wrote to Maestro Pastrini, proprietor of the London Hotel, asking him to reserve a comfortable apartment for us.

Although it was only the eighth of January, we were already a bit late; the entire hotel had been engaged a month before, save for two bedrooms and a cabinet situated *al secondo piano*, which he offered us at the modest rate of one louis per day. We accepted immediately, asking Maestro Papini to hold both rooms for us beginning Saturday, February 10. Then, our lodgings assured, Albert went directly to Naples, intending to see Rome only upon his return, while I continued my walks in the Cascine and at Bellosguardo.

On Saturday evening, as planned, we met at the customs square, Albert arriving by the Angrisani stagecoach and myself by mail coach.

Rome was already in the grip of that muffled, unfriendly hubbub that precedes its great festivals, for there were only four in Rome every year: Carnival, Holy Week, Corpus Christi, and the festival of Saint Peter.

The rest of the year, the city reverted to a glum apathy, a state somewhere between life and death that made it resemble a station between this world and the next.

A sublime station, to my mind, a stop full of poetry and character that I had already visited six times, finding it each time more marvelous and fantastic.

We arrived at the London Hotel in the middle of a crowd that was already growing and agitated; at our first inquiry, we were told with that impertinence of which only innkeepers and the drivers of hired coaches are capable that there were no rooms for us at the London Hotel, at which point I sent my card to Maestro Pastrini, requesting a moment of his time.

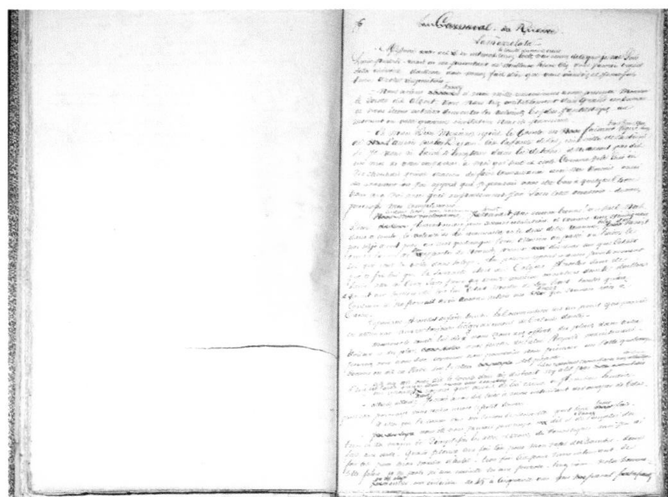

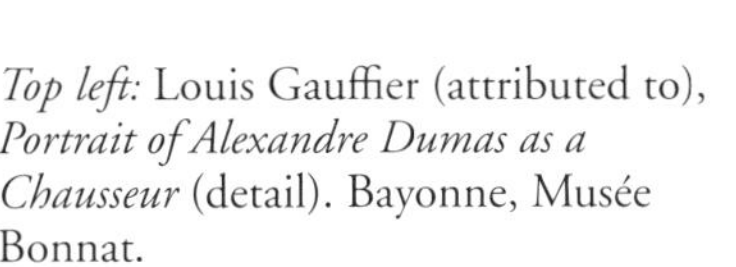

Top left: Louis Gauffier (attributed to), *Portrait of Alexandre Dumas as a Chausseur* (detail). Bayonne, Musée Bonnat.
Left and opposite: Pages from the autograph manuscript of the first draft of *The Count of Monte Cristo.* Villers-Côtterets, Musée Municipal Alexandre Dumas.

Le Comte de Montecristo

Impressions de Voyage dans Paris
tout chemin mene à Paris

Vers le Commencement de l'annee 1838 j'avais rencontré a florence un de mes amis Parisiens le Comte albert de Morcerf et il avait été convenu entre nous que nous irions passer le Carnaval de la meme annee à Rome

or comme Ce n'est pas une petite affaire que d'aller passer le Carnaval à Rome surtout quand on tient à ne pas coucher place du peuple ou dans le Campo Vaccino, nous nous empressames d'ecrire, à Maitre Pastrini proprietaire de l'hotel de Londres place d'espagne pour le prier de nous retenir un appartement confortable

quoique nous ne fussions encore qu'au 8 Janvier, il etait deja un peu tard tout l'hotel etait retenu depuis un mois à l'exception de deux Chambres d'un cabinet situé al secondo Piano qu'on nous offrait Moyennant la modique retribution d'un Louis par jour. Nous nous empressames d'accepter et nous repondimes a maitre Pastrini de tenir les deux Chambres a notre disposition pour Samedi 10 fevrier puis tranquilles desormais au moins sur notre Logis Albert partit directement pour Naples ne Comptant voir Rome qu'à son retour et moi je Continuai mes promenades quotidiennes aux Cascines et à Bello Sguardo

Le Samedi soir fideles tous deux au rendez vous donnés nous arrivions à la Place de la Douane, albert par la Diligence d'angrisani, et moi par la Malle poste

Rome etait deja en proie à cette rumeur sourde et febrile qui precede les grands evenements or à Rome il y a quatre grands evenements par an le Carnaval, la Semaine Sainte, la Fete Dieu Et la Saint Pierre

Tout le reste de l'annee La Ville retombe dans sa morne apathie etat intermediaire entre la vie et la mort et qui la rend Semblable à une espece de Station entre ce monde ci et l'autre

Station sublime mon ami Halte pleine de poesie et de Caractere que j'ai faite deja six fois et qu'à Chaque fois j'ai trouvee plus fantastique et plus Merveilleuse

Nous arrivames à l'hotel de Londres au milieu d'une foule deja grossissante et agitée. sur notre premiere demande il nous fut repondu avec cette impertinence particuliere aux cochers de fiacre retenus et aux aubergistes au complet qu'il n'y avait pas de place pour nous a l'hotel de Londres. sur quoi j'envoyai ma carte

The Devil's Pool

George Sand, 1846

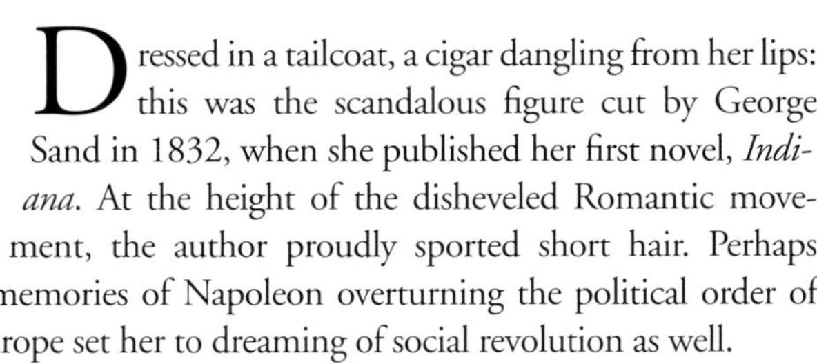

Dressed in a tailcoat, a cigar dangling from her lips: this was the scandalous figure cut by George Sand in 1832, when she published her first novel, *Indiana*. At the height of the disheveled Romantic movement, the author proudly sported short hair. Perhaps memories of Napoleon overturning the political order of Europe set her to dreaming of social revolution as well.

The future novelist was born Amandine Lucile Aurore Dupin in 1804 and spent most of her childhood at Nohant, her grandmother's country house in central France. Here she read voraciously and enjoyed an active outdoor life.

At eighteen she married Casimir Dudevant, a country squire, by whom she became the mother of two children. Nine years later, the couple parted, and Mme. Dudevant embarked on her life as a journalist, novelist, political pamphleteer, and intimate of writers and composers. Her life as George Sand had begun.

Many of her novels are autobiographical, and these often address social issues. Her later works are simple stories of rustic life. One of these, *La Mare au diable* (*The Devil's Pool*) is perhaps her best work—a gem of narrative clarity and exquisite language. Sand was impetuously honest. Initially, this feisty spirit had a hard time; her letters are a monument of complaint, overflowing with invective against a world of men determined to exclude her. As a letter-writer, she bears little resemblance to the thoughtful writer of Nohant, yet they are one and the same person. An exceptional woman, Sand had to experience and endure a great deal before she could find peace with herself as a gifted writer who happened to be a woman. Perhaps her experiments in gender nonconformity enabled her to find her path and her voice.

Pierre-Emmanuel Prouvost d'Agostino

Chapter 4
Beneath the Great Oaks

"Ah, that," said Germain, when they had taken a few steps. "What will they think at the house when the little man doesn't come in? The family will be worried, they'll look everywhere for him."

"You can tell the man who's mending the road up there that you're taking him along, and ask him to tell your people."

"Excellent, Marie, you think of everything. I'd forgotten that Jeannie must be up there."

"He lives very close to the farm and will surely deliver the message." When they had taken this precaution, Germain got the mare trotting again, and Petit-Pierre was so delighted that for a time he forgot that he hadn't eaten. But after a mile or so, the movement of the horse having upset his stomach, he started to gape, turned pale, and said he was dying of hunger.

"Here we go," said Germain. "I knew we wouldn't get very far before this little gentleman started to complain of hunger or thirst."

"I'm thirsty, too!" said Petit-Pierre.

"Well then! Let's stop at Mother Rebec's in Corlay, the Daybreak, a fine name for a poor establishment. Come on, Marie, you'll have a spot of wine, too."

"No, no, I don't need a thing," she said. ["I'll hold the mare while you go in with the child."]

Top left: Thomas Couture, *Portrait of George Sand* (detail). Paris, Musée de la Vie Romantique.
Left: Marsh with Waterlilies (*The Devil's Pool*), dendritic watercolor by George Sand. Private Collection.
Below: George Sand's inkwell. Collection Christian Sand.
Opposite: Page from the autograph manuscript of *The Devil's Pool*. In the final version of the novel, these lines appear at the beginning of chapter 7, "The Moor." Paris, Bibliothèque Nationale de France.

54

Ch 4.

Sous les grands chênes.

— Ah ça, dit Germain, lorsqu'ils eurent fait quelques pas, que va-t-on dire à la maison, en ne voyant pas rentrer ce petit bonhomme? les parens vont être inquiets, et le chercheront partout?

— Vous allez dire au cantonnier qui travaille là-haut sur la route, que vous l'emmenez et vous lui recommanderez d'avertir votre monde.

— C'est vrai, Marie, tu t'avises de tout, toi! moi, je ne pensais plus que Jeannie devait être par là.

— Et justement il demeure tout près de la métairie, il ne manquera pas de faire la commission.

Quand on eut avisé à cette précaution, Germain remit la jument au trot, et petit Pierre était si joyeux qu'il ne s'apperçut pas tout de suite qu'il n'avait pas dîné. mais le mouvement du cheval lui creusant l'estomac, il se prit au bout d'une lieue à bailler, à pâlir, et à confesser qu'il mourait de faim.

— Voilà que ça commence, dit Germain. je savais bien que nous n'irions pas loin sans que ce monsieur criât la faim, ou la soif.

— J'ai soif aussi! dit petit Pierre.

— Eh bien, nous allons donc entrer dans le cabaret de la mère Rebec, à Corlay, au Point du jour? belle enseigne, mais pauvre gîte! allons, Marie, tu boiras aussi un doigt de vin.

— Non, non, je n'ai besoin de rien dit-elle,

"Tomorrow, at dawn"

Victor Hugo, 1847

Early in September of 1843, Victor Hugo turned forty-one. He was already a famous and celebrated writer, having behind him his *Odes*, his *Ballads*, *The Orientals*, *Autumn Leaves* and *Twilight Songs*, *Han of the Island*, *The Hunchback of Notre-Dame*, *Cromwell*, *Hernani*, and *Ruy Blas*. Two years earlier, he had become a member of the Académie Française. For a decade, he had carried on a passionate affair with Juliette Drouet, who every year looked forward to the summer, when her "Toto" could sometimes get away from his family long enough to take a trip with her, thereby briefly enlivening her life as a reclusive, oft-betrayed mistress.

Thus Hugo abandoned both his wife Adèle and his daughter Léopoldine, who had asked him to vacation with them in the valley of the Seine. For several weeks, he traveled in Spain with Juliette as "Monsieur and Madame Georget." Their escapade was nearing its end. For several days, the poet had been strangely sad and nostalgic. "There is death in my soul, it seems to me that this island is a large coffin set down in the sea," he wrote about the island of Oleron, which they had just visited. On September 9, in Rochefort, on the way home, he learned from the newspaper *Le Siècle* that Léopoldine had drowned accidentally five days before, along with her husband Charles Vacquerie and the child she was carrying. A few days later, Léopoldine and Charles were buried in the same coffin in front of the small church in Villequier.

For the next ten years, until the rebirth that was his exile, Hugo continued to write but published nothing. He fled his pain by pursuing power, honors, and fleeting liaisons. His suffering never subsided: the pain became ever more intense, to such an extent that four years later, when he wrote "*Demain, dès l'aube*" ("Tomorrow, at dawn"), he neglected to capitalize the first word of its lines. He filled his notebooks with verses dedicated to his daughter, unfinished poems inspired by the one he called "the angel of his youth," she "whose gaze mirrored the clarity of her soul," and whose long black hair continued to haunt him to the end.

And why this wind that forgets me but takes her,
She a green leaf, and myself a dead one.

Jean-Pierre Guéno

Tomorrow, at dawn, when the countryside turns
white,
I will leave. You see, I know that you await me.
I will go through forest, I will go through mountains.
I can remain distant from you no longer.

I will walk with my eyes fixed on my thoughts.
Seeing nothing outside of myself, hearing not a
sound,
Alone, unknown, with bent back and crossed hands,
Sad, and the day will be for me like night.

I will look neither at the golden twilight,
Nor at the sails approaching Honfleur,
And when I arrive, I will place on your tomb
A bouquet of green holly and flowering heather.

October 4, 1847

Victor Hugo

Top left: Nicolas-François Chifflart, *Portrait of Victor Hugo* (detail), ca. 1868. Paris, Maison de Victor Hugo.
Right: Chatillon, *Léopoldine Hugo with a Book of Hours*. Paris, Maison de Victor Hugo.
Opposite: Autograph manuscript of "Tomorrow, at dawn" a poem from *Contemplations*, published in 1847. Paris, Bibliothèque Nationale de France.

269

—

demain, dès l'aube, à l'heure où blanchit la campagne,
je partirai. vois-tu, je sais que tu m'attends.
j'irai par la forêt, j'irai par la montagne.
~~car je ne puis rester~~
je ne puis demeurer loin de toi plus longtemps.

je marcherai les yeux fixés sur mes pensées,
sans rien voir au dehors, sans entendre aucun bruit,
seul, inconnu, le dos courbé, les mains croisées,
triste, ~~et~~ le jour pour moi sera comme la nuit.

je ne regarderai ni l'or du soir qui tombe,
ni les voiles au loin descendant vers Harfleur,
et quand j'arriverai, je mettrai sur ta tombe
un bouquet de houx vert et de bruyère en fleur.

—

4 octobre 1847.

et de la sauge
une branche de ~~houx et de bruyère~~ en fleur.

—

The Lady of the Camellias

Alexandre Dumas the Younger, 1848

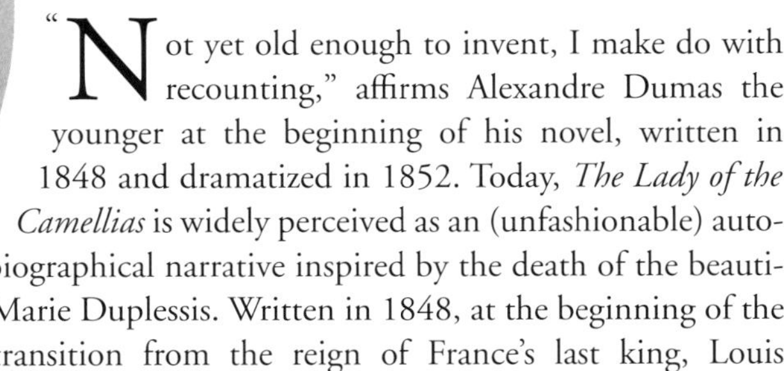

"Not yet old enough to invent, I make do with recounting," affirms Alexandre Dumas the younger at the beginning of his novel, written in 1848 and dramatized in 1852. Today, *The Lady of the Camellias* is widely perceived as an (unfashionable) autobiographical narrative inspired by the death of the beautiful Marie Duplessis. Written in 1848, at the beginning of the violent transition from the reign of France's last king, Louis Philippe, to the Second Empire of Napoleon III, it tells of a love condemned by the hypocritical conventions of a world in which adultery was commonplace. Everything was against the union of Marguerite Gautier, a courtesan who had made the camellia her emblem, and Armand Duval, a respectable young man. The story has its subversive aspect, for it dared challenge the legitimacy of a rotting moral code.

The great-grandson of a marquis and a slave, the natural son of a laundress and the writer Alexandre Dumas, the young Alexandre, who was placed in a foster home by the police at age seven after an argument between his parents, could not help but be sensitive to social prejudices that had made him a bastard twice over. In a volatile world dominated by former aristocrats and would-be rentiers, men were at the mercy of women, themselves held hostage by a society which treated them like a form of currency, arranging their marriages on the basis of their dowries and keeping them for sensual pleasure. It is hardly surprising that the younger Dumas should have tried to open his contemporaries' eyes.

When the novel was made into a play (known in English as *Camille*) Dumas watered it down to assure its success with the theatrical public, which was indeed taken in by it: somewhat disingenuously, they gave it a triumphant welcome, not realizing that its author was himself torn between his sexual drives and his need for authenticity, between his taste for vice and his longing for virtue.

The role of Marguerite has been performed by many great actresses, from Sarah Bernhardt to Greta Garbo and Isabelle Adjani—not to mention by many great sopranos in Verdi's *La Traviata*. The dialogue of this well-crafted play, ironically shallow and flat, is more akin to Ionesco's theater of the absurd than to conventional boulevard fare; it conveys the disquiet of a man who had understood that the hypocrisies of the demi-monde were shared by society as a whole, one intimately familiar with corrupt values that often unjustly condemned human beings to marginality.

Jean-Pierre Guéno

Act II
Scene 8

ARMAND: Good day, my dear Prudence. Here I am, Marguerite. What's the matter? How pale you are. You're shaking. Are you ill? What's happened?

MARGUERITE: I'm fine, my friend. But you, how is it you're in Paris?

ARMAND: My father has arrived and I had a long discussion with him. He wanted to separate us, Marguerite, but nothing in the world could separate me from you. He threatened me! What are such threats to me? He said he would cancel my pension. So I'll work. What work could be hard for me when I have your love at the end of the day?

MARGUERITE: My god, how he loves me.

ARMAND: Let's go, Marguerite; it's getting late, and there's nothing to keep us in Paris. Let's get going.

MARGUERITE: Not yet.

ARMAND: But what's the matter? In heaven's name.

MARGUERITE: Something about your unexpected arrival seems unlucky, that's why I'm upset. I can't be the cause of a break between you and your father, my friend. You have to see him again, go to him. Perhaps we should stop seeing each other (Armand becomes alarmed) for a time. I no longer know what I'm saying. I'm going mad, and all my courage is disappearing.

ARMAND: My father will reconsider. Calm yourself, and let's be off. I hate Paris. I feel it's unlucky for me.

MARGUERITE: So we'll return to our little house, and we'll love each other as before, and we'll be happy, as we've been for the last three months. Tell me so, Armand, tell me that you love me. I very much need to hear you say it.

ARMAND: Yes, I love you, Marguerite, you know it well. But you've become ill thinking about something that you're hiding from me. [illegible].

MARGUERITE: Nothing, my friend, nothing, I swear it. Apart from my love, which easily alarms you, I'm fine. There's nothing new in my life. I was chatting with Prudence about some business when you arrived. She came to fetch me, didn't you, Prudence, to see a man who is waiting at her place. You know, the man who's to handle my sale. I did not want you to run into him, so I asked him to go to her place, that's all. In a few minutes I'll be with you and we'll never be apart from one another again. Wait for me, I'll be right back, my adored Armand. Come, Prudence, come (Prudence urges her offstage).

ARMAND: Don't be long.

Top left: Léon Bonnat, *Portrait of Alexandre Dumas the Younger* (detail). Châteaux de Versailles et de Trianon.
Left: The Lady of the Camellias, watercolor by Maxime Rebière.
Opposite: Two pages of the autograph manuscript of the play *Camille,* Dumas's dramatization of his novel *The Lady of the Camellias*. Paris, Bibliothèque Nationale de France.

11 51

Marguerite

Oui, je veux vous charger de quelque chose.

Prudence

De quoi ?

Marguerite

De cette lettre.

Prudence

Pour qui.

Marguerite

Regardez.

Prudence lisant l'adresse.

M. de Varville.

Marguerite

Silence, voici Armand.

Scène 8.

Marg. Prud. Armand.

Armand.

Bonjour, ma chère Prudence, me voici Marguerite. Qu'as-tu. Comme tu es pâle. Tu trembles. Es-tu malade, que t'est-il arrivé ?

Marguerite

Je n'ai rien, mon ami. mais toi. comment s'est passé que tu es à Paris.

Armand

Mon père est arrivé et j'ai eu avec lui une longue explication. Il voulait nous séparer, Marguerite, mais rien dans le monde ne pourra me séparer de toi. Il m'a menacé ! que peut-il contre moi ? Il m'a dit que ma supposée ... ma perte. Eh bien, je t'ai vue aussi. Quel bonheur ... quand j'aurais ton amour à lui faire oublier.

Marguerite

Comme il t'aime mon Dieu.

Armand

Allons, Marguerite, il se fait tard, nous n'avons plus rien à faire à Paris. Partons !

Marguerite

Pas encore.

Armand

Mais qu'as-tu ? au nom du ciel.

Marguerite

~~Je craignais un malheur~~. J'avais pressenti un malheur dans ton arrivée inattendue. Voilà ma nature et mon émotion. Je respire, je te brouiller avec ton père, mon ami. Il faut le revoir. Va chez lui. Peut-être devrions-nous cesser de nous voir (mouvement d'Armand) pendant quelques jours. Je ne sais plus ce que je dis. Je deviens folle et tout mon courage s'en va.

12 52

Armand.

Mon père me rendra ce qu'il a dit. Je suis tranquille par ce côté. J'ai promis de dîner, il me semble que ce n'est rien de malheureux pour nous.

Marguerite

Est-ce que nous allons ~~repartir~~ retourner là-bas, dans notre petite maison, et nous aimer comme auparavant, et nous serons heureux comme nous le sommes depuis trois mois. Dis-moi cela, mon Armand, dis-moi que tu m'aimes, j'ai ~~bien~~ ~~tu~~ bien besoin de l'entendre dire.

Armand

~~Mais~~ Oui, je t'aime, Marguerite, tu es bien malade. Il y a quelque chose que tu me caches. Je veux le savoir.

Marguerite

Moi, mon ami, rien, je t'assure. C'est mon amour qui s'alarme facilement. Je me porte bien. Il n'y a rien de nouveau dans ma vie. Je causais d'affaires avec Prudence quand tu es venu. Elle venait me chercher, n'est-ce pas Prudence, pour voir un homme qui m'attend chez elle, un homme dont j'ai besoin pour ma vente. Je voulais partir que tu te trouvais avec ton père. Je suis revenue chez elle, voilà tout. Je vais être ici dans quelques minutes. Je vais auprès de lui et nous quitterons Paris. Attends-moi. Je reviens, mon Armand, adieu. Venez, Prudence, venez. (~~Elle~~ Prudence l'entraîne)

Armand

Reviens vite.

Scène 9.

Armand seul.

Bonne Marguerite. Comme elle s'effraie à l'idée d'une séparation. Comme elle m'aime. Dans quelle agitation elle est. ~~Sept~~ huit heures déjà. Voici la chambre où je l'ai connue ! Que de choses se sont passées depuis ce jour. Elle était alors entourée de moqueries qui allaient prendre une si large place dans sa vie. Ce Varville qui était là, comme elle le traitait. Comme elle m'avait traité, moi-même, mais elle m'aime, moi. Quelle éloquence il y a dans les objets inanimés. ~~Comme~~ Que de choses me ~~disent~~ dit cette chambre muette. — Mon père est peut-être irrité. Qu'a-t-il fait ? Il réfléchira. Il pardonnera. Demain j'irai le voir. Si je pouvais le faire trouver avec Marguerite, il serait convaincu tout de suite, que la

Aurélie

Gérard de Nerval, 1855

He was perhaps the only real French Romantic—or, more precisely, the only German Romantic in French literature, with all that this entails in the way of curses, madness, daydreaming, and fantasy, of flagrant yet longed-for failure.

Nerval never exploited lyricism for financial gain, never sought large print runs or high-profile publicity. Unlike Lamartine, he did not write to bring tears to beautiful eyes, nor to nourish the dreams of women in the provinces; unlike Hugo, he caressed only chimeras, rejecting social and political ambitions as too secular and constraining. As with Racine's Phaedra, his sickness, despite its affinities with his own time, came from far away. Like Musset the misunderstood and ill-loved, he suffered, in body and soul, from a split personality; like Hoffmann, he fled from something within himself—a sarcastic, even diabolical *doppelgänger*—to the point of self-destruction. He felt many affinities with the eponymous hero of Goethe's *Faust*, a work that he translated with great care.

He sought escape from his inner landscape, a paradise of shadow and fog, of impossibly idealized love, outside of Paris, near Chantilly. There, in green fields and still pools, below the gently changing skies of the Ile-de-France, he set young girls dancing in robes of dawn and twilight destinies. Living shades who spread the petals of their blossoming youth on the tomb of the "inconsolable and desperate widow" who was Gérard de Nerval.

Pierre-Emmanuel Prouvost d'Agostino

Memories of Gérard de Nerval

It was in 1840 that my *vita nuova* began. I was in Belgium, where I was staying in rue Brûlée, near the large market. I went regularly to dine, on the Montagne de la Cour, at the home of a beautiful lady friend, and then went to the Théâtre de la Monnaie, to which I had an author's pass. There I had the intoxicating pleasure of hearing again a charming singer whom I had known in Paris and who was performing as a principal at the Brussels opera. Occasionally, another beautiful lady signaled to me in the orchestra from her box, and I went up to see her. We chatted about the singer, whom she thought gifted. She was good and indulgent about my old Parisian passion, and I was almost always permitted to accompany her to her house at the Schaarbeck gate.

One evening she invited me to a magnetism seance, where I saw a somnambulist for the first time. That very day, Napoleon's ashes had been returned to Paris. The somnambulist gave a detailed description of the ceremony that agreed perfectly with the accounts in the next day's Paris newspapers. But she added that, at the moment Napoleon's body made its triumphal entry into the Invalides, his soul escaped the casket and, flying away to the north, came to rest on the plain at Waterloo.

I was struck by this idea, as were the others in the assembled company, which included the Bishop of Malines. Two days later, there was a brilliant concert at the Salle de la Grande Harmonie. Two queens were in attendance. The queen of song was the woman I shall henceforth call Aurélie. The second was the queen of Belgium, no less beautiful and younger still. They were coiffed identically, their hair hanging over their necks in gold Medici hairnets.

This concert made a great impression on me. From that moment, I thought only of returning to Paris, in hopes of obtaining a commission that would send me back to Flanders in a more brilliant position.

Gérard de Nerval

Top left: Gérard de Nerval, daguerreotype by Adolphe Legros, 1853 or 1854.
Left: A theater box in the nineteenth century, watercolor by Maxime Rebière.
Opposite: Page from an early draft of *Aurélie*, autograph manuscript. Paris, Bibliothèque Nationale de France.

Souvenirs de Gérard de Nerval. 1. 2

Ce fut en 1840 que commença pour moi cette — Vita nuova. —

Je me trouvais à Bruxelles, où je demeurais rue Brûlée, près le grand marché. J'allais ordinairement dîner, montagne de la Cour chez une belle dame de mes amies, puis je me rendais au théâtre de la Monnaie où j'avais mes entrées comme auteur. Là je m'enivrais du plaisir de revoir une charmante cantatrice que j'avais connue à Paris et qui tenait à Bruxelles les premiers rôles d'opéra. Parfois une autre belle dame me faisait signe de sa loge aux places d'orchestre où j'étais et je montais près d'elle. Nous causions de la cantatrice, dont elle aimait le talent. Elle était bonne et indulgente pour cette ancienne passion parisienne et presque toujours j'étais admis à la reconduire jusque chez elle à la porte de Schaarbeck.

Un soir on m'invita à une séance de magnétisme. Pour la première fois je voyais une somnambule. C'était le jour même où avait lieu à Paris le convoi de Napoléon. La somnambule décrivit tous les détails de la cérémonie, tels que nous les lûmes le lendemain dans les journaux de Paris. Seulement elle ajouta qu'au moment où le corps de Napoléon était entré triomphalement aux Invalides son âme s'était échappée du cercueil et prenant son vol vers le Nord, était venue se reposer sur la plaine de Waterloo.

Cette grande idée me frappa, ainsi que les personnes qui étaient présentes à la séance et parmi lesquelles on distinguait Mgr l'Évêque de Malines. — A deux jours de là il y avait un brillant concert à la Salle de la Grande Harmonie. Deux reines y assistaient. La reine du chant était celle que je nommerai désormais Aurélie. La seconde était la reine de Belgique, non moins belle et plus jeune. Elles étaient coiffées de même et portaient à la nuque derrière leurs cheveux tressés, la résille d'or des Médicis.

Cette soirée me laissa une vive impression. Dès lors je ne songeai plus qu'à retourner à Paris espérant me faire charger d'une mission qui me mettrait plus en lumière à mon retour dans les Flandres.

Sophie's Misfortunes

Comtesse de Ségur, 1858

Like her heroine, her first name was Sophie. Her family name was Rostopchine, which carried associations of fire and destruction. Her father had burned Moscow to spite Napoleon. Little inclined to such follies, the countess led an uneventful life. Having married badly, she decided, once she had become a grandmother, to transform her world into art.

Her stories unfold around 1850, a moment when the first daguerreotypes were appearing and photography remained a pastime pursued by provincial landowners. Sentimental children's stories? Not quite! It would be unjust to reduce them to the level of a well-bred young lady's "accomplishments": below their innocuous surface there lurks a mischievous cruelty. The presiding spirit of her fiction is devilish but charming, and it is situated at the threshold of the lost, verdant paradise of our first loves. Children perceive the absurdities of grownups with the brutal clarity of innocence. The countess adopted the point of view of these grave little judges, conveying something of their relentless clear-sightedness.

Paradoxically, her world of little girls appealed to young boys. Her heroines, given deliciously old-fashioned names, were their first loves: Camille and Madeleine, too well behaved to be true; the reasonable Marguerite de Rosebourg; and the incorrigible Sophie, and her dear cousin Paul to whom, reunited with him after countless adventures, she avows: "I didn't forget you. You were asleep in my heart, and I woke you up sometimes to tell you that I still loved you."

Pierre-Emmanuel Prouvost d'Agostino

Bread for the Horses

Sophie liked to eat. Her mama knew that overeating was bad for you, so she forbade Sophie to eat between meals. But Sophie, who was always hungry, ate everything she could get her hands on.

Every day after lunch, around two o'clock, Madame de Réan fed bread and salt to Monsieur de Réan's horses. There were more than a hundred of them. Sophie followed her mama with a basket full of pieces of dark bread and gave her one at every stall; but her mama severely forbade her to eat any of it, since this black, scarcely cooked bread would give her a stomachache.

Her last stop was the pony stable. Sophie had a pony of her own, which her father had given her; it was a little black horse, no larger than a small donkey. She was permitted to feed the bread to her pony. She often took a bite out of it before giving it to him.

One day, when she was more [desirous of this black bread than usual, she held it between her finger, such that only a small part of it was exposed.]

Cte de Ségur née Rostopchine.

Top left: The Comtesse de Ségur at age forty-two, watercolor by Gaston de Ségur.
Right and below: Sophie's Misfortunes, watercolors by Maxime de Rebière.
Opposite: Page from the autograph manuscript of *Sophie's Misfortunes*. Paris, Bibliothèque Labadens.

Le pain des chevaux

Sophie était gourmande. Sa Maman savait que de trop manger est mauvais pour la santé; aussi défendait-elle à Sophie de manger entre ses repas.

Mme de Réan allait tous les jours après déjeuner, vers deux heures, donner du pain et du sel aux chevaux de Mr de Réan; il y en avait plus de cent. Sophie suivait sa Maman avec un panier plein de morceaux de pain bis et dans chaque stalle elle lui en présentait un. Sophie aurait bien voulu en manger parce que ce pain noir lui faisait envie, mais sa Maman lui défendait sévèrement d'en manger parce que ce pain noir et mal cuit lui faisait mal à l'estomac. Elle finissait par l'écurie des poneys. Sophie avait son poney à elle; c'était un tout petit cheval noir, pas plus grand qu'un petit âne, que lui avait donné son Papa; on lui permettait de donner elle-même du pain à son poney. Souvent elle mordait dedans avant de le lui présenter. Un jour, qu'elle avait plus

The Goncourt Brothers, 1858

Despite an age difference of eight years, Jules and Edmond de Goncourt exemplified an extreme form of twinship that Edmond evokes beautifully in his novel, *The Zemganno Brothers*: "The two brothers did not only love one another; they were linked by mysterious ties, by psychic attachments, by the curious affinities between twin natures, and this despite a considerable discrepancy in their ages and their having diametrically opposed characters. Their first, instinctive responses to things were identical. They experienced sudden feelings of sympathy or antipathy simultaneously, and when they went out, they seemed indistinguishable to everyone who saw them."

Each of them was an engraver, a draftsman, a painter, a historian, a novelist, a journalist, an art critic, a collector, a playwright. Twenty years before it became fashionable, the two brothers, sizing up the world with a gaze that was lucid, often cynical and disabused but ever curious, laid the groundwork for literary naturalism, exploring the dark recesses of a bourgeois society that was, politically and socially, at an impasse.

In 1851, they began to keep a common diary whose daily entries were made for the first nineteen years in Jules's hand, then, for twenty-six years after Jules's death, by Edmond. Long before Proust, they embarked upon a kind of "search for present time," discussing a forty-four-year span of literary life with an acidity and, on occasion, a malevolence that have become legendary. They wielded their shared pen like a razor, using it to slash, slice, and dice. Their cynicism and misanthropy fostered the development of an astonishing visual acuity, a permanent distancing from a world that they never stopped scrutinizing through magnifying lenses, the better "to see beings and things through unaccustomed glasses."

Jean-Pierre Guéno

Top left: Edmond and Jules de Goncourt, photograph by Nadar. *Opposite and below:* Page (with passages in both authors' hands) from the autograph manuscript of *A Journal of Literary Life*. Paris, Bibliothèque Nationale de France.

[April] 25
At Monsieur Norblin's, a true collector, providential for the dealers and sales rooms. Small, modest interior populated by children, full of five-hundred-franc Claude Lorrains. Shows us his rich collection of Dutch works: Jan Steens for which he paid top dollar. All of these masters bore me; when I think about the men who drew all these trivialities, I see them as coarse and stocky, with big behinds, pissing into the fireplace, their caps over their ears, wearing a baker's outfit, a little kneading apron—ugly and ill-bred like Tenier's work, lacking ideals.

[April] 28 [1858]
I've been inside the Hôtel de Ville only twice.

Once in 1848, I saw in the Salle Saint-Jean the bodies of those killed in February, neatly arranged in coffins.

Another time, in the same room, I was stripped nude as a worm wearing blue glasses; and, despite my myopia, given that I was a property owner, the review board decided that I would make a charming hussar.

This evening I went to the Hôtel de Ville for the third time, for a ball. It was rich and it was poor. Much gold, and then there was the magnificence of the rooms and galleries. Damask everywhere, little velvet; not a single old tapestry. Fabric everywhere, art nowhere. And on the walls, crammed with insipid allegories painted by second-rate artists whose names I don't care to know, even less art than elsewhere. Ah! Take me back to the Louvre! But the dazzle of the twelve thousand pairs of eyes present was not exactly demanding . . .

I glimpsed, over a fireplace, a large portrait of the emperor that's worthy of Horace Vernet. As for the ball, it was a ball; at least people elbowed one another and even danced. I saw a uniform and an institution as old as General Foy, or the expression "It's the best of Republics," a myth, a symbol, a flag, a relic: students of the École Polytechnique dancing en masse, furiously, with bits of gowns made of blue or white gauze caught on the buttons of their tails.

I was most struck—and they were beautiful things—by the siphon-shaped inkstands in the Conseil Municipal: they are visible on these great occasions. They are monumental, serious, grave, restrained, foursquare, opulent, and imposing; they have something of the Pyramids and something of the belly of Monsieur Prudhomme [an archetypal puffed-up egoist featured in the lithographs of Daumier]: they resemble the good sense and prosperity of a bourgeois! Oh! The inkwells of Maurepas [a government minister], of Meissonnier [a virtuoso rococo silversmith]!

E. J. de Goncourt

25. Été chez Mr Norblin. un véritable amateur, la providence des marchands et des ventes; petit intérieur modeste et peuplé d'enfants, tout plein de Claude Lorrain de cinq cents francs. nous montre collection riche d'hollandais, des Jean Steen payés au poids de l'or. — Tous ces maîtres là m'ennuient: je pense aux hommes qui ont dessiné tous ces magots là, et je les vois vilains, trapus, gros culs, pissant dans la cheminée; leurs bonnets sur l'oreille, leur veston de boulanger, leur petit valet de pétun: — de laids ~~et bêtes~~ comme des Teniers: sans plus d'idéal.

28. Je n'étais entré que deux fois dans ma vie à l'hôtel de ville; une fois en 48, j'avais vu dans la salle St Jean, ~~tous les morts~~ tous les tués de février bien proprement garnalisés dans des cercueils; une autre fois, dans la même salle, je m'étais mis nu comme un ver, avec des lunettes bleues, et malgré ma myopie, et attendu que j'étais propriétaire, le Conseil de révision avait déclaré que je ferais un charmant hussard. — Ce soir je vais pour la troisième fois à l'hôtel de ville, mais au bal. Cela est riche, et cela est paré; de l'or, et puis c'est toute la magnificence des salles et des galeries, du damas partout, à peine du velours, pas une tenture de vieille tapisserie; le tapissier partout, nulle part l'art, et sur les murs chargés de plates allégories peintes par des Vasari dont je ne crois pas savoir le nom, moins d'art encore qu'ailleurs; Ah! qu'on me ramène ~~au plafond~~ à la galerie d'Apollon! Mais l'éblouissement des douze mille paires d'yeux qui sont là. n'est pas bien exigeant. X Pour le bal c'est un bal: au moins l'on se coudoie et même l'on danse: et où l'on danse, j'ai vu un uniforme et une institution vieille comme le général Foy, ou le mort: c'est la meilleure des Républiques; un mythe, un symbole, un drapeau, une relique: des deux de l'École polytechnique. valsant en masse ~~furieusement~~ avec des morceaux de robe de gaze bleues ou blanches accrochées aux boutons de leurs pans d'habit; Ce qui m'a le plus frappé, et c'est une belle chose, ce sont les encriers syphoïdes des conseil municipal: on les voit ces grands jours là, ils sont monuments; sérieux, graves, recueillis, carrés, opulents, imposants: ils ont quelque chose des pyramides. et quelque chose du ventre de Mr Prudhomme. ils ressemblent au bon sens et à la prospérité d'un bourgeois. X Puis çà et là de grandes pancartes qui ressemblent à des pages d'écriture de Brard et St Omer: ce sont de solennelles poignées de main en anglais de la cité de Londres à la municipalité de Paris. ~~Il y a des femmes, des femmes~~ Point de parisiennes: une parisienne ~~joyeuses et laides~~ ~~sans type~~ n'est une femme au bal. Il n'y a de parisiennes que dans la rue ou en omnibus: des femmes sans type, laides et joyeuses, qui peuvent la misère décente des ménages de petits employés, des fortunes perdues des Malvina de la maison Nucingen. parfois une jolie fille au bras de son vieux père général, une jolie fille n'...

X J'ai aperçu au dessus d'une cheminée un grand portrait de l'Empereur qui mérite bien d'être d'Horace Vernet. ~~Ce serait une grande économie un rabais du vingtième siècle que de~~ J'aime à croire que le cadre est un panneau partout. Il faut songer au lendemain.

X Oh! l'ordre de Mr de Maurepas de Meissonnier!

My Heart Laid Bare

Charles Baudelaire, 1859

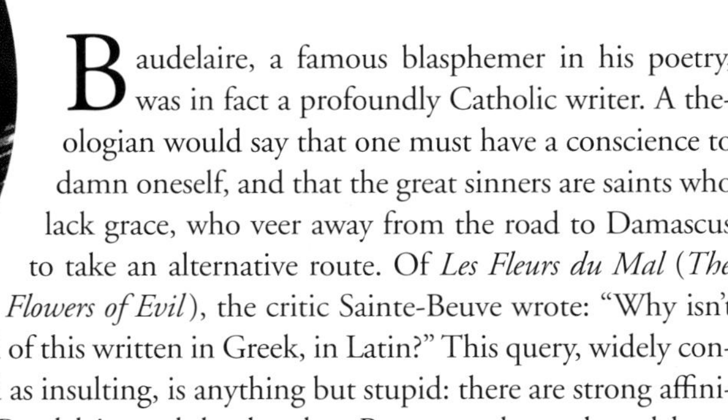

Baudelaire, a famous blasphemer in his poetry, was in fact a profoundly Catholic writer. A theologian would say that one must have a conscience to damn oneself, and that the great sinners are saints who lack grace, who veer away from the road to Damascus to take an alternative route. Of *Les Fleurs du Mal* (*The Flowers of Evil*), the critic Sainte-Beuve wrote: "Why isn't all of this written in Greek, in Latin?" This query, widely construed as insulting, is anything but stupid: there are strong affinities between Baudelaire and the decadent Roman authors who celebrate the Christian faith—"in an indolent language in which dances the gold of the sun," as Verlaine would say, another renegade believer.

What are these explosive sensibilities, these eruptions of conscience that spangle despair with stars? As a poet, Baudelaire was in many ways the last of the eighteenth-century moralists. A dandy who decked himself out in epigrams, he preferred lines alive with intelligence to the slack diction of the preacher. He never stooped to making the pathetic vulgar; although he attacked an era that Nietzsche would stigmatize as mortal to superior souls, his pen was never inelegant. An Old-Regime decorousness shapes this calligraphy, as if with curling tongs. This rich vein of contradiction would issue in the shattered face visible in Carjat's photograph: a mask of half-crazed contempt, a face as enigmatic as a tale by Edgar Allan Poe. The teeth part only to utter an obscenity! "Defeated hope / Weeps."

Pierre-Emmanuel Prouvost d'Agostino

My heart laid bare

Torture is, as a technique for discovering truth, a barbaric idiocy; it is to use a material means to a spiritual end.

The death penalty results from a mystical idea that is completely misunderstood today. The aim of the death penalty is not to *save* society, at least materially. It aims to effect the *spiritual* salvation of society and the guilty party. For the sacrifice to be perfect, there must be assent and joy on the victim's part. It would be impious to give a condemned man chloroform, for this would rob him of awareness of his grandeur as a victim and deny him his chance to enter Paradise.

As for torture, it issued from an infamous part of the heart of Man, thirsty for pleasure of the flesh. Cruelty and voluptuousness, identical sensations, like extreme cold and extreme heat.

Charles Baudelaire

Top left: Charles Baudelaire, *Self-Portrait.* Paris, Musée du Louvre. *Opposite and below:* Page from the autograph manuscript of *Mon coeur mis à nu* (*My Heart Laid Bare*). Paris, Bibliothèque Nationale de France.

Quant à la torture, elle est née de la partie infâme du coeur de l'homme, assoiffé de voluptés. Cruauté et volupté, sensations identiques, comme l'extrême chaud et l'extrême froid.

21

Mon cœur mis à nu

La question (torture) est, comme art de découvrir la vérité, une niaiserie barbare ; c'est l'application d'un moyen matériel à un but spirituel.

La peine de Mort est le résultat d'une idée mystique, totalement incomprise aujourd'hui. La peine de Mort n'a pas pour but de sauver la société, matériellement du moins. Elle a pour but de sauver (spirituellement) la société et le coupable. Pour que le sacrifice soit parfait, il faut qu'il y ait assentiment et joie de la part de la victime. Donner du chloroforme à un condamné à mort serait une impiété, car ce serait lui enlever la conscience de sa grandeur comme victime et lui supprimer les chances de gagner le Paradis.

Quant à la torture, elle est née de la partie infâme du cœur de l'homme, assoiffé de voluptés. Cruauté et volupté, sensations identiques, comme l'extrême chaud et l'extrême froid.

"The Morlaisian Complaint"

Tristan Corbière, 1863

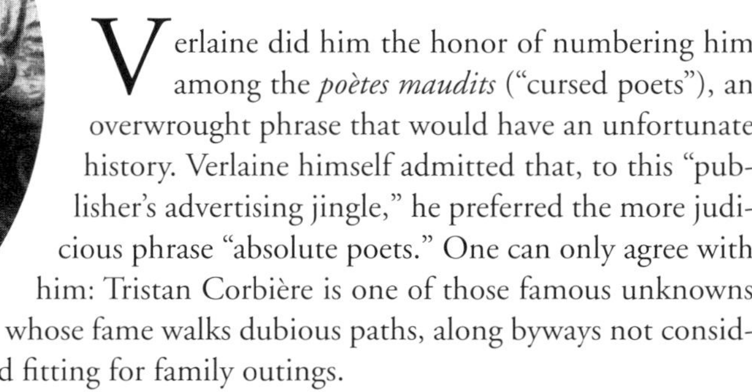

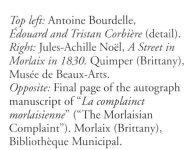

Verlaine did him the honor of numbering him among the *poètes maudits* ("cursed poets"), an overwrought phrase that would have an unfortunate history. Verlaine himself admitted that, to this "publisher's advertising jingle," he preferred the more judicious phrase "absolute poets." One can only agree with him: Tristan Corbière is one of those famous unknowns whose fame walks dubious paths, along byways not considered fitting for family outings.

Dead at the age of thirty, ravaged by the strong liquor of *le mot juste* ("the precise word") and wickedly oblique verse, this native of Brittany wrote much as lovers carve their interlocking initials on trees, as sailors have the names of their beloveds tattooed on their skin, as a suicide opens his veins, as a jealous lover stabs his rival in an alley. He belonged to that school of the street that cultivates the uncouth, makes grace wince, and experiences truth like a blow to the stomach. A vagrant, one imagines him emptying bottles of sparkling but mortal eau-de-vie, a liquor transparent like the eyes of some beloved captured and lost in a moment of drunken transcendence. Corbière had no time to master himself, to transform his flashes of genius into inner light, to transmute his penchant for blasphemy into lofty indifference. It is a harsh fate to die before attaining self-discipline, before having managed to exert full control over one's art. No matter! Whether from illness or disgust, whether in a spirit of farce or out of impatience to be done with it, his *Jaundiced Lovers* spoke of emotions that were yellow like the fevers brought back from distant colonies.

Pierre-Emmanuel Prouvost d'Agostino

Top left: Antoine Bourdelle, *Édouard and Tristan Corbière* (detail).
Right: Jules-Achille Noël, *A Street in Morlaix in 1830.* Quimper (Brittany), Musée de Beaux-Arts.
Opposite: Final page of the autograph manuscript of "*La complainct morlaisienne*" ("The Morlaisian Complaint"). Morlaix (Brittany), Bibliothèque Municipal.

14

The commissioner, son of a dog
And a boring crocodile,
Like old Nero set fire
To a Venetian lantern
That he had, my faith,
Taken on credit at Leroy's.

15

But here's Leroy, an angel
(some angels are firemen)
With a big nose, who clasps the feet
Of the gendarmes in formation.
They will never unsheathe
Before the people of Morlaix!!

16

That is so staggering
For future generations.
There was some question
Of setting Leroy to music;
Music for violin.
Subtle minds will understand me.

17

Here's the tribunal in the hall,
A president of Hell born;
but as regards the nose,
truly the filthy Collinet,
having stuffed it too soon
In the case of the delinquents!

18

Collinet and d'Amphernet
Quickly pursue the enquiry,
For they both had noses
To spy on our behinds.
And noses that they unloaded
against the people of Morlaix.

19

The prosecutor lifts above the troop
a noble head with white hair
that the guilty ones would often
see rising up from their soup . . .!
A beautiful old man's head
that is very eloquent, for . . .

20

He convicts them to hard labor
By way of punishment
and without more ado
Slaps them into prison!
They will never unsheathe
Against the people of Morlaix.

Tristan Corbière

14

Le commissaire, fils de chienne
Et crocodile ennuyeux
comme feu Néron mit le feu
à un' lanterne vénitienne
qu'il avait, de par ma foy,
prise à crédit chez Leroy

15

Mais v'là Leroy qui est un ange
(G n'a des anges qui sont pompiers)
D'un nez fort embrasse les pieds
des gens d'armes en phalanges
On ne dégainera jamais
devant l' peuple de Morlaix !!

16

Celà est si mirifique
Pour les générations
Futures, qu'il est question
De mettre Leroy en musique;
musique de violon
gens subtils me comprendront.

17

V'là l'tribunal dans la salle,
Un président d'enfer vrait
mais pour ce qui est du nez
vraiment Collinet l'a sâle
l'ayant fourré trop avant
Dans le cas des délinquants !-

18

Bien vite instruisent l'affaire
Collinet et D'amphernet
Car ils avaient tous des nez
pour espionner nos derrières
et des nez qu'ils déguénaient
contre le peuple de Morlaix-

19

L'procureur lèsur la troupe
Une noble tête à cheveux blancs
que les coupables doivent souvent
voir se dresser dans leur soupe....!
Un belle tête de vieillard
qui est très éloquente, car...

20

Il les condamne à la peine
Pour cause de chatiment
et sans plus de sacrement
En prison on les rengaine !
On ne dégainera jamais
Contre le peuple de Morlaix

Captain Fracasse

Théophile Gautier, 1863

Before managing to escape from the desolation of his miserable château, before being obliged to use word, mask, cape, and sword to conquer his Isabelle, the hero of *Captain Fracasse* had another adventure: that of his creation. Between 1836, when the work's publication was first announced, and 1863, when it finally appeared in the pages of the *Revue nationale et étrangère*, there intervened an extended period of gestation that was punctuated by two trials. During this span, Gautier also, with some reluctance, ceded to his publisher's request that he provide a happy ending. Thus, time affected Gautier's life as it had that of his hero.

The novel begins as comedy but ends as tragedy, and thus is best described as tragicomic: "In the end," as one character remarks, "since theater represents life, life should resemble it as a sitter does his portrait." *Captain Fracasse* is a hymn to theatricality and to painting, for in its pages Gautier performs as novelist, scene painter, and playwright. So artfully does he manipulate his material that the reader has no chance to settle into the narrative. Rife with overwrought descriptions, exalted diction, *coups de théâtre*, and improbable plot developments, it succeeds in demonstrating the virtuosity of an author whose aim is to amuse both himself and his readers. Literature and poetry are made to smooth over life's rough spots; but they also reveal destiny's eternal oscillation between pleasure and violence, between fairy-tale sweetness and the bitter taste of tragedy.

The theme of deception is ubiquitous in *Captain Fracasse*. Between Gautier's portrait of the Baron de Sigognac, chiseled with words in the opening pages of his manuscript, and the scene of the burial of the baron's cat at the end of the book, time unwinds its thread, spinning out strands of flight and nostalgia. By the time Sigognac discovers the family treasure at the close, it matters little to him, for he has already regained his wealth. But then, such ironic outcomes touch the core of the great tragicomedy that is human existence.

Jean-Pierre Guéno

Top left: Jean-Baptiste Clésinger, *Portrait of Théophile Gautier* (detail), pastel and charcoal. Châteaux de Versailles et de Trianon.
Left: Nicolas-Antoine Taunay, *Itinerant Players*. Reims, Musée des Beaux-Arts.
Opposite: First page of the autograph manuscript of *Captain Fracasse*. Paris, Bibliothèque de l'Institut.

Captain Fracasse

In the reign of Louis XIII, there stood on the slope of one of the bare hills that rise here and there on the Landes, between Dax and Mont-de-Marsan, a country-seat of the sort commonly met with in Gascony, and which the peasantry call châteaux.

Two round towers with conical roofs flanked the corners of the building; and on the façade two deeply cut grooves betrayed the previous existence of a drawbridge, reduced to a state of sinecure by the filling up of the moat. With their pepper-pot look-outs and their swallow-tailed vanes, they gave the manor house a feudal aspect, while the deep green mantel of ivy that covered one of them contrasted happily with the gray tones of the masonry, which was already old.

A traveler spying the castle from a distance and noting its pointed gables standing out against the sky, above the broom and the heath, would have concluded it was a very suitable habitation for a country nobleman; but, drawing nearer, he would have changed his mind. Invasive mosses and parasitical plants had reduced the road leading to the dwelling from the road to a narrow white path that looked like a faded braid on a well-worn cloak. Two ruts filled with rainwater and inhabited by frogs testified to the fact that carriages had once driven that way, but the sense of security exhibited by the batrachians indicated that they had long been in possession and were certain of not being disturbed.—On a path worn through the weeds and soaked by a recent downpour, there was not a single human footprint; the twigs of the scrub, laden with sparkling droplets of water, seemed not to have been parted for some time.

Large yellow, leprous-looking patches mottled the loose brown tiles on the roofs, whose rotten rafters had given way in places. The vanes were rusted and, unable to turn, pointed in different directions; the dormer windows were closed with wooden shutters, worn and split. Stones filled the barbicans of the towers; of the twelve windows on the façade, eight were boarded up with planks; the others were glazed with flawed glass that, at the slightest breeze, shook in the lead settings. Between these windows, the plaster had fallen away in flakes like the skin of an invalid, exposing disjointed bricks and fill eroded by the pernicious influence of the moon. The door, framed by a stone lintel whose regular bumps corresponded to old ornament dulled by time and neglect, was surmounted by a dilapidated coat of arms that the cleverest herald could not have deciphered, and whose foliate motifs curled fantastically, not without many breaks. The leaves of the door still retained, toward the top, vestiges of red paint and seemed to blush at their dilapidated state; diamond-headed nails held together the split planks, forming symmetrical designs that were interrupted here and there.

(1) 3

Le Capitaine Fracasse

Sur le revers d'une de ces collines decharnées qui bossuent les landes entre Dax et Mont de Marsan s'elevait au commencement du regne de Louis XIII une de ces gentilhommières si communes en Gascogne et que les villageois decorent du nom de chateau

deux tours rondes coiffées de toits en eteignoir flanquaient les angles d'un batiment sur la facade duquel deux rainures profondement entaillées trahissaient l'existence primitive d'un pont levis reduit à l'etat de sinécure par le nivelage du fossé et donnaient au manoir un aspect assez feodal avec leurs echauguettes en poivrière et leurs gironettes à queue d'aronde. une nappe de lierre enveloppant a demi l'une des tours tranchait heureusement par son vert sombre sur le ton gris de la pierre deja vieille à cette epoque

Le voyageur qui eut apperçu de loin le castel dessinant ses faitages pointus sur le ciel au dessus des genets et des bruyères l'eut jugé une demeure convenable pour un hobereau de province mais en approchant son avis se fut modifié. le chemin qui menait de la route à l'habitation s'etait reduit par l'envahissement de la mousse et des vegetations parasites à un etroit sentier blanc semblable a un galon terni sur un manteau rapé. deux ornières remplies d'eau de pluie et habitées par des grenouilles temoignaient qu'anciennement des voitures avaient passé par là mais la securité de ces batraciens montrait une longue possession et la certitude de n'etre pas derangé — sur la bande frayée à travers les mauvaises herbes et detrempée par une averse recente on ne voyait ~~d'autre~~ empreinte de pas humain et les brindilles de broussailles chargées de gouttelettes brillantes ne paraissaient pas avoir eté ecartées depuis long temps

de larges plaques de lèpre jaune marbraient les tuiles brunies et desordonnées des toits dont les chevrons pourris avaient cedé par places la rouille empechait de tourner les gironettes qui indiquaient toutes un vent different. les lucarnes etaient bouchées par des volets de bois dejeté et fendu. des pierrailles remplissaient les barbacanes des tours — sur les six fenetres de la facade il y en avait quatre barrées par des planches; les deux autres montraient des vitres bouillonnées tremblant à la moindre pression de la bise dans leur reseau de plomb. entre ces fenetres le crepi tombé par ecailles comme le derme d'une peau malade mettait à nu des briques disjointes, des moellons effrités aux pernicieuses influences de la lune; la porte encadrée d'un linteau de pierre dont les rugosités regulières indiquaient une ancienne ornementation emoussée par le temps et l'incurie etait surmontée d'un blason fruste que le plus habile heraut d'armes eut eté impuissant a dechiffrer et dont les lambrequins se contournaient fantasquement non sans de nombreuses solutions de continuité. les vanteaux de la porte ~~la porte~~ offraient encore vers le haut quelques restes de peinture sang de boeuf et semblaient rougir de leur etat de delabrement; des clous a tete de diamant contenaient leurs ais fendillés et formaient des symetries

Journal

Jules Michelet, 1865

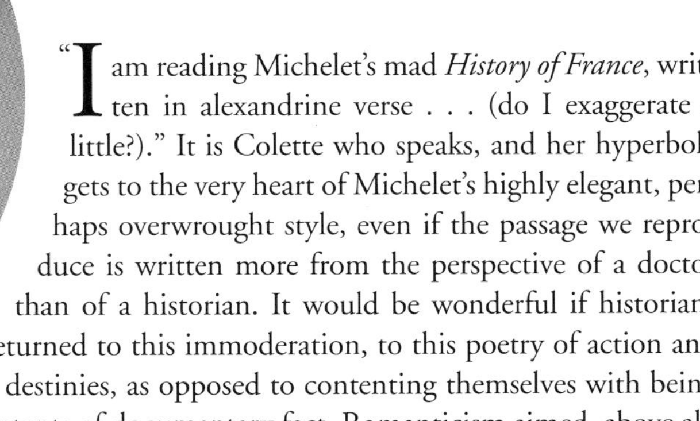

"I am reading Michelet's mad *History of France*, written in alexandrine verse . . . (do I exaggerate a little?)." It is Colette who speaks, and her hyperbole gets to the very heart of Michelet's highly elegant, perhaps overwrought style, even if the passage we reproduce is written more from the perspective of a doctor than of a historian. It would be wonderful if historians returned to this immoderation, to this poetry of action and great destinies, as opposed to contenting themselves with being chilly accountants of documentary fact. Romanticism aimed, above all, to impose a lyrical point of view. Napoleon wrote and epic of France in mortal thrusts and cannon discharges, in military reports drafted in ink, gunpowder, and thunder. Chateaubriand did likewise in *Mémoires d'outre-tombe* (*Memoirs from Beyond the Grave*), combining lucid foreknowledge of events with elegiac evocations of a lost world. This was the tradition that Michelet claimed as his own. He satisfied perfectly Léon Bloy's requirements for a genuine prophet: "Not a doctrinal charlatan or a pontificating prognosticator, but above all a visionary of the past." In his view, the art of inspired history was akin to the incandescence of Homer, to Jeremiah's lamentations at the fall of Babylon. He sought to elevate all things, all disciplines to the level of original creation, to blend the genres into a mode of expression that was "worthy and superior."

These days, philosophers and scientists who embrace intellectual transparency and stylistic clarity are regarded with suspicion. But esthetic emotion—in this context, produced by a combination of judicious erudition and vigorous diction—is inseparable from the desire for knowledge. The French tradition of such writing has become lost in a brackish swamp of dubious concepts and methodological zeal. It is refreshing to revisit works full of vivid images, texts whose epic narratives speak to the heart and the soul: in short, books as splendidly evocative as Michelet's. The frescos in the Panthéon no longer seem as bad as was once thought; they influenced our childhood much as did the illustrations in the Hetzel edition of Jules Verne. When a writer like Michelet tackles the basic stuff of our history, it again becomes a field of dreams, an inexhaustible source of marvels.

Pierre-Emmanuel Prouvost d'Agostino

August 18, 1865. When the difference in ages is so great, shouldn't one be content that the agreeable young woman, who wants very much to love you, accepts your expressions of love amicably and without displeasure? Such profound delight is an immense happiness even when the pleasure is all on one side. But what a delicate cause for concern! Isn't this a sacrifice made out of docility, out of goodness? These are perfectly natural questions, and I put them to myself at the time of our marriage. Quite naturally so. By contrast with fiery, plethoric women who have copious, forceful periods, it was not to be hoped that she would surrender herself on certain days (on particular days every month, for example), if not to the husband, then at least to the marriage. When I received her she was so pale, so white, so anemic! Would she live? It seemed doubtful. There wasn't one of her functions that didn't seem compromised. I had to make her live, first by reviving her, giving her the strength to live. How would I make her eat, digest, etc.? This had to be tended to every day. As to conjugal relations, there was a congenital problem, as with her mother, and also a spasmodic contraction (a consequence of her grave illness). But her heart and will were mine, her imagination, too; her impressions of the Collège de France. Her ready sensitivity to what she called my genius, to the indignant outbursts with which I heated up the crowd, touched her below my words, and when we returned to our little retreat, made our relations very sweet.

The very age that seemed so much against me has, to the contrary, been favorable to me. The person she most loved was her father (her protector against her mother's severity). She lost him early without being able to express her tender love for him. This sweet and profound feeling was effectively set aside, postponed, becoming a blend of past and present. She scarcely distinguished between us. She was the little girl as much as she was the innocent wife, happy to find him again and make him happy in me.

I was her father, and in a very particular way, when I discovered her talent, helping her to write *L'Oiseau*. Our child had not lived, and seeing her so fragile, I dared not commit another offence. But in *L'Oiseau*, in *L'Insecte*, in *La Mer*, etc. I assisted her. Here she was my daughter and my wife. She created under me, with me. This helped her to relax physically. She was the complete woman, possessed of an extra sense. Something infinitely touching, this chaste and sickly child.

J. Michelet

Top left: Iphigénie Dupont-Zipcy, *Portrait of Jules Michelet* (detail). Châteaux de Versailles et de Trianon. *Left and opposite:* Pages from the autograph manuscript of Michelet's *Journal*. Paris, Bibliothèque de l'Institut.

ces, troubles, lourdes, vulgaires chez tant d'autres, sont chez elle marqués de signes très fins qui pourtant révéleraient à des yeux cet mystère pudique, qui se passe alors au sein de la femme, mystère de

S. Gervais
vendr. 18 a. 69

Dans une telle différence d'âge ne doit-on pas être heureux que la personne jeune, agréable, qui veut bien vous aimer, accepte avec amitié, reçoive sans déplaisance vos témoignages d'amour? Une si profonde jouissance serait un bonheur immense quand même tout le plaisir devrait être d'un seul côté. Mais quel sujet cependant de délicate inquiétude! n'est-ce pas un sacrifice de docilité, de bon cœur? Ce sont les questions naturelles qu'on s'adresse, que je m'adressai au temps de notre mariage. Elles étaient bien naturelles. On ne pouvait espérer que, comme les f. sanguines, pléthoriques obligées de verser un trop plein de force, elle serait à certains jours [à tel jour du mois par exemple] tirée, sinon au mari, tout au moins au mariage. Je l'avais reçue si pâle, si blanchie, avec si peu de sang!

Vivrait-elle? on en doutait. Par une de ses fonctions qui ne parût compromise. Il me fallait la faire vivre, la ressusciter d'abord, lui donner la force d'aimer. Comment la ferais-je manger, digérer, etc., c'était l'affaire de chaque jour. Pour l'union, elle y avait une difficulté de naissance, comme sa mère, et de plus une contraction spasmodique (suite de sa grande maladie). Mais le cœur, la volonté étaient meilleurs, l'imagination aussi, ses impressions du collège de France, sa vive sensibilité à ce qu'elle appelait génie, à l'effusion morale dont je réchauffais les foules, s'émouvait sous ma parole, et quand nous étions revenus dans notre petit ermitage, lui rendait nos rapports très doux.

L'âge même qui semblait tellement contre moi, tout au contraire me servit. Ce qu'elle avait le plus aimé, c'était son père (son protecteur contre les duretés de sa mère). Elle le perdit de bonne heure sans pouvoir lui dire sa tendresse; ce suave et profond sentiment fut comme réservé, ajourné, mêlé du passé, du présent. Elle ne nous distinguait guère; elle était la petite fille autant que l'innocente épouse, heureuse de le retrouver et de le rendre heureux en moi. J'étais son père, et je le fus de façon bien personnelle, quand je lui formai son talent, que je l'aidai à faire l'Oiseau. Notre enfant n'avait pas vécu, et la voyant si fragile, je n'osais récidiver; mais dans l'Oiseau, dans l'Insecte, dans la Mer, etc., je la fécondai; elle y fut ma fille et ma femme. Elle créa sous moi, avec moi. Cela la détendit physiquement. Elle fut femme tout à fait, en un sens de plus. Chose infiniment touchante que ce chaste enfant maladif,

Sentimental Education

Gustave Flaubert, 1869

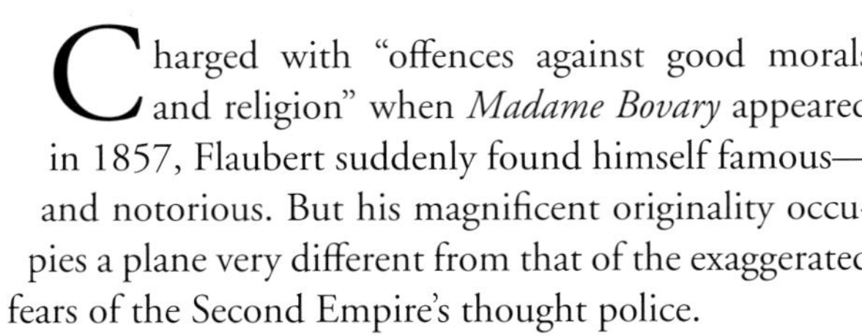

Charged with "offences against good morals and religion" when *Madame Bovary* appeared in 1857, Flaubert suddenly found himself famous—and notorious. But his magnificent originality occupies a plane very different from that of the exaggerated fears of the Second Empire's thought police.

Some liken Flaubert's achievement to that of Balzac; they suggest that he merely pushed the acute social observations of *The Human Comedy* a bit farther, treating with frankness matters that, thirty years before, had been considered off-limits. Such was the view of Émile Zola, who praised the "reality at once so meticulous and so epic" of Flaubert's work. A letter written by Flaubert himself to Guy de Maupassant, however, suggests that such an affiliation is ill-founded: "Don't talk to me of realism, naturalism, or experimentation. I've had enough. What empty nonsense!"

Flaubert sought to write novels that were independent works of art, affairs of style. Going beyond Honoré de Balzac's documentary ambitions, dismissing the Romantics' idealist approach to fiction, he cultivated irony, multiplicity of viewpoint, and copious description. Dreaming of writing " a book about nothing," conceived under the aegis of that "impersonality which is a sign of strength," he produced in *L'Éducation sentimental* (*Sentimental Education*) a novel of idiocy: the idiocy of characters caught up in their own desires, and of the base means to which they resort to satisfy them. In other words, a novel of failure, which is the most pervasive thing in the world.

Going still farther, Flaubert embarked on the inhuman enterprise of sizing up universal idiocy in a work to be entitled *La Copie* (*The Copy*). All that we have of it is *Bouvard and Pecuchet*, an attempt by a writer of genius to skewer the mediocrity of minds stocked only with "received ideas."

Pierre Chalmin

Despite what seemed to him insurmountable obstacles, his soul was full of hope, of a distant happiness that he could scarcely formulate. He felt brighter, stronger, gentler, braver. Prodigious undertakings seemed easy to him—the universe had suddenly expanded, and she was in his mind the fixed, luminous point where everything converged.

Seized with impatience, he climbed into the seat and began to drive.

He whistled, between his teeth, a brilliant Italian air.

The two horses struck the ground in cadence, the carriage rocked; lulled by this motion, his eyes half closed, inhaling the evening air, he abandoned himself to a dreamy, limitless joy.

At Bray he didn't wait for the horses to be fed their oats, he continued on his way, alone—and he said to himself as he walked:

> You are neither pale nor dark
> It seems you've been gilded
> With a ray of sunlight

He repeated "with a ray of sunlight" several times.

Arnoux had called her Marie. He shouted "Marie" and his voice vanished in the air.

A broad band of purple lit up the western sky and was reflected at ground level, making the puddles in the road shimmer like gold; the large wheat stacks that rose here and there above the stubble cast giant shadows. The branches of the bare elms were silhouetted against the horizon. A dog on a distant farm began to bark.

Top left: Eugène Giraud, *Portrait of Gustave Flaubert* (detail), ca. 1866. Châteaux de Versailles et de Trianon. *Right and opposite:* A page from the autograph manuscript of an early draft of Flaubert's *Sentimental Education*, quite different from the final text. Paris, Bibliothèque Nationale de France.

Malgré les obstacles insurmontables qu'il entrevoyait, il avait ~~une~~

Au fond ~~du cœur~~ [espérance & ~~comme~~ la certitude d'un bonheur lointain qu'il ne pouvait cependant guères formuler. Il se sentait plus intelligent, plus fort, plus tendre plus brave. Les ~~œuvres~~ entreprises prodigieuses lui apparaissaient faciles – L'univers venait, tout à coup, de s'élargir, & elle était dans sa pensée le point fixe & lumineux où l'ensemble des choses convergeait

[[Une impatience \ l'esprit] il monta sur le siège & se mit à conduire]

Il sifflait, entre ses dents, un air de bravoure italien.

Les deux chevaux battaient la terre en cadence, la voiture oscillait & bercé par ce mouvement, les pensées entr[illegible] ~~les pensées entr[illegible]~~ [il s'abandonnait [illegible] humant le vent du soir ~~regard perdu dans les nuages~~ à une joie rêveuse & infinie.

Il n'attendit ~~pas dans~~ à Bray qu'on eut donné l'avoine, il continua la route, seul, ~~à pied~~ – & il se disait ~~[illegible]~~ tout ~~haut~~, en marchant

Tu n'es point blanche ni rosée

Mais il semble qu'on t'a dorée

Avec un rayon du soleil

Il se répéta plusieurs fois « Avec un rayon de soleil » ~~il avait entendu~~ il avait appelé Arnoux l'appeler Marie. Il cria « Marie » sa voix se perdit dans l'air]

Une ~~large~~ couleur de pourpre enflammait ~~largement~~ le ciel à l'occident. [& se reflétant à ras du sol elle faisait briller ~~comme~~ de l'or les flaques d'eau dans les fossés, de grosses meules de blé qui se levaient au milieu des chaumes, çà & là, projetaient des ombres géantes. – Des ormes sans ~~feuilles~~ ~~[illegible]~~ dessinaient en noir sur l'horizon la silhouette de leurs ~~branches~~ branchages] un chien se mit à aboyer dans une ferme très loin.

"Letter of the Seer"

Arthur Rimbaud, 1871

"One isn't serious at the age of seventeen." As penned by the young Rimbaud, this was either an outright lie or an instance of poetic licence, for he had left high school after taking first prize in Latin verse, had read and consumed everything that might aid him in setting off a literary bombshell. Nothing could be more serious, more considered and judicious, than the program articulated in his so-called "letter of the seer." The phrase "controlled disorder of all the senses," worthy of Saint Teresa of Avila or San Juan de la Cruz, caught the attention of Claudel, who discerned behind this hoax of a precocious literary adolescent a dangerously engaged soul, the dazzling art of an "undomesticated mystic."

The victim of gross misunderstanding, Rimbaud is effectively a public nuisance for those weathering the storms of adolescence. Instead of regarding him as an articulate adolescent who poured out his feelings, we do better to focus on his flawless mastery of a liberty that, like a wild horse, hurtles one, at one's own peril, toward the terrible and exacting discipline of poetic expression. We should also steer clear of construing his liaison with Verlaine in politically correct terms. The hirsute, redheaded faun and the androgynous Adonis made for an odd couple; they would become the Infernal Bridegroom and the Foolish Virgin in *A Season in Hell*, which takes us far beyond a soothing justification of pederasty. "'I' is somebody else," even in the grip of intense passion. The gunshot in Brussels was only a well-placed period, a violent gesture of closure. There followed, as a postscript, Rimbaud's flight to find himself, the ultimate illumination: a blinding retreat to the desert and sun of Africa.

Pierre-Emmanuel
Prouvost d'Agostino

Top left: Henri Fantin-Latour, portrait of Rimbaud, detail of *Corner of a Table*, 1872. Paris, Musée d'Orsay.
Right: Prose passage from the autograph manuscript of Rimbaud's "Letter of the Seer" (translated above right). Paris, Bibliothèque Nationale de France.
Opposite: Opening page from the autograph of Rimbaud's "Letter of the Seer," with his poem "Parisian War Song." Paris, Bibliothèque Nationale de France.

To Paul Demeny, May 15, 1871

For "I" is somebody else. If brass wakes up to find itself a trumpet, that is certainly not its fault. This is obvious to me: I am present at the hatching of my thought: I watch it, I listen to it: I let fly an arrow: the symphony stirs in the depths, or leaps onto the stage. If the old imbeciles hadn't found only false meanings of "Me," we wouldn't have to sweep away the millions of skeletons that, interminably, have accumulated the products of their blinkered intellects, claiming to be their authors!

In Greece, as I said, verse and lyre set Action to rhythm. After that, music and rhyme were games, diversions. The study of this past delights the curious: some rejoice in reviving these antiquities:—let them. The universal intelligence has always thrown up its ideas naturally; men gathered a portion of these fruits of the brain: people acted through them, wrote books about them; things continued thus, man not working on himself, not yet being awake, or not yet in the plenitude of the great dream. Bureaucrats, writers: author, creator, poet, such men never existed!

The first study of the man who would be a poet is full knowledge of himself; he looks for his soul, inspects it, tempts it, learns it. As soon as he knows it, he should cultivate it! That seems simple: in every brain there is a natural development; so many *egoists* proclaim themselves authors; many others credit themselves for their intellectual progress! But what's in question is making the soul monstrous: like kidnappers who mutilate children. Picture a man implanting and cultivating warts on his face.

I am saying that one must be a *seer*, make oneself a *seer*.

The Poet makes himself a *seer* by a protracted, immense, and studied *disturbance of all the senses*. All forms of love, of suffering, of madness; he looks for himself, he exhausts all the poisons within him, keeping only their quintessence. Indescribable torture for which he will need all faith, all superhuman strength, in which he becomes for all the Great Unwell, the Great Criminal, the Great Accursed,—and the supreme Knower!—For he reaches the *unknown*! Because he has cultivated his soul, already rich, more than anyone! He reaches the unknown, and when, bewildered, he ends by losing the intelligence of his visions, he has seen them! May he die bounding through unheard of and unspeakable things: other horrible workers will come; they will begin from the horizons where the other one collapsed!

—more in six minutes—

I 1

Charleville, 15 mai 1871.

J'ai résolu de vous donner une heure de littérature nouvelle. Je commence de suite par un psaume d'actualité :

Chant de guerre Parisien

Le Printemps est évident, car
Du cœur des Propriétés vertes,
Le vol de Thiers et de Picard
Tient ses splendeurs grandes ouvertes !

Ô Mai ! quels délirants culs-nus !
Sèvres, Meudon, Bagneux, Asnières,
Écoutez donc les bienvenus
Semer les choses printanières !

Ils ont schako, sabre et tam-tam
Non la vieille boîte à bougies
Et des yoles qui n'ont jam, jam...
Fendent le lac aux eaux rougies !

Plus que jamais nous bambochons
Quand arrivent sur nos tanières [XX quand viennent sur nos fourmilières]
Crouler les jaunes cabochons
Dans des aubes particulières :

Thiers et Picard sont des Éros,
Des enleveurs d'héliotropes,
Au pétrole ils font des Corots :
Voici hannetonner leurs tropes...

Ils sont familiers du Grand Truc !..
Et couché dans les glaïeuls, Favre
Fait son cillement aqueduc,
Et ses reniflements à poivre !

La Grand ville a le pavé chaud,
Malgré vos douches de pétrole,
Et décidément, il nous faut
Vous secouer dans votre rôle...

Et les Ruraux qui se prélassent
Dans de longs accroupissements,
Entendront des rameaux qui cassent
Parmi les rouges froissements ! A. Rimbaud

Quelles rimes ! ô quelles rimes !

Around the World in Eighty Days

Jules Verne, 1873

Fed up with the "green paradise of infantile love," Jules Verne concocted the laboratory of a mad scientist, a submarine engine room, an entire country of fantastical geared machinery obscured by jets of steam, and rich in mysterious, fog-draped islands. Working to this tune, he transformed the knights of old picture books into captains of industry, without surrendering a jot of their heroism. Kings become superb if misanthropic conquerors, courageous sea captains, or aeronautical Prometheuses. Only princesses are absent—distant, rather, idealized. They are present only for the final scene, where they embrace their savior against the background of a spectacular Indian sunset or an aurora borealis. After which little boys can sleep and (especially) dream in all tranquility.

Verne was the most discrete man in the world, a provincial bourgeois imbued with all the domestic virtues, a prominent figure in Amiens, where he ran for office. Outwardly, he seemed a bureaucrat, an elegant and erudite rentier, as behooves great eccentrics who carry within them entire universes. As a result, he was widely regarded as a harmless writer of children's books.

Some say that he suffered as a result. But consider another writer, this one English: Lewis Carroll. As the Reverend Charles Dodgson of Christ Church, Oxford, he was a respectable mathematician who gave boring lectures, but under his pseudonym he contrived wickedly humorous limericks with pessimistic overtones, and used his persona as a teller of abracadabrous tales simultaneously to mask and to facilitate the indulgence of his fascination with little girls. Verne's motivations are somewhat more opaque. He made do with hitching his dreams to iron horses and other baroque modes of transportation of his time. The poetry of his work revealed itself only gradually, like one of those strange figures that the eye picks out in oxidation stains on the metal sides of old machines and cargo ships in port. Behind the prophet of the future, the visionary of technology and "progress," we can now discern an author who was uneasy, sensitive, capable of plumbing strange and mysterious depths.

Pierre-Emmanuel Prouvost d'Agostino

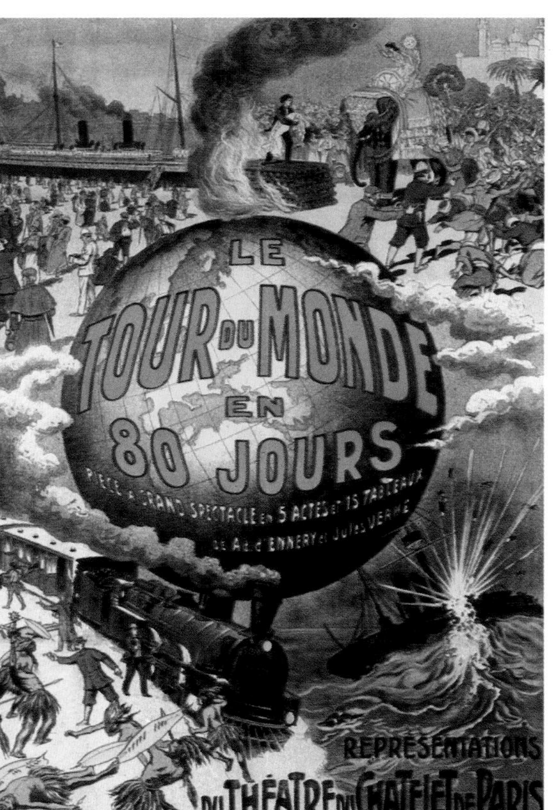

Top left: Jules Verne, photograph by Nadar (detail).
Left: Poster for a stage production of *Around the World in Eighty Days* mounted at the Théâtre du Châtelet, Paris. Nantes, Musée des Beaux-Arts.
Opposite: First page of the autograph manuscript of *Around the World in Eighty Days*. Paris, Bibliothèque National de France.

Around the World in Eighty Days
I
In which Phileas Fogg and Passepartout accept each other,
the one as master, the other as servant

In the year 1872, No. 7 Saville Row, Burlington Gardens, the house in which Sheridan died in 1814, was occupied by Mr. Phileas Fogg, Esq., one of the most singular and remarked members of the Reform Club, despite his efforts to avoid attracting attention.

One of the greatest orators ever to honor England, then, was succeeded by this Phileas Fogg, an enigmatic personage about whom little was known, save that he was a polished member of English high society. People said that he resembled Byron, at least facially (his feet were beyond reproach); but he was a Byron with whiskers, an imperturbable Byron who might live on a thousand years without growing old.

Certainly an Englishman, it was more doubtful whether Phileas Fogg was a Londoner. He had never been seen at the Exchange, nor at the Bank, nor in the counting rooms of the City; no ship owned by him had ever come into the London docks. This gentleman figured on no administrative boards. His name had never resounded in any of the Inns of Court, either at the Temple, or at Lincoln's Inn, or at Gray's Inn. Nor had he litigated in the Court of Chancery, or in the Exchequer, or in the Queen's Bench, or in the Ecclesiastical Courts. He was neither industrialist, nor businessman, nor merchant, nor gentleman farmer. He belonged neither to the Royal Institution nor to the London Institution; neither to the Artisan's Association nor to the Russel [*sic*] Institution; neither to the Literary Institution of the West, nor to the Institution of Law, nor to the Institution of Arts and Sciences placed under the direct patronage of His Gracious Majesty. In short, he belonged to none of the many societies that swarm in the English capital, from the Harmonic to the Entomological, established primarily to extirpate pernicious insects.

Phileas Fogg belonged to the Reform Club, and that was all.

To anyone curious as to how so mysterious a gentleman came to belong to this honorable association, the response would be that he was recommended by the Barings, with whom he had unlimited credit. This fostered a degree of surface respectability, for his checks were consistently paid on presentation from his account current, which was invariably flush.

Was Phileas Fogg rich? Undoubtedly. But even the best informed could not say how he had made his fortune, and Mr. Fogg was the last person to whom to apply for the information. In any event, he was never prodigal, but neither was he avaricious, for whenever he knew that funds were needed for a noble, useful, or benevolent cause, he provided them quietly, even anonymously.

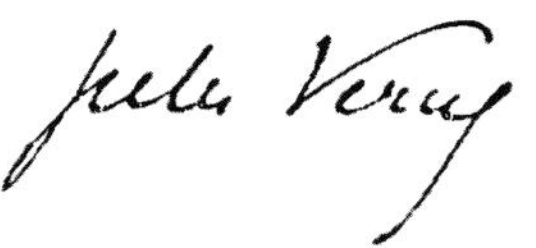

Le Tour du Monde en quatre-vingts jours.

—

1.

Dans lequel Phileas Fogg et Passe-partout s'acceptent réciproquement l'un comme maître, l'autre comme domestique.

En l'année 1872, la maison portant le n.° 7 de Saville-row, Burlington gardens — maison dans laquelle Shéridan mourut en 1814, — était habitée par Phileas Fogg, esq. l'un des membres les plus singuliers et les plus remarqués du Reform-Club de Londres, bien qu'il semblât prendre à tâche de ne rien faire qui pût attirer l'attention.

A l'un des plus grands hommes d'état qui honorent l'angleterre, succédait donc ce Phileas Fogg, personnage énigmatique, dont on ne savait rien, sinon que c'était un fort galant homme, et l'un ~~et~~ des plus beaux gentlemen de la haute société anglaise. On disait qu'il ressemblait à Byron — par la tête, ~~[illegible]~~ car il était irréprochable quant aux pieds, mais un Byron sans passion, refroidi, impassible, qui aurait vécu mille ans sans vieillir physiquement.

[Anglais, à coup sûr, Phileas Fogg n'était peut-être pas Londonner. On ne l'avait jamais vu ni à la Bourse, ni à la Banque, ni dans aucun des comptoirs de la cité. Ni les bassins ni les docks de Londres n'avaient jamais reçu un navire ayant pour armateur Phileas Fogg. Ce gentleman ne figurait dans aucun comité d'administration. Son nom n'avait jamais retenti dans un collège d'avocats, ni au Temple, ni à Lincoln's-inn, ni à Gray's-inn. Jamais il ne plaida ni à la cour du Chancelier, ni au banc de la Reine, ni à l'Échiquier, ni en cour ecclésiastique. ~~Il ne faisait partie~~ Il n'était ni industriel, ni négociant, ni marchand, ni agriculteur. Il ne faisait partie ni de l'Institution Royale de la Grande Bretagne, ni de l'Institution de Londres, ni de l'Institution des artisans, ni de l'Institution Russel, ni de l'Institution littéraire de l'Ouest, ni de l'Institution du Droit, ni de cette Institution des arts et des sciences réunies, qui est placée sous le patronage direct de sa Gracieuse Majesté. Il n'appartenait enfin à aucune des nombreuses sociétés qui pullulent dans la capitale de l'angleterre, depuis la Société de l'armonica jusqu'à la Société entomologique, fondée principalement dans le but de détruire les insectes nuisibles.

Phileas Fogg était membre du Reform-Club, et voilà tout.

A qui s'étonnerait de ce qu'un gentleman aussi mystérieux comptât parmi les membres de cette honorable association, on répondra qu'il passa sur la recommandation de M.M. Baring frères, chez lesquels il avait un crédit ouvert. De là, une certaine « surface » due à ce que ses chèques étaient régulièrement payés à vue par le débit de son compte courant, invariablement créditeur.

Ce Phileas Fogg était-il riche ? Incontestablement. Mais comment il avait fait fortune, c'est ce que les mieux informés ne pouvaient dire, et Mr. ~~et~~ Fogg était le dernier auquel il convînt de s'adresser pour l'apprendre. En tout cas, il n'était prodigue de rien, mais non avare, car partout où il manquait un appoint pour une

Cruel Tales

Villiers de L'Isle-Adam, 1874

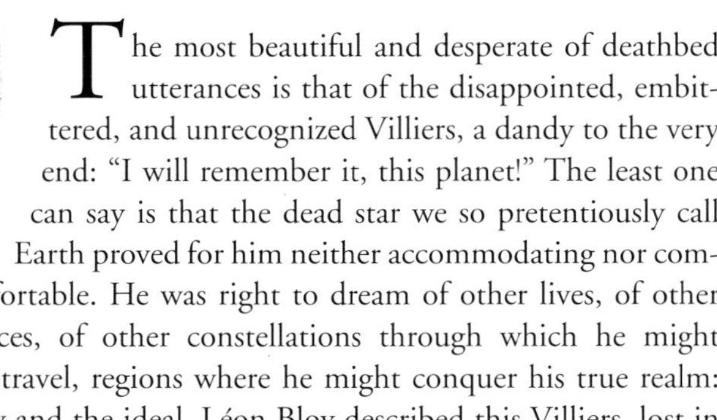

The most beautiful and desperate of deathbed utterances is that of the disappointed, embittered, and unrecognized Villiers, a dandy to the very end: "I will remember it, this planet!" The least one can say is that the dead star we so pretentiously call Earth proved for him neither accommodating nor comfortable. He was right to dream of other lives, of other places, of other constellations through which he might dream-travel, regions where he might conquer his true realm: that of fantasy and the ideal. Léon Bloy described this Villiers, lost in the fantastic light of his imagination, writing *L'Ève future* (*The Future Eve*): "flat on his belly on a filthy garret floor, never having had the wherewithal to buy even the most rickety of tables."

This pure writer, intractable and incorruptible, was one of the accursed who endured poverty with pride, leaving a final accounting to God. He was the last, completely legitimate descendant of the knight-kings of Malta; aware of his nobility, this superbly oblivious being took it into his head to pretend to the Greek throne, solely on the basis of his prestigious lineage, even as he regretted "not having five francs in my pocket, so that I might lend them to someone poorer than I." Irony rendered this extreme case elegant; the very idea of "The Glory Machine" is redolent of the author of *Contes cruels* (*Cruel Tales*): an impeccable visionary, an unalloyed poet—and his own smiling executioner, ever ready, like Poe, to caw "nevermore" in a grating deadpan.

Pierre-Emmanuel Prouvost d'Agostino

The Glory Machine
—S.G.D.G.—
To Stéphane Mallarmé
Sic itur ad astra*

I

What a model century! What movement! Can we never stop it? In fact, how would we, and why? Hurtling forward as we do, any such attempt would be virtual suicide. We are animated by a spirit of discovery. To discover! Anything whatever! That says it all. Thanks to tireless effort, the most extra-normal chimeras materialize at every moment, and are put to the most dazzling uses.

Don't these new manifestations of our very intellectual instincts set us apart, just a bit, from earlier humans? Yes, we are different. We are conscious of our elevation toward the Useful! We also know that our solar system advances unsteadily toward Hercules' *Byta*, toward the fabulous, sidereal deadpan that attracts the Universe by blinking its fiery eye from way yonder, at the bottom of the sky. Thus Courage and Hurray! That will be our motto.

Away with these sterile, coprograde, pusillanimous spirits who, conniving with their hallucinations, pose a threat to such a future! Mounted on that hippopotamus of Understanding known as the Absurd, and preaching who knows what breathless, worthless, and quibbling logic, they strive, spurring their impermeable accomplice on frightfully, to buck the current? Madness, pure madness!

Villiers de l'Isle-Adam

*"Thus does one rise to the stars": a citation from Virgil, *Aeneid*, IX, 641.

Top left: Joseph Delteil, *Auguste de Villiers de L'Isle-Adam,* 1896. *Right:* James Ensor, *Christ's Entry into Brussels in 1889,* 1888, J. Paul Getty Museum, Los Angeles. *Opposite:* First page of the autograph of "The Glory Machine," a short story published in *Cruel Tales.* Paris, Bibliothèque Nationale de France.

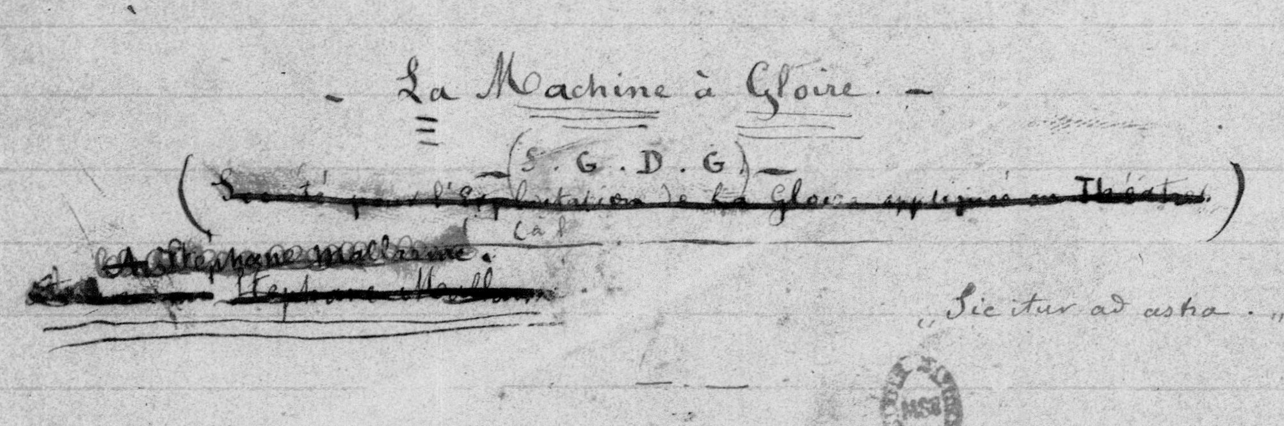

La Machine à Gloire
(S.G.D.G.)
„Sic itur ad astra."

I

Quel maître-siècle! Quel mouvement! Pourrons-nous jamais nous arrêter?... — Au fait, comment et pourquoi? Lancés comme nous le sommes, tout temps d'arrêt serait un véritable suicide. Un esprit de découverte nous anime. Découvrir! N'importe quoi! Tout est là. Grâce à d'incessants efforts, les chimères les plus extra-normales s'incarnent, à chaque instant, dans l'application la plus éblouissante.

Ne différons-nous pas, quelque peu, par cette nouveauté de nos instincts intellectuels, de la précédente espèce humaine? Oui, nous en différons. Nous avons conscience de notre assomption vers l'Utile! Nous savons également que notre système solaire chemine, en titubant, vers le Lyra d'Hercule, vers ce fabuleux prince-sans-rire sidéral qui attire l'Univers en lui clignant son œil de feu tout là-bas, au fond du Ciel: — aussi courage et hurrah! voilà notre devise. Arrière ces esprits bréhaignes, pusillanimes et tardigrades, qui, connubant avec leurs hallucinations, se font un épouvantail d'un tel avenir! À cheval sur cet hippopotame de l'entendement qu'on appelle l'Absurde, et prêchant on ne sait quelle Logique essoufflée, caduque et ratiocinante, ils s'évertuent, en éperonnant, avec effroi, leur imperméable acolyte, à remonter le courant?... C'est folie. Folie

"It weeps in my heart"

Paul Verlaine, 1874

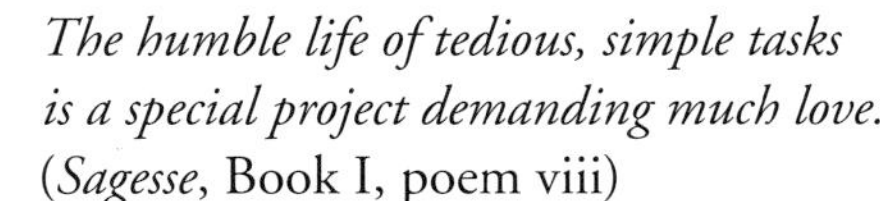

The humble life of tedious, simple tasks
is a special project demanding much love.
(*Sagesse*, Book I, poem viii)

Verlaine's entire life bore the stamp of his never having accepted such a humble lot, preferring to undertake rare and difficult work that left him wretchedly poor, tasks that likewise demanded much love but were scarcely remunerative. It was amidst profound abjection that Verlaine found his most dulcet accents.

The only son of a military man who died young, spoiled as a child by a female cousin ten years his senior who soon perished in turn, then raised by a mother who waxed nostalgic for her uncompleted pregnancies (in a drunken rage, Paul obtained vengeance by smashing the jars containing his aborted brothers and sisters), Verlaine assumed in succession the roles of unworthy son, bad husband, scandalous lover of the young Rimbaud, and precocious drunkard, as if goading his contemporaries to outrage: "A curse on this Verlaine, on this drunkard, this pederast, this assassin, this coward beset from time to time by fears of hell that make him shit his pants." As the author of this indictment is Edmond de Goncourt, we should not be surprised by its viciousness.

Before he met Rimbaud, he had already published *Poèmes saturniens* (*Saturnian Poems*) and *La Bonne Chanson* (*The Good Song*), but the scabrous miracle of their liaison completely transformed his poetry. From their wanderings in Belgium and England, he brought back *Ariettes oubliées* (*Forgotten Songs*), a sequence republished in *Romances sans paroles* (*Romances Without Words*). His masterpieces remain *Sagesse* (*Wisdom;* 1881), *Jadis et Naguère* (*Once and Yesterday;* 1884)—where he articulated his core poetic precept: "Music above everything"—and *Amour* (*Love;* 1888). The greatest of all French Catholic poets died alone, in a whore's hovel.

Pierre Chalmin

III
It rains gently on the town
(Arthur Rimbaud)

It weeps in my heart
as it rains on the town.
What is this languor
that pierces my heart?

Oh, sweet sound of the rain
on the earth and on the roofs!
For a heart that is numbed
oh, the song of the rain!

It weeps without reason
in my disheartened heart.
What! no treason?
This is grief without reason.

It is the far worst pain
not to know why,
without love, without hatred,
my heart has so much pain.

P. Verlaine

Top left: F. A. Cazals, *Portrait of Paul Verlaine* (detail). Paris, Musée de la Vie Romantique.
Right: William Samuel Horton, *The Tuileries*. Paris, Musée d'Orsay.
Opposite: Autograph manuscript of "*Il pleure dans mon coeur*" ("*It weeps in my heart*") from the set of *Ariettes oubliées* ("*Forgotten Songs*") published in *Romances sans paroles* ("*Romances Without Words*"). Paris, Bibliothèque Littéraire Jacques-Doucet.

III

~~It rains and the wind is never weary.~~
(~~Longfellow~~)
"Il pleut doucement sur la ville"
(Arthur Rimbaud)

Il pleure dans mon coeur
Comme il pleut sur la ville
Quelle est cette langueur
Qui pénètre mon coeur ?

O bruit doux de la pluie
Par terre et sur les toits!
Pour un coeur qui s'ennuie
O le chant de la pluie!

Il pleure sans raison
Dans ce coeur qui ~~s'afflige~~ s'écoeure
Quoi! nulle trahison!...
~~Ce deuil~~ Le deuil est sans raison

~~O bruit doux de la pluie~~
~~Par terre et sur les toits~~
~~Pour un coeur qui s'ennuie~~
~~O le chant de la pluie~~

C'est bien la pire peine
De ne savoir pourquoi
Sans amour et sans haine
Mon coeur a tant de peine!

The She-Devils

Jules Barbey d'Aurevilly, 1876

By nature contemptuous, haughty as a rooster surrounded by capons, Barbey d'Aurevilly could have been the model for Edmond de Rostand's *Chantecler*. Crested with insolence, sporting a musketeer's whiskers and endowed with a piercing gaze whose fierceness was accentuated by thick eyebrows, this worthy descendent of Beau Brummel dared all—save for modesty, an affectation of parvenus. In his view, "the world would be a better place if we still had the right to thrash those of lower station than ourselves." There was also a bit of Don Quixote in this enemy of frauds: attracted to celestial and infernal extremes, he was a devilish adherent to Holy Roman orthodoxy, perfumed with old incense in which one detects a hint of sulphur.

This *grand seigneur* was obliged to live in a manner that fell far short of his dreams of magnificence. Heir to a noble lineage of heroic cast, disdainful of the modern world, he imbued his fiction with an exaggerated version of his ancestral ethos, developing Stendhal's contrast between the red and the black to a level of intensity bordering on cruelty. He shows us a world in which ordinary bedrooms harbor, behind crimson curtains, entire hells of secret desire. With his delusions, his canes, his repartee, his superb insolence, and his razor-sharp wit, Barbey draped himself in the last remnants of Romanticism, brandishing all the while an intelligence and a sense of entitlement worthy of an eighteenth-century aristocrat.

Pierre-Emmanuel Prouvost d'Agostino

Top left: Émile Levy, *Portrait of Jules Barbey d'Aurevilly* (detail), 1881. Châteaux de Versailles et de Trianon.
Right: Félicien Rops, frontispiece for Barbey d'Aurevilly's *Les Diaboliques* (*The She-Devils*). Paris, Musée du Louvre.
Opposite and detail at right: Page from the autograph of "Happiness in Crime," a story published in *The She-Devils*. Paris, Bibliothèque National de France.

"My dear fellow, I must dig deep for that story, as for a bullet over which the flesh has healed; for oblivion is like the flesh of living things, reforming over events and obscuring our view of them: after a time, of everything about them, even where they took place.

"It was in the early years of the Restoration. A regiment of the Guards passed through the town of V—; and, as it was obliged, for some military reason or other, to remain there two days, the officers decided to organize a bout of swordsmanship in the town's honor. As it happens, there was good reason for the officers of the Guards to so honor the town. It was, to use an expression current at the time, 'more royalist than the king.' Considering its size, it was positively swarming with nobility. More than thirty of its young men were then serving either in the Life Guards or the Prince's Regiment, and the officers passing through V—knew almost all of them. But the principal inducement for organizing such a bout was the town's exceptional reputation for swordsmanship; known as the 'duellers' redoubt,' it remained more smitten with the blade than any other town in France. The Revolution of 1789 may have deprived male nobles of their traditional right to wear swords, but in V—they demonstrated that, although no longer permitted to wear them, they could still wield them. The officers' bout was quite brilliant. All of the best swordsmen in the region rushed to it, even amateurs of the younger generation, who had not, as was previously the norm, cultivated the difficult and complex art of fencing; and all of them displayed such enthusiasm for manipulation of the blade, the glory of our forefathers, that an old provost marshal of the regiment, who had served his time three or four times over, and whose sleeve was covered with decorations, thought it would be a good idea to end his days running a school of arms in V—; and the colonel, informed of the plan and approving of it, granted him his discharge and left him there. As it turned out, the idea of the provost marshal, whose family name was Stassin but who was known to his fellow soldiers as the 'Body-Thrust,' was a stroke of genius. There had not been a proper fencing school in V—for some time; this had long been a subject of regret among the nobility, who were obliged to instruct their sons themselves, or to impose upon newly discharged comrades-in-arms whose command of what they were teaching was tenuous at best. The inhabitants of V—prided themselves on being particular. They were possessed of the sacred fire. For them, simply killing their man did not suffice; it had to be done with cunning and artistry, according to rules. What mattered most to them was that a man bear arms handsomely, and they had nothing but contempt for vigorous but inelegant swordsmen who, while perhaps dangerous antagonists, were not, in the true and strict sense, what are known as 'fencers.'

Mon cher, c'est là une histoire qu'il faut aller chercher déjà loin,
comme une balle perdue sous des chairs revenues, car l'oubli, c'est comme une chair de
choses vivantes qui se reforme par dessus les événements et qui empêche d'en voir rien,
d'en soupçonner rien au bout d'un certain temps, même la place ! C'était dans les premières
années qui suivirent la Restauration. Un régiment de la Garde passa par la ville de V... et ayant été obligé
d'y rester deux jours, pour je ne sais quelle raison militaire, les officiers de ce régiment s'avisèrent
de donner un assaut d'armes en l'honneur de la ville. La ville en effet, avait bien
tout ce qu'il fallait pour que ces officiers de la Garde lui fissent honneur et fête. Elle était
– comme on disait alors – plus royaliste que le Roi. Proportion gardée avec sa dimension
(ce n'est guères qu'une ville de cinq à six mille âmes) elle foisonnait de noblesse. Plus de trente
jeunes gens de ses meilleures familles servaient alors soit aux Gardes du Corps, soit à ceux
de Monsieur, et les officiers du régiment en passage à V... les connaissaient presque tous.
Mais la principale raison qui décida de cette martiale fête d'un assaut, fut la réput-
-ation d'une ville qui s'était appelée « la bretteuse », et qui était encore, dans ce moment
là la ville la plus bretteuse de France. La Révolution de 1789 avait eu beau enlev-
-er aux nobles le droit de porter l'épée. A V... ils prouvaient que s'ils ne
la portaient plus, ils pouvaient toujours s'en servir. L'assaut donné par les offici-
-ers fut très brillant. On y vit accourir toutes les fortes lames du pays, et même tous les amateurs,
plus jeunes d'une génération, qui n'avaient pas cultivé comme on le cultivait autrefois un art
aussi compliqué et aussi difficile que l'escrime, et tous, montrèrent un tel enthousiasme pour
le maniement de l'épée, la gloire de nos pères, qu'un ancien prévôt du régiment qui avait fait
trois et quatre fois son temps, et dont le bras était couvert de chevrons, s'imagina que ce serait une
bonne place pour y finir ses jours qu'une salle d'armes qu'on ouvrirait à V... et le colonel à qui
il communiqua et qui approuva son dessein lui délivra son congé et l'y laissa. Ce prévôt qui
s'appelait Stassin, en son nom de famille et La Pointe-au-corps, en son surnom de guerre, avait eu là tout
simplement une idée de génie. Depuis longtems il n'y avait plus à V... de salle d'armes, conven-
-ablement tenue et c'était même une de ces choses dont on ne parlait qu'avec mélancolie entre ces
nobles obligés de donner eux-mêmes des leçons à leurs fils ou de
les leur faire donner par quelque compagnon, revenu du service, qui savait à peine ou qui
savait mal ce qu'il enseignait. Les habitants de V... se piquaient d'être difficiles. Ils avaient réell-
-ement le feu sacré. Il ne leur suffisait pas de tuer leur homme, ils voulaient le tuer savam-
-ment et artistement par principes. Il fallait avant tout, pour eux qu'un homme comme
ils disaient, fût beau sous les armes, et ils n'avaient qu'un profond mépris pour ces robustes et
maladroits qui peuvent être très dangereux sur le terrain, mais qui ne sont pas, au strict

Jack

Alphonse Daudet, 1876

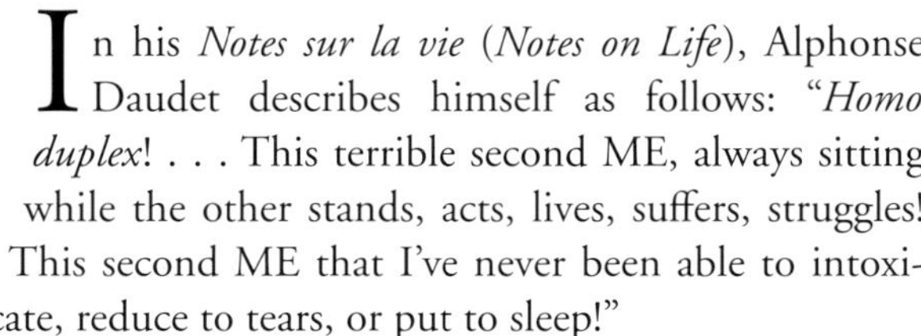

In his *Notes sur la vie* (*Notes on Life*), Alphonse Daudet describes himself as follows: "*Homo duplex*! . . . This terrible second ME, always sitting while the other stands, acts, lives, suffers, struggles! This second ME that I've never been able to intoxicate, reduce to tears, or put to sleep!"

This man, who sought to nourish his work with life's vicissitudes and depravities, was never fooled by this doubling. The second Me—the "nice Daudet," the writer who couldn't help but write and suck the blood of reality as well as that of all the stories he heard or read—was as fanatically active as his first Me, whose appetite for life was prodigious: he was a libertine with a decided taste for debauchery and loose women, for "things agreeable and swinish."

At the end of his life, consumed by syphilis and tuberculosis, the writer was reduced to meditating upon his own suffering: that of a bon vivant paralyzed by *doulou* (Provençal for *douleur*, pain or suffering). Having contracted syphilis during a brief fling at age eighteen, he passed it on to Marie Rieu, with whom he had a tumultuous affair, before marrying Julie Allard. Marie died from the illness, which would later claim Daudet's friends Guy de Maupassant and Gustave Flaubert as well as Jules de Goncourt—just as, earlier, it had felled Théophile Gautier, Honoré de Balzac, Stendhal, and Charles Baudelaire.

Before his death, Daudet kept a diary recording his experiences as a "man-orchestra of pain," an individual reliving the torments of Christ. He registered their nuances and shifts, which were sometimes subtle and sometimes obscenely violent: "My pain occupies the horizon, fills everything. Gone is the phase in which the illness makes one better; likewise that in which it embitters, makes the voice and all the gears creak. At present, it is a hard, stagnant, painful torpor. Indifference to everything." By 1897, when he died, he had ceased to be the *homo duplex* who caused all of those who loved him to suffer. Pain, his Way of the Cross, had gradually reintegrated him.

Jean-Pierre Guéno

He glimpsed vaguely, near the altar, the shadowy figure of a woman kneeling in the rude folds of a nun's habit; but he could not quite construe what she was reciting in her lively, singsong voice, for she was so used to praying that the words passed her lips without breaks or breaths. But his attentive ear managed to make out her last words.—"O my God, protect my friends, my enemies, prisoners, travelers, the ill and the dying. . . ."

Jack then fell into a feverish, agitated sleep in which the nearby groans of the dying blended with visions of prisoners rattling their chains, and of travelers wandering endless roads.

[. . .] He was himself one of the travelers. He was walking down the road, which resembled the one to Étiolles but was longer and more sinuous, and lengthened with every step. His mother Cécile preceded him without waiting for him, and he could discern the flutterings of their two robes between the trees. He was prevented from joining them by enormous machines arrayed along the ditches, frightening, roaring, their gaping mouths and smoking shafts belching hot air towards him. Steam planers, steam saws: they were all there, their rods, teeth, and pistons operating with deafening hammer blows. Jack, trembling, decided to pass through them. He was struck, snatched up, torn apart; strips of his flesh were carried off with bits of his smock, his legs were burned by large molten ingots, and his entire body enveloped by raging fires whose hell penetrated his chest. What a dreadful struggle to break free from all this, to seek refuge in the forest of Sénart, which bordered this cursed road! And here, under the freshness of the large branches, Jack became little again. He was ten years old. He was coming back from one of his extended forays with the warden; but over there, at the corner of an allée, old Salé, billhook in hand, was sitting on her bundle of wood, watching him. He wanted to flee; the old woman dashed after him, gave furious chase through the immense forest, now so dark that night was descending over the trees. He ran and ran. . . . The old woman was faster than he was . . . He heard her step getting closer, the wood scraping against her, her panting breath. Finally she grabbed him, struggled with him, threw him to the ground, and sat on his chest with all her weight, crushing the child with her prickly branches. . . .

Jack woke up with a start. He recognized the large room lit by night-lights, the row of beds, the labored breathing, the coughs breaking the silence. He dreamed no more.

Top left: Alphonse Daudet and his Daughter Edmée (detail). Paris, Musée d'Orsay.
Left: La Doulou (*Suffering*), autograph manuscript. Private collection.
Opposite: Page from the first draft of *Jack*, autograph manuscript. Private collection. The translation (top right) is of the corresponding passage in the final, published text.

Monologue of a Faun

Stéphane Mallarmé, 1876

There is no need to visit unknown lands or wage war to find adventure. It can be had without leaving one's room—and adventurers can be English professors lost in their daydreams, heckled by their students and seemingly not in full possession of their faculties. Mallarmé risked the only asset in a penniless intellectual's portfolio: the good health of his mind. Some who do so never recover, for example, Nietzsche. Mallarmé, however, compelled admiration with his madness. On his famous Tuesdays, when he received his guests in his apartment in the rue de Rome, he held forth like an oracle. The poet Paul Valéry quipped that it was sufficient to frequent him to have genius.

As so often happens in such cases, if not always, his creative adventure began with a resounding "No!" "No" to the facile charms of glib rhetorical verse. "No" to poetry conceived as a fancier form of prose. Before the study of linguistics had developed, Mallarmé distinguished the referential operation of language from its poetic function. The former, in his view, boiled down to "universal reportage," to the instrumental use of words to convey an idea in much the same way that currency enables exchange transactions: no sooner used than forgotten. The poet proceeds differently. Without disappearing altogether, the idea becomes secondary. The poet achieves his effects by exploiting the non-intellectual properties of language: rhythm, the play of sonorities and associations, networks of images and sounds. Within language, he contrives a language of his own.

Mallarmé, and especially the Mallarmé of "Afternoon of a Faun" (originally entitled "Monologue of a Faun"), went farther than Baudelaire in this search for a "sorcery of evocation." In effect, he liberated *Les Fleurs du mal* (*The Flowers of Evil*) from lingering vestiges of hoary poetic diction. The Symbolist poets, like the Impressionist painters, sought the active participation of the reader-viewer in the elaboration of artistic content.

Mallarmé staked everything on this quest for a poetic Holy Grail. His life became inextricable from his oeuvre, but from his perspective things scarcely could have been otherwise. "For me, the case of the poet, in this society that makes it impossible for him to survive, is the case of a man who isolates himself to fashion his own tomb."

Paul Desalmand

Top left: Édouard Manet, *Portrait of Stéphane Mallarmé* (detail), 1876. Paris, Musée d'Orsay.
Left: Paul Gauguin: *Afternoon of a Faun*, tamanu wood. Vulaines, Musée Stéphane-Mallarmé.
Right: Binding of *Monologue d'un faune*. Paris, Bibliothèque Littéraire Jacques-Doucet.

Opposite: Monologue of a Faun, first page of autograph preliminary draft, which differs radically from the final version. Paris, Bibliothèque Littéraire Jacques-Doucet.

Monologue of a Faun

(A faun, seated, allows two nymphs to escape from his arms. He rises.)

I had nymphs!
Was it a dream? No: the clear
Rubies of lifted breasts continue to embrace the still air.

(Breathing)

and I drink sighs

(Stamping his foot.)

Where are they?

(Appealing to the setting.)

O foliage, if you are protecting these mortals,
Surrender them to me, by that April which swells
your nubile
Branches, (I still languish in such pain!)
And by the nudity of roses, o foliage!

Nothing.

(Stamping heavily)

I want them!

(Pausing)

And if this beautiful, pillaging pair
Was but an illusion of my deceptive senses?

Stéphane Mallarmé

Monologue d'un Faune.

—

(Un faune, assis, laisse de l'un et de l'autre de ses bras s'enfuir deux nymphes.

Il se lève.)

J'avais des nymphes!

Est-ce un songe? Non: le clair
Rubis des seins levés embrase encore l'air
Immobile,

(Respirant.)

et je bois les soupirs.

(Frappant du pied.)

Où sont-elles!

(Invoquant le décor.)

O feuillage, si tu protèges ces mortelles,
Rends-les moi, par Avril qui gonfla tes rameaux
Nubiles, (je languis encore des tels maux!)
Et par la nudité des roses, ô feuillage!

Rien.

(A grands pas.)

Je les veux!

(S'arrêtant)

Mais si ce beau couple au pillage

The Bachelor

Jules Vallès, 1878

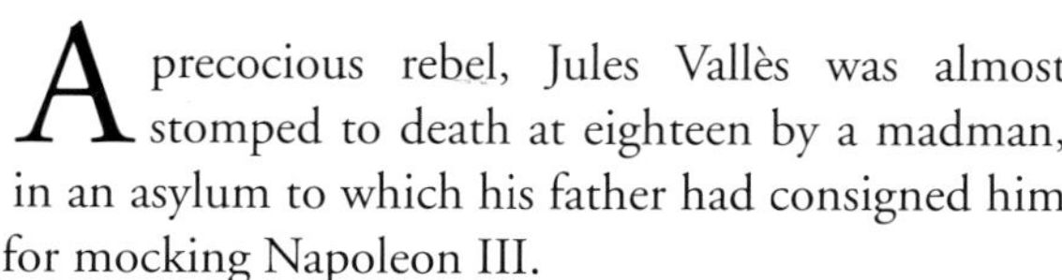

A precocious rebel, Jules Vallès was almost stomped to death at eighteen by a madman, in an asylum to which his father had consigned him for mocking Napoleon III.

A child martyr, a scrawny bachelor who dedicated his memoirs "to all those who, fed Greek and Latin, died of hunger," he was an active supporter of the Commune uprising of 1871 during which he helped to prevent the burning of the Panthéon and the massacre of several innocents. He miraculously survived the ensuing mass executions—which prompted him to write of "all those who, victims of social injustice, took up arms against an ill-made world, those who, under the banner of the Commune, would form the great federation of pain." He is best known for his long autobiographical novel, whose three volumes (entitled *The Child, The Bachelor*, and *The Insurgent*) guarantee him a place in the French literary history.

Vallès was preeminently a utopian, and he founded several successive newspapers, all named *La Rue* (*The Street*). He was forthright about wanting to remake this imperfect world, for he had been obliged to swallow more than his share of its idiocies. Calling himself a "Rualist" (from rue (["street," a wordplay on "Realist"], he put his faith in the people, and in reality. Victimized by a cruel Paris, alert to a thousand subtle colorings of the city's ethical and social life (the rich culture of its *petits métiers* [crafts], the progressive "dejoying" of labor, the dignity of the working poor and of legitimate rebellion), he was in many ways the ultimate witness to the doomed struggle of an archaic labor force. He aspired to a "liberty without bounds," and he never compromised when it came to his political ideals—or to his literary standards, for he was an impeccable French stylist.

After returning from political exile, Vallès died, destitute, on the Boulevard Saint-Michel in February of 1885. At the time, preparations were underway for the grandiose funeral of Victor Hugo, who was thirty years his senior. The younger man had just turned fifty-two. Reportedly, his last words were: "I have suffered greatly." More than a superb writer, he was an exemplary man, almost a secular saint.

Pierre Chalmin

But they've mutilated my thought, they've removed a sentence!

The removed sentence was precisely the one that most mattered to me! I had written the article for it—it was the final blow.

I knew it by heart; I had worked so hard on it!

I went to bed, covered my head with the sheets, and closed my eyes, the better to envision it.

I pronounced the moral:

"Such is often the lot of those who burn their ships before the paternal hearth to throw themselves into life's stormy seas! How many have I seen stumble, because they wanted to jump feet-first over their hearts!"

Did they know at the paper that I had never seen anyone jump feet-first over his heart? This image of people bringing their ships before their house to burn them and then embark, did it strike them as too bold?

Were they classicists?

I lost myself in conjecture.

I would find out when I went to collect my fee.

I was told:

"Come to the till on Saturday."

I would have written my article for nothing.—Almost all novices sacrificed the first fruits of their inspiration.

The *Revue des Deux Mondes* never paid for first articles. The *Pierrot* had paid, but perhaps I was the first one in its history. Doubtless I had made a big hit!

They had edited out the passage about ships and feet-first. That was no reason for the piece not to have made an impression, and they probably wanted to win my loyalty, they made a financial sacrifice for it.

I couldn't refuse this money! Anyway, I could use it to pay for some alterations a tailor had done for me.

I didn't, however, want to come across as a man in a hurry, as having entered the world of letters to make money.

I dallied a bit on Saturday—the designated day—before going to collect the fee for my copy.

On the other hand, I mustn't make them wait too long!

I entered the office.

Jules Vallès

Top left: Gustave Courbet, *Portrait of Jules Vallès* (detail), ca. 1861.
Opposite and below: page from the autograph manuscript of *Le Bachelier* (*The Bachelor*), chapter 26, "Le Journaliste." Paris, Bibliothèque Nationale de France.

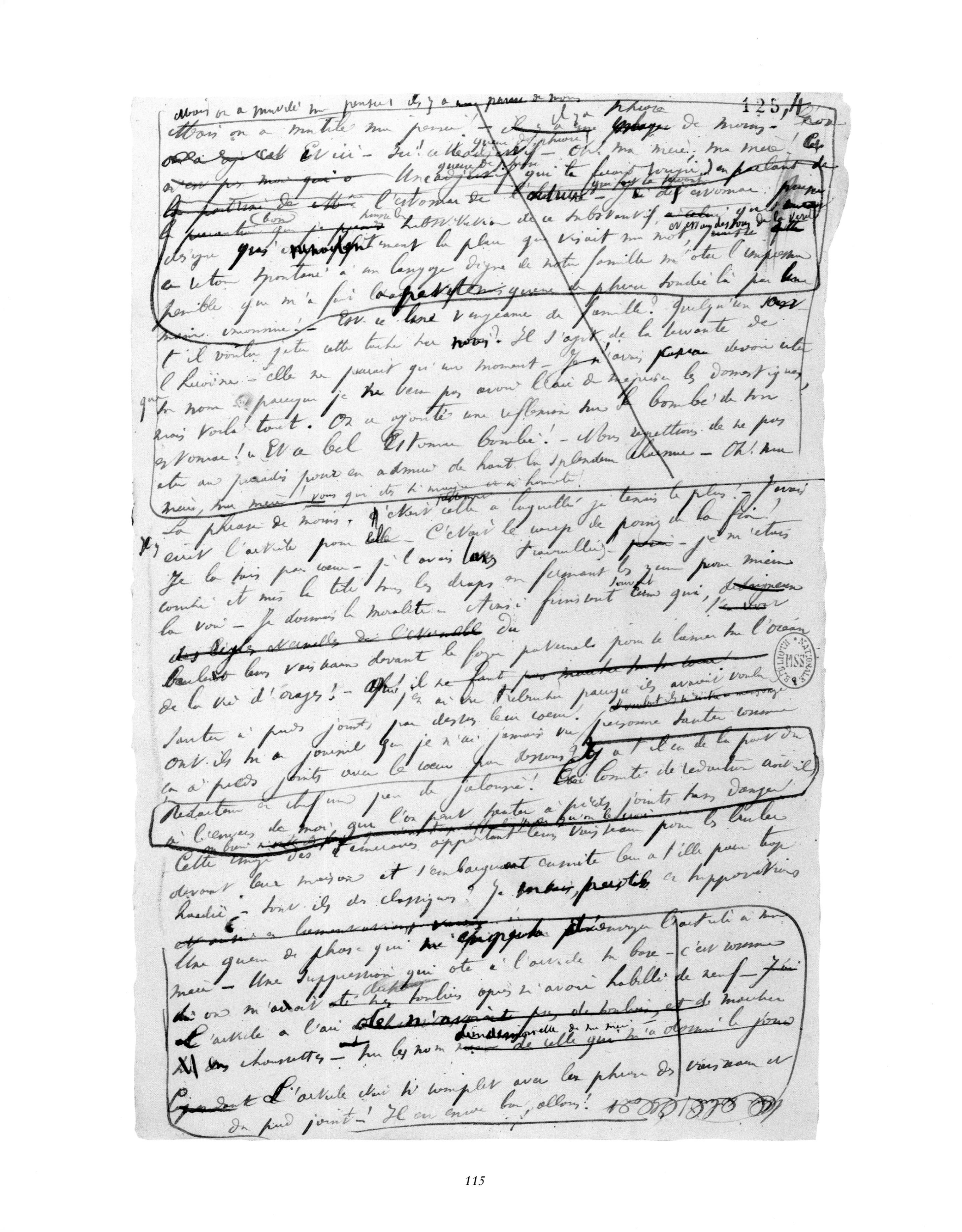

125

Recollections of My Youth

Ernest Renan, 1883

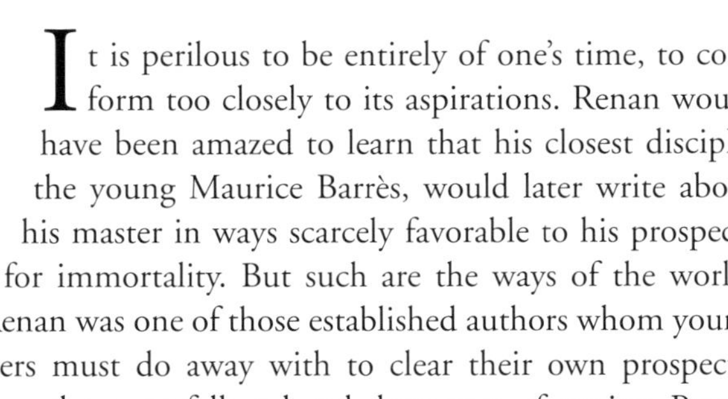

It is perilous to be entirely of one's time, to conform too closely to its aspirations. Renan would have been amazed to learn that his closest disciple, the young Maurice Barrès, would later write about his master in ways scarcely favorable to his prospects for immortality. But such are the ways of the world: Renan was one of those established authors whom young writers must do away with to clear their own prospects. Somehow, the poor fellow lured detractors of genius: Proust accused him of describing biblical Jerusalem in a platitudinous style better suited to a tourist guide. But the bilious disparagement of formidable critics is the price of talent. It is difficult for us today to imagine the extent of Renan's influence, especially of his *Vie de Jésus* (*Life of Jesus*). Highly controversial in its time, its style was admired by many: André Breton wrote of its "inspired heights," which he situated between Golgotha and the Acropolis. Had Renan heeded his innermost desires, he would have become a poet. But the second half of the nineteenth century demanded certainties, and Victor Hugo was already ensconced as the Homer of universal suffrage. Renan had to make do with university amphitheaters and, instead of a throne, with a chair of philosophy. His spirituality and sense of wonder found outlet in a vague pantheism. Like Leconte de Lisle and Louis Ménard, he aspired to antique paganism, but without renouncing the comforts of modern positivism and the ambiguities of doubt.

The "Prayer on the Acropolis" is more than a classic excerpt suitable for elementary-school readers. It made a lasting impression on several generations in the late nineteenth century and beyond. The faith in beauty, in the harmony of art and the universe, to which it gives voice might seem ill-suited to an age of scientism that, nursery to future disenchantment and despair, ushered in terrifying weapons of destruction.

This fervent, ideology-laden lesson proved congenial to such writers as Barrès, Montherlant, and Maurras, who, reading between the lines, responded to its sense of wonder. Renan, a large but rather melancholy gentleman of whom Daudet remarked that he "never relaxed until the end of a meal, after the wine and the liqueurs," passed on the precious torch of the humanities to a century all too prone to barbarity.

Pierre-Emmanuel Prouvost d'Agostino

"Prayer on the Acropolis"

. . . For several years, my dreams were of the burned chain of Galaad, of the pick of Safed in which the Messiah appeared, of Carmel and its fields of anemones sown by God, of the abyss of Aphaca from which issues the river Adonis. A singular thing! It was in Athens, in 1865, that I first experienced a strong feeling of going backwards, an effect like that of a cool, piercing breeze come from far, far away.

Athens made an impression on me that was much the strongest I have ever received. There is a place in the world where perfection exists—only one, not two—and that place is Athens. I had never imagined anything remotely like it. What was revealed to me was an ideal crystallized in Pentelic marble. Previously, I had held the view that perfection was not of this world; only one thing seemed to me proximate to the absolute. I had long since ceased to believe in miracles, in the literal sense; however, the unique destiny of the Jewish people, culminating in Jesus and Christianity, seemed to me something completely apart. For me, the Jewish miracle was now joined by the Greek one, the fact that a people had created a beauty that is eternal, unmarred by local or national stain, something that existed only once and would never be seen again, but whose effect would last forever. I knew that Greece had created science, art, philosophy, civilization, but I had no sense of the scale of this achievement. When I saw the Acropolis, I had a revelation of the divine, as when I first read the Gospels, as the Gospels come alive for me when I saw the valley of the Jordan from the Casyonne Heights. Then the whole world seemed barbaric to me. . . . The Romans were but coarse soldiers; the majesty of the most beautiful Romans, of Augustus, of Trajan, seemed to me mere pose by comparison with the easy, simple nobility of these proud and tranquil citizens.

E. Renan

Top left: Émile Cohl, *Caricature of Ernest Renan* (detail).
Left: Gabriel Prieur, *The Statue of Demosthenes in Athens,* 1847.
Opposite: Page from the autograph manuscript of *Souvenirs d'enfance et de jeunesse* (*Recollections of My Youth*) with the beginning of the "Prayer on the Acropolis." Paris, Bibliothèque Nationale de France.

entièrement nouvelles que j'y trouvai les visions que j'y eus d'un monde divin totalement étranger à nos froides et mélancoliques contrées, m'absorbèrent tout entier. Mes rêves pendant quelques années, furent la chaine brulée de Galaad, le pic de Safed où apparaîtra le Messie, le Carmel et ses champs d'anémones semés par Dieu, le gouffre d'Aphaca d'où sort le fleuve Adonis. Chose singulière! ce fut à Athènes en 1865, que j'éprouvai pour la première fois un vif sentiment de retour en arrière, un effet comme celui d'une brise fraiche, pénétrante, venant de très loin.

L'impression que me fit Athènes est de beaucoup la plus forte que j'aie jamais ressentie. Je n'avais jamais rien imaginé de pareil. C'était l'idéal cristallisé en marbre pentélique qui se montrait à moi. Jusque là j'avais cru que la perfection n'est pas de ce monde; une seule chose me paraissait se rapprocher de l'absolu. Je ne croyais plus depuis longtemps au miracle, dans le sens propre du mot; cependant la destinée unique du peuple juif, aboutissant à Jésus et au christianisme, m'apparaissait comme quelque chose de tout à fait à part. Or voici qu'à côté du miracle juif, venait se placer pour moi le miracle grec, ce fait d'un peuple créant un type de beauté éternelle, sans aucune tache locale ou nationale, une chose qui n'a existé qu'une fois, ne s'était jamais vue, ne se reverra plus, mais dont l'effet durera éternellement. Je savais bien avant cela que la Grèce avait créé la science, l'art, la philosophie, la civilisation, mais l'échelle me manquait. Quand je vis l'Acropole, j'eus la révélation du divin, comme je l'avais eue la première fois que je lus l'Évangile; le monde entier alors me parut barbare; sans Celtes, Germains, Slaves m'apparurent comme des lourdauds,

The Horla

Guy de Maupassant, 1883

The career of Guy de Maupassant was almost as meteoric as that of Rimbaud. The short story *Boule de Suif* (*Ball of Fat)* began his ascent to literary glory. Initially, the writers in Zola's circle, which he frequented, thought of him as a pleasure-seeker with literary pretensions. Then came a decisive moment. In 1880, the group decided to publish a collective volume of stories about the recently ended Franco-Prussian War, and each writer was asked to read his contribution aloud to the others. When it was Maupassant's turn, he read *Boule de Suif,* after which Zola and his guests, startled to discover how gifted he was, rose and approached him in silence, a gesture more telling than ordinary praise. The next year, Maupassant published *La Maison Tellier* (*Madame Tellier's Establishment*), and his literary reputation was made.

There followed several years of frenetic production, which netted six novels, three hundred short stories, and more than two hundred essays. To sustain this furious pace, Maupassant resorted to every possible aid, however noxious, including ether. However, neither amorous conquests, nor excursions on his sailboat (christened the Bel Ami, after his novel of that name), nor his work regimen sufficed to keep his demons at bay. Already seriously depressed when *Boule de Suif* appeared, he remained obsessed by feelings of life's ultimate futility. As this anguish began to consume him, he tried to channel it into a novel—even two, for there are two versions of *The Horla*. The second is unquestionably the better of them. It is cast as a diary, a form that, as in Gogol's *Diary of a Madman*, proves ideal for communicating the narrator's inexorable descent into madness. He tries to kill the Horla, a hostile being made all the more unnerving by its invisibility, by setting fire to his own house. Afterwards, suspecting that this tactic has failed, he postulates that the creature has possessed his own body: "No . . . No . . . there's no doubt, no doubt . . . He isn't dead . . . So . . . So . . . I'll just have to kill myself!" An unsettling notion, given the sad particulars of Maupassant's own end. Twelve years after the appearance of *Boule de Suif,* Maupassant tried to kill himself by cutting his throat. He was admitted to an asylum, where a cycle of psychiatric crises followed by periods of remission continued until his death the following year.

Paul Desalmand

The Horla

May 8
What a fine day! I spent the whole morning reclining on the grass in front of my house, under the enormous plane tree that covers, shelters, and shades it. I love this country. And I love living here because my roots are here, those deep and delicate roots that connect a man to the earth where his ancestors were born and died, that connect him to what people think and eat, to the customs as well as the cooking, to local turns of phrase, to peasant inflections, to the smell of the soil, the towns, and the very air.

I love the house where I grew up. From my windows I can see the Seine flowing the length of my garden, behind the road but close to the house, the great and broad Seine, which goes from Rouen to Le Havre, covered with passing boats.

Over to the left, Rouen, a vast city with blue roofs below a pointed population of Gothic towers. Numberless, some thin and some wide, they are dominated by the cast-iron spire of the cathedral, and are full of bells that ring in the blue air on beautiful mornings, sending my way their sweet and distant metallic drone, their bronze song brought to me by the breeze, sometimes stronger and sometimes weaker, depending on whether they are waking up or dozing off.

Top left: François-Nicolas Feyen-Perrin, *Portrait of Guy de Maupassant* (detail). Château de Versailles et de Trianon.
Right: Edvard Munch, *The Scream*, 1893. Oslo, Najonalgalleriet.
Opposite: First page of an autograph manuscript of *The Horla*. Paris, Bibliothèque Nationale de France.

1

Le Horla

. . . .

8 mai.

Quelle journée admirable ! J'ai passé toute la matinée étendu sur l'herbe, devant ma maison ~~blanche~~, sous l'énorme platane qui la couvre, l'abrite et l'ombrage tout entière. J'aime ce pays, et j'aime y vivre parce que j'y ai mes racines, ces profondes et délicates racines qui attachent un homme à la terre où sont nés et morts ses aïeux, qui l'attachent ~~[illegible]~~, à ce qu'on pense et à ce qu'on mange ~~[illegible]~~ ~~[illegible]~~ aux usages et ~~[illegible]~~, ~~au goût spécial~~ aux nourritures, aux ~~intos~~ locutions locales, aux intonations des paysans, aux odeurs du sol, des villages et de l'air lui-même.

J'aime ma maison où ~~je suis né~~ j'ai grandi. De mes fenêtres je vois la Seine qui coule ~~devant ma porte~~, le long de mon jardin, derrière ~~le chemin~~ la route presque ~~et qui semble~~ chez moi, la grande et large Seine qui va de Rouen au Havre, couverte de bateaux qui passent. ~~La~~ vaste ville à gauche, là-bas Rouen ~~[illegible]~~ ~~[illegible]~~ aux toits bleus ~~qui domine~~ sous le peuple pointu des clochers ~~[illegible]~~ gothiques. Ils sont innombrables, frêles ou larges, dominés par la flèche de fonte de la cathédrale, et pleins de cloches qui sonnent dans l'air bleu des belles matinées, ~~et jetant jusqu'à~~ ~~moi~~ jetant jusqu'à moi leur doux et lointain bourdonnement de fer, leur chant d'airain que la brise m'apporte ~~tantôt~~ tantôt plus fort et tantôt plus affaibli, suivant qu'elle s'éveille ou s'assoupit.

Against the Grain

Joris-Karl Huysmans, 1884

To cast oneself as the head of a school is to court ridicule. In his assumption of the role, Zola was not shy when it came to disciplining errant disciples. When one of them, Joris-Karl Huysmans, devised, in *À Rebours* (*Against the Grain*), what would become a rosary for an entire generation of decadents, the members of Zola's circle tut-tutted like scandalized prudes. "And *this* young man, who held out such promise as a naturalist writer! Lost in the vaporous realm of idealism, in the land of incense and estheticism!" Their self-righteous rebukes continued: "The only smells tolerated by naturalist dogma are the hearty aroma of petit-bourgeois stews, the musty fragrance of the latrine, the acrid odor of workers' sweat." The author of *Les Soeurs Vatard* (*The Vatard Sisters*) had isolated himself in an ivory tower with a chrysoberyl floor, perfumed by the dubious effluvia of vetiver and opoponax, and collected rare and complicated vices as if they were orchids. He had become enamored of a titled nobleman, Jean des Esseintes, inspired by a certain Count Robert de Montesquiou! The literary left cringed in horror. But the young generation was enchanted: finally, they found in Symbolism an alternative to the dreary positivism that had long been the only option under the Third Republic. And to top everything, Huysmans, after experimenting with black masses, threw himself at the foot of the Cross and became a Trappist monk. What strange ironies undergird the zigzags of literary modernism and the froufrou of the Belle Époque!

Pierre-Emmanuel Prouvost d'Agostino

Languorously ensconced in an immense wing chair, his feet resting on the vermeil pears of the firedogs, his slippers warmed by the fire, which darted and crackled as if blown by a bellows, des Esseintes placed the old quarto he had been reading on a table, drew himself up, lit a cigarette, and began to daydream deliciously, following at full gallop a trail of memories that, obscured for months, had reemerged because of his having suddenly, for reasons unknown, recalled a name.

With surprising clarity, he saw in his mind's eye how uncomfortable his friend d'Aigurande had been, when, at a gathering of confirmed bachelors, he had been obliged to admit he was about to marry. There were general cries of dismay, and the company tried to evoke for him the abomination of sharing his bed. To no avail. D'Aigurande had lost his head: he believed in the intelligence of his future wife, and claimed to have discerned in her an exceptional capacity for devotion and tenderness.

Alone among the company, des Esseintes had supported his intentions from the moment he learned that d'Aigurande's fiancée wanted them to live on the corner of one of the new boulevards, in one of the new apartment buildings with round towers.

Convinced of the pitiless power of marital squabbles, more disastrous for merely resilient spirits than for great ones, and aware that d'Aigurande had no fortune and that his wife's dowry was virtually nil, he foresaw the endless problems that would result from this simple wish.

In effect, d'Aigurande commissioned a complete ensemble of made-to-order furnishings: consoles with rounded backs, curved curtain rods, crescent-shaped carpets, etc.

Top left: Jean-Louis Forain, *Portrait of Georges-Charles, known as Joris-Karl Huysmans* (detail). Châteaux de Versailles et de Trianon.
Right: Nadar, photograph of Robert de Montesquiou, the model for Huysmans's Jean des Esseintes.
Opposite: Autograph manuscript of *À Rebours* (*Against the Grain*), beginning of chapter 6. Paris, Bibliothèque Nationale de France.

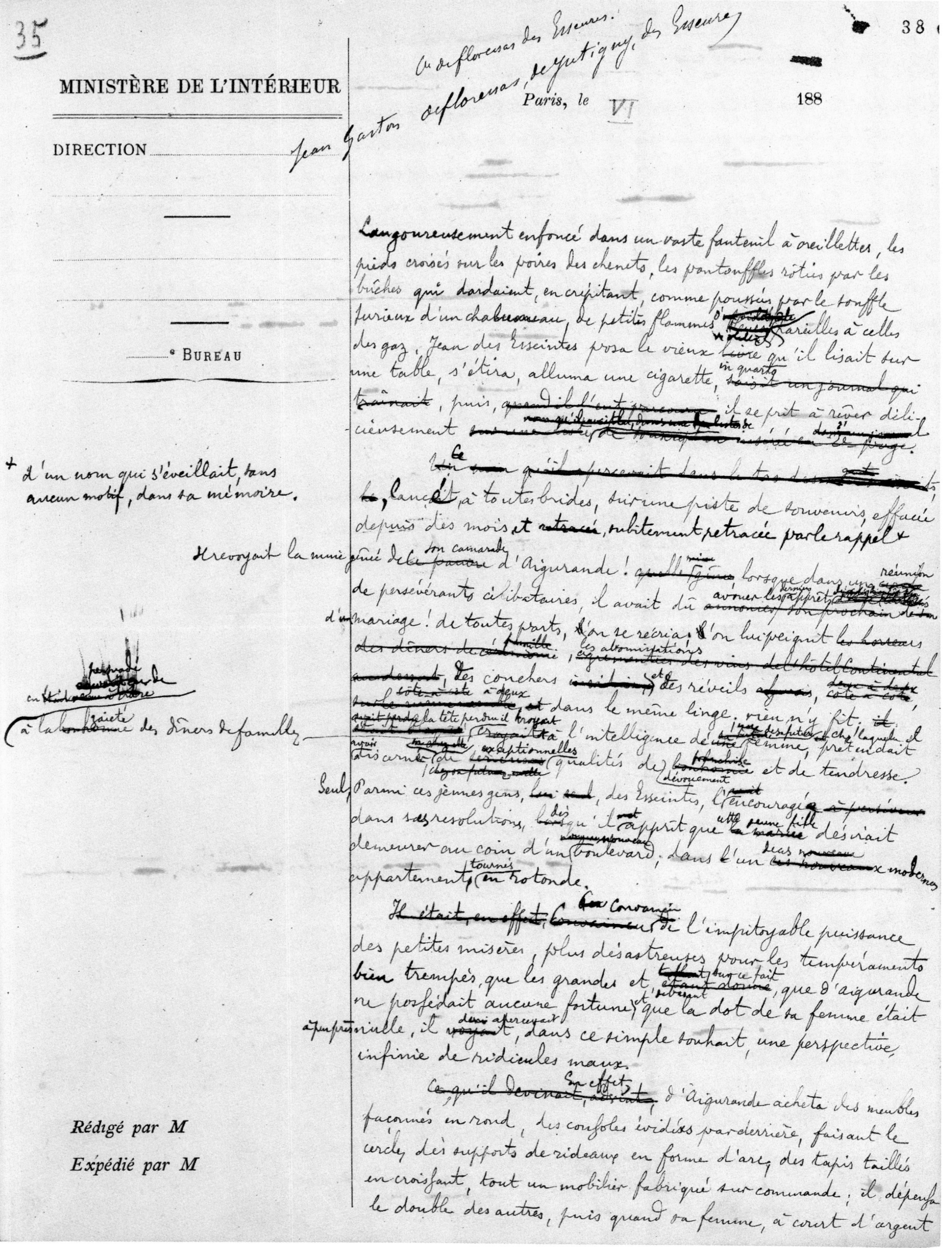

35

38

MINISTÈRE DE L'INTÉRIEUR

DIRECTION

Bureau

Paris, le VI 188

ou de Floressas des Esseintes.

Jean Gaston de Floressas, de Lutigny, des Esseintes

Langoureusement enfoncé dans un vaste fauteuil à oreillettes, les pieds croisés sur les poires des chenets, les pantoufles rôties par les bûches qui dardaient, en crépitant, comme poussées par le souffle furieux d'un chalumeau, de petites flammes pareilles à celles des gaz, Jean des Esseintes posa le vieux in quarto qu'il lisait sur une table, s'étira, alluma une cigarette, puis il se prit à rêver délicieusement + d'un nom qui s'éveillait, sans aucun motif, dans sa mémoire.

Ce ... lancé, à toutes brides, sur une piste de souvenirs effacée depuis des mois et subitement retracée par le rappel + [illegible] son camarade d'Aigurande! Il revoyait la mine ... lorsque dans une réunion de persévérants célibataires, il avait dû avouer les derniers apprêts d'un mariage! de toutes parts, on se récria, on lui peignit les abominations ..., des couchers et des réveils côte à côte ... à la ... des dîners de famille ... rien n'y fit. ... à l'intelligence de sa future chez laquelle il croyait ... exceptionnelles qualités de dévouement et de tendresse.

Seul parmi ces jeunes gens, des Esseintes l'encouragea dans ses résolutions, dès qu'il apprit que cette jeune fille désirait demeurer au coin d'un boulevard, dans l'un des modernes appartements tournés en rotonde.

Convaincu de l'impitoyable puissance des petites misères, plus désastreuses pour les tempéraments bien trempés que les grandes et, sur ce fait, que d'Aigurande ne possédait aucune fortune et que la dot de sa femme était à peu près nulle, il avait aperçu, dans ce simple souhait, une perspective infinie de ridicules maux.

En effet, d'Aigurande acheta des meubles façonnés en rond, des consoles évidées par derrière, faisant le cercle, des supports de rideaux en forme d'arcs, des tapis taillés en croissant, tout un mobilier fabriqué sur commande; il dépensa le double des autres, puis quand sa femme, à court d'argent

Rédigé par M

Expédié par M

The Rougon-Macquart Novels

Émile Zola, 1893

For Émile Zola's largely middle-class readership, such novels as *La Terre* (*The Earth*, about the provincial peasantry), *L'Assommoir* (about the world of Parisian laundresses and day-laborers) and *Germinal* (about coal miners) were rather exotic fare. The everyday lives of such people were as strange to the middle class as are, for most of us, those of Amerindians or residents of Bali. In a sense, such works functioned for their original public much like journalism does for us today.

Naturalism, a prolongation of the realist movement, sought to depict reality as it was. Its adherents eschewed euphemism and moralizing commentary, holding that a work's lessons should be self-evident. Zola, leader of the naturalist school, saw himself as an objective anatomist of the social body, but even he allowed that a degree of attenuation was necessary. Nonetheless, his work became a focus of controversy. Although avid for respectability, he found himself vilified by his own class.

Did the uproar caused by his fiction help to change contemporary attitudes? Undoubtedly. Above all, however, it changed Zola himself. He was a tireless researcher, and the more he learned about the lives of ordinary workers, the more indignant he became about their shameless exploitation. As a result, his world view was utterly transformed, and he became increasingly sympathetic to socialist ideals.

So much so that when the Dreyfus Affair erupted, he quickly grasped which was the side of right. He committed his entire being to defending the unjustly accused Dreyfus, a decision for which he was rewarded with exile. But it also won him recognition. As one critic put it, "He was a moment in the evolution of human conscience." And in that of the consciousness of the miners from northern France who traveled to Paris for his funeral and, parading behind his casket en route to the cemetery of Montmartre, chanted in homage: "Germinal! Germinal! Germinal!"

Paul Desalmand

The Ladies' Paradise

I

Denise had walked from the Gare Saint-Lazare, where she and her two brothers had gotten off a train from Cherbourg, having spent the night on the hard bench of a third-class carriage. She held Pepe by the hand and Jean followed behind, all three of them exhausted by the trip, bewildered and lost in the middle of the vast city, looking at the houses, asking at every corner for directions to the rue de la Michodière, where their uncle Baudis lived. But as they finally entered the Place Gaillon, the startled young girl came to a dead stop.

"Oh!" she said. "Jean, just look!"

And there they stood in a huddle, all dressed in black, still in mourning for their father. She, rather puny for her twenty years and looking impoverished, carried a small parcel; beside her, her little brother, five years old, clutched her arm, while over her shoulder stood her older brother, a blooming sixteen, his arms dangling.

Émile Zola

Top left: Jean-François Raffaëlli, *Portrait of Émile Zola* (detail), 1892, from the cover of a parchment binding of the original edition of *L'Assommoir*. Paris, Bibliothèque Nationale de France.
Left: At "The Ladies' Paradise," watercolor by Maxime Rebière.
Opposite: The first pages of autograph manuscripts of four novels in the *Rougon-Macquart* series: *The Ladies' Paradise*, *Germinal*, *L'Assommoir*, and *The Earth*. The last is in the hand of Zola's wife Alexandrine, who notes at the bottom that, as the original first page had been lost, she had reconstituted it on June 9, 1904.

AU BONHEUR DES DAMES

Mr Barbazange 37. 2 pts 1606

I

Denise était venue à pied de la gare Saint-Lazare, où un train de Cherbourg l'avait débarquée avec ses deux frères, après une nuit passée sur la dure banquette d'un wagon de troisième classe. Elle tenait par la main Pépé, et Jean la suivait, tous les trois brisés du voyage, effarés et perdus au milieu du vaste Paris, le nez levé sur les maisons, demandant à chaque carrefour la rue de la Michodière, dans laquelle leur oncle Baudu demeurait. Mais, comme elle débouchait enfin sur la place Gaillon, la jeune fille s'arrêta net de surprise.

— Oh! dit-elle, regarde un peu, Jean!

Et ils restèrent plantés, serrés les uns contre les autres, tout en noir, achevant les vieux vêtements du deuil de leur père. Elle, chétive pour ses vingt ans, l'air pauvre, portait un léger paquet; tandis que, de l'autre côté,

6 1

GERMINAL

Première partie

M Roc...

I

Dans la plaine rase, sous la nuit sans étoiles, d'une obscurité et d'une épaisseur d'encre, un homme suivait seul la grande route qui va de Marchiennes à Montsou, dix kilomètres de pavé coupant tout droit, à travers les champs de betteraves. Devant lui, il ne voyait même pas le sol noir, et il n'avait la sensation de l'immense horizon plat que par les souffles du vent de mars, des rafales larges comme sur une mer, glacées d'avoir balayé des lieues de marais et de terres nues. Aucune ombre d'arbre ne tachait le ciel, le pavé se déroulait avec la rectitude d'une jetée, au milieu de l'embrun aveuglant des ténèbres.

L'homme était parti de Marchiennes vers deux heures. Il marchait d'un pas allongé, grelottant sous le coton aminci de sa veste et de son pantalon de velours. Un petit paquet, noué dans un mouchoir à carreaux, le gênait beaucoup; et il le

1

L'ASSOMMOIR

1 F

18 heures

I

Gervaise avait attendu Lantier jusqu'à deux heures du matin. Puis, toute frissonnante d'être restée en camisole à l'air vif de la fenêtre, elle s'était assoupie, jetée en travers du lit, fiévreuse, les joues trempées de larmes. Depuis huit jours, au sortir du Veau à deux têtes, où ils mangeaient, il la plantait là sur le trottoir de la rue des Poissonniers, l'envoyait se coucher avec les enfants et ne reparaissait que tard dans la nuit, en racontant qu'il cherchait du travail. Ce soir-là, pendant qu'elle guettait son retour, elle s'était imaginé le voir entrer au bal du Grand-Balcon, dont les dix fenêtres flambantes éclairaient d'une nappe d'incendie la coulée noire des boulevards extérieurs; et, derrière lui, elle avait aperçu la petite Adèle, une brunisseuse qui dînait à leur restaurant, marchant à cinq ou six pas, les mains ballantes, comme si elle venait de lui quitter le bras, pour ne pas passer ensemble sous la clarté crue des globes de la porte.

Quand Gervaise s'éveilla, vers cinq heures, raidie, les reins brisés, elle éclata en sanglots. Lantier n'était pas rentré. Pour la première fois, il découchait. Elle resta assise au bord du lit, sous la lam-

 1

La Terre

Première partie

I

Jean, ce matin-là, un semoir de toile bleue noué sur le ventre, en tenait la poche ouverte de la main gauche, et de la droite, tous les trois pas, il y prenait une poignée de blé, que d'un geste, à la volée, il jetait. Ses gros souliers trouaient et emportaient la terre grasse, dans le balancement cadencé de son corps; tandis que, à chaque jet, au milieu de la semence blonde toujours volante, on voyait luire les deux galons rouges d'une veste d'ordonnance, qu'il achevait d'user. Seul, en avant, il marchait, l'air grandi; et, derrière, pour enfouir le grain, une herse roulait lentement, attelée de deux chevaux, qu'un charretier poussait à longs coups de fouet réguliers, claquant

Première page égarée que je viens de reconstituer le neuf Juin 1904. Alexandrine E. Zola

Carrot-Head

Jules Renard, 1893

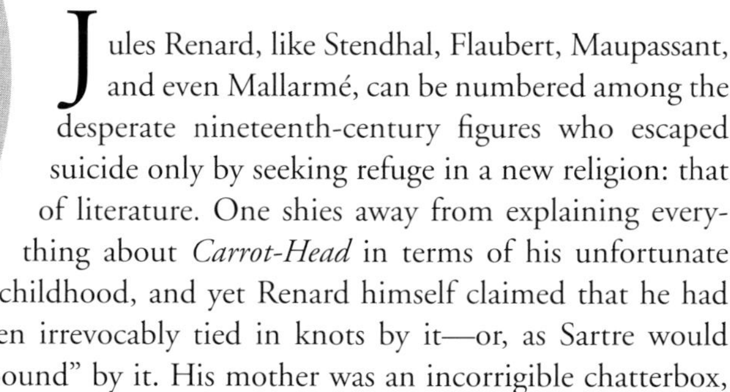

Jules Renard, like Stendhal, Flaubert, Maupassant, and even Mallarmé, can be numbered among the desperate nineteenth-century figures who escaped suicide only by seeking refuge in a new religion: that of literature. One shies away from explaining everything about *Carrot-Head* in terms of his unfortunate childhood, and yet Renard himself claimed that he had been irrevocably tied in knots by it—or, as Sartre would say, "bound" by it. His mother was an incorrigible chatterbox, bigoted, and malevolent; he would never forget her and dreamed of revenge. We get a sense of his feelings towards her from this dream fragment, entered into his diary in October 1896: "Immediately afterwards, we were enemies again. . . . Using the arms with which I had passionately embraced her, I threw her down and crushed her; I walked on her and ground her face into the kitchen tiles."

As often happens, this feeling of emptiness, later named existential anguish, coexisted with a profound love of life. Every morning, Jules Renard rejoiced at being alive, and he admitted: "Paradise is not of this earth, but parts of it are." A paradise of parts, but paradise nonetheless.

He never stopped testifying to this earthly richness. The same man who joked about seeing life *en rosse* ("as a redhead"; a play on the phrase *la vie en rose*) knew that he had a pronounced sentimental streak. As mayor of his village, he saw to it that the local roads were maintained properly, but as a poet he preferred to see them overrun by wild oats.

His writing is economical (perhaps a reaction to his mother's logorrhoea) and compact, in ways suggestive of Japanese haiku. He tried to purge his work of all trace of individuality, seeking to become a spokesperson for nature: "Poet, strive only for that. You were brought into the world to be the consciousness of what lacks consciousness." One critic mocked this extreme concision by pretending that, at the end of a life devoted to literature, Jules Renard would be satisfied with writing "*La Poule Pond*" ("The hen lays").

Paul Desalmand

Carrot-Head had heard that nothing worked better as a lure for crayfish than a bit of cat flesh, not even hen intestines or butcher's waste. Now he knew of a cat that was unloved because it was old, sick, and a bit mangy. Carrot-Head invited it to come and have a cup of milk with him, in his hut. It would be just the two of them. It was always possible that a rat would venture out from the walls, but Carrot-Head promised only the cup of milk. He pushed it into a corner and urged the cat towards it, saying:

"Enjoy."

He stroked its back, called it sweet names, observed the rapid movement of its tongue, then grew tender.

"Poor old fellow, enjoy what's left you."

The cat emptied the cup, dried the bottom, licked the edges, and then turned its attention to its own sugared lips.

"Are you done, all done?" asked Carrot-Head, still stroking it. "I'm sure you'd drink another cup, but that's all I could steal. And then, a little sooner, a little later, what's the difference?"

On saying these words, he placed the tip of his gun on the cat's forehead and fired.

The blast deafened Carrot-Head. He thought he'd knocked down the shack, and when the smoke cleared, he saw, at his feet, the cat looking at him with one eye. Half its head was gone, and blood was running into the cup.

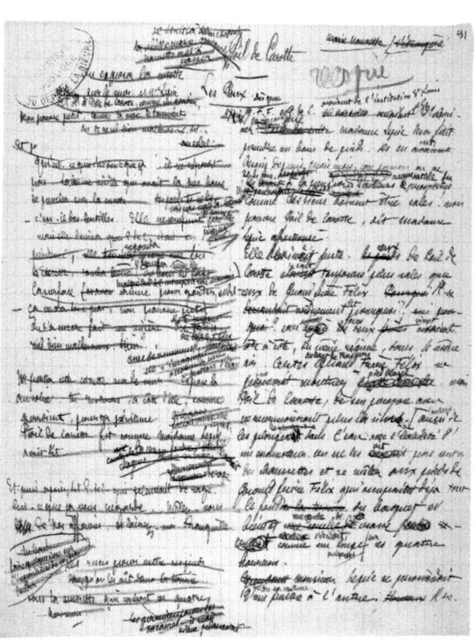

Top left: Jules Renard, photograph by Philippe Bert.
Left, right, and opposite: Table of contents and two pages of text from the autograph manuscript of *Poil de Carotte* (*Carrot-Head*). The passage illustrated at the right is from the vignette entitled "The Cat."
Nevers, Archives Départementales de la Nièvre.

~~Fables sans morale~~ Poil de Carotte

—

Le chat ~~[illegible]~~

Poil de Carotte l'a entendu dire : rien ne vaut la viande de chat pour pêcher les écrevisses, ni les tripes d'un poulet, ni les déchets d'une boucherie. Or il connaît un chat méprisé, ~~dont personne ne veut plus~~, parce qu'il est vieux, malade et ~~[illegible]~~ çà et là, pelé. Poil de Carotte l'invite à venir prendre une tasse de lait chez lui, dans son toiton. Ils seront seuls, ~~à moins qu'~~un rat s'aventure hors des ~~[illegible]~~ murs. Poil de Carotte ne promet que la tasse de lait. Il l'a posée dans un coin, ~~et le chat entre~~, il pousse le chat ~~vers elle~~, et dit :

— Régale-toi, ~~[illegible]~~

Il lui flatte l'échine, lui donne des noms tendres, observe ses vifs coups de langue, puis s'attendrit.

— Pauvre vieux, jouis de ton reste.

Le chat vide la tasse, nettoie le fond, ~~lèche le bord~~ essuie le bord, et il ~~n'a plus à~~ ne lui reste plus à lécher que ses lèvres sucrées.

— As-tu fini, bien fini, demande Poil de Carotte qui le caresse toujours. Sans doute tu ~~en voudrais~~ boirais volontiers une autre tasse, mais je n'ai pu voler que celle-là. D'ailleurs un peu plus tôt, un peu plus tard.

À ces mots, il lui applique au front le canon d'une carabine ~~[illegible]~~ et fait feu.

La détonation étourdit Poil de Carotte, il croit que le toiton même a sauté, et quand le nuage de fumée ~~[illegible]~~ se dissipe, il voit à ses pieds, le chat qui le regarde d'un œil. Une moitié de sa tête est emportée et le sang coule dans la tasse de lait.

Il travaille dans un enfer étroit.

Fait un léger tableau, tandis qu'il dort, de la pêche aux écrevisses. Au milieu des roseaux se lève. Le regarde d'un œil.

On entend le souffle de veaux qui viennent boire, touchent le bord de poils de carotte de leurs mufles et quand ils se retournent,

Des femmes flottent sur l'onde, glissent comme des draperies de ~~[illegible]~~

Les rayons de lune remuent comme des aiguilles à tricoter.

Se colorent ~~[illegible]~~ en battant le sol de coups sourds.

Tout le décor tremble mais les écrevisses avancent. Poil de Carotte essaie de fuir, mais il a perdu ses jambes. Il tend vainement les bras, fraternité ~~[illegible]~~ d'angoisse, avec ~~[illegible]~~ entendant.

Et ne peut déplacer sa ~~[illegible]~~ Et les écrevisses s'approchant, avancent déjà leurs pinces.

Le bateau

Quand le chat expire, Poil de Carotte tombe assis,

une pièce

~~[illegible]~~ d'un peu

My Diary

Léon Bloy, 1896

Léon Bloy was born in 1846, a few months before the apparition of the Virgin on the mountain of La Salette. He devoted his life and his work to conveying the "message of La Salette," which amounted to *iste sacerdos cloaca immunda* ("this clergy is a filthy sewer"), and to the Virgin's assertion that she would not be able to restrain the avenging arm of her Son much longer. The end of time would come this evening, and the return of Christ, weary of the outrages inflicted upon him by a humanity no longer in his own image, would come tomorrow . . . Léon Bloy produced a body of work unique in the history of French literature, full of zeal and imbued with the impatience of a Paracelsus. In his first book, *Le Désespéré* (*The Despairing One*), he announces with startling intensity: "If a rich man of bad faith gives a sou to a poor man, this sou will pierce the poor man's hand, fall, make a hole in the stars, and upset the balance of the world." In essays on Christopher Columbus, Marie-Antoinette, Louis XVII, and Napoleon, Bloy forecasts an impending disaster tempered by the Communion of Saints, both living and dead. "Our liberty is one with the equilibrium of the world," he writes, trying to convey how the least of our acts has unsuspected consequences. *Femme Pauvre* (*The Poor Woman*), Bloy's second and final novel, tells the story of Saint Clotilde and her painful rejection of all satanic temptation.

Better remembered is Bloy's diary, celebrated for its viciousness, whose first volume is entitled *Le Mendiant Ingrat* (*The Thankless Beggar*). So oblivious was Bloy here of literary niceties that he entitled its second volume *Mon Journal* (*My Diary*), a publication that won him a mere four hundred readers. During Bloy's lifetime, none of his books sold more than a thousand copies; his *Exégèse des lieux communs* (*The Wisdom of the Bourgeoisie*), an ironic masterpiece, interested almost no one. Nevertheless, Léon Bloy remains one of the most remarkable French stylists of the last two hundred years.

Pierre Chalmin

From a letter to M. E. Marlier, Brussels
February 1, 1896

—"So you are finally buried, once and for all!" he seems to say. "And not a moment too soon. Compared to you, I resemble a cesspool cleaner, and my twenty volumes fell from adolescents' hands when they heard your verse. But now I triumph. I am made of iron and granite, I never sweat, I earn 400,000 francs per annum, and I don't give a damn about the poor. I want everybody to know, tell everyone, I couldn't care less about the poor, and it's a very good thing that they should starve in ignominy. Strength, justice, real glory, true nobility, unsurpassable grandeur: that is riches. Only then is one master, does one have a right to be admired. Long live my money, long live my gut, and bully for Poetry! Of all geniuses of all times, I am the one most worthy of adoration."

If there should be any doubt about Verlaine's status as the finest contemporary poet, a porphyry-maker and child-king of Poetry lost among riffraff, what better proof could there be than the rage of this super-rich potentate of the boors? We should admire this indigestible porcine's sense of smell. We have seen laments brayed over the carcasses of Dumas the son and other pontificators who knew easy success, without his bothering to intervene. The impending end of the glabrous [François] Coppée won't trouble him, either. That one doesn't irritate him or condemn him. But Verlaine, that's another story.

So he rushes forward, like a furious landlord attacking an unfortunate tenant trying to move out on the sly.

"Just a minute," he shouts. "You forget that there's Me and that I am Me and that everything here belongs to Me! Literary recognition is my exclusive property; and I won't let anything leave. I work hard, I do! I've sold a lot of shit, I've produced even more, and I vituperate against dreamers who don't pay their rent."

"Having been an infinitely greater pig than any man before me, having vilified, with incomparable success, everything there is to vilify, I want to be recognized as the boss, the absolute chief, the caliph, and I call to witness the whole of the bourgeois rabble whose votes have exalted me. I am the Unique One, and it is an insupportable breach of order for anyone to be admired save at my command or with my permission."

Unfailingly, it is the *quality* of the votes that Zola scents out. He has an old Jew's instinct for distinguishing good money from the bad that is always his remuneration, and with which he must always content himself . . .

Léon Bloy

C'est la qualité des suffrages que subodore infailliblement Zola. Il a un instinct de vieux juif pour discerner la bonne monnaie d'avec la mauvaise que, pour son compte, il reçoit toujours & dont il est forcé de se contenter. Les raisons, très-soigneusement dissimulées, de sa fureur apparaissent malgré lui dans l'ostentation de ses «haines». Quoi qu'il fasse, il se sent goujat & il est inconsolable de ne trôner derrière, lui qu'une goujate multitude.

petit texte

Top left: Léon Bloy, *Self-Portrait*, November 1863. Private collection. *Above and opposite:* Page (detail and full view) from the autograph manuscript of *Mon Journal* (*My Diary*). La Rochelle, Bibliothèque Municipal.

tractivement à lui-même, afin qu'éclatassent les supériorités infinies du sale négoce de la vacherie littéraire sur la Poésie des Séraphins. Il a tenu à piaffer, à promener toute sa sonnaille de brute autour du cercueil de cet indigent qui avait crié merci dans les plus beaux vers du monde.

« — Te voilà donc, une bonne fois, enterré! semble-t-il dire. Ce n'est vraiment pas trop tôt. À côté de toi, je ressemblais à un vidangeur & mes vingt volumes tombaient des mains des adolescents [illegible] ils entendaient tes vers. Mais, à cette heure, je triomphe. Je suis de fer, moi, je suis de granit, je ne me soûle jamais, je gagne quatre cent mille francs par an & je me fous des pauvres. Qu'on le sache bien, que tous les peuples en soient informés, je me fous absolument des pauvres & c'est très-bien fait qu'ils crèvent dans l'ignominie. La force, la justice, la gloire solide, la vraie noblesse, l'indépassable grandeur, c'est d'être riche. Alors seulement on est un maître & on a le droit d'être admiré. Vive mon argent, vivent mes tripes & bran pour la Poésie! Je suis le plus adorable génie des siècles. »

Si on pouvait douter que Verlaine ait été véritablement le plus haut poète contemporain, le porphyrogénète & l'enfant-roi de la Poésie égaré parmi la crapule, quel témoignage plus certain que cette rage du richissime potentat des mufles?

Admirons le flair de cet incomestible pourceau. On a pu braire des lamentations sur la charogne du fils Dumas ou de tels autres bonzes du succès facile, sans qu'il intervînt. La fin prochaine du glabre Coppée ne le troublera pas davantage. Ceux-là ne le gênent ni ne le condamnent. Mais Verlaine, c'est autre chose.

Il s'élance alors comme un proprio furibond sur un locataire malheureux qui déménagerait à la cloche de bois.

« — Un instant, gueule-t-il, vous oubliez qu'il y a moi & que je suis moi & que tout ici appartient à Moi. Le garno littéraire est mon exclusive propriété & je ne laisserai rien sortir. Je suis un travailleur, Moi! j'ai vendu beaucoup de merde, j'en ai fait encore plus & je vitupère les rêveurs qui ne paient pas leur loyer.

« Ayant été infiniment plus cochon qu'aucun homme ne l'avait jamais été, ayant avili, avec un succès incomparable tout ce qui pouvait être avili, je veux qu'on reconnaisse en moi le patron, le chef absolu, le calife, & j'en appelle à toute la racaille bourgeoise dont les suffrages m'ont exalté. Je suis l'Unique & c'est un désordre insoutenable que quelqu'un soit admiré sans mon ordre ou ma permission. »

C'est la qualité des suffrages que subodore infailliblement Zola. Il a un instinct de vieux juif pour discerner la bonne monnaie d'avec la mauvaise que, pour son compte, il reçoit toujours & dont il est forcé de se contenter. Les raisons, très-soigneusement dissimulées, de sa fureur apparaissent malgré lui dans l'ostentation de ses « haines ». Quoi qu'il fasse, il se sent goujat & il est inconsolable de ne traîner derrière lui qu'une goujate multitude.

Verlaine raté! Barbey d'Aurevilly raté! Villiers de l'Isle-Adam raté! Il y en a peut-être un quatrième dont le nom est à l'extrémité de sa plume, mais il ne l'écrira pas, parce que le titulaire est encore vivant & que cela pourrait lui faire un bout de réclame. Parbleu! ceux-là régnèrent & règnent encore, sans argent, sur l'aristocratie de la jeunesse que dégoûte le mercantilisme populacier du croquant de lettres. Et voilà ce qui ne se pardonne pas.

Tout de même, avouons-le, c'est une chose un peu stupéfiante que le dédain de ce compilateur assommant & malpropre pour de tels artistes. J'ai connu surtout d'Aurevilly dans l'intimité de qui j'eus l'honneur de vivre plus de vingt ans & je me rappelle l'espèce d'agonie du très-haut & très-magnanime écrivain quand ses fonctions de critique l'obligeaient à lire un roman de Zola. Imaginez un aigle captif dans une fosse d'aisances, ne fût-ce qu'une heure, un quart d'heure, une minute même qui lui semblerait les siècles des siècles!

Et maintenant, cher monsieur, vous allez me demander sans doute comment il est possible, malgré tout, que Zola ait commis la gaffe d'un article aussi insolent & aussi grotesque. Mon Dieu! la réponse est simple. Zola est un sot. Porté par le caprice de la Fortune à une situation littéraire inouïe, il est devenu, par excellence, le « mime » de cette déesse,

A Tale of the Pyrenees

Pierre Loti, 1897

Bourget, Maupassant, and Loti
Are sold in all the gares.
They can be found with the rôti
The oranges, and the cigars.

This witty quatrain by Laurent Tailhade is premised on the immense popularity of the author of *Aziyadé* (translated into English as *Constantinople*). Women tended his cradle, in the austere shape of two generations of the widows commonly found in port cities, for the sea once claimed many men. Women would also haunt his work, elusive beauties from the end of the world, more imaginary than real. Loti collected such tropical flowers. His is a sensuality perfumed with regret. In these frail heroines—chosen victims, the doomed princesses of remote lands—Loti saw only exotic toys subject to his European whims.

It would be easy to criticize him for his prejudices, which were pervasive in his day. But there is another Loti, a writer who rejected love stories redolent of rose water and palm wine in favor of masculine adventure tales. *Ramuntcho* (translated as *A Tale of the Pyrenees*) was born of his enthusiasm for the Basque country. To this proud man with sensitive nerves, its no-nonsense hospitality proved irresistible, as did its mixture of damp sea air and the dry climate of nearby Spain.

Loti is one of those writers whose reputation is belied by his work. At his house at La Rochelle, which he decorated like a seraglio, the most telling attraction is his bedroom, whose modest iron bed speaks volumes. Thanks to literature, a little boy named Julien Viaud, who later rechristened himself Pierre Loti, managed to contrive extravagant tales of love and travel.

Pierre-Emmanuel Prouvost d'Agostino

And while she dreamed, gazing upwards, her eyes lost in the dark clouds and imprisoning mountain tops, Ramuntcho felt his pulse run faster, his heart beat stronger, for what she had just said so spontaneously filled him with intense joy. Bending his head towards her, speaking in an infinitely soft, childlike voice, he asked her, almost jokingly:

"*We'll go?* Isn't that what you said: *we'll go*, you with me? Does that mean that, when you are of age, you will consent to our marriage?"

In the darkness, he could see the soft black sparkle of Gracieuse's eyes, as she looked up at him with an expression of astonishment and reproach:

"You mean . . . you didn't know?"

"I wanted you to say it, don't you see? You had never told me, you know."

He squeezed the arm of his little fiancée, and their pace slowed. It was true that they had never told one another, less because it seemed obvious than because whenever they started to speak they were overtaken by fear: the fear of having been wrong, of discovering it wasn't true. . . . And now they knew, now they were sure. They were suddenly aware of having crossed, together, the grave and solemn threshold of life. Leaning on one another, they were a bit unsteady as they advanced slowly, like two children drunk on youth, joy, and hope.

"But do you think she'll agree, your mother?" asked Ramuntcho, after a long, delicious silence.

"Ah! That. . . ." answered his little fiancée, with an uneasy sigh. "Arrochkoa, my brother, will probably be for us. But Mama! Will Mama agree? And then, it wouldn't be soon in any case. . . . You still have to do your stint in the army."

"No, not if you don't want me to. No, I can get out of my military service! I am Guizpuzcoan, like my mother, so my enlistment is voluntary. So that will be however you like; I'll do whatever you want."

"Then, my Ramuntcho, I'd prefer to wait longer for you so you can be naturalized and become a soldier like the others. That's what I'd like, since you ask me!"

"Really, that's what you want? So much the better, for that's what I want, too."

P. Loti

Top left: M. Amilly, *Pierre Loti in Oriental Costume* (detail), 1912. Private collection.
Left: Edmond Hedouin, *The Pork Market at Saint-Jean-de-Luz*. Bayonne, Musée Bonnat.
Opposite. Page from the autograph manuscript of *Ramuntcho* (*A Tale of the Pyrenees*). Paris, Bibliothèque Nationale de France.

plus fort, dans l'intense joie de ce qu'elle venait de si spontanément dire. Et, la tête penchée vers elle, la voix infiniment douce et enfantine, il lui demanda, comme un peu pour plaisanter:

—« Nous irions? C'est bien comme ça que tu as parlé: nous « irions, toi avec moi? Ça signifie donc que tu serais consentante, un peu « plus tard, quand nous serons d'âge, à nous marier tous deux?»

Il perçut, à travers l'obscurité, le gentil éclair noir des yeux de Gracieuse qui se levaient vers lui avec une expression d'étonnement et de reproche:

—« Alors..... tu ne le savais pas?»

—« Je voulais te le faire dire, tu vois bien ... C'est que tu ne me « l'avais jamais dit, sais-tu ....»

Il serra ~~[illegible]~~ contre lui le bras de sa petite fiancée et leur marche devint plus lente.. C'est vrai, qu'ils ne s'étaient jamais dit cela; non pas seulement parce qu'il leur semblait que ça allait de soi, mais surtout parce que, au moment de parler, ils se sentaient arrêtés par une terreur quand même, — la terreur de s'être trompés et que ce ne fut pas vrai... Et à présent, ils savaient, ils étaient sûrs. Alors ils prenaient conscience qu'ils venaient de franchir à deux le seuil grave et solennel de la vie. Et, appuyés l'un à l'autre, ils chancelaient presque dans leur promenade ralentie, comme deux enfants ivres de jeunesse, de joie et d'espoir ....

—« Mais, est-ce que tu crois qu'elle voudra, ta mère?» reprit ~~Ramoudcho~~ Ramuntcho timidement, après le long silence délicieux...

—« Ah! voilà .... répondit la petite fiancée, avec un soupir « d'inquiétude.. ~~Olhatxe~~ Arrochkoa mon frère sera pour nous, c'est ~~sûr~~ bien probable. Mais « maman?.. Maman voudra-t-elle?...

« Et puis, ce ne serait pas pour bientôt, dans tous les cas.. Tu as ton « service à faire à l'Etat.»

—« Non, si tu le veux! Non, je peux ne pas le faire, mon service! « Je suis un Guipuscoa, moi, comme ma mère était; alors, on ne me « prendra ~~[illegible]~~ pour la Conscription ~~[illegible]~~ que si je le demande.. Donc, ce sera « comme tu l'entendras; comme tu voudras, je ferai..»

—« Ça, mon ~~Ramoudcho~~ Ramuntcho, j'aimerais mieux plus longtemps t'attendre et que « tu te fasses naturaliser, et que tu sois soldat comme les autres. C'est mon idée à moi, « puisque tu veux que je te la dise!.

—« Vrai, c'est ton idée!. Eh bien tant mieux, car c'est la mienne aussi.

Cyrano de Bergerac

Edmond Rostand, 1897

To write nothing that issues not from thyself,
And to counsel modestly thusly: "My friend,
Rest content with flowers, fruit, even leaves,
If they are gathered from your own garden!
Then, if a little glory should happen your way,
Needing to render nothing to Caesar,
Keeping all the credit for yours truly,
In short, disdaining to be parasite ivy
When one is oneself neither oak nor ash,
You may not rise high, but you will rise alone!

Fate seemed well disposed indeed toward the young Edmond Rostand, who at the hundredth performance of his *Cyrano de Bergerac* was awarded the Legion of Honor by a President of the Republic who declared, not altogether in jest: "Rostand, you have saved France." It seemed that all Paris adored the playwright, who was elected to the Académie Française at age thirty-four and made his way through the city sporting a frock coat pulled in at the waist, the enterprising moustache of a low-ranking officer, and the silken gaze of an indifferent womanizer. But this neurasthenic man, all but smothered by the excessive adulation, sought relief from his asthma in the pure air of the Basque country, in the lunar Versailles of Arnaga.

Was his well of inspiration running dry? No, but it is disconcerting for a writer who knows himself to be a minor master to hear himself everywhere proclaimed a national treasure. *Cyrano*, lauded to the skies, is merely an extravagant play that arrived at the right moment. Upon rereading, it reveals itself to be an odd amalgam of baroque and romantic elements, a work in which a fake Louis XIII idiom—language redolent of Góngora, Scudéry, and Viau—is set in convoluted verse, with results analogous to a flashy piece of Art Nouveau jewelry. This unclassifiable theatrical object, simultaneously patriotic and sentimental, farcical and melodramatic, is a startling and unique creation.

There followed *L'Aiglon*, an extended, lyrical celebration of failure, and *Chanticleer*, which was a spectacular disappointment. Rostand, aware of the disproportionate extent of his fame, tried to live up to it but proved unequal to the task. Nonetheless, he remains a touching, disquieting, and sensitive poet, a fantasist given to preciosity who was mistakenly compared to Hugo in a period desperate for epic.

Pierre-Emmanuel Prouvost d'Agostino

Top left: Edmond Rostand in academic garb, photograph by Van Bosh, 1901. Paris, Bibliothèque Nationale de France.
Right: Cyrano de Bergerac, watercolor by Maxime Rebière.
Opposite: In lieu of the autograph manuscript of *Cyrano de Bergerac*, which is lost, we reproduce this page from a guest register on which Rostand inscribed, at his host's request, part of a speech from the play (*Cyrano*, Act 2, scene 8). His wife did likewise, inscribing a quatrain.

N'écrire jamais rien qui de soi ne sortît,
Et modeste d'ailleurs se dire : mon petit,
Sois satisfait des fleurs, des fruits, même des feuilles,
Si c'est dans ton jardin à toi que tu les cueilles !
Puis, s'il advient d'un peu triompher, par hasard,
Ne pas être obligé d'en rien rendre à César,
Vis à vis de soi-même en garder le mérite,
Bref, dédaignant d'être le lierre parasite,
Lors même qu'on n'est pas le chêne ou le tilleul,
Ne pas monter bien haut, peut-être, mais tout seul !

(Acte II - Cyrano)

Edmond Rostand

Les cigales, ces bestioles,
Ont plus d'âme que les violes ;
Les cigales, les cigalons
Chantent mieux que les violons !

(Les Pipeaux)

Rosemonde Rostand

Diary of a Chambermaid

Octave Mirbeau, 1900

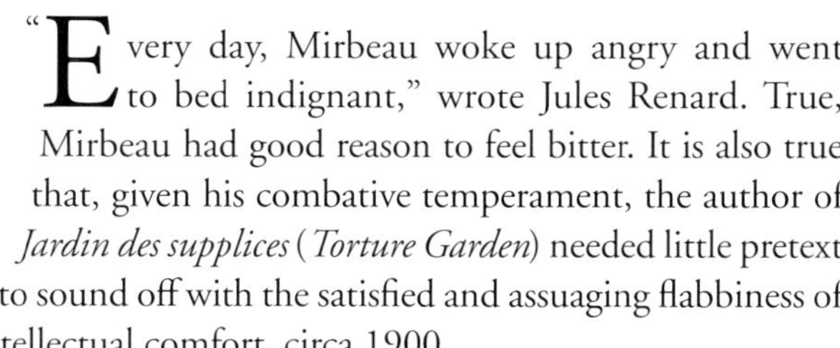

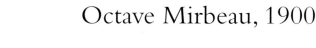

"Every day, Mirbeau woke up angry and went to bed indignant," wrote Jules Renard. True, Mirbeau had good reason to feel bitter. It is also true that, given his combative temperament, the author of *Jardin des supplices* (*Torture Garden*) needed little pretext to sound off with the satisfied and assuaging flabbiness of intellectual comfort, circa 1900.

One either loves or hates the vehemently expressed biases of this great injustice collector, who often contradicted himself but never lied to or deceived himself. His contemporary Forain, whose draftsman's pencil was as sharp as his intelligence, caricatured some servants under the heading: "Our Enemies." Mirbeau's chambermaid corroborates the accuracy of this designation. What better observation post from which to study the dubious reverses of respectable fronts than the keyhole? What better position from which to rummage through desks and trash baskets? Do we know them, these strangers whom we welcome into our homes and authorize to do our housekeeping: in other words, to commit the most indiscrete acts without fear of punishment?

The fictional author of this imaginary diary is a veritable virago, a dismissed maid who wreaks revenge by exposing all the secrets of her former employers, washing their dirty linen in public. Given this premise, is it justifiable to complain of the work's excesses, of the bleakness of the world it pictures, so sordid as to make the reader uncomfortable? "I would prefer to write only of beauty," claimed Mirbeau, "but I am an artist; I observe my time, and I scarcely see it proliferating around me."

Pierre-Emmanuel Prouvost d'Agostino

Top left: Photograph of Octave Mirbeau (detail). Paris, Bibliothèque Nationale de France.
Left: Proposed design by Mirbeau himself for the cover of *Journal d'une Femme de Chambre* (*Diary of a Chambermaid*). Paris, Bibliothèque Labadens.
Opposite: First page, autograph manuscript of *Journal d'une Femme de Chambre* (*Diary of a Chambermaid*). Paris, Bibliothèque Labadens.

Diary of a chambermaid

I

September 14

Today, September 14, at three in the afternoon, in mild weather, gray and rainy, I assumed my new post. It is the twelfth one in two years. Needless to say, I don't mention the ones I held before that. It would be impossible for me to count them. Ah, I can boast of having seen quite a few interiors, and faces, and filthy souls.... And it's not over yet ... How difficult masters are these days.... It's unbelievable!

The hire was arranged through the job listings in Le Figaro, and without my having seen Madame. We wrote to one another, and that was that; a risky business that can lead to surprises on both sides. Madame's letters are well written, it's true. But they reveal a fussy and meticulous character. Well! She felt obliged to offer so many explanations and commentaries, so many whys and wherefores! I don't know if Madame is stingy; in any case, she didn't exactly break the bank for her stationery, which comes from the Magasin du Louvre. I'm not rich myself, but I'm more stylish; I write on beautiful textured paper, some of it pink and some pale blue, that I collected from my former mistresses. Some of it even has a countess's crown letterhead. That must have impressed her.

Finally, here I am in Normandy, at Mesnil-Roy. Madame's property, which is not far from the town, is called the Prieuré. That's about all I know about the place where I'll be living from now on. I have some concerns and regrets about burying myself, on impulse, in the depths of the provinces. What little I've seen of the place scares me, and I ask myself what will happen to me here. Nothing good, I daresay, and there's sure to be man trouble. That's a perk we can always count on. For every one of us who succeeds, which is to say for every one of us who marries a fine young man or settles down with an old one, how many of us are destined to misfortune, to being swept away by the great whirlwind of poverty? In the end, I had no choice; and this was better than nothing.

This is not the first time I've been engaged in the provinces. Four years ago, I took a post.... Oh! Not for long ... and under circumstances that were truly exceptional. I remember that adventure as if it were yesterday. Although some of the details are a bit coarse, even horrible, I want to tell the story anyway.

Octave Mirbeau

Le Journal d'une femme de chambre

I

14 septembre.

Aujourd'hui, 14 septembre, à trois heures de l'après-midi, par un temps doux, gris et pluvieux, je suis entrée dans ma nouvelle place. C'est la douzième, en deux ans. Bien entendu, je ne parle pas des places que j'ai faites durant les années précédentes. Il me serait impossible de les compter. Ah! je puis me vanter que j'en ai vu des intérieurs, et des visages, et de sales âmes. Et ça n'est pas fini!... À la façon vraiment extraordinaire, vertigineuse dont j'ai roulé successivement, ici et là, de maison en bureau et de bureau en maison, du Bois de Boulogne à la Bastille, de l'Observatoire à Montmartre et des Ternes au Marais, et de Paris en province, partout, sans pouvoir jamais rester nulle part, faut-il que les maîtres soient difficiles à servir, maintenant!

L'affaire s'est traitée par l'intermédiaire des Petites Annonces du Figaro, et sans que je voie Madame. Nous nous sommes écrit des lettres et c'est tout; moyen chanceux où l'on a, de part et d'autre, des surprises, souvent. Les lettres de Madame sont bien écrites, ça c'est vrai, mais elles révèlent un caractère tatillon et méticuleux... Ah! lui en faut des explications et des commentaires et des pourquoi et des parce que... Je ne sais si Madame est avare, en tout cas, elle ne se fend guères pour son papier à lettres... Il est acheté au Louvre!... Moi qui ne suis pas riche, j'ai plus de coquetterie... J'écris sur du papier parfumé à la peau d'Espagne, du beau papier, tantôt rose, tantôt bleu pâle, que j'ai collectionné chez mes anciennes maîtresses. Cela a dû lui en boucher un coin!

Enfin, me voilà en Normandie au Mesnil-Roy... La propriété de Madame qui n'est pas loin du pays, s'appelle: le Prieuré... C'est, à peu près, tout ce que je sais de l'endroit où désormais je vais vivre.

Je ne suis pas sans inquiétudes, ni sans regrets d'être venue, à la suite d'un coup de tête, m'ensevelir dans ce fond perdu de province. Ce que j'en ai aperçu m'effraie un peu et je me demande ce qui va encore m'arriver ici. Rien de bon, sans doute, et, comme d'habitude, des embêtements!... Les embêtements, c'est le plus clair de notre bénéfice!... Pour une qui réussit, j'entends pour une qui épouse un brave garçon ou qui se colle avec un vieux, combien sont destinées aux malchances, emportées dans le tourbillon de la misère!... Après tout, je n'avais pas le choix, et cela vaut mieux que rien.

Ce n'est pas la première fois que je suis engagée en province. Il y a quatre ans, j'y ai fait une place... oh! pas longtemps... mais dans des conditions véritablement exceptionnelles. Je me souviens de cette aventure comme si elle était d'hier... Bien que les détails en soient un peu lestes et même horribles, je veux la conter. D'ailleurs,

"Imprint"

Anna, Countess de Noailles, 1901

Anna de Noailles, née Brancovan, blessed with high cheekbones, hair "blue like prunes," and immense green eyes, vigorously led the "invasion of women" into the bastion of French literature. A Greco-Roman princess, born in Paris and a French citizen by election, the young countess—a Dreyfusard, and the model for the Vicomtesse de Réveillon in Proust's *Jean Santeuil*—won fame at age twenty-four with two volumes of poetry, *Le Coeur innombrable* (*The Elusive Heart*, 1901) and *L'Ombre des jours* (*The Shadow of Days*, 1902), both characterized by an idiosyncratic naturalism haunted by the transience of all things ("Yet one day you will leave me, Youth"). Her three novels also met with success, especially *Le Visage émerveillé* (*The Wondering Visage*), the fictional diary of an amorous nun, a work informed by her own passionate liaison with Maurice Barrès, whose fascination with the Orient and with death also inflects the sunny jubilation of *Éblouissements* (*Bedazzlements*, 1907). Was she merely a "garden muse," a "pagan" and "oriental" drunk on life and the dance? Solitude (from 1908), an encounter with the young poet Henri Franck, his death soon after, the horrors of war, and reconciliation with Barrès (1917) variously left their mark on *Les Vivants et les Morts* (*The Living and the Dead*, 1913) and *Les Forces Éternelles* (*Eternal Forces*, 1920). Here one discovers a mystic (unable to forget herself) and an astonishing poet of love able to encompass its tender, carnal, and cruel aspects. Despite doubts and infidelities (she reflects on one such encounter in *Poème d'amour*, 1924), the death of Barrès elicited from her the dense and terrible collection *L'Honneur de souffrir* (*The Honor of Suffering*, 1927), whose bleakness also colors *Derniers Vers* (*Final Poems*, 1934). Her small but agile hand continued to inscribe the volutes of her script in manuscripts and letters until the end (her correspondents included Proust, Colette, Loti, Jammes, Gide, and Cocteau). Despite illness, this lesser but indefatigable Sybil, who claimed she wrote "so as not to die," produced seventeen books. Of this oeuvre, all that is currently in print, in French, are an anthology (*L'Offrande*) and the love poems published in an appendix to the *Correspondance Noailles-Barrès*. She used traditional metric schemes but stretched them to the limit, filling them with the concrete imagery of sensation and figures of fierce emotional urgency. A lyricist of the fleeting moment, she left behind a body of poetry that testifies to the vicissitudes of love in the face of death.

Claude Mignot

Imprint

I will press myself against life with such force,
Embrace it with such ardor and strength,
That before the day's sweetness is denied me.
It will be warmed by my entwining arms.

The sea, spread widely over the world,
Will retain, in the errant wandering of its waters,
The taste of my pain, which is acrid and salted
And rolls on the surging days like a ship.

I will leave of myself in the folds of hills
The warmth of my eyes which have seen them
in flower,
And the cicadas sitting on thornbush branches
Will resonate with the piercing cry of my desire.

In the spring fields the new greenery
And the tufted grass at the ditches' edge
Will sense, throbbing and elusive like wings,
The ghosts of my hands which have pressed
them so strongly.

Nature, which was my joy and my domain,
Will breathe in the air my persistent ardor,
And on the despondency of human sadness
I will impress the unique form of my heart . . .

Top left: Philip Alexis de Laszlo, *Portrait of Countess Anna de Noailles* (detail). Paris, Musée d'Orsay.
Left: Photograph of Maurice Barrès by Nadar. Anna de Noailles dedicated her collection *Le Coeur innombrable* (*The Elusive Heart*) to Barrès.
Opposite: Autograph of *"L'empreinte"* (*"Imprint"*), from *Le Coeur innombrable* (*The Elusive Heart*). Paris, Bibliothèque Nationale de France.

13

L'empreinte

Je m'appuierai si bien et si fort à la vie
D'une si rude étreinte et d'un tel serrement,
Qu'avant que la douceur du jour me soit ravie
Elle s'échauffera de mon enlacement.

La mer abondamment sur le monde étalée
Gardera dans la route errante de son eau
Le goût de ma douleur qui est âcre et salée
Et sur les jours mouvants roule comme un bateau.

Je laisserai de moi dans le pli des collines
La chaleur de mes yeux qui les ont vu fleurir,
Et la cigale assise aux branches de l'épine
Fera vibrer le cri strident de mon désir.

Dans les champs printaniers la verdure nouvelle
Et le gazon touffu sur le bord des fossés
Sentiront palpiter et fuir comme des ailes
Les ombres de mes mains qui les ont tant pressés

La nature qui fut ma joie et mon domaine
Respirera dans l'air ma persistante ardeur,
Et sur l'abattement de la tristesse humaine
Je laisserai la forme unique de mon cœur...

29

Ubu in Montmartre

Alfred Jarry, 1901

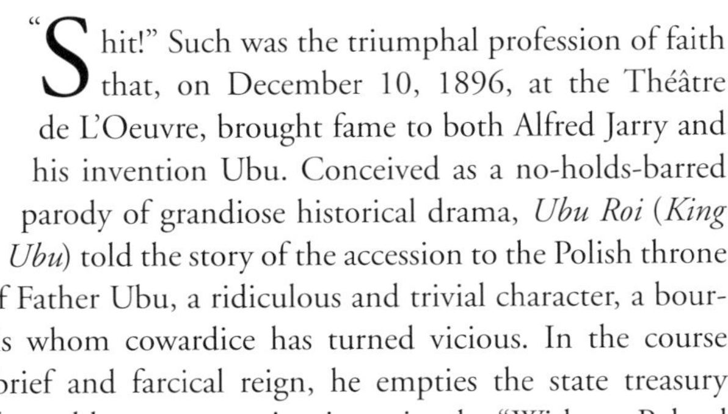

"Shit!" Such was the triumphal profession of faith that, on December 10, 1896, at the Théâtre de L'Oeuvre, brought fame to both Alfred Jarry and his invention Ubu. Conceived as a no-holds-barred parody of grandiose historical drama, *Ubu Roi* (*King Ubu*) told the story of the accession to the Polish throne of Father Ubu, a ridiculous and trivial character, a bourgeois whom cowardice has turned vicious. In the course of his brief and farcical reign, he empties the state treasury and "brains" the nobles, pronouncing imperiously, "Without Poland there would be no Poles!"

Jarry was fond of practical jokes and black humor. As an elaborate hoax, he invented "pataphysics," the "science of imaginary solutions in symbolic accord with the lineaments of objects described by their virtuality." As he put it: "To the law of bodies falling towards a center, why not prefer that of the ascension of emptiness towards a periphery?" Deep in the country at Coudray, near Corbeil, he lived in a cart filled with discarded merchandise that he dubbed the "Tripod," surrounded with a rabbit pen. He wrote several "sequels" to *Ubu Roi* (*Ubu Enchained, Ubu Cuckolded, Ubu in Montmartre*), as well as narrative fictions *(L'Amour Absolu, Messalina, The Supermale*).

During a stint as critic for *La Revue Blanche*, he foundered. Destitute and at a loss, lacking basic amenities and ruining his health with drink, he contracted tubercular meningitis. After being brought to a hospital in Paris from Laval, his native town, where he had sought refuge, he asked for a toothpick and died. He was thirty-four. He left behind him the first pieces of the "machine to overturn the mind" (Louis Aragon) that would be constructed by Dada. Rabelaisian, romantic, and absurd, skeptical to the point of anarchy, Alfred Jarry heralded the Surrealist revolt, of which he remains an extreme and precocious incarnation.

Pierre Chalmin

Father Ubu: And shit! Down the trap door. Bring anybody important who's left (procession of current figures, with commentary ad lib). You who so strangely resemble a famous thief of the Élysée Palace, down the trap! And you, prefect of police, with all the respect you deserve, down the trap! Down goes the English minister, and to make sure nobody's jealous, bring a French minister, too, it doesn't matter which one. And you, noted anti-Semite, down the trap. And you, Semitic Jew, and you, ecclesiastic, and you, apothecary, down the trap, and you, censor, and you, damaged goods, down you go! Well now, here's a singer who came in the wrong door; that's enough of you, down the trap! Come on, everybody down the trap, down the trap, down the trap! Hurry up, down the trap, down the trap!

Curtain—end of Act 4

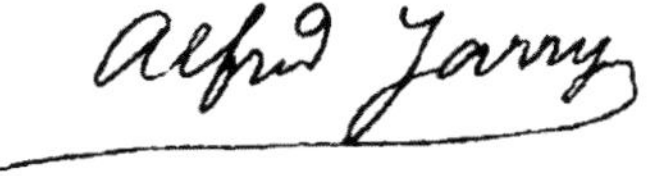

Top left: Hermann-Paul, *Portrait of Alfred Jarry* (detail). Paris, Musée Picasso.
Above: Alfred Jarry, *True Portrait of Monsieur Ubu*, 1896. Published in the original edition of the play.
Left: Edmond Heuzé, lithograph for an edition of *Ubu Roi* published by Tériade, 1966. Laval, Bibliothèque Municipal.
Opposite: Page from the autograph of *Ubu sur la Butte* (*Ubu in Montmartre*). Laval. Bibliothèque Municipal.

la trappe! dans la trappe ça 6

ministre anglais, et pour ne pas faire de jaloux amenez aussi un ministre français, n'importe lequel; et toi, notable antisémite, dans la trappe; et toi l'ecclésiastique et toi l'apothicaire! dans la trappe [et toi le censeur et toi l'avare! dans la trappe]. Tiens, voici un chansonnier qui s'est trompé de porte, on t'a assez vu, dans la trappe. oh oh! celui-ci ne fait pas de chansons, il fait des articles de journal mais ce n'en est pas moins toujours la même chanson dans la trappe! allez, passez tout le monde dans la trappe, dans la trappe, dans la trappe! dépêchez-vous, dans la trappe, dans la trappe!

R. Radiguet. — Fin du 1er

R. de Arté

The Ageless Ones

Victor Segalen, 1903

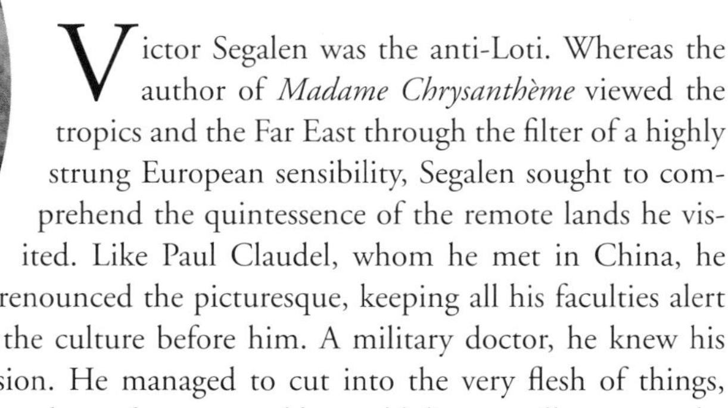

Victor Segalen was the anti-Loti. Whereas the author of *Madame Chrysanthème* viewed the tropics and the Far East through the filter of a highly strung European sensibility, Segalen sought to comprehend the quintessence of the remote lands he visited. Like Paul Claudel, whom he met in China, he renounced the picturesque, keeping all his faculties alert to the culture before him. A military doctor, he knew his profession. He managed to cut into the very flesh of things, accessing their color and poetry, and he could diagnose illnesses on the evidence of the subtlest of symptoms. He familiarized himself with the anatomy of civilizations—and of letters—from the inside, probing their innermost reaches. When he wrote, he did not so much describe things as operate on them. The results are more penetrating, and more affecting, than books of images.

Like Baudelaire and Rimbaud, he was haunted by the exotic, but the literary motifs he drew from it were neither charming nor precious. For him, the most inaccessible sites lay within ourselves, in the depths of language. "'I' is somebody else" (Rimbaud), but only when a restless Me dares to explore its own farthest reaches. Debussy, who was fascinated by the Balinese music he heard at the Universal Exposition of 1900, absorbed this influence so fully as to make his borrowings seem wholly organic. In the same way, Segalen internalized the shock of the unfamiliar, getting at its core and installing it at the heart of his creative imagination.

Pierre-Emmanuel Prouvost d'Agostino

I

Now the god that illuminates the Tahitian sky every day—Oro is his name—had just disappeared slowly beyond the reef. The lower genies, the ones presiding over Daytime Desires, fled the darkness, and in the limpid shadows the furtive Night Desires took their place. Dressed in impalpable flesh, but violent and hateful, they descended on gentle breezes from the sleeping peaks, flowed into the valleys, and tormented fishermen at their nocturnal fishing, and the fearful living, with dubious dreams and aggressive strokes. But they dreaded the gleam of torches made of dried bamboo, and above all the consoling clarity of the moon, gazes cast by Great-Hina-of-the-Sky, whom Oro chose for his wife, and whose changing face . . .

Victor Segalen

Top left: Daniel de Monfreid, *Portrait of Victor Segalen* (detail).
Left: Victor Segalen, *Bora-Bora,* watercolor from *Journal des Îles,* his Polynesian diary-sketchbook of 1903–04. Paris, Bibliothèque Nationale de France.
Opposite: Page from the autograph manuscript of *Les Immémoriaux* (*The Ageless Ones*). Paris, Bibliothèque Nationale de France.

I

Or, le dieu qui chaque jour illumine le Ciel Tahitien — Oro est son nom — venait de disparaître ~~dans~~ ~~au loin~~ en la mer — extérieure, ~~très au~~ ~~delà du~~ bien au delà du récif. Les Génies

Or, le dieu qui chaque jour illumine le ciel Tahitien, — Oro est son nom, — venait lentement de disparaître, ~~au loin en la~~ au loin du récif en la ~~au delà du récif.~~ Les Génies de rang inférieur

de rg. inférieur ceux-là qui président aux Désirs-du-Jour fuyaient devant l'obscurité, et dans l'ombre limpide erraient à leur place les furtifs Désirs-de-la-Nuit. ~~Impalpables~~ Impalpables et cependant violents, haineux ~~aux~~ Vie Vêtus de chairs impalpables & cependant violents et haineux, ils descendaient avec la brise lente ~~et fraîche~~ des sommets endormis, ~~glissaient~~ & coulaient aux vallées, et venaient tourmenter de songes équivoques ou de frôlements hargneux ~~la vie nocturne~~ ~~les pêcheurs dans leurs~~ pêches nocturnes, ou les vivants épeurés. Mais ils redoutaient les lueurs des grandes torches de bambous secs, et surtout la ~~clarté~~ ~~l'apparition~~ la consolante clarté lunaire, regard apaisant jeté par la changeante ombre lunaire par la grande Hina Du ciel

~~regard~~ regards jetés par la Face ~~éternelle~~ changeante ~~de Hina~~ de la grande Hina-du-Ciel, dont regards jetés par la Grande-Hina-du-Ciel que choisit Oro pour époux, et dont la Face changeante

1 fois

Clearing at Noon

Paul Claudel, 1905

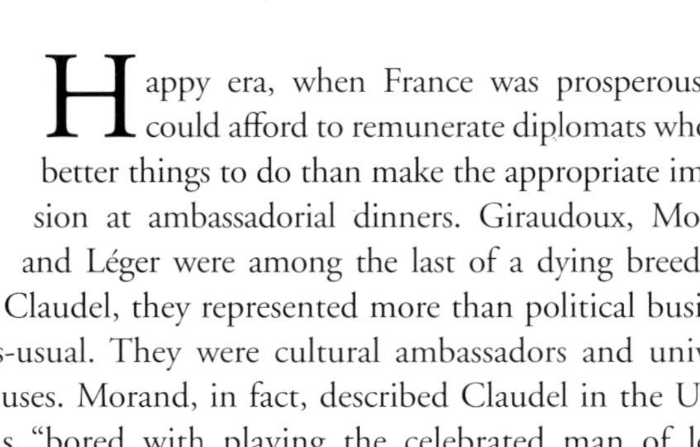

Happy era, when France was prosperous and could afford to remunerate diplomats who had better things to do than make the appropriate impression at ambassadorial dinners. Giraudoux, Morand, and Léger were among the last of a dying breed; like Claudel, they represented more than political business-as-usual. They were cultural ambassadors and universal geniuses. Morand, in fact, described Claudel in the United States as "bored with playing the celebrated man of letters expected to offer insightful remarks to the unlettered." Claudel brought his young colleague along to witness dawn over the Grand Canyon. "Before this grandiose spectacle, he was in his element; one would have said the sun rose exclusively for his pleasure." Claudel does not have a good press, partly because Catholic writers with a mystical bent are now unfashionable. Incomprehensible yet passionate, they embrace difficulty and obscurity. Like Pascal and Bloy, Claudel weighed his words as the Archangel Michael weighs souls at the Last Judgment. His flashes of inspiration are sometimes redolent of Apocalypse, unsettling our moral complacencies, and sometimes they manifest a firm belief in immortality, revealing our shortsightedness. Too long, *Le Soulier de Satin* (*The Silken Slipper*)? Only if one is too impatient to wait for miracles. Obscure, *Partage du Midi* (*Clearing at Noon*)? Only if you resist making your spirit accessible to its inspirational breath. Like Hugo, Claudel heard God speaking of the love of humanity even in the song of tropical storms, even in the mysterious voices of corporal desire.

Pierre-Emmanuel Prouvost d'Agostino

YSÉ: You know that we'll remain in Hong Kong for some time. Where you are, I think. (Silence.) Well, don't you like that?

MESA: I won't spend much time in China. Just long enough to see to my affairs.

YSÉ: A year, perhaps two?

MESA: Yes . . . Perhaps . . . more or less.

YSÉ: And then?

MESA: Nothing!

YSÉ: A year or two, more or less, and then nothing?

MESA: And then nothing! Yes. What concern is that of yours? Your life is arranged, I'm a yellow dog! What does my life matter to you? Everyone loves you.

YSÉ: Does that make you angry?

MESA: Live your life. As for me, I never wanted anything. I've left men behind.

YSÉ: Nonsense! You've brought the whole lot of them with you.

MESA: Laugh! You are beautiful and joyful. Myself, I am sinister and alone. And I want nothing to do with you; what do you want with me? What is there between us? (Pause.)

YSÉ: Mesa, I am Ysé. It's me.

MESA: It's too late. Everything's over. Why do you come looking for me?

YSÉ: Haven't I found you?

MESA: It's over. My withdrawal from the world, it was all arranged! Why do you come looking for me? Why do you bother me?

YSÉ: That's what women are for.

MESA: What have I to do with you? What have you to do with me? I tell you it's all over. You mean no more to me than another! What's to be expected, what's to understand about women? What do they give you, in the end? They want you to give yourself to them completely, which is totally impossible. And what's the point? There's no way for me to give you my soul. That's why I began to look elsewhere. . . .

P. Claudel

Top left: Paul Claudel in 1953, shortly after the premiere of *Partage du Midi* (*Clearing at Noon*).
Left: Félix Labisse, set design for the first production of *Partage du Midi*, staged by Jean-Louis Barrault in 1948.
Opposite: Page from the autograph first draft of *Partage du Midi*. Paris, Bibliothèque Nationale de France.

Vous savez que nous allons rester quelque temps à Hong Kong
Où vous êtes, je crois.

Silence

Eh bien, cela ne vous plait pas?

Mesa

Je ne suis pas pour longtemps en Chine. Le temps que j'y règle mes intérêts.

Ysé

Un an, peut-être, deux ans?

Mesa

Oui, peut-être, plus ou moins.

Ysé

Et puis?

Mesa

Rien!

Ysé

Un an, deux ans, peut-être, plus ou moins, et puis rien?

Mesa

Et puis rien! Quoi? qu'est-ce que cela vous fait?
Votre vie est arrangée, je suis un chien jaune! que vous importe la mienne? Chacun vous aime.

Ysé

En êtes-vous fâché?

Mesa

Vivez votre vie. Mais pour moi, je n'ai rien voulu avoir.
J'ai quitté les hommes.

Ysé

Bah!
Vous emportez toute la collection avec vous.

Mesa

Riez! Vous êtes belle et joyeuse, et moi, je suis sinistre et seul.
Et je ne veux rien de vous; qu'auriez-vous à faire de moi?
Qu'y a-t-il entre vous et moi?

Pause

Ysé

Mesa, je suis Ysé. C'est moi.

Mesa

Il est trop tard. Tout est fini. Pourquoi venez-vous me rechercher?

Ysé

Ne vous ai-je pas trouvé?

Mesa

Tout est fini! J'avais si bien arrangé
De me retirer, de me sortir d'entre les hommes, c'était fait!
Pourquoi venez-vous me rechercher? pourquoi venez-vous me déranger?

Ysé

C'est pour cela que les femmes sont faites.

Mesa

Qu'ai-je à faire avec vous? qu'avez-vous à faire de moi?
Je vous dis que tout est fini!
Pas plus vous qu'aucune autre! Qu'est-ce qu'il y a attendre, qu'est-ce qu'il y a à comprendre chez les femmes?
Qu'est-ce qu'elle vous donne après tout? et ce qu'elle demande,
Il faudrait se donner à elle tout entier,
Et il n'y a absolument pas moyen, et à quoi cela sert-il?
Il n'y a pas moyen ~~que je~~ vous donner mon âme.
C'est pourquoi je me suis tourné d'un autre côté.
Et maintenant pourquoi est-ce que vous venez me déranger? pourquoi est-ce que vous venez me rechercher? Cela est cruel.
Pourquoi est-ce que je vous ai rencontrée? pourquoi est-ce que vers moi
Vous tournez ce visage insupportable? Il est trop tard!
Vous savez bien que c'est impossible. Je sais que vous ne m'aimez pas.
D'une part, ~~je sais que~~ vous êtes mariée, et d'autre part je sais que vous avez goût

"The Tendrils of the Vine"

Colette, 1905

After twelve years of marriage, there were signs of tension between Colette and her husband Willy. They had written six novels together (four in the Claudine series, two in the Minne series), but all of them had been published, with Colette's approval, only under her husband's name.

But the young woman, still only thirty-two, was beginning to feel an irrepressible desire to make her own mark. She began by scribbling the refreshing playlets of *Sept Dialogues des Bêtes* (recently translated as *Barks and Purrs*), which were published in the *Mercure de France, La Vie Heureuse,* and *La Vie Parisienne* in 1904.

She was a regular contributor to the *Mercure Musical* from its beginnings, and in its first issue, dated May 15, 1905, she published "*Les Vrilles de la Vigne*" ("*The Tendrils of the Vine*"). This brief fable recounts how, initially, the nightingale did not sing by night. One morning, however, it awoke to discover that it was caught in tendrils that had shot up while it slept on a grapevine. It managed to escape only "at the cost of a thousand pains," and swore it would never again slumber while the tendrils grew. To make sure that it didn't succumb to sleep, it resolved to sing all night: "And I let loose with a lament that revealed my voice to me." This is the nightingale speaking, but thereafter the narrator seems indistinguishable from Colette herself, especially when she writes (in the definitive, slightly revised final text) of the bird's desire "to tell, tell, tell everything I know, all my thoughts, all my surmises, all that enchants or hurts or astounds me." In effect, Colette Willy here declared her independent identity as a writer, as the Colette who, twenty years later, was prompted to write in *La Naissance du Jour* (*Break of Day*): "Why suspend the course of my hand over the paper that, for so many years now, has been the repository of all that I know about myself, of whatever I try to hide, invent, and figure out about myself?" After another twenty-year interval, she wrote in *Le Fanal Bleu* (*The Blue Lamp*): "With humility, I intend to keep writing. There is no other option for me. But when does one stop writing? . . . I used to think that it was a task like any other, that you put down your implement, joyfully cried out 'Done!,' and wiped your hands, from which rained down grains of sand that one held to be precious. . . . But then you see that the grains of sand have spelled out: 'To be continued . . .'"

The story's title became that of the first book published by Colette Willy (1908), a collection drawn from the many short texts she had written over the three preceding years. These prose poems attracted the attention of Guillaume Apollinaire and were admired by Sacha Guitry. The critic André Fresnoy sensed her rare gift and was touched by her avowal in "The Tendrils of the Vine": "It is not our place to penetrate the symbol or to determine whether the deliverance was painful. But can we regret the suffering that revealed to you your voice, bird, and your genius, poet?"

Alain Brunet

The Tendrils of the Vine

Inflexible, tenacious, avid, and treacherous, the tendrils of a bitter vine wrapped around me while, in the middle of my springtime, I had fallen into a happy and trusting sleep. But with a frightened lunge, I burst all of those twisting threads, whose double, claw-like sprigs already gripped my flesh, and I fled. . . .When the torpor of another honeyed night weighed on my eyelids, I again feared the tendrils of the vine, and I let loose with a lament that revealed my voice to me . . .

Alone, wakeful, agitated, I saw rise before me in the ash-blue night a star voluptuous and morose . . . To make sure I no longer fall into a happy sleep in treacherous Spring, when flourishes the gnarly vine, I listen to the sound of my voice. Sometimes I feverishly say things usually left unsaid or whispered very low. . . . and then my voice languishes to a murmur because I dare not say things that have been said, have been screamed long before me, for millions of years. . . .

I want to tell, tell, tell all that I think, all that I know, all that enchants me, all that hurts me, all that astounds me, all that revolts me . . . But every morning, a cool, sensible hand is placed on my mouth. . . .And my exalted cry reverts to moderate verbiage, to the loquacity of a child who talks out loud only to calm himself. I no longer know happy sleep—but I no longer fear the tendrils of the vine. . . .

End, "Tendrils of the Vine"

Top left: Photograph of Colette ca. 1900. Private collection.
Left: A mandarin yellow Parker U.S.A Duofold Senior pen like the one with which Colette wrote.
Below: Watercolor by Maxime Rebière.
Opposite: Three pages from the autograph manuscript of "*Les Vrilles de la Vigne*" ("*The Tendrils of the Vine*"). Paris, Bibliothèque Nationale de France.

30
35

pages 9
et 10

Les Vrilles de la Vigne

Cassantes, tenaces, aiguës et traîtresses, les vrilles d'une
vigne amère m'ont liée, tandis que
dans mon printemps je
reposais d'un somme heureux
et sans défiance. Mais j'ai rompu,
d'un sursaut épouvanté, tous ces fils
tors, dont la double corne crochue
déjà tenait à ma chair, — et
j'ai fui ... Quand la torpeur d'une
nouvelle nuit de miel pesa
sur mes paupières j'ai craint
de nouveau les vrilles de la
vigne, et j'ai
jeté tout haut
une plainte qui m'a révélé ma
voix ...

31
36

Toute seule, éveillée, agitée,
je regarde monter devant moi dans
la nuit couleur de cendre bleue
un astre voluptueux et morose ... Pour
me défendre de retomber dans
l'heureux sommeil dans
le printemps menteur où fleurit
la vigne crochue, j'écoute le
son de ma voix.

Parfois je
dis fiévreusement
ce qu'on a coutume
de taire ou de chuchoter
très bas ... et puis
ma voix languit jusqu'au murmure
parce que je n'ose pas dire ce que

37 32

tous ont ont crié bien
(avant moi,
depuis des milliers d'années ...
Je voudrais dire, dire, dire tout ce
que je pense, tout ce que je sais,
tout ce qui m'enchante, tout
ce qui me blesse, tout ce qui
m'étonne, tout ce qui me
révolte ... Mais il y a toujours,
au matin, ta invisible sage main
fraîche qui se pose sur ma
bouche ... Et mon cri qui s'élevait
descend au verbiage modéré
à la volubilité de l'enfant
qui parle haut seulement pour
s'étourdir ... Je ne connais plus
le somme heureux, — mais je
ne crains plus les vrilles de
la vigne ...

fin Vrilles de la Vigne

Strait Is the Gate

André Gide, 1906

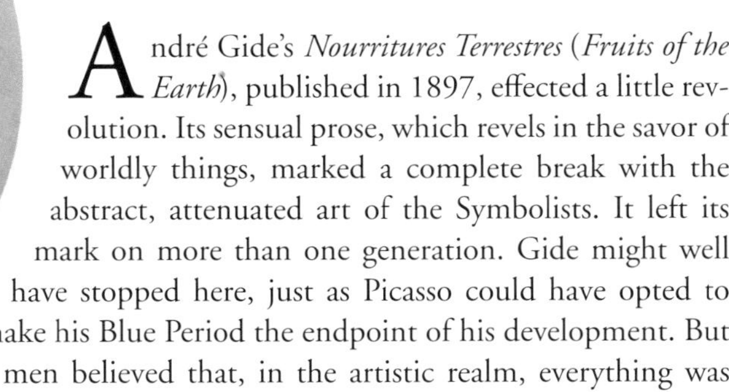

André Gide's *Nourritures Terrestres* (*Fruits of the Earth*), published in 1897, effected a little revolution. Its sensual prose, which revels in the savor of worldly things, marked a complete break with the abstract, attenuated art of the Symbolists. It left its mark on more than one generation. Gide might well have stopped here, just as Picasso could have opted to make his Blue Period the endpoint of his development. But both men believed that, in the artistic realm, everything was permissible—except repeating oneself. Materially, there would have been much to gain from exploiting a formula whose success was assured. To his public's chagrin, Gide preferred perpetually to reinvent himself as a writer. In every project, he killed one part of himself so that another might blossom.

L'Immoraliste (*The Immoralist*), published in 1902, drew upon the same North African experiences as did *Nourritures Terrestres*, but its classical narrative structure constitutes an implicit critique of the earlier work's hedonism. *La Porte Étroite* (*Strait is the Gate*, 1909), while thematically related, is imbued with aspirations completely at odds with the sensibility of *Nourritures Terrestres*. Its heroine Alissa tries to escape carnal desire by seeking refuge in God.

La Symphonie Pastorale (*The Pastoral Symphony*, 1919) is a parable quite remote from these preoccupations. *Les Faux-Monnayeurs* (*The Counterfeiters*) again placed Gide's career at risk, along with the genre on which it had been premised. In this novel about the writing of a novel, a conceit that reveals the form's artifices in the most artificial way possible, Gide created a commonplace, an achievement that Baudelaire regarded as a mark of genius.

Gide realized that the life of the mind is always threatened by stagnation in routine. His favorite motto, perhaps borrowed from Goethe, was: "*Meurs et deviens,*" "Die and evolve."

Paul Desalmand

I kept aloof from my new comrades, going out little and avoiding pleasure; I moved forward holding my heart high as if it were full of a precious liqueur, and I placed my steps carefully, trying to spill nothing. I had utter contempt for everything that intoxicates others, and intoxicated myself with my renunciations.

The correspondence between Genevieve and myself became more frequent. I was careful to direct my thoughts along paths that she herself might have chosen, such that, step by step, she would come to like accompanying me. Rather than troubling her with my doubts, I pretended not to have any and lovingly kept my mind in a state of faith that might please her.... How absurd! I now have nothing but contempt for what then made me happy.

When Easter approached, my desire to see her again became so intense that I couldn't wait for vacation. Advancing it by several days, I suddenly announced my return. What a reunion! The word "engagement" remained unspoken, but it sang in our hearts. To solemnize the mute promise we had already made to one another, we took communion together on Easter Sunday. Marguerite also took communion. I remarked, on this visit, that she had become much more serious; she was fully aware of our love; at the moment of receiving the host, I met her gaze, which then fell upon Genevieve; and, since her lips were trembling, I thought she must be asking God to bless us. A moment later she looked at me again, and I smiled at her as a brother smiles at his sister.

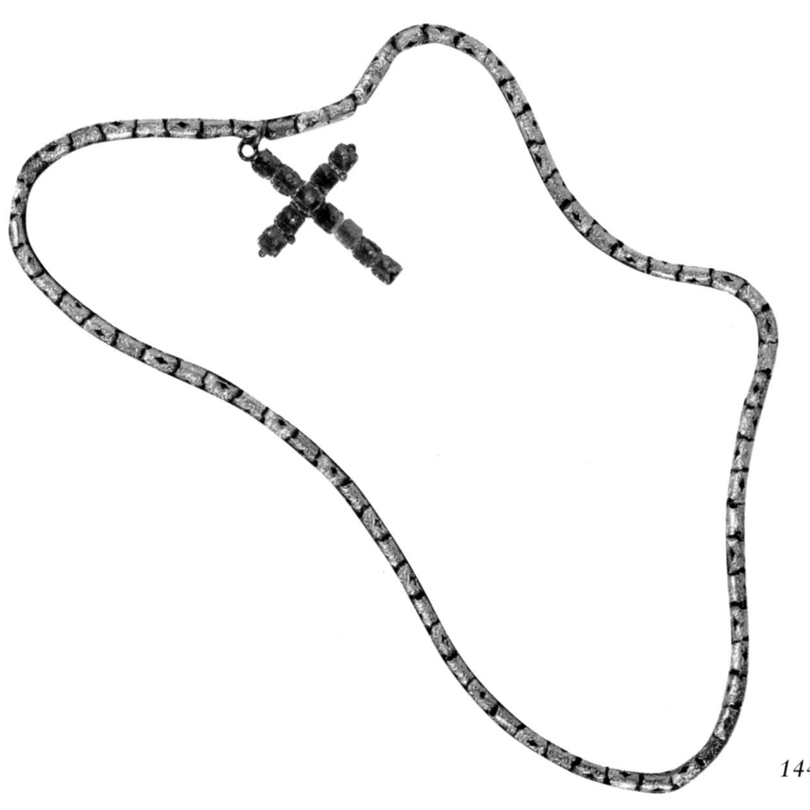

Top left: Paul Albert Laurens, *Portrait of André Gide* (detail), 1924. Paris, Musée d'Orsay.
Left: The "necklace of Alissa," with its emerald cross, belonged to Madeleine Rondeaux, Gide's cousin. It inspired the one worn by the heroine of *La Porte Étroite* (*Strait is the Gate*). Paris, Bibliothèque Littéraire Jacques Doucet.
Opposite: Page from an early draft of *La Porte Étroite* (*Strait Is the Gate*), 1906. Gide revised the text several times; this passage differs significantly from the corresponding one in the final version. Paris, Bibliothèque Nationale de France.

comme plein d'une liqueur précieuse, et je dirigeais droit mes pas, veillant à n'en rien renverser. Je méprisais intensément tout ce dont les autres se grisent et me prisais de mes renoncements.

La correspondance entre Geneviève et moi devint fréquente. Je ~~fis~~ prenais soin de n'aventurer ma pensée qu'en des chemins qu'elle aurait pu choisir d'elle même, de manière que, pas à pas, elle aimât m'y accompagner. Plutôt que de la troubler par des doutes, je prétendais n'en pas avoir et maintenais amoureusement mon esprit dans un état de foi qui put lui plaire... Absurdité! Je n'ai plus aujourd'hui que du mépris pour ce dont je faisais alors mon bonheur.

Quand approcha le temps de Pâques, mon désir de la revoir devint si vif que je ne pus attendre les vacances. Les devançant de plusieurs jours, j'annonçai mon retour brusquement. Quel revoir! Le mot fiançailles, s'il n'éclatait pas sur nos bouches du moins chantait déjà dans nos cœurs. Pour solenniser la muette promesse que déjà nous nous faisions l'un à l'autre, le jour de Pâques nous approchâmes ensemble de la table sainte. ~~Juliette~~ Marguerite aussi communia. Je remarquai, à ce nouveau séjour, qu'elle était devenue beaucoup plus grave; elle n'ignorait rien de notre amour; à l'instant de communier je rencontrai son

A Flea in Her Ear

Georges Feydeau, 1907

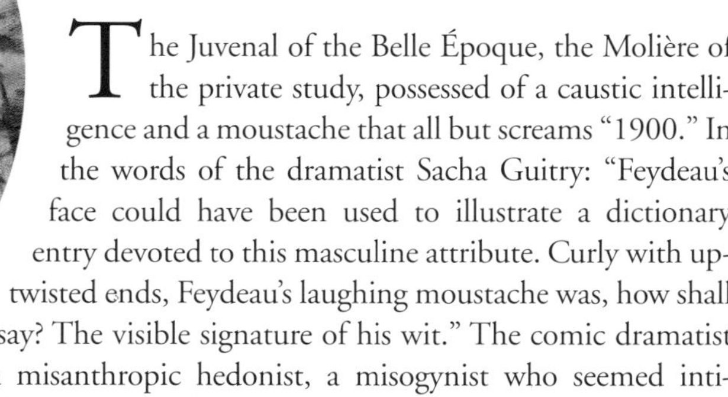

The Juvenal of the Belle Époque, the Molière of the private study, possessed of a caustic intelligence and a moustache that all but screams "1900." In the words of the dramatist Sacha Guitry: "Feydeau's face could have been used to illustrate a dictionary entry devoted to this masculine attribute. Curly with up-twisted ends, Feydeau's laughing moustache was, how shall I say? The visible signature of his wit." The comic dramatist was a misanthropic hedonist, a misogynist who seemed intimately versed in women and the arts of seduction. Although a specialist in the light comedies known as *vaudevilles*, he transcended the limitations of the genre; along with several other playwrights, Feydeau invented a type, the "lady from Maxim's" who pursues a career in the "duchy of the Folies-Bergère." One critic wrote of *A Flea in Her Ear*: "So extraordinary is this creation that its author, following Wagner's example, should make a tetrology of it."

Feydeau did not rest content with mining a seam of hilarity. Although a bon vivant and a dandy, he was obsessed with death and treated his fits of depression with cocaine and champagne. Ultimately, he mixed bile with his rosewater, writing ghastly marital comedies in which doors slam like so many slaps in the face of surface respectability. Grimaces leave crevices in the makeup, and the family circle becomes a matrimonial ring of Hell worthy of Dante's *Inferno*. The bitter truths about love first explored by Stendhal seem to underlie one of his titles: *But Don't Walk around in the Nude!*

Pierre-Emmanuel Prouvost d'Agostino

Top left: Charles-Émile Carolus-Duran, *George Feydeau Reading* (detail). Lille, Musée Des Beaux-Arts. *Left:* Scene from a 1967 production of *A Flea in Her Ear* at the Théâtre Marigny in Paris, directed by Jacques Charron. Left to right: Daniel Ceccaldi, Jean-Claude Brialy, Micheline Presle, and Marco Perrin. *Opposite:* Page from an autograph manuscript of *A Flea in Her Ear*. Paris, Bibliothèque Nationale de France.

LUCIENNE (reading the label): Hotel Cuddly Kitten!

RAYMONDE: And at Montretout, my dear! Another name that speaks volumes! Yes, the whole thing is quite unseemly conveniences (she puts the box on the table, stage right). There's no mistake, you know, everything is clear: I'm onto him.

LUCIENNE: Oh!

RAYMONDE: Good god, I already had my doubts, when I saw my husband a bit . . . a bit . . .

LUCIENNE: Manzaranes?

RAYMONDE: Yes! I said to myself: "Well! So what? What of it?" But really, this! No! This has put a flea in my ear!

(She returns the box to the cabinet from which she had taken it)

LUCIENNE: Yes, but of course!

RAYMONDE: And if you saw that hotel, my dear! It looks like it just came from the confectioner's.

LUCIENNE: What do you mean, "If I saw it?" You've been there?

RAYMONDE: Of course; I just got back.

LUCIENNE: Eh?

RAYMONDE: That's why I was late.

LUCIENNE: Oh!

RAYMONDE: You'll understand that I wanted to be absolutely sure. I said to myself: there's only one thing to do: talk to the manager. Ah! Well! And if you think questioning a manager is easy! It's dreadful, how vice makes allies, my dear! He didn't want to know a anything about it.

LUCIENNE: Well, it's the ABC of his profession.

RAYMONDE: Exactly! You can't imagine what he said to me: "But madame, if I divulged the names of the people who patronized my hotel, you would be the first to avoid it!" Yes, to me! And I couldn't get him to say another word. I tell you, a real carp!

LUCIENNE (making a face): Oh! You flatter him!

RAYMONDE: So its quite clear that we can only count on ourselves. Men help each other out, we must do the same. You're much cleverer than I am. You know the score. What should I do?

LUCIENNE: Goodness! There you catch me off guard!

RAYMONDE: Oh! Please try! A flash of genius!

LUCIENNE: Yes! Let's see . . . (she thinks). I know! Why don't you demand an explanation from your husband?

RAYMONDE: What! *You* tell me this? You know perfectly well he'll lie to me. Men are the biggest liars there are . . . except for women.

Lucienne
oui c'est vrai je crois les deux seuls êtres au monde qui... tu n'as pas essayé de faire revenir ton mari... il y a des agences...

Raymonde
Elles vous traînent en longueur pour augmenter les frais, et n'arrivent généralement à rien quand elles ne vous trahissent pas.

Lucienne
Écoute il y aurait peut être un moyen que j'ai vu servir souvent au théâtre

Raymonde
ah! Quoi? Quoi?

Lucienne
Oh! il n'est pas génial: seulement on adresse une lettre à votre mari comme si c'était d'une autre femme bien entendu et on lui donne un rendez-vous auquel on a soin d'aller. Si le mari vient eh! bien on est fixé...

Raymonde
oui oui, tu as raison. Ce n'est peut-être pas génial, mais ce sont généralement les moyens les plus classiques qui réussissent le mieux. Nous allons écrire tout de suite à Victor Emmanuel

Lucienne
Écrivons à Victor Emmanuel.

Raymonde
ah! oui mais... il connaît mon écriture, écoute! toi, tu vas lui écrire

Lucienne
Moi! ah! non, non, c'est trop délicat

Raymonde
eh! bien je fais appel à ta délicatesse... voilà tout! Es-tu ma meilleure amie ou ne l'es tu pas

Lucienne
ah! tu me conduiras en enfer...

Raymonde
eh! bien, tu y retrouveras mon mari

Lucienne
grand bien me fasse. allons donc du papier à lettre...

Raymonde
ah! oui mais pas le mien... attends... j'ai quelque chose qui sera peut être l'affaire. Du papier que j'ai acheté pour les enfants de ma sœur pour leurs compliments... avec de la dentelle et des fleurs peintes

Lucienne
il croirait qu'il a affaire à une cuisinière Il n'irait pas. non? tu n'as pas du papier un peu suggestif

Raymonde (tirant une boîte de son meuble)
J'ai celui de la maison... il... je venais de l'acheter pour la campagne... il n'est pas très suggestif

Lucienne
Il n'est pas extraordinaire mais enfin ça fera l'affaire non. Enfin en le parfumant fortement.

Raymonde
ah! Pour ça j'ai ce qu'il faut. un certain trèfle incarnat

Presentation from the Beauce Region to the Virgin of Chartres

Charles Péguy, 1912

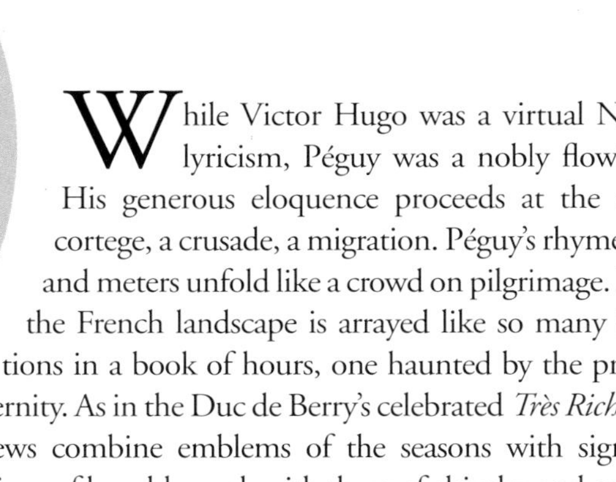

While Victor Hugo was a virtual Niagara of lyricism, Péguy was a nobly flowing river. His generous eloquence proceeds at the rate of a cortege, a crusade, a migration. Péguy's rhyme schemes and meters unfold like a crowd on pilgrimage. En route, the French landscape is arrayed like so many illuminations in a book of hours, one haunted by the prospect of eternity. As in the Duc de Berry's celebrated *Très Riches Heures,* his views combine emblems of the seasons with signs of the zodiac, depictions of humble work with those of chivalry and courtly life, all beneath changeable French skies populated by angels wearing the mantle of time, blessed with gentle smiles and curls the color of champagne.

Péguy was like the craftsmen who built the great cathedrals: with his simple hands, he fashioned his masterpiece with modesty. In his art, lofty lancet windows are reinforced by strong buttresses. He chose his words as carefully as the cathedral builders placed their keystones and pierced their pinnacles. Like Joan of Arc, he heard the voice of France in the wind and the song of the forest, read his mission and his destiny in the undulating promise of ripe wheat. He heard holy voices magically coming from trees. For him, the earth of France, once pagan, was decked out with Christian marvels and shone with wonders of popular piety. The soil would reclaim this man of the earth who addressed himself to the heavens. In 1914, like so many peasants who were massacred during the first mechanized war, he was mowed down in the unfertile furrow of a trench, a young shaft in a sacrificial harvest.

Pierre-Emmauel Prouvost d'Agostino

Presentation from the Beauce
Region to the Virgin of Chartres

Star of the Sea, here the heavy cloth
And the deep swell and the ocean of wheat
And the moving foam and our granaries full,
Here your gaze on this immense cope.

And here your voice on this heavy plain
And our absent friends and our depopulated hearts,
Here alongside us our loosened fists
And our lassitude and our full strength.

Star of the Morning, inaccessible queen,
Here we march towards your illustrious court,
And here the plateau of our poor love,
And here the ocean of our immense pain.

A lament hovers and spreads beyond the horizon.
The few roofs resemble an archipelago.
From the old bell tower there issues a kind of appeal.
The thick church seems a lowly house.

Péguy

Top left: Léon Deshairs, *Portrait of Charles Péguy,* 1894.
Right: Jean-Baptiste Corot, *Chartres Cathedral,* 1830 (retouched 1872). Paris, Musée du Louvre.
Opposite: Autograph manuscript of "*Presentation of the Beauce Region to the Virgin of Chartres.*" Orléans, Centre Charles-Péguy.

1o)

Présentation de la Beauce

à Notre Dame de Chartres

Étoile de la mer voici la lourde nappe

Et la profonde houle et l'océan des blés

Et la mouvante écume et nos greniers comblés,

Voici votre regard sur cette immense chape

2o)

Et voici votre voix sur cette lourde plaine

Et nos amis absents et nos cœurs dépeuplés,

Voici le long de nous nos poings désassemblés

Et notre lassitude et notre force pleine.

3o)

Étoile du matin, inaccessible reine,

Voici que nous marchons vers votre illustre cour,

Et voici le plateau de notre pauvre amour,

Et voici l'océan de notre immense peine.

4o)

Un sanglot rôde et court par delà l'horizon.

A peine quelques toits font comme un archipel.

Du vieux clocher retombe une sorte d'appel.

L'épaisse église semble une basse maison.

The Gods Are Thirsty

Anatole France, 1912

The playwright Sacha Guitry called him Monsieur France, adding: "As one might have called Cervantes Monsieur Spain." When the writer introduced himself to Sarah Bernhardt, the following exchange ensued:

"It is you, Monsieur, who bear such a name?"

"Yes, madame."

"Change it: it is too much for one man. Take Anatole or France, not both!"

One has attained true fame when, given an impossible name, one sees it become commonplace. In this respect, Anatole's destiny was ambiguous. His real patronymic was Thibault, and in *Time Regained*, in the guise of Bergotte, Proust blessed him with an enviable death, passing away peacefully in front of a painting by Vermeer. A disciple of the poet Leconte de Lisle, France rejected texts by Mallarmé and Verlaine during his editorship of *Le Parnasse Contemporain.* "I cannot, gentlemen," he wrote them. "We would become a laughing-stock." As regards style and idea, Anatole France would always prefer the path of moderation, avoiding all extreme positions. Although allied with anticlerical circles, his proclivities were not unlike those of an old-regime abbé: he relished fine food, pretty women, and beautiful books. For him, the perusal of a rare edition was a sensual experience.

Debussy once dismissively characterized Saints-Saëns as "the man of the world most knowledgeable about music." Anatole France was the Saint-Saëns of letters. To a question posed by the young Marcel Proust (for whose *Les Plaisirs et les Jours* [*Pleasures and Days*] he wrote a preface), he sharply retorted: "You ask how I became so erudite. The answer is simple: as a youngster, I was neither as pretty-boy nor as snobbish as you; I didn't play the social game; I spent my time in libraries." This quasi-official author of a limply liberal Third Republic was an eighteenth-century dilettante smack in the middle of the Belle Époque.

As a title for his fictionalized account of the Terror, he co-opted Saint-Juste's celebrated call for a purge in the name of the public good, "the gods are thirsty." He did so ironically, however, for the novel is an exposé of political madness and an attack on the pernicious effect of doctrinaire intransigence. The character of Évariste Gamelin, a frustrated painter turned bloodthirsty informant, is the epitome of the resentful failure. The worthiest causes can have dreadful outcomes: such is the moral of the novel, conceived by its author as a scathing rebuttal of Clémenceau's well-known claim that "la *Révolution est un bloc,*" "the Revolution is a unity."

Pierre-Emmanuel Prouvost d'Agostino

. . . gave him the strength to look death coldly in the face, because at age twenty-eight he was tired of life, and showed neither terror nor dejection. His gaze, falling on Gamelin, registered utter contempt. Then his expression of distaste gave way to an ironic smile. He mused on this idiot's having mistaken a pomegranate flower, a souvenir of the adorable Nieves, dead in his arms at age twenty, for a carnation. No one applauded the sentence.

Gamelin rushed to the "Amour Peintre" and burst into the white room where Élodie waited for him every night. "You are avenged. Tomorrow Maubel will be no more."

She understood. "Wretch! It's you who have killed him, and he was not my lover."

She fainted. But in the darkness of this little death, her hands groped for her lover. Returning to consciousness, she gave him a suffocating embrace, sunk her nails into his flesh, and called him between clenched lips the most dreadful and endearing names. She loved him with her whole body; the more terrible and cruel he seemed, the more she saw him drenched in his victims' blood, the more she hungered and thirsted for him.

Top left: Marie-Louise-Clémentine Breslau, *Portrait of Anatole-François Thibault, known as Anatole France* (detail). Châteaux de Versailles et de Trianon.
Below: Charles Louis Muller, *Summons of the Last Victims of the Terror* (sketch), ca. 1850. Paris, Louvre.
Opposite: Page from a working draft (incomplete) of *Les Dieux Ont Soif* (*The Gods Are Thirsty*), with an early version of the end of Chapter sixteen. Paris, Bibliothèque Nationale de France.

lui donnaient la force de regarder froidement la mort en face, lors qui ... de la vie, il ne montrait ni terreur ni abattement. Ses regards rencontrant le visage de Gamelin le souffletèrent de leur mépris. Puis à son expression de dégoût succéda presque aussitôt un sourire ironique. Il songeait que le misérable était aussi un imbécile qui avait pris pour un oeillet la grenade effeuillée, souvenir de l'adorable ... qu'ils montrent les bras à vingt ans. Personne n'applaudit la sentence.

Gamelin courut à l'amour peintre, s'élança chaque nuit dans la chambre blanche où l'attendait Elodie.

— Tu es vengée. Demain Maubel ne sera plus.

Elle comprit : C'est toi qui l'as tué et ce n'était pas mon amant.

— Misérable !...

Elle tomba évanouie. Mais dans les ombres de cette mort légère, ses mains qui battaient l'air, cherchaient son amant. Revenue à elle, elle le pressa dans ses bras à l'étouffer, lui enfonça profondément les ongles dans la chair, et lui donna de ses lèvres les noms les plus atroces et les plus chers. Elle l'aimait de toute sa chair, et plus il lui apparaissait terrible, cruel, plus elle le voyait couvert du sang de ses victimes, plus avait faim et soif de ses baisers.

135 52

XVI, 241-243

"The Pont Mirabeau"

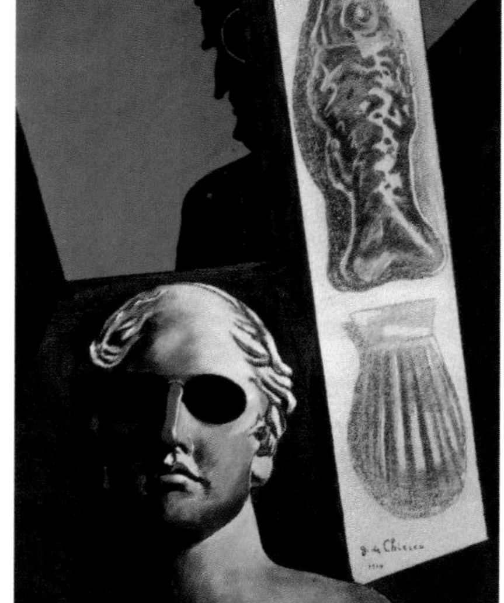

Guillaume Apollinaire, 1913

The origins, existence, and love life of Apollinaire all bore the imprint of a precarious existence. An illegitimate child in life as in literature, he was a literary shooting star, an errant poet without roots or ties. Simultaneously nostalgic and ahead of his time, he disdained theory and affiliation with any school, but he had a genius for pure poetic magic.

Although claimed by the Spanish Flu in 1918, he had previously received two grave wounds: his 1912 breakup with Marie Laurencin; and in March 1916, on the battlefield, the blow delivered by a piece of shrapnel that pierced his temple.

Apollinaire probably first learned of Marie from his friend Picasso. As the poet later recalled, when he met her in 1907, in the shop of the picture dealer Clovis Sagot in the rue Lafitte, she had "the somber, childlike face of those destined to make others suffer." Her face "glittered with blinking eyes like birds with brilliant plumage. Her unkempt hair, cut short to expose her neck, was thick and dark like a nocturnal forest."

Among the many women who haunted the poet's short life, and who eventually populated the procession of his former loves—from Maria Dubois to Jacqueline Kolb, by way of Linda Molina, Annie Playden, Louise de Coligny-Châtillon, Madeleine Pagès, and a few others—Marie Laurencin occupies a special place. She left an indelible mark on his work, one as insistent as the imperturbable flow of the Seine. Apollinaire himself proposed this analogy in "Le Pont Mirabeau," which he wrote when their relationship was falling apart: "The river is like my pain, it flows and never ceases." The Bibliothèque Nationale de France preserves a recording of Apollinaire reading this poem in a voice that is grave, sententious, and sad. As much as anything, this vocal timbre immortalizes Marie's silhouette and her "bun of chestnut hair." It resounds with the nostalgia of a jilted lover who knew perfectly well that

> *Memories are hunting horns*
> *Whose sound dies in the wind.*

Jean-Pierre Guéno

The Pont Mirabeau

Below the Pont Mirabeau flows the Seine.
And must it remind me of our love?
There was always joy after the pain.

Come, night, sound the hour,
The days slip by, I remain.

Let us remain hand-in-hand, face-to-face,
While under the bridge of our arms pass
The so weary waters of eternal gazes.

Come, night, sound the hour,
The days slip by, I remain.

Love slips by like this running water
Love slips by; how slow is life,
And how violent is hope!

Come, night, sound the hour,
The days slip by, I remain.

The days pass and the weeks pass
Neither time past nor love returns;
Below the Pont Mirabeau flows the Seine.

Come, night, sound the hour,
The days slip by, I remain.

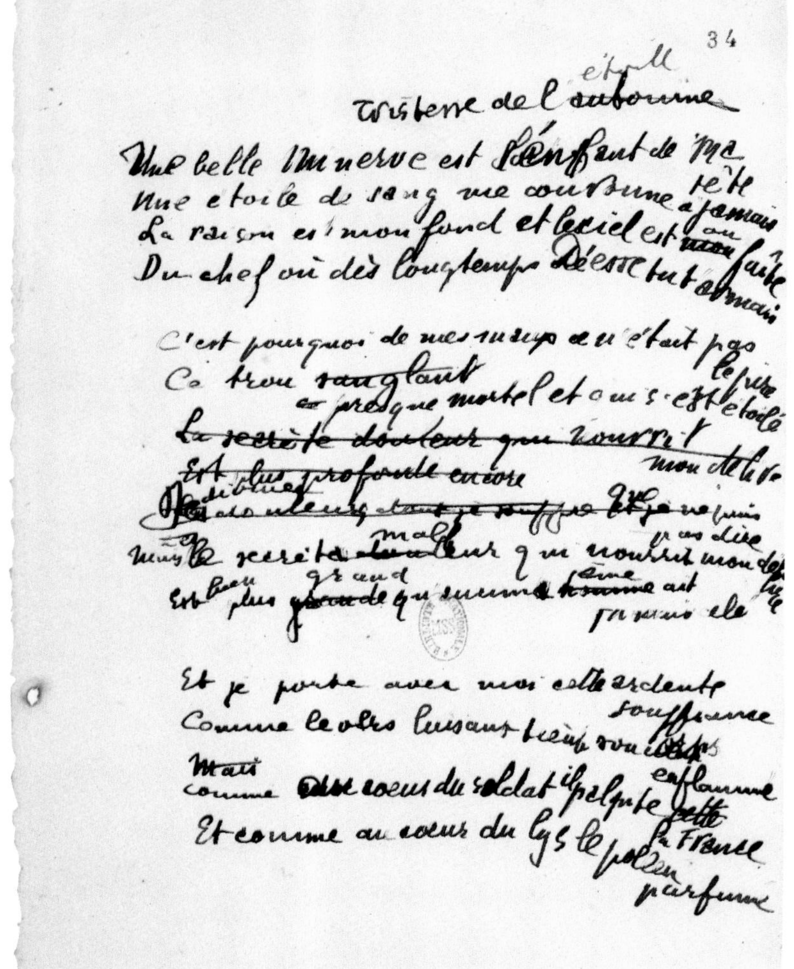

34

Tristesse de l'étoile

Une belle Minerve est l'enfant de ma tête
Une étoile de sang me couronne à jamais
La raison est au fond et le ciel est au faîte
Du chef où dès longtemps Déesse tu t'armais

C'est pourquoi de mes maux ce n'était pas le pire
Ce trou sanglant presque mortel et qui s'est étoilé
Mais le secret malheur qui nourrit mon délire
Est bien plus grand qu'aucune âme ait jamais celé

Et je porte avec moi cette ardente souffrance
Comme le ver luisant tient son corps enflammé
Comme au coeur du soldat il palpite la France
Et comme au coeur du lys le pollen parfumé

Top left: Giorgio de Chirico, *Premonitory Portrait of Apollinaire,* 1914. Paris, Musée National d'Art Moderne.
Right: Autograph manuscript of "*Tristesse d'une Étoile*" ("*Sadness of a Star*"), published in *Calligrammes* (1918). Paris, Bibliothèque Nationale de France.
Opposite: Autograph manuscript of "*Le Pont Mirabeau*" ("*Mirabeau Bridge*"). Paris, Bibliothèque Nationale de France.

Le pont Mirabeau

1

Sous le pont Mirabeau coule la Seine.
Et nos amours faut-il qu'il m'en souvienne ?
La joie venait toujours après la peine.

Vienne la nuit, sonne l'heure,
les jours s'en vont, je demeure,

~~Restons~~ Les mains dans les mains, restons face à face,
Tandis que sous le pont de nos bras passe
Des éternels regards l'onde si lasse.

Vienne la nuit, sonne l'heure,
les jours s'en vont, je demeure

L'amour s'en ~~va~~ ~~cette~~ comme cette eau courante,
l'amour s'en va ; comme la vie est lente
Et comme l'espérance ~~est~~ violente !

Vienne la nuit, sonne l'heure,
les jours s'en vont, je demeure.

Passent les jours ~~et~~ passent les semaines
Ni temps passé, ni les amours reviennent,
Sous le pont Mirabeau coule la Seine

Vienne la nuit, sonne l'heure
Les jours s'en vont je demeure.

Swann's Way

Marcel Proust, 1913

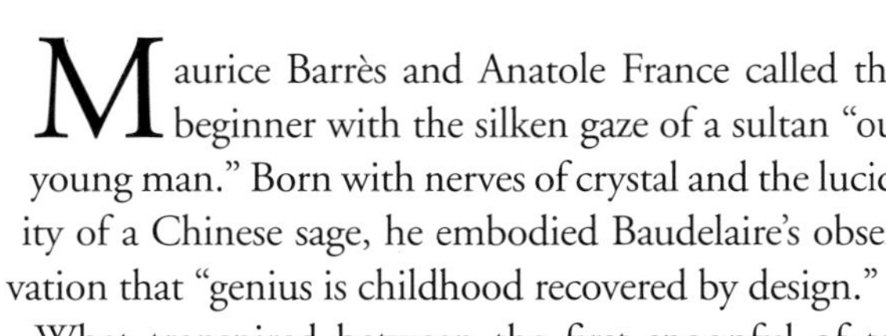

Maurice Barrès and Anatole France called this beginner with the silken gaze of a sultan "our young man." Born with nerves of crystal and the lucidity of a Chinese sage, he embodied Baudelaire's observation that "genius is childhood recovered by design."

What transpired between the first spoonful of tea containing soaked morsels of a madeleine and the recognition of a familiar footstep in the courtyard of the Hôtel de Guermantes? Nothing, and yet everything: the essential, the immutable. An existence? All existence, for what is in question is a "work of art": a dream-life that sparkles with a thousand reflections, like one of Monet's suns pulverized into countless points of light by the surface of the sea.

À la Recherche du Temps Perdu (*In Search of Lost Time*) was a paper monster that, like Prometheus's vulture, consumed its author. Proust longed to transcend the limits of estheticism, he wanted to transform flesh into word, to burn his body at the stake of a sickbed. In this mirage of truth, the ether smells of rain-soaked gardens, the universe becomes visible from a bedroom alcove; reality is placed between parentheses, like a perilous leap between two rolls of the drum, between the sounds of nocturnal carriages transporting Marcel, an entomologist of passion, to so-called houses of love, where he experimented, on insects with human faces, with the cruelties of jealousy and the torments of desire. A worldly executioner risen from Hell in impeccable tailcoat and butter-soft gloves, a Mephistopheles of the Ritz, but above all executioner of himself: nothing that is too human, which is to say inhuman, was foreign to him.

Pierre-Emmanuel Prouvost d'Agostino

Top left: Jacques-Émile Blanche, *Portrait of Marcel Proust,* ca. 1895. *Right:* Autograph manuscript of *Le Temps Retrouvé* (*Time Regained*), with attached sheets of revisions. Paris, Bibliothèque Nationale de France. *Opposite:* Early draft (1909) of a passage from *Du côté de chez Swann* (*Swann's Way*). Paris, Bibliothèque Nationale de France. The translation is of the corresponding passage of the final text, published in 1913 (closing paragraphs of the "Overture").

And suddenly the memory came to me. The taste was that of the morsels of madeleine that, on Sunday mornings in Combray (because on that day I never went out before mass time), when I went into her bedroom to say good morning, my Aunt Léonie used to give me after she had dipped them in tea or lime-tea. The sight of the little madeleine recalled nothing to me before I had tasted it; perhaps because, as I had seen them on the trays of pastry shops many times since without eating them, their image had dissociated itself from those Combray days to become linked with more recent ones; perhaps because, of the memories so long left undisturbed, nothing survived, everything had crumbled; the forms—like that of the little pastry shell, so lushly sensual beneath its austere and pious ridges—had been done away with, or, lying dormant, had lost the expansive force that would have enabled them to reenter consciousness. But when nothing of a remote past survives, after the death of its people, after the destruction of its objects, only odors and tastes, frailer but more vivid, more immaterial, more persistent and accurate, linger for a time on the ruins of the rest like souls, ready and hoping to be recalled, to bear without flinching, on their almost impalpable sensory traces, the immense edifice of memory.

And no sooner had I recognized the taste of the morsels of madeleine soaked in lime-tea that my aunt had given me (although I still did not know why this memory made me so happy, a revelation that must be postponed until much later), than the old gray house on the street, where her bedroom was, superimposed itself, like a theatrical decor, over the little pavilion overlooking the garden that my parents had added to the rear (until then, I had been able to recall only this truncated wall); and with it the house, the town, from morning until evening and in all sorts of weather, the square where I was sent before lunch, the streets where I ran errands, the paths we took when the weather was fine.

And as in the game in which the Japanese amuse themselves by submerging, in a porcelain bowl filled with water, little pieces of paper that, hitherto indistinguishable, almost immediately upon being plunged into it stretch, twist, take on color, differentiate themselves, become flowers, houses, figures that are substantial and recognizable; likewise, now all of the flowers in our garden and those in the park of Monsieur Swann, and the water lilies on the Vivonne, and the good people of the town and their little dwellings and the church and all of Combray and its environs, all of this sprang forth, town and gardens alike, from my cup of tea.

Marcel Proust

6

dans le thé et quand elle fut amollie la portai à ma bouche ~~a bout me gorgée~~ en même temps me gorgée de thé. Mais ~~il n'y fut pas plus tôt que~~ à l'instant même [tressaillis, attentif] ~~un~~ plaisir délicieux m'avait envahi, ~~isolé~~ plaisir qui était, ~~isolé~~ détaché de la notion de sa cause, ~~qui était~~ ~~totalement ... vague ... me remplissait~~ ~~d'une essence précieuse~~ encore une ~~...~~ me remplissait ~~...~~ d'une essence précieuse ~~...~~ qui m'avait rendu les vicissitudes de la vie indifférentes, ses ~~...~~ désastres inoffensifs, sa brièveté illusoire. ~~...~~ [illegible] cette essence n'était pas en moi, elle était moi, ~~...~~ Je ne me sentais plus médiocre, contingent, mortel. ~~...~~ D'où m'était venue cette félicité, cette ~~...~~ qui était plus que moi de l'ennui, ~~et~~ des peines de la vie, la triste journée, mon moi médiocre. Je sentais bien qu'elle ~~était~~ liée au goût de la biscotte ~~...~~ et qu'en fait elle le dépassait infiniment. Qu'était-elle, ~~...~~ d'où venait-elle, que signifiait-elle, où l'appréhender? ~~Grande tâche~~ quand l'esprit est le quêteur ~~...~~ incertain ~~chercher~~ ~~...~~ à la fois ~~...~~ qui cherche et ~~...~~ qui ne sait ~~...~~ lui-même ~~...~~ le chercheur ~~...~~ où il ~~...~~ chercher et où tout son bagage ne lui servirait de rien. et une partie de lui que lui, lumière, ~~...~~ pas? Quelque chose qui n'est pas encore, qui seul peut

[Marginal additions:] que / à ce qui d'abord / de ce passé / et / les avait / ou plutôt / qu'il était / elle était ce que j'étais devenu / quel de la biscotte avait touché ma [illegible] qu'elle devait être liée à ce goût / elle le dépassait infiniment. / quand il faut / [illegible]

Meaulnes: The Lost Domain

Alain-Fournier, 1913

"A misfortune frequently visited upon masterpieces has befallen *Le Grand Meaulnes* (*Meaulnes: The Lost Domain*)," wrote Jean Prévost. "It has been betrayed by its readers." He was commenting on the general tendency to reduce the novel to its first three parts: to the story of the strange party at which Augustin Meaulnes meets Yvonne de Galais, and thus to a dream-like tale of adolescent love and friendship. However, the book encompasses much more than youth, which is only its point of departure. Overall, it proceeds from dreams to harsher realities. Although largely autobiographical, the novel—elaborated over more than eight years—transcends its genre to tell the compelling tale of our "hard, short lives."

If it remains widely read, that is because it has the fascination of an objective assessment of human existence, of the agitated fall of our lives, in which concessions, petty betrayals, and fleetingly paradisal loves apply a soothing but illusory balm to our existential wounds. Fournier lures us into his book, making us empathize with the surrogates for himself—and for ourselves—that are Augustin Meaulnes, François Seurel, and Frantz de Galais. Although professing reservations ("No human construct is sufficiently vast to encompass the world I carry within myself"), he manages to evoke, with considerable power, the inevitable rift between our thirst for absolute meaning and the reality of our finitude. *Meaulnes: The Lost Domain* is a saga of souls searching for one another, and whose paths sometimes cross without their realizing it. It is a chivalric novel for those in quest of the Grail, but who flee happiness for fear that it will be the end of them.

Fournier himself had no time to attain this absolute realm, for he was mowed down prematurely in 1914. Nonetheless, through his style, through his salvaging of words' original meanings, he sometimes brushed up against it. Which should not surprise us, given his fervent commitment to "the protracted search for words able to restore the first and complete impression."

Jean-Pierre Guéno

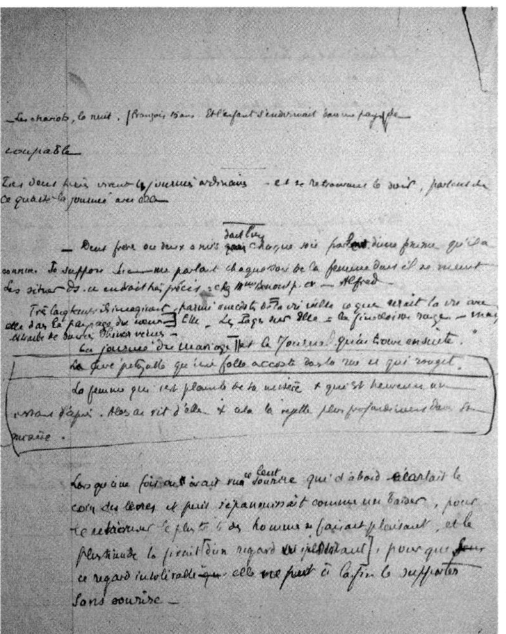

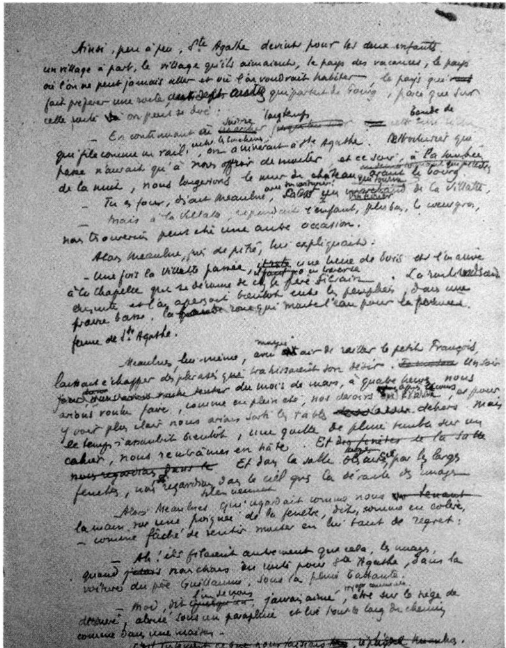

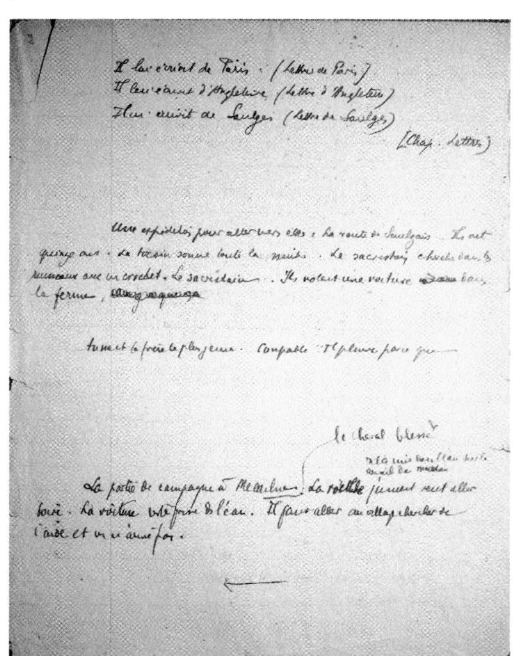

Top left: Photograph of Alain-Fournier (detail).
Left: Watercolor by Maxime Rebière.
Right and opposite: Pages from an early draft of *Le Grand Meaulnes* (*Meaulnes: The Lost Domain*). Archives Alain Rivière.

Tous mes jeux d'aubépines sont finis. Je m'enfermais dans le cabinet des archives, plein de mouches mortes et d'affiches battant au vent, et je lisais assis sur une vieille bascule. Après quatre heures sous le préau, je découvrais parfois dans les paniers oubliés des gamins un livre de lecture que je ne connaissais pas. Et lorsque la nuit venait, que le carreau dépoli de notre petite cuisine s'illuminait tandis que déjà les chiens dans la cour de la ferme commençaient à hurler à la lune, je rentrais. Ma mère avait commencé le repas et j'étais seul avec elle. Je montais trois marches de l'escalier et tout dans le noir, appuyé sur la rampe de fer, je la regardais allumer son feu dans l'étroite cuisine où vacillait la flamme d'une bougie.

Depuis que Meaulnes est chez nous, tout a très changé. Il m'entraîne tard avec lui le soir dans les rues de Sainte-Agathe. Nous nous trouvons, à la nuit, dans des lieux du pays que je ne connaissais pas. Je me revois à la queue d'une bande de gamins, suivant un étroit chemin plein de paille et de purin, entre des granges et des cours de ferme où les chiens aboient, dans le faubourg de la Belle-Étoile. Meaulnes connaît déjà tous les endroits où vont les gamins. Je crois bien qu'il est entré déjà dans presque toutes les maisons et même dans les plus mystérieuses. Seul ou avec les autres gamins, il entre partout

"The Marching Wood"

Jean Cocteau, 1914

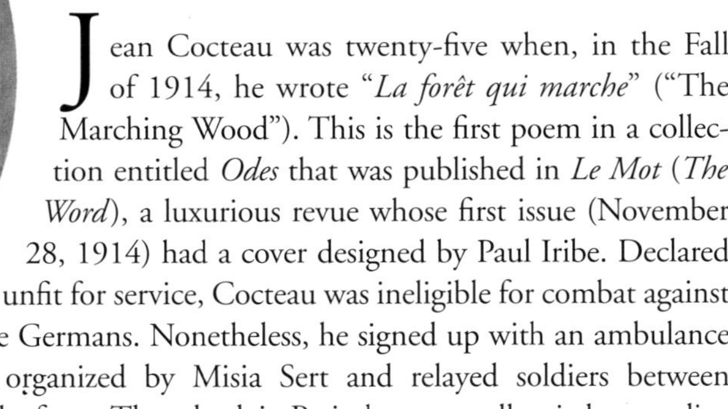

Jean Cocteau was twenty-five when, in the Fall of 1914, he wrote "*La forêt qui marche*" ("The Marching Wood"). This is the first poem in a collection entitled *Odes* that was published in *Le Mot* (*The Word*), a luxurious revue whose first issue (November 28, 1914) had a cover designed by Paul Iribe. Declared unfit for service, Cocteau was ineligible for combat against the Germans. Nonetheless, he signed up with an ambulance corps organized by Misia Sert and relayed soldiers between Rheims and the front. Then, back in Paris, he repeatedly tried to reenlist.

"The Marching Wood" evokes the advance of English troops toward combat. According to Cocteau, the poem consists of three lexical "ensembles," the first of which was to be printed conventionally, in roman typeface, the second in italics, and the third entirely in capital letters. Two manuscripts of the poem are known. In one of them, the text is arranged in free verse so as to resemble conventional stanzas. In the other (see opposite), the use of different colors (purple, green, and red) is an organizing factor and indicates Cocteau's interest in the presentation of this text. There is every reason to think that Apollinaire's "*La Lettre Océan*" ("The Letter Ocean") was the model here, for Cocteau admired the poet's ideograms. Cocteau inscribed the words and sentence fragments in all directions, but in configurations that suggest what the poem would become. The handwriting differs from the one later used by Cocteau. He has often been criticized for imitating the fanciful conceits of the poet Anna de Noailles, whose work he greatly admired after meeting her in 1911. This text corroborates the observation.

Dominique Marny

I came across the English near the battle
On their large motorized lorries
Their faces of brick red
And their songs of evenings on the Thames.
Their uniforms had not the drab invisibility
Of gunpowder, filth, and fatigue
Of the enemy's uniforms.
I saw the English roll towards the battle
Like Shakespeare's marching wood
Like an uprising of young laborers
Like the sap of foliage.

They were on the road that smells of apples
(We heard the cannon wreaking havoc on the
pink hill)
Like a soccer team
Like a large school out for a walk
Like a ship's crew on shore leave
Perfumed with a tar of ginger salt and iodine . . .
For the sweet earth where we are . . .

Jean Cocteau

Top left: Jacques-Émile Blanche, *Study for a Portrait of Jean Cocteau* (detail). Rouen, Musée des Beaux-Arts.
Right: Jean Cocteau, *Self-Portrait* (in a letter to Paul Valéry, October 1924). Paris, Bibliothèque Nationale de France.
Opposite: Autograph manuscript of "*La forêt qui marche*" ("The Marching Wood"), 1914. Paris, Bibliothèque Historique de la Ville de Paris.

Ces grands camions automobiles Soulèvement de jeunes labours

feuillages

Bonjour! Conserves de thon rose

6 heures 20 du soir juste Les figures Brique rose Dans l'herbe la pomme

Les phares neufs

sous son auto vite inverse arbre mouillé embaume le crépuscule

Entre les pommiers jusqu'à

75 155

LE CANON: ——— ——— — — ——— bous-cule

Bonjour Bonjour!

la colline rose

17 ans Foot Ball Collège MATCH

Des lèvres la gangrène son doucéâtre musc monotone la colline rose

Obus Bonjour! LUNE

gateaux secs à terre l'équipage Navire natal goudron

Je me souviens

Conserves gingembre bonjour!

20 ans

Gin Pipes Douce terre où nous sommes

Chemises de rechange

sel

lads d'autres

TAMISE

du globe

Octobre

Aéroplanes

17 ans

Chevaux de courses en Seine et Oise

tabac cuirs tubs

ciel Chantaient

Brouillards 1815 1915

67

Thé

Chine

Le peuple de marins

Ils

Tron escale

Steerforth

SHAKSPEARE

Auf tonnant qui tombe d'un aigle rose

Chantaient LUNE

Champignons faisan

its a long long way to go!

SHAKSPEARE

29 ans bonjour!

fougères ROI GEORGES

Le gibier se déjouent

crache de la poussière

prairies

Ile qui chante

mousse le chasseur champignons

genoux nus

mousse

la couleur du Wisky et des faubourgs de LONDRES

forêt qui roule

DIMANCHE

SHAKSPEARE 20 ans

souffle avec

Match à mélinite

X — L'obus chante — sa

Tes noirs séraphins durs LUNE

Choral

Shubert

Broc de bière écumeuse glaciale

to the

blanc joufflus de fumée Colonies!...

REIMS

22 ans

Etudiants BACH L'ennemi

parabole — et déflagre — X

I know

Les

Les Vandales

chameau vert

machines d'agriculture

Henri Heine

aux rives du Neckar

1815 harangues anniversaire Remords Revanches

match

20 ans

LUNE Equipe vers

Stra té gie des per spectives

Les phares remuent le grand

Nul

ROCAILLE de BE[?]

Orion

la laie de pierre

Mitrailleuse: son doux balancement de palme son bruit au loin la suture

la suture qui craque entre un champs de trèfle et un champs d'orge

LA LUNE

Six heures et demie du soir

Le dernier camion

its a long long way to Tipperary

La couleur des rochers de Corse, des moutons de Lorraine

The Dice Cup

Max Jacob, 1916

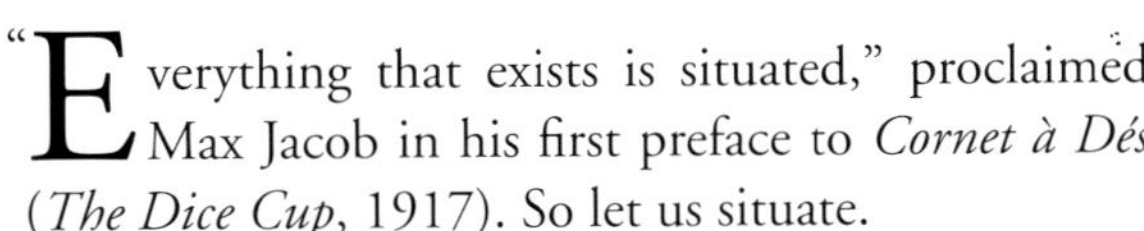

"Everything that exists is situated," proclaimed Max Jacob in his first preface to *Cornet à Dés* (*The Dice Cup*, 1917). So let us situate.

Born in 1876, in Quimper, to a Jewish family from Lorraine, Max Jacob tried his hand at an array of jobs (legal clerk, salesman, piano teacher, art critic, painter) whose range reflects both his impoverished background and his exceptional gifts. In 1901, Picasso, Apollinaire, and André Salmon introduced him to the artistic Bohemia of Montparnasse, but toward the end of 1909, in his room on Rue Ravignan, he had a vision of Christ. "What beauty! What elegance and sweetness! His shoulders, his gait! He wears a robe of yellow silk and blue frontals. He turns around and I see his peaceful and radiant face." He converted to Catholicism and henceforth lived in retreat at Saint-Benoît-sur-Loire, surviving on revenue from the sale of his gouaches. "I will die a martyr," he remarked hopefully.

On February 24, 1944, as he was leaving morning mass in the crypt of the basilica, he was arrested by the Gestapo. He died the following March 5, in the Drancy internment camp. Of his many Parisian friends, only Sacha Guitry had attempted to free him. Although he was a mystical poet, his work is also droll, disarming, and unclassifiable (*La Défense de Tartuffe* [*In Defense of Tartuffe*], *Le Cabinet Noir* [*The Black Cabinet*], *Filibuth ou la Montre en Or* [*Filibuth, or the Gold Watch*]). Treasured by his friends in the Montmartre and Montparnasse circles—not only Apollinaire, but Cocteau, Francis Carco, Pierre Mac Orlan, and Maurice Sachs, who left a sensitive portrait of him—he was the victim of formidable artistic predators. But not unknowingly. In *Petit Historique du "Cornet à Dés"* (*Short History of "The Dice Cup"*), dated 1943, he wrote: "They came in the morning, 7, Rue Ravignan, to read the "Poem of the Night" . . . the neighbors, Picasso, Salmon, Mac Orlan, etc. 'How they'll feast on that!' said Mac Orlan."

Pierre Chalmin

Frontispiece

Yes, it fell from the nipple of my breast and I didn't notice. As a ship full of sailors heads out of port without the sea's becoming any more agitated, without the earth's sensing this new adventure, there fell from my breast of Cybele a new poem and I didn't notice.

Poem of the Moon

There are on the night three mushrooms that are the moon. Abruptly, like the song of a cuckoo clock, they rearrange themselves at midnight every month. There are in the garden rare flowers that are little recumbent men, a hundred, they are mirror reflections. There is in my dark room a lurking luminous censer, then two . . . phosphorescent aerostats, they are mirror reflections. There is in my head a bee that talks.

Rue Ravignan

"One cannot bathe in the same river twice," said the philosopher Heraclitus. But it is always the same ones who come back! At the same times, they pass by, gay or sad. All of you, passersby of Rue Ravignan, I have given you the names of history's dead! Here Agamemnon! There Madame Hanska![1] Ulysses is a milkman! Patroclus is at the end of the street while a Pharaoh is close by. Castor and Pollux are the ladies from the fifth.[2] But you, old ragpicker, you who come in the magical morning to take away the still-living rubbish when I extinguish my great big lamp, you whom I know not, mysterious and poor ragpicker: to you I assign a name that is celebrated and noble. I call you Dostoevsky.

Max Jacob

1. Ève Hanska, Balzac's mistress.
2. From the fifth *arrondissement* of Paris.

Top left: Marie Laurencin, *Portrait of Max Jacob*, 1907. Orléans, Musée des Beaux-Arts.
Left: Max Jacob, illustration for *The Dice Cup*. Orléans, Bibliothèque Municipale.
Right: Autograph page with three prose poems from *The Dice Cup*. Orléans, Bibliothèque Municipale.

20

Frontispice

Oui ! il est tombé du bouton de mon sein et je ne m'en suis pas aperçu. Comme un bateau sort de l'antre du rocher avec les marins sans que la mer en prenne davantage, sans que la terre sente cette aventure nouvelle, il est tombé de mon sein de Cybèle un poème nouveau et je ne m'en suis pas aperçu

× ×

Poème de la lune

Il y a sur la nuit trois champignons qui sont la lune. Aussi brusquement que chante le coucou d'une horloge ils se disposent autrement à minuit chaque mois. Il y a dans le jardin des fleurs rares qui sont de petits hommes couchés et qui s'éveillent tous les matins. Il y a dans ma chambre obscure une navette ~~[illegible]~~ lumineuse qui rôde puis deux .... aérostats phosphorescents, c'est les reflets d'un miroir. Il y a dans ma tête une abeille qui parle

La rue Ravignan

On ne se baigne pas deux fois dans le même fleuve, disait le philosophe Héraclite. Pourtant ce sont toujours les mêmes qui remontent. Aux mêmes heures, ils passent gais ou tristes. Vous tous, passants de la rue Ravignan, je vous ai donné les noms des défunts de l'Histoire ! Voici Agamemnon ! Voici Mme Hanska ! Ulysse est un laitier ! Patrocle est au bas de la rue qu'un Pharaon est près de moi. Castor et Pollux sont les dames du cinquième. Mais toi, vieux chiffonnier, toi qui, au féerique matin viens enlever les débris encore vivants quand j'éteins ma bonne grosse lampe toi que je ne connais pas, mystérieux et pauvre chiffonnier toi, chiffonnier, je t'ai nommé d'un nom célèbre et noble, je t'ai nommé Dostoïewsky

Elastic Poems

Blaise Cendrars, 1919

Cendrars chose from the start to be *modern*, which is not the same thing as fashionable. For him, poetry was not a matter of nostalgic complaints about an intractable universe. He was very much of this world, and was quite comfortable in it. Trains, automobiles, skyscrapers, moving pictures, speed: why complain about them? They had a beauty of their own that the poet could turn to account. He had only to find an appropriately syncopated language. If the camera company in question had not objected, he would have entitled one of his poetry collections *Kodaks*. How better to express his aim to fix the fleeting instant? In his view, it was the poet's role to express what doesn't happen in what happens.

Du monde entier au coeur du monde (*From the Whole World to the Heart of the World*), the title under which he gathered his poems, is consistent with this ambition. Although Cendrars the adventurer, the world traveler, is fondly regarded, he was above all a stylist, one who influenced the Apollinaire of *Zone*. His work stands up better than that of his contemporaries who put too much stock in exoticism. This bard of the new beauty, this veteran of the Foreign Legion—a truculent bon vivant—was also, however paradoxical this might seem, a mystic. He was nostalgic not for the past but for the sacred. One need only read *Le Plan de l'Aiguille* (*Antarctic Fugue*), *Les Confessions de Dan Yack* (*Confessions of Dan Yack*), or *Le Lotissement du Ciel* (*Sky: Memoirs*) to become convinced of this. "The windows of my poetry are open wide to the boulevards," he wrote in *Poèmes Élastiques* (*Elastic Poems*). But sometimes, as in "*Les Pâques à New York*" ("Easter in New York"), he spoke about God, and regretted that "mystic fires no longer gleam in stained-glass windows."

Paul Desalmand

Diary

Christ
It's been a year now since I last thought about
you
Since I wrote my next to last poem "Easter"
My life is much changed since then
But I am still the same
I even wanted to become a painter
Here are the paintings that I made and that
hang on the walls tonight
I have strange thoughts about myself that
make me think about you.

Christ
Life
Here's what I've dug up
My paintings are painful to me
I am too passionate
Everything is orangish
[I spent a sad day today thinking
about my friends and reading

Christ
Life crucified in the wide-open diary that I hold
in my outstretched arms
Wingspan
Rockets
Turmoil
Screams
One would say an airplane was falling
It's me
Passion
Fire
Serial novel
Shrieks of light
It's all very well to not want to talk about oneself
Sometimes you have to scream
I am the other
Too sensitive

Blaise Cendrars
August 17, 1913]

Top left: Photograph of Blaise Cendrars, roughly contemporary with *Poèmes Élastiques* (*Elastic Poems*). *Left, right, and opposite:* Two pages (with detail) from an illustrated autograph manuscript of *Poèmes Élastiques*. Paris, Bibliothèque Nationale de France.

4
JOURNAL
Christ
voici plus d'un an que je n'ai plus pensé à vous
Depuis que j'ai fait mon avant dernière Pâques
Ma vie a bien changé depuis
Mais je suis toujours le même
Voir les tableaux que j'ai fait et
qui se sont pendant aux murs
Ils m'ouvrent d'étranges vues
sur moi-même qui me font
penser à vous
Christ
La vie
voilà ce que j'ai souillé
Mes peintures me font mal
Je suis trop passionné
Tout est orangé

André Breton and Philippe Soupault, 1920

La Glace sans Tain 1

Prisonniers des gouttes d'eau nous ne sommes que des animaux perpétuels nous courons dans les villes sans bruits et les affiches enchantées ne nous touchent plus. A quoi bon ces grands enthousiasmes fragiles ces sauts de joie desséchés? Nous ne savons plus rien que les astres morts, nous regardons les visages et nous soupirons de plaisir. Notre bouche est plus sèche que les plages perdues et nos yeux tournent sans but sans espoir. Il n'y a plus que ces cafés où nous nous réunissons pour boire ces boissons fraîches ces alcools délayés et les tables sont plus poisseuses que ces trottoirs où sont tombées nos ombres mortes de la veille. Quelquefois le vent nous entoure de ses grandes mains froides et nous attache aux arbres découpés par le soleil. Tous nous rions nous chantons mais personne ne sent plus son cœur battre
La fièvre nous abandonne
Les gares merveilleuses ne nous abritent plus jamais les longs couloirs nous effraient. Il faut donc étouffer

The Unstained Mirror

Imprisoned in drops of water we are only perpetual animals we run noiselessly in the towns and the enchanted posters no longer move us. What's the good of these fragile enthusiasms these wasted jumps for joy? We no longer know anything but dead stars, we look at faces and we sigh with pleasure. Our mouth is drier than lost beaches and our eyes turn pointlessly hopelessly. All that remains are those cafes where we meet to drink those cold beverages those mixed drinks and the tables are stickier than the sidewalks onto which our dead shadows fell the day before. Sometimes the wind surrounds us with its large cold hands and attaches us to trees cut by the sun. We all laugh we sing but no one still feels his heart beating

The fever leaves us

The wondrous train stations shelter us no more the long corridors frighten us. So we must smother . . .

It is the dream of every poet, sometimes unacknowledged, to attain the raw, original quintessence of poetic language. Baudelaire spoke of spinning gold from mud, Rimbaud of submitting the word to a fecund alchemy. Lautréaumont sought to access the darker reaches of consciousness, while the Surrealists, more ambitious and considerably madder, spurred by the work of the psychiatrist Janet and the psychoanalyst Freud, dreamed of bypassing rational thought to reach the unknown riches of the unconscious, the subliminal truths of being. In 1920, this unprecedented program resulted in a collection entitled *Les Champs Magnétiques* (*Magnetic Fields*).

The title itself is suggestive, for it evokes a subterranean, drive-driven, extra-personal dynamic that was central to the surrealist movement. Breton, who initially favored the title "*Les Précipités*" (Precipitates), spoke of his "desire to write a dangerous book." Perhaps it is this danger that explains his willingness to collaborate with Soupault. Nonetheless, the book is largely Breton's; in addition to being responsible for the initial idea, the organizational scheme, and most of the poems, he fine-tuned the manuscript prior to its publication. But the collaborative dynamic made it possible to downplay the role of the individual voice, which here cedes pride of place to a shared mental force (ostensibly) free from the shackles of reason.

les Champs magnétiques
(suite)

II. Saisons

J'ai quitté les Salles Dolo de bon matin avec grand-père. Le petit voudrait une surprise. Ces cornets d'un sou n'ont pas été sans grande influence sur ma vie. L'aubergiste s'appelle Tyran. Je me retrouve souvent dans cette belle pièce avec les mesures de volume. Le chromo du mur est une rêverie qui se représente toujours. Un homme dont le berceau est dans la vallée atteint avec une jolie barbe à quarante ans le faîte d'une montagne et se met à décliner doucement. Les mendiants prononçaient le château. Il y avait d'adorables colères d'enfant à propos de ces plantes grasses qu'on applique sur les cors, il y avait les fleurs de lis conservées dans l'eau de vie quand tu tombais. J'ai commencé à aimer les fontaines bleues devant lesquelles on se met à genoux. Quand l'eau n'est pas troublée (troubler l'eau nuit, paresser dans ce monde) on voit jaillir des pierres, des parcelles d'or qui fascinent les crapauds. On m'explique les sacrifices humains. Comme j'écoute les tambours dans la direction du douët! C'est ainsi qu'on nomme l'endroit un

II. Seasons

I leave the Salles Dolo early in the morning with grandfather. The little one wanted a surprise. These penny trumpets were not without influence on my life. The innkeeper's name was Tyran. I often find myself back in this beautiful room with measures of volume. The cheap color print on the wall is a dream that always represents itself. A man whose cradle is in the valley reaches with a pretty beard at age forty the summit of a mountain and begins a slow decline. There were adorable childish fits over the plump plants that are applied to the horns, there were fleurs-de-lys preserved in eau-de-vie when you fell.

I began to love blue fountains before which people kneel. When the water is untroubled (troubling the water harms, lazing about in this world) one sees stones gush forth, bits of gold that fascinate toads. Human sacrifice is explained to me. As I listen to drums coming from the douët! That is what they call the place....

The principle of automatic writing exerts considerable fascination. The first *Surrealist Manifesto*, published in 1924, proposed rules for its functioning. In a state of half-sleep, words, and phrases—striking, illogical, obstinate—rise to the surface, "banging against the glass," imposing their "very high degree of manifest absurdity." After which, in "the most passive or receptive state," one has only to transcribe the message, writing very quickly, "without preconceived subject" and without rereading.

This is how one revs up the machine. Often, of course, it produces gratuitous idiocies. But sometimes, if spurred into action by receptive and audacious creative imaginations, it can trigger miraculous explosions, stylistic flashes of dazzling brilliance. For example: "The wondrous train stations shelter us no more"; or: "The gutters of paradise are well acquainted with the white rats that run under the throne of God." Such visionary effusions may make the literal-minded laugh, but they have considerably enlarged our capacity for esthetic response. It would scarcely be an exaggeration to say that *Magnetic Fields* wrought havoc with the triumphant rationalism of modernity, for which it substituted the prerogatives of dreams, the virtues of delirium, and the epiphanies of the imagination.

Yves Stalloni

Top left and top right: Francis Picabia, portraits of Philippe Soupault (left) and André Breton (right), 1920. *Above:* Autograph manuscripts of Philippe Soupault (left) and André Breton (right) for *Les Champs Magnétiques* (*Magnetic Fields*). Paris, Bibliothèque Nationale de France.

"Love of Homonyms"

Robert Desnos, 1922

It was in the celebrated periodical *Littérature*, a Dadaist organ, that the young Robert Desnos first declared himself a writer committed to the "absolute Surrealist act." "Surrealism is the order of the day and Desnos is its prophet," declared André Breton in 1924. Taking part in experiments with hypnosis, he explored the full gamut of subversive language games in the 150 sentences of his poem *Rrose Sélavy* [*sic*] ("109: The laws of our desires are dice without spare time").

His *La Liberté ou l'Amour* (*Liberty or Love*, 1927), a lyrical and erotic narrative about a club of sperm-drinkers, prompted a conviction for "immorality." At about the same time, he began to distance himself from the Surrealist group, whose support of the communist party he found intolerable. An authentic anarchist, he was soon cast out by Breton, to whom he retorted: "Surrealism is now in the public domain, and is at the disposal of heretics, schismatics, and atheists."

In 1930, he published *Corps et Biens*, an anthology of poetry written between 1919 and 1929, a "balance sheet" and a "history through example of all the poetic innovations of recent years." But his masterpieces are the collections *L'Aumonyme, Les Ténèbres*, and *À la Mystèrieuse*. Desnos began to live with Youki Foujita, his future wife, and began a decade of radio broadcasts, for which he produced dramatic adaptations of his poetry as well as advertising slogans. He continued to publish in periodicals until early in 1944, when he was arrested by the Gestapo as a member of the Resistance. He was deported, and died of typhus and starvation at the Terezin concentration camp on June 8, 1945. The following text was found scribbled on a piece of paper in his uniform: "I have dreamed of you so much, walked, talked, slept with your ghost so much, that the only thing left me, perhaps, and still, is to be a ghost among ghosts and a hundred times more shadow than the shadow who strolls and will stroll cheerfully on the sundial of your life."

Pierre Chalmin

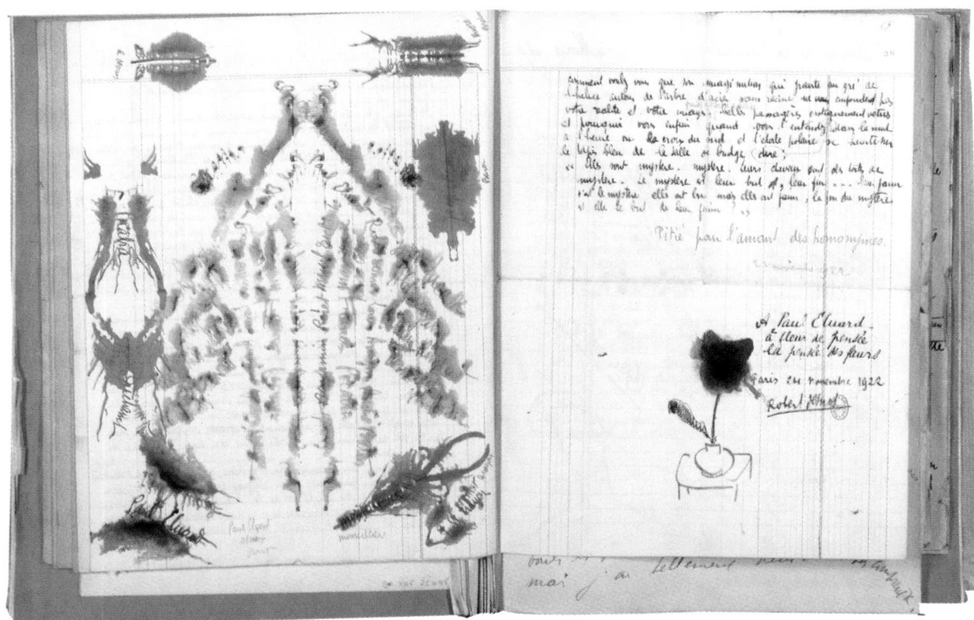

Love of Homonyms

"It's a vexing business, creating mystery around our loves. Perhaps not so vexing as that.

I love it, it drives so fast, the big white automobile. From time to time, at bends in the road, the white and black chauffeur, more majestically than a frigate captain, slowly lowers his arm into the space that drives, drives, drives so fast, in white waves like the wheels of the automobile that I love.

But the mystery that unfolds concentrically around her breasts has captured in its labyrinth of tear-stained macadam the big white automobile that undulates rather than rolls, generating in the space around it great invisible and concentric waves of mystery. The aerial target that men pierce without realizing it slowly falls to pieces to the great pleasure of lovers, and the sphere, circled by parallel lines like her breasts, collapses like a balloon. Dirigibles and hot-air balloons, airplanes and steamers, locomotives and automobiles, all is mystery in my motionless love for her breasts."

After having spoken, I looked:

The desert that stretched out around me was populated with echoes that placed me cruelly in the presence of my own image reflected in the mirror of mirages. The women holding these hand mirrors were nude, except for their hands, which were gloved, their left breasts, sheathed in black moiré taffeta that made my gums scream with lust, except also for their hair, hidden below thin yellow wool scarves. When these women turned around, I could see the whole of their wondrous backs, except the necks, the backbones, and the smalls above their rumps, hidden as these were by the scarves. Did this partial nudity, cunningly irritating to me, cause my madness? Tell me, you whose mystery is the end, the goal.

Flee no longer, first-class passengers, when the clandestine immigrant, tied to the propeller to make the crossing at little expense, calls to you in the evening, when, bending over the shaft, you seek to identify your hair, the undulations of the banner and the waves. Your faces and the reflections of your faces present themselves in turn above and below him. How could his imagination, which revolves, at the propeller's pleasure, around the rootless tree of steel, help but confuse your reality and your image, fruits of the propeller tree, fleeting beauties erotically attired, and why flee when you hear it said by night, at the hour when the Southern Cross and the Polar Star collide on the blue carpet of bridge rooms:

"They are mystery, mystery. Their hair is a canvas of mystery. . . Mystery is their goal, their end. . . Their hunger is the mystery. They have drunk, but they are hungry. Is the end of the mystery the goal of their hunger?"

Take pity on the lover of homonyms.

Top left: Photograph of Robert Desnos by Man Ray. Published in *Corps et Biens*, 1930.
Left and opposite: pages from the autograph manuscript of "*Amour des Homonymes*," published in the collection *Corps et Biens*. Paris, Bibliothèque Nationale de France.

Amour et homonymes

« C'est une fâcheuse aventure que : créer le mystère autour de nos amours. Pas si fâcheux que ça.

Je l'aime elle roule si vite la grande automobile blanche. De temps à autre, au tournant des rues, le chauffeur blanc et noir plus mystérieusement qu'un capitaine de frégate abaisse lentement le bras dans l'espace qui roule roule roule si vite en mâts blancs comme les roues de l'automobile que j'aime. Mais le mystère qui se déroule concentriquement autour de ses seins a capturé dans son labyrinthe de macadam taché de larmes la grande automobile blanche qui vogue plutôt qu'elle ne roule en faisant naître autour d'elle dans l'espace les grandes ondes invisibles et concentriques du mystère. Le câble aérienne que les hommes traversent sans s'en douter se déloque lentement au gré des amants et la sphère cerclée de parallèles comme ses seins crève comme un ballon dirigeable et ballons, aéroplanes et vapeurs, locomotives et automobiles tout est mystère dans notre immobile amour pour ses seins. »

Après avoir parlé je regardai.

Le désert qui s'étendait autour de moi était peuplé d'échos qui me mirent cruellement en présence de ma propre image reflétée dans le miroir des mirages. Les femmes qui tenaient ces glaces à main étaient nues hormis leurs mains qui étaient gantées, leur sein gauche qui était gainé de taffetas moiré noir à faire hurler de volupté mes gencives, hormis aussi leurs cheveux dissimulés sous une écharpe de fine laine jaune. Quand ces femmes se retournaient je pouvais tout voir de leurs dos merveilleux tout hormis la nuque la colonne vertébrale et cette partie de la croupe où la cambrure prend naissance cachées qu'elles étaient par les pans de l'écharpe. Cette nudité partielle et savamment irritante pour moi a-t-elle causé ma folie ? Dites le moi vous dont le mystère est la fin, le but.

Ne vous enfuyez plus passagers de 1ère classe quand l'émigrant clandestin lié à l'hélice pour faire à peu de frais la traversée vous appelle le soir à l'heure où penché près de la hampe vous cherchez à identifier vos cheveux l'ondoiement de l'étendard et les flots. Vos visages et le reflet de vos visages se présentent tour à tour au dessus et au dessous de lui

Count d'Orgel's Ball

Raymond Radiguet, 1923

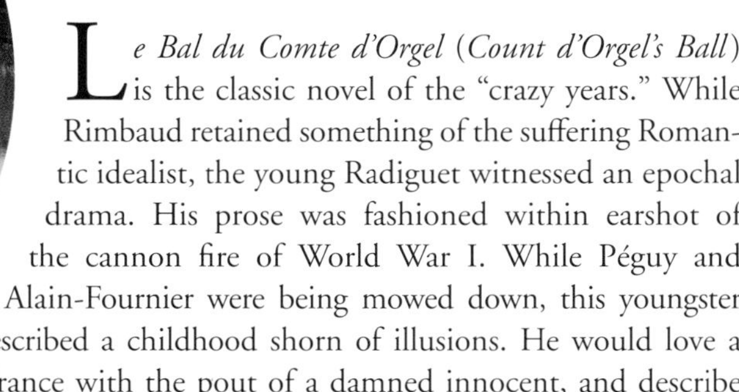

Le Bal du Comte d'Orgel (*Count d'Orgel's Ball*) is the classic novel of the "crazy years." While Rimbaud retained something of the suffering Romantic idealist, the young Radiguet witnessed an epochal drama. His prose was fashioned within earshot of the cannon fire of World War I. While Péguy and Alain-Fournier were being mowed down, this youngster described a childhood shorn of illusions. He would love a lost France with the pout of a damned innocent, and describe the diversions of his era—carefree but already edged with black—in language that went straight to its target. His accounts of emotional turmoil and sexual indulgence have a classical rigor reminiscent of Madame de La Fayette and Saint-Simon. He adored "badly-written" eighteenth-century novels, diabolical works of casual elegance that he felt had culminated in *Dangerous Liaisons*. Radiguet, a budding Laclos on the banks of the Marne, would never utter the cry of Rimbaud's *The Drunken Boat*: "True! I have wept too much!"

Le Diable au Corps (*Devil in the Flesh*) was entitled *Les Yeux Secs* (*Dry Eyes*) before Cocteau and Grasset hit upon the alternative as a provocative marketing hook. Publishers are not the only ones who get rich on books that become notorious; authors do, too, and not only in monetary terms. Having experienced and survived the ensuing literary scandal, Radiguet chose to produce subtler entertainments. After peering into the little gardens of Saint-Maur, he was weary of family dramas and turned his attention to the acrobatics of unbridled passion. In *Count d'Orgel's Ball*, the little knight from Faublas becomes a myopic Don Juan, a cruel de Sade of impossible love.

Pierre-Emmanuel Prouvost d'Agostino

Countess Orgel was creole. By birth, she belonged to the illustrious house of Grimoard de la Verberie. Few families could compete with its lineage, which could be traced back to the Frankish Count Grimoard, sometimes confused by our medieval chroniclers with the mayor of Grimoald Palace, an ancestor of the Grimaldis. The Grimoards prided themselves on the fact that their name had already lost its luster in an era when those attached to the families now regarded as our most venerable stood out for their novelty.

Top left: Jacques-Émile Blanche, *Study for a Portrait of Raymond Radiguet at Age Twenty* (detail). Rouen, Musée des Beaux-Arts.
Below left: Kees Van Dongen, *The Archangel's Tango*, 1930. Nice, Musée des Beaux-Arts Jules-Chéret.
Below right: Kees Van Dongen, *The Revellers*. Troyes, Musée d'Art Moderne.
Opposite: Page from an autograph draft of *Le Bal du Comte d'Orgel* (*Count d'Orgel's Ball*). The text was revised considerably before publication. Paris, Bibliothèque Nationale de France.

1

(1)

La comtesse d'Orgel était créole. Elle appartenait par sa naissance à l'illustre maison des Grimoard de la Verberie. Peu de familles pouvaient rivaliser ~~en ancienneté~~ avec ~~celle-ci~~ elle, qui établissait sa filiation depuis le comte franc Grimoard, que nos chroniqueurs du moyen-âge confondent parfois avec le maire du palais Grimoald, dont descendent les Grimaldi. Les Grimoard ~~de la Verberie~~ se glorifiaient de ce que l'éclat de leur nom fut déjà éteint, à une époque, où les noms qui, aujourd'hui, sont ceux de nos plus vieilles familles, frappaient par leur nouveauté.

• Mais cette famille n'était glorieuse qu'à ses ~~que pour~~ yeux, ~~elle-même~~ ~~, et les~~ était ceux des historiens. Ce nom qui ~~[illegible]~~ pouvait faire prétendre les Grimoard aux premiers rangs dans le royaume, les paralysait. Car il leur aurait fallu flatter des grands, qui, pensaient ~~les Grimoard~~ ils, auraient dû être leurs vassaux.

? (Il ne faudrait pas croire que nous allons essayer de tracer un historique, toujours fastidieux,

Doctor Knock

Jules Romains, 1923

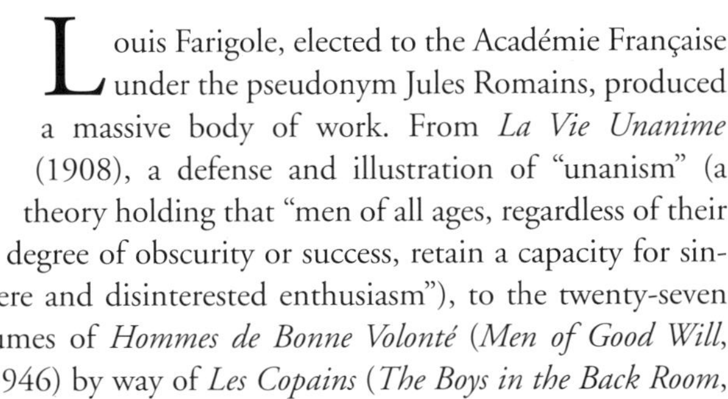

Louis Farigole, elected to the Académie Française under the pseudonym Jules Romains, produced a massive body of work. From *La Vie Unanime* (1908), a defense and illustration of "unanism" (a theory holding that "men of all ages, regardless of their degree of obscurity or success, retain a capacity for sincere and disinterested enthusiasm"), to the twenty-seven volumes of *Hommes de Bonne Volonté* (*Men of Good Will*, 1930–1946) by way of *Les Copains* (*The Boys in the Back Room*, 1913) and *Knock ou le Triomphe de la Médecine* (*Doctor Knock*, 1923), Jules Romains wrote almost 30,000 pages, in all genres (poetry, fiction, plays, essays) and on all literary registers (from odes to hoaxes).

Men of Good Will, a vast novel whose narrative unfolds over the quarter century extending from 1908 to 1933, is quite original in conception. An evocation of an entire period, of a "historical wave," it has multiple narrative lines, all of which pass through the crucible of World War I (two volumes are devoted to the battle of Verdun). Hugely successful in both France and the United States, it has since been forgotten, partly because of its formidable length.

In France, however, two of his other works remain popular: *The Boys in the Back Room*, a hilarious tale of hoaxes devised by a small group of friends to wreak vengeance on a stuffy, hypocritical society, and, especially, his play *Doctor Knock*, an indestructible comedy. Some have seen in this fable of a doctor with blind faith in his profession—"Healthy people are sick but don't know it"—a prefiguration of the mass hypnosis wrought by Hitler and Stalin. Jules Romains aspired to produce a "modern epic narrative," but it would seem that he was destined merely to "tickle" and "scratch" the surface of his era without ever putting his finger on its wound.

Pierre Chalmin

Act 2

KNOCK: Careful, don't confuse us! Does it tickle or does it itch?

LE TAMBOUR: It itches, but it also tickles a bit.

KNOCK: Good. And show me exactly where.

LE TAMBOUR: Here.

KNOCK: Here? Or here?

LE TAMBOUR: There, or perhaps there, between the two.

KNOCK: Right between the two. Isn't it just a little farther to the left, where I put my finger?

LE TAMBOUR: Yes, I think so.

KNOCK: Ah hah! (He reflects with a serious air.) Does it itch more after you've had *tête de veau à la vinaigrette*?

Top Left: Photograph of Jules Romains (detail) taken on the occasion of a 1947 revival of *Doctor Knock*.
Below left: Louis Jouvet and Guy Favières in the first production of *Doctor Knock*, December 1923.
Below: Becan, known as Cahn, poster for the first production of *Doctor Knock*. Paris, Bibliothèque Nationale de France.
Opposite: Page from the autograph manuscript of *Doctor Knock*. Paris, Bibliothèque Nationale de France.

Où est-ce que ça vous grattouille ?

Le T6

Ça me grattouille, (après réflexion) mais ça me chatouille bien un peu aussi.

Knock.

Bon. Et montrez-moi exactement l'endroit.

Le T6

Par ici.

Knock.

Par ici ? ou par ici ?

Le T6

Là, ou peut-être là. Entre les deux.

Knock.

Juste entre les deux. Est-ce que ça ne serait pas plutôt un rien à gauche, là où je mets mon doigt.

Le T6

Il me semble bien.

Knock.

Ah ah ! (il médite d'un air sombre) Est-ce que ça ne vous grattouille pas ~~ne le sentez~~ ~~pas~~ davantage quand vous avez mangé de la tête de veau à la

The Will-o'-the-Wisp

Pierre Drieu La Rochelle, 1931

"I want to tell a story. Will I ever manage to tell a story that's not my own?" asks Pierre Drieu La Rochelle at the beginning of *État Civil*. The question is resonant, for his best books are autobiographical: *Interrogation*, *Fond de Cantine* (*The Back of the Canteen*), and *La Comédie de Charleroi* (*The Comedy of Charleroi*), which draw upon his experience as a heroic combatant in World War I; *État Civil* and *Rêveuse Bourgeoisie* (*The Distracted Bourgeoisie*), which evoke his childhood and his milieu; *Gilles*, which, although disappointing as a novel, offers a splendid panorama of France between the wars; *Le Feu Follet* (*The Will-'o-the-Wisp*), a limpid narrative in which, after *La Valise Vide* (*The Empty Suitcase*), he responds to a friend's suicide; *Récit Secret* (*Secret Story*), published posthumously; and his *Journal* (1939–1945), a masterpiece that has only recently been published.

Unforgiving of the political writings that he published before the war, reproaching him for having taken on the editorship of *La Nouvelle Revue Française* during the Occupation (during which stint he wrote of the triumphal premiere of Sartre's *The Flies* before an audience peppered with Nazi commandants), many have castigated him as a fascist collaborator, obliterating an author who had sufficient nobility to refuse to be judged by people worth less than he.

No writer of the period lived it with the same intensity as Drieu, nor were any more disdainful of it than he was. "I have a horror of mediocrity," proclaims Alain Leroy, the protagonist-suicide of *Feu Follet*. Modeled after Jacques Rigaut, a dadaist—like Leroy—whom Drieu met through the periodical *Littérature* and who committed suicide in 1929, this disaffected bourgeois is Drieu's double. In March 1945, refusing to flee the purgers, Drieu committed suicide by gassing himself. "I had gotten it into my head that I mustn't live beyond fifty."

Pierre Chalmin

Around five o'clock, Alain woke up; someone was knocking at his door. It was Dr. La Barbinais.

"I woke you, my dear friend; I'm sorry, for you need rest."

"Sit down, doctor." Alain was still lying in bed. The return to life after a deep sleep gave him a desolate look that made the doctor's goatee twitch.

"You spent the night outside; no matter, unless you've done something stupid."

"No, I didn't take anything; I was with someone."

"Ah, very good." The doctor seemed delighted. He was counting on women to distract Alain from drugs. But for that to happen, Alain would have to like women pretty well, and one of the ones he knew would have to have certain ideas about virility. But Alain raised his eyebrows in a way that put an end to La Barbinais' delight.

"I'm going to start up again."

"Don't do that."

"What else do you want me to do?"

"Still no letter from America?"

"I won't get one."

"Oh yes you will. Be patient."

"I haven't got much patience left, I've done nothing but wait all my life."

"Wait for what?"

"I don't know."

"But today you know very well what you're waiting for. You say that you love your wife and that she loves you. When she learns that you're trying to break the habit, surely she'll want to help."

"She left me because she understood that I'd never break free."

"But you're breaking free right now."

"You know very well that I'm not."

"It seems to me that you're doing much better."

"That won't last. Beginning tonight . . .

Top left: Photograph of Pierre Drieu La Rochelle. Collection Madame Jean Drieu La Rochelle.
Right: Writing implements of Pierre Drieu La Rochelle. Collection Madame Jean Drieu la Rochelle.
Opposite: Page of the autograph manuscript of *Le Feu Follet* (*Will-o'-the-Wisp*). Collection Madame Jean Drieu La Rochelle.

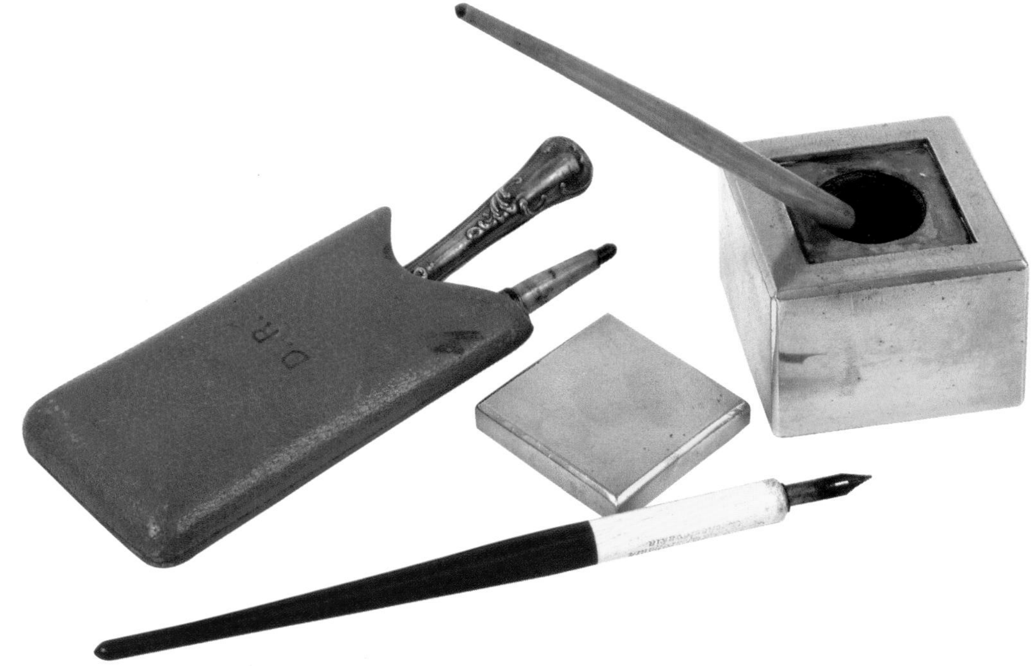

3

1

Vers cinq heures, Alain se réveilla : on frappait à sa porte. C'était le docteur de la Barbinais.

- Je vous réveille, mon cher ami, je le regrette, car vous avez besoin de vous reposer.

- Asseyez-vous, docteur.

Alain resta étendu sur son lit. Le retour à la vie, après ce lourd sommeil, mettait sur son visage une désolation qui fit frémir la barbiche du docteur.

- Vous avez passé la nuit dehors, ce n'est rien, si vous n'avez pas fait de bêtises.

- Non, je n'en ai pas pris. J'étais avec quelqu'un...

- Ah, très bien.

Le docteur parut enchanté. Il comptait sur les femmes pour distraire Alain de la drogue. Mais pour cela il aurait fallu qu'Alain aimât beaucoup les femmes et que l'une d'entre ~~elles~~ celles qu'il connaissait au moins eût des idées sur la virilité. Mais Alain fronça les sourcils de telle sorte que l'enchantement de la Barbinais disparut.

- ~~Mais~~ Je vais en reprendre.

- Mais non, voyons.

- Qu'est-ce que vous voulez que je fasse d'autre ?

- Pas encore de lettre d'Amérique ?

- Je n'en recevrai pas.

- Mais si, vous allez en recevoir. Soyez patient.

- Je ne suis guère patient, bien que je n'aie fait qu'attendre toute ma vie.

- Attendre quoi ?

- Je ne sais pas.

- Mais aujourd'hui, vous savez très bien ce que vous attendez. Vous avouez que vous aimiez votre femme et qu'elle vous aime. Quand elle va savoir que vous faites un effort pour sortir de vos habitudes, elle va sûrement venir à votre aide.

X

- Elle m'a quitté parce qu'elle a compris que je ne pouvais pas sortir de la drogue.

- Mais vous en sortez en ce moment.

- Vous savez bien que non.

- Je constate que vous êtes beaucoup mieux.

- Cela ne durera pas. Dès ce soir...

The Vipers' Tangle

François Mauriac, 1932

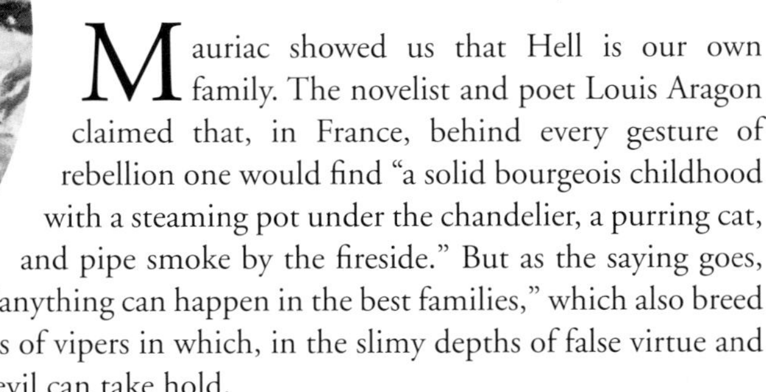

Mauriac showed us that Hell is our own family. The novelist and poet Louis Aragon claimed that, in France, behind every gesture of rebellion one would find "a solid bourgeois childhood with a steaming pot under the chandelier, a purring cat, and pipe smoke by the fireside." But as the saying goes, "anything can happen in the best families," which also breed knots of vipers in which, in the slimy depths of false virtue and deception, evil can take hold.

Initially, Mauriac was a literary darling who held forth the promise of a long and brilliant career. He brought to a state of unprecedented perfection the recipe for arsenic-in-the-stew, a dish best served at Sunday dinner after mass, and ideally suited to impatient heirs, and to wives wishing to get rid of troublesome husbands. In a pot, soak two or three generations' worth of family secrets and resentments, season with the spice of latent hatred, add a pinch of scandal, cover, and let simmer a long, long time. In the silence of kitchens where, to all appearances, the pots and pans are impeccably clean, listen to the song of this slow simmer: an infernal boiler that envelopes characters who, while they might seem like exemplary citizens of Bordeaux, are in fact worthy of Dante's *Inferno*.

Such is the mean music of boredom and cruelty spun by Mauriac's prose. He has few peers when it comes to evoking respectable people who, with their seemingly spotless hands, hide mortal weapons in piles of suspiciously clean laundry, hoping to obliterate the stench of their crimes with lavender.

Pierre-Emmanuel Prouvost d'Agostino

I

You will be astonished to discover this letter in my safety deposit box in Westminster Bank, on top of a packet of stock certificates. It would have been simpler to entrust it to a notary, with instructions that he give it to you in the event of my death, or to leave it in my desk drawer. The one that my children will force open first, while my body is still warm. But I've been rewriting this letter in my head for years, and always, in my sleepless nights, I have imagined its being removed from the metal coffer—a coffer otherwise empty, containing nothing but this text of vengeance cooked up over almost half a century. Don't worry. Doubtless you've already seen for yourself: "The certificates are there." I can almost hear your voice in the vestibule, after returning from the bank, saying to the children through your veil: "The certificates are there." But they very nearly weren't, and I had planned things carefully: if I had wished it, today you would have nothing except the house and some land worth almost exactly as much as the dowry. Luckily for you, I outlived my hatred. For a long time I thought my hatred was the thing about me that was most alive. And now it's all gone, and the old man that I've become finds it difficult to imagine the furious man, the sick fellow whose doctors had abandoned all hope and who, instead of spending his nights plotting vengeance—the time bomb had already been set with a meticulous care that made me proud—was trying to find some way to enjoy it. Yes, I would have liked to live long enough to see your face when you came back from the bank. The problem was, how could I get you to open the box at just the right moment, just in time for me to have the final, frightful joy of hearing your desperate queries: "Where are the certificates?" It seemed to me that even the most horrible pain would be unable to destroy this [pleasure.]

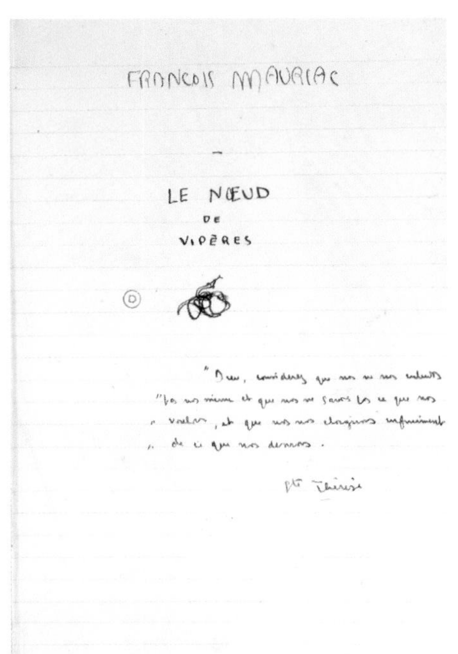
FRANCOIS MAURIAC

LE NŒUD
DE
VIPÈRES

Top left: Jacques-Émile Blanche, *Study for a Portrait of François Mauriac* (detail). Rouen Musée des Beaux-Arts. *Right:* Gustave Moreau, *Studies of Snakes (after Johann Wagler, "Descriptiones et Icones Amphibiorum")* for "Hercules and the Lernaean Hydra." Paris, Musée Gustave Moreau. *Left and opposite:* Autograph manuscript of *Le Noeud de Vipères* (*The Vipers' Tangle*): title page and first text page. Paris, Bibliothèque Littéraire Jacques-Doucet.

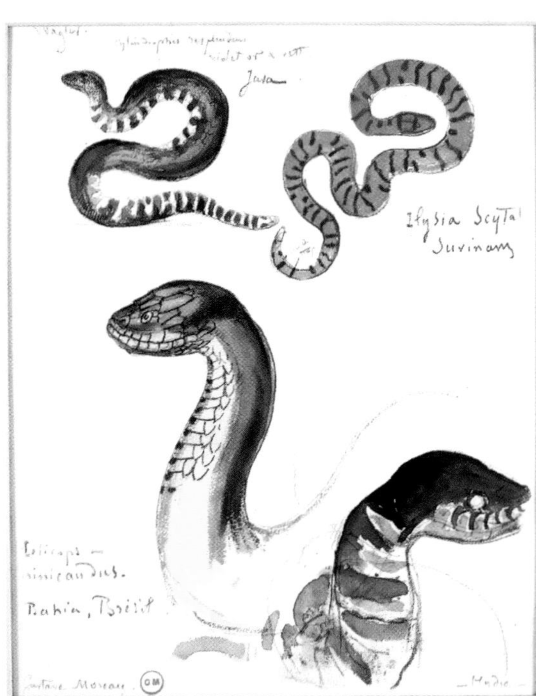

16 fév 31

I

Tu seras étonnée de découvrir cette lettre dans mon coffre de la Westminster Bank, sur un paquet de titres. Il aurait été plus simple de la confier au notaire qui te l'eût remise après ma mort ou bien de la ranger dans le tiroir de mon bureau — le premier que les enfants forceront avant que j'aie commencé d'être froid. Mais c'est que pendant des années j'ai refait en esprit cette lettre et des [illegible] durant mes insomnies, [illegible] sur le métal du coffre — d'un coffre vide, et ne contenant rien d'autre que cette vengeance durant [illegible] un demi-siècle, cuisinée. Rassure-toi. Tu es d'ailleurs déjà rassurée : « les titres y sont » Il me semble entendre de quel ton dès le [illegible] au retour de la banque, tu diras aux enfants à travers ton crêpe : « les titres y sont. » Il s'en est fallu de peu qu'ils n'y fussent pas et j'avais eu les mesures : si j'avais voulu vous seriez aujourd'hui dépouillés de tout sauf de la maison et des terres que représentent la dot quelques francs très [illegible], Vous avez la chance que j'aie survécu à ma haine. J'ai cru longtemps que ma haine était ce qu'il y avait en moi de plus vivant. Mais il est vrai qu'elle n'est pas la même aujourd'hui et [illegible] la veillait que [illegible] le [illegible] [illegible] le représenter l'homme furieux qui durant des nuits ne [illegible] ma vengeance — elle était [illegible] avec une infection [illegible] — cette haine relativement [illegible] [illegible] avec une [illegible] dont j'étais fier — mais [illegible] de Louis en [illegible]. Oui, j'aurais voulu voir [illegible] votre tête à tous au retour de la banque. [illegible] Le problème consistait à ne pas te donner trop tôt la [illegible] pour ouvrir le coffre, à te la donner juste assez tard pour que j'aie [illegible] de t'entendre [illegible] : « Où sont les titres ? » Il me semblait que la plus atroce agonie ne m'eût gâté la [illegible]

Man's Fate

André Malraux, 1933

In the somewhat stay-at-home French literary crowd, the peripatetic Malraux stands very much apart. At age twenty he left for Indochina, where he saw things that made him a staunch anti-colonialist. In 1924, at age thirty-three, he was in Moscow with other writers to combat the rise of fascism. Two years later, he created the "España" squadron and fought alongside Spanish republicans. Enlisted in the tank corps and taken prisoner at the beginning of World War II, he joined the Resistance rather at the last minute. There is no denying Malraux's penchant for self-dramatization, but there has never been any question about his energy and his courage.

With Malraux, action is never a mere *diversion*, a means whereby individuals manage to avoid confronting their mortality. His main characters are constantly interrogating themselves about the meaning of their actions and of history, or, more precisely, about the possibility of their bestowing meaning on something that is essentially meaningless. The man of action resembles the artist insofar as he reveals himself to be greater than what weighs him down. Political leaders, like creative figures, try to make sure that their lives are not insignificant It is no accident that Malraux spent his last years writing books about de Gaulle and Picasso.

La Condition Humaine (translated as *Man's Fate*) is a meditation on both the social condition (exploiter or exploited) and the metaphysical condition (what is a life?). In prose that is dense and sometimes overwrought, the novel explores the ways in which various characters deal with difficult circumstances that present them with hard choices. Everyone responds differently. Kyo gambles on the revolution; Tchen tries to forget his humiliation, and that of his family, through terrorism; Gisors chooses drugs, Ferral the will to power.

Man's Fate is at the heart of Malraux's work, a kind of core in which all of it gestated and from which all of it issued. Some critics have never forgiven him for his unconditional support of de Gaulle. Nonetheless, this novel remains a key work in the French literature of the first half of the twentieth century.

Paul Desalmand

[March 21, 1927
12:30 P.M.]

Should Tchen try to lift the mosquito net, or should he strike through it? Wouldn't the sound of the ripping muslin wake the sleeping man? The knife would move as quickly as any noise. Doubtless this hesitation was only his flesh resisting the murderous gesture that agitated his insides like a sob. He knew he was resolved, but at that moment all he could think about, in a fascinated stupor, was the pile of white muslin that fell from the ceiling over a body that seemed mere shadow, and from which emerged only an inclined foot, asleep but alive—human flesh. The only light came from the neighboring building: a large, pale rectangle of electricity traversed by the bars of the window; one of their shadows fell just above the foot as if to accentuate its volume and life. Four or five car horns honked at once. Discovered? To fight, to fight against enemies capable of defending themselves, enemies who were awake!

The racket died down; some sort of traffic jam (there were still traffic jams out there, in the world of men . . .). He again found himself facing the limp patch of muslin and the rectangle of light, motionless in a night in which time had ceased to exist.

He repeated to himself that this man had to die. Mechanically, for he knew that he would kill him. Captured or not, executed or not, it scarcely mattered. Nothing existed but this foot, this man against whom he had to strike without letting him defend himself—for if he defended himself, he would cry out.

His eyes blinking, Tchen discovered within himself, to the point of nausea, not the combatant he expected to find but a sacrificer. And not only to his chosen gods: below his sacrifice to the revolution there swarmed a world of dark depths compared with which this night of crushing anguish seemed like clarity. "To assassinate is not merely to kill . . ."

Top left: André Malraux in April 1945, when he was commander of the Alsace-Lorraine brigade.
Below and opposite: Pages from the autograph manuscript of *La Condition Humaine* (*Man's Fate*). Paris, Bibliothèque Nationale de France.

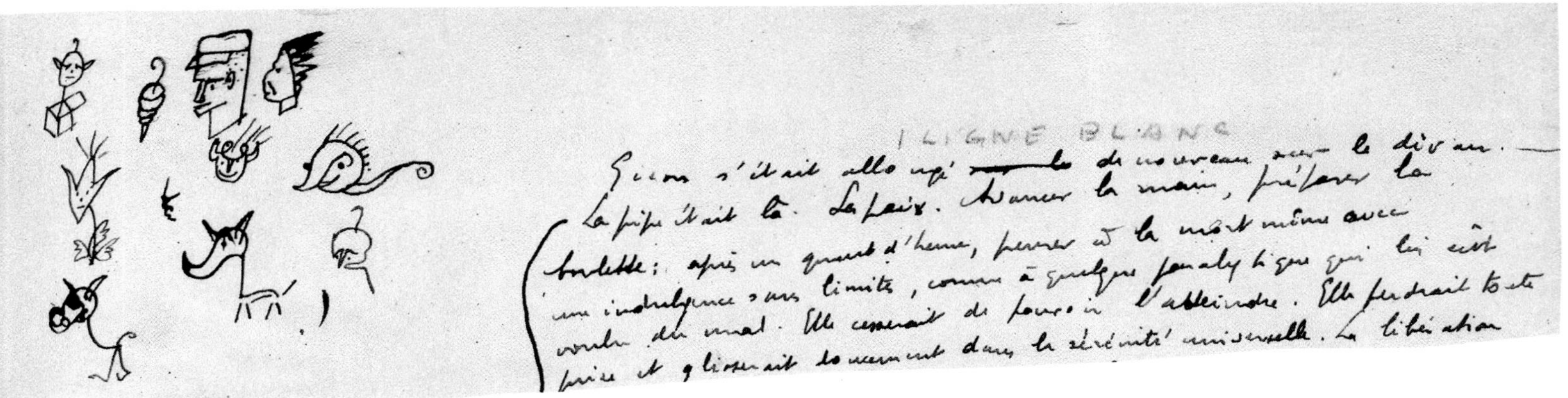

I.

Tchen Tenterait-il de ~~s~~lever la moustiquaire, ou frapperait-il au travers? ~~Il craignait~~ Le bruit de la mousseline déchirée n'éveillerait-il pas le dormeur? ~~Abandon~~ Le couteau irait aussi vite que tout bruit. Cette hésitation dégoûtante n'était sans doute que la défense de sa chair contre le geste meurtrier qui bougeait en lui comme un sanglot. ~~Dégoûtante~~? Il connaissait sa fermeté, mais n'était capable, en cet instant, que d'y songer avec hébétude, fasciné par ce tas de mousseline blanche qui tombait du plafond sur un corps moins visible qu'une ombre, et d'où sortait seulement ~~cette~~ ce pied ~~main grasse~~ à ~~demi~~ incliné ~~fléchie~~ par le sommeil, vivant quand même — de la chair d'homme. ~~dans la lumière que l'immeuble d'en face projetait~~ La seule lumière venait de l'immeuble voisin, ~~pâle~~ : un grand rectangle d'électricité pâle coupé par les barreaux de la fenêtre, dont l'un rayait ~~coupait~~ le lit juste au-dessous du pied comme pour en accentuer le volume et la vie. Quatre ou cinq klaxons grincèrent à la fois ~~Wang Tchong s'efforce de ne pas respirer~~. Découvert? Combattre,

The Green Mare

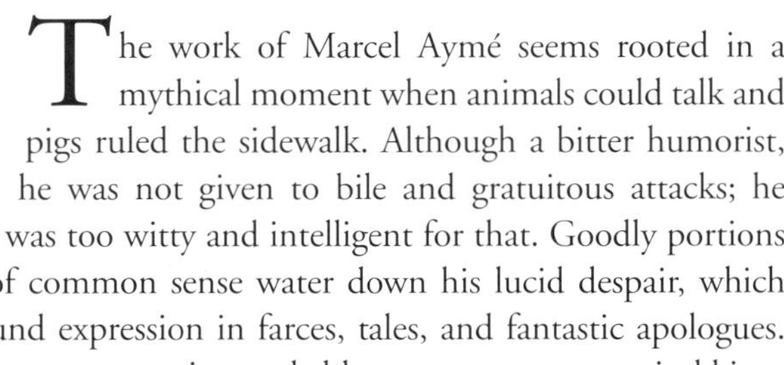

Marcel Aymé, 1933

The work of Marcel Aymé seems rooted in a mythical moment when animals could talk and pigs ruled the sidewalk. Although a bitter humorist, he was not given to bile and gratuitous attacks; he was too witty and intelligent for that. Goodly portions of common sense water down his lucid despair, which found expression in farces, tales, and fantastic apologues. His pen was a magic wand able to summon up magical kingdoms, realms where animals and young girls flourish, love one another, and sing in dream landscapes. As sorcerers go, Aymé could be scoffing, foiling ill intentions and punishing bad subjects, dressing down, with scathing humor, anyone guilty of disgraceful behavior, pretension, or bad faith. He is by turns indulgent, bemused, and pitiless with his creatures.

In *La Jument Verte* (*The Green Mare*), which made him famous in 1933, the ease with which he combines grittiness with refinement, and dreadful events with comedy that chills your spine are notable. Aymé is a La Fontaine with a difference: the seventeenth-century writer gave animals human vices, but Aymé describes men who have assumed the faces of animals. For he saw how his contemporaries had swapped their human features for short-lived and idiotic satisfactions, becoming hyenas or asses to guarantee their intellectual comfort. An excellent vintage from the fountain of youth, the work of Marcel Aymé tastes like new wine; although a bit astringent at first sip, it has not yet released its full bouquet.

Pierre-Emmanuel Prouvost d'Agostino

Top left: Marcel Aymé in 1933. Collection Madame Françoise Arnaud.
Right: Green glass mare that Marcel Aymé kept on his desk until his death. Collection Madame Françoise Arnaud.
Opposite: First page, autograph manuscript of *La Jument Verte* (*The Geen Mare*). Collection Madame Colette Magne and Madame Françoise Arnaud.

I

One day, in the village of Claquebue, there came into the world a mare who was green. Not the washed-out green of decrepit, white-haired old hags, but a pretty jade green. Upon seeing the creature appear, Jules Hardouin could scarcely believe his eyes, nor the eyes of his wife. "It's not possible," he said. "How could I be so lucky?"

A farmer and horse trader, Hardouin had never been rewarded for being wily, untruthful, and money-grabbing. His cows died by twos, his pigs by sixes, and his seeds sprouted in their sacks. He was scarcely luckier with his children: in order to keep three, he had to have six. But children, they were less of a bother. He had a good cry the day of their burial, wrung out his handkerchief when he got home, and hung it on the line to dry. In the course of the year, as a result of his pouncing on his wife, he always managed to make another. That was the convenient thing about children, and where they were concerned, he didn't complain too much. He had three boys who were very much alive and three daughters in the cemetery, which suited him pretty well. A green mare was a great novelty, there being no known precedent. The thing seemed remarkable, for in Claquebue almost nothing ever happened. There was still talk of how Maloret deflowered his daughters, but after a hundred years the story had lost interest; the Malorets had always used their daughters thus; people were used to it. From time to time, the republicans, a half-dozen in all, took advantage of a moonless night to sing the Carmagnole below the priest's windows and bellow "down with the Empire." Otherwise, nothing ever happened. Then people became bored. And as time didn't pass, the old didn't die. There were twenty-eight centenarians in the community, without counting those aged between seventy and a hundred, who made up half the population. A few had been cut down, but such executions were of necessity private initiatives, and the village, sleepy, crippled, ossified, was as sad as Sunday in paradise.

The news escaped the stable, zigzagged between the woods and the river, made the circuit of Claquebue three or four times, and began to make the rounds of the square in front of the town hall. Immediately, everyone headed for the house of Jules Hardouin, some running or galloping, others limping or hobbling. Everyone was dying to get there first, and the old men, scarcely more reasonable than the women, added their quivering murmurs to the immense clamor that filled the countryside:

"Something's happening! Something's happening!"

Marcel Aymé

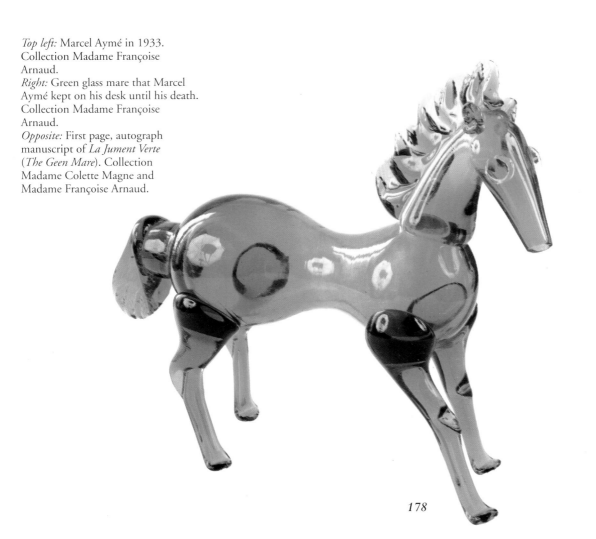

I

Au village de Claquebue naquit un jour une jument verte, non pas de ce vert pisseux qui accompagne la décrépitude chez les carnes de poil blanc, mais d'un joli vert jade. En voyant apparaître la bête, Jules Haudouin n'en croyait ni ses yeux, ni les yeux de sa femme. – Ça n'est pas possible, disait-il, j'aurais trop de chance.

Cultivateur et maquignon, Haudouin n'avait jamais été récompensé d'être rusé, menteur et grippe-sous. Ses vaches crevaient par deux à la fois, ses cochons par six, et son grain germait dans les sacs. Il était à peine plus heureux avec ses enfants et, pour en garder trois, il avait fallu en faire six. Mais les enfants, c'était moins gênant. Il pleurait un bon coup le jour de l'enterrement, tordait son mouchoir en rentrant et le mettait sécher sur le fil. Dans le courant de l'année, à force de sauter sa femme, il arrivait toujours bien à lui en faire un autre. C'est ce qu'il y a de commode dans la question des enfants, et de ce côté-là, Haudouin ne se plaignait pas trop. Il avait trois garçons bien vifs et trois filles au cimetière, à peu près ce qu'il fallait.

C'était une grande nouveauté qu'une jument verte et qui n'avait point de précédent connu. La chose parut remarquable car à Claquebue, il n'arrivait jamais rien. On se racontait que Maloret dépucelait ses filles, mais l'histoire n'intéressait plus, depuis cent ans qu'elle courait; les Malorets en avaient toujours usé ainsi avec leurs filles; on y était habitué. De temps à autre, les républicains, une demi-douzaine en tout, profitaient d'une nuit sans lune pour aller chanter la Carmagnole sous les fenêtres du curé et beugler "à bas l'Empire." À part cela, il ne se passait rien. Alors, on s'ennuyait. Et comme le temps ne passait pas, les vieillards ne mouraient pas. Il y avait vingt-huit centenaires dans la commune, sans compter les vieux d'entre soixante-dix et cent ans, qui formaient la moitié de la population. On en avait bien abattu quelques-uns, mais de telles exécutions ne pouvaient être que le fait d'initiatives privées, et le village, sommeillant, perclus, ossifié, était triste comme un dimanche au paradis.

La nouvelle s'échappa de l'écurie, zigzagua entre les bois et la rivière, fit trois fois le tour de Claquebue, et se mit à tourner en rond sur la place de la mairie. Aussitôt, tout le monde se porta vers la maison de Jules Haudouin, les uns courant ou galopant, les autres clopinant ou béquillant. On se mordait aux jarrets pour arriver des premiers, et les vieillards à peine plus raisonnables que les femmes, mêlaient leurs chevrotements à l'immense clameur qui emplissait la campagne:

– Il arrive quelque chose ! il arrive quelque chose !

Dans la cour du maquignon, le tumulte fut à son comble, car les habitants de Claquebue avaient déjà retrouvé la hargne des temps anciens. Les plus pieux sollicitaient le curé d'exorciser la jument verte, et les six républicains de la commune lui criaient: "à bas l'Empire!" dans le nez, sans se cacher. Il y eut un commencement de bagarre, le maire reçut un coup de pied dans les reins qui lui fit monter un discours à la gorge. Les jeunes femmes se plaignaient d'être pincées, les vieilles de n'être pas pincées, et les gamins hurlaient sous les gifles. Enfin, Jules Haudouin parut sur le seuil de l'écurie. Hilare, les mains sanglantes, il confirma:

– Elle est verte comme une pomme !

Joy of Man's Desiring

Jean Giono, 1935

The work of Jean Giono does not fall into two periods; it constitutes a whole. In *Que Ma Joie Demeure* (*Joy of Man's Desiring*), as in *Un Roi Sans Divertissement* (*A King without Diversions*), it remains focused on the confrontation between man and the world around him, its unifying thread being the veritable dialectic of the "Gionian" hero. For Giono, there are two kinds of "kings" who confront the great enigma of the universe and the depths of human anguish. Those of the first kind experience a rift, an absurd and definitive incoherence, in human condition; crucified by ennui and pierced by mortality, they are torn between the infinitely great and the infinitely petty. "Man is minuscule. He forgets this. Even to describe him as a thinking reed is too much."[1] And these "kings" rebel, especially when winter snows or the crushing summer sun deprive them of the natural "diversions" that are perfumes, colors, and sounds, of the "extraordinary roar of colors and smells" evoked in *Noé*. At such moments, the only "habitable" place for them, the only one "where one can imagine a world in peacock colors, is the bed." So they resolve to drive away "that most horrible of wolves . . . boredom" (*Le Déseurteur*). They transform themselves into sacrificers and, like Monsieur V in *A King without Diversions*, shed the blood of others. The other "kings," by contrast, strive to transcend the experiential rift in hopes of attaining a supreme harmony. Unlike Langlois in *A King without Diversions*, they do not need to smoke a cartridge of dynamite to take the true measure of the universe. They learn that the universe is within as well as around them, that they are links in a great chain of universal coherence. They become "protectors" and "smugglers" of souls, disseminators of joy and wisdom; they save others, and if a sacrifice to the gods is called for, they calmly elect themselves for the honor, like Bobi the acrobat in *Joy of Man's Desiring*. "Writing almost always gives me a satisfying angle on things. A book provides me with answers to my anguish," wrote Giono in 1965, five years before his death.

Jean-Pierre Guéno

1. An allusion to a remark by Blaise Pascal.

Rise up and fight with a resolute heart. Indifferent to pleasure and pain, to gain and loss, to victory and defeat, fight with all your might.

Krishna

Life is worth suffering for.

I

It was an extraordinary night. There had been wind, but it had stopped, and the stars sparkled like grass. They were in clusters with golden roots. There were some that resembled trapped animals with brilliant squirts of blood around them.

Jourdan couldn't sleep. He tossed and turned. "The sky is so clear, it's so beautiful," he said. He had never seen that.

The sky trembled like metal. You couldn't say why, almost everything was motionless. It wasn't the wind. It was just the sky descending to touch the earth, scrape the plains, strike the mountains, and make the corridors of the woods resound. Afterwards, it reascended to the highest of heights.

Jourdan tried to wake his wife. He had an idea. "That made you a little giddy. The drum of the sky, and then the color of the night . . ."

Jean Giono

Top left: Photograph of Jean Giono by Gisèle Freund, 1965. Avignon, Bibliothèque Municipale Classée.
Below and opposite: First pages of the autograph manuscript of *Que Ma Joie Demeure* (*Joy of Man's Desiring*). Avignon, Bibliothèque Municipale Classée.

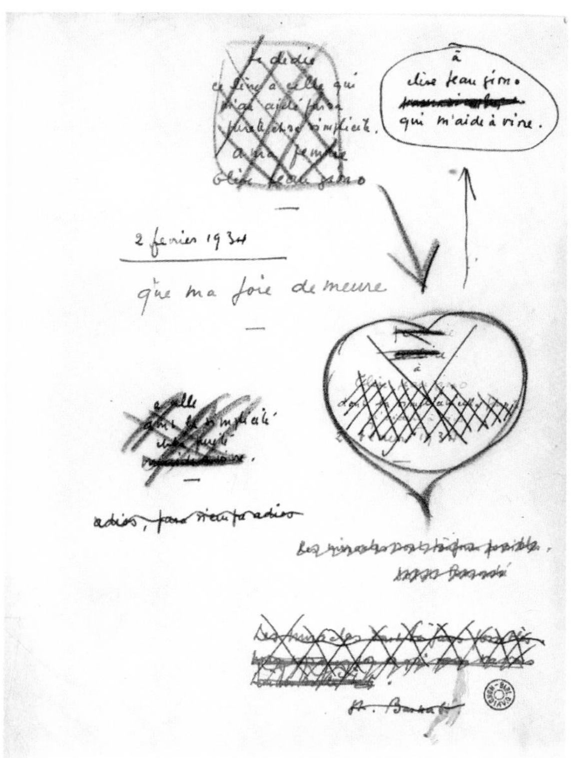

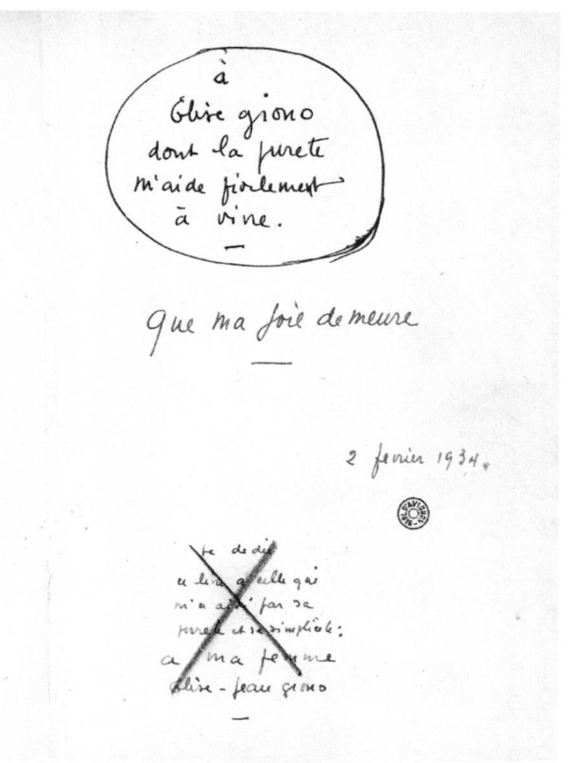

1

Lève-toi, et combats d'un cœur résolu. Indifférent au plaisir et à la douleur, au gain et à la perte, à la victoire et à la défaite, combats de toutes tes forces

Krishna.

La vie vaut de souffrir.

—

I

C'était une nuit extraordinaire. Il y avait eu du vent, il avait cessé, et les étoiles avaient éclaté comme de l'herbe. Elles étaient en touffe avec ses racines d'or, ~~épanouies, enfoncées dans les ténèbres et qui soulevaient des mottes luisantes de nuit~~. Il y en avait qui étaient comme des bêtes écrasées avec du sang de lumière giclé tout autour.

Jourdan ne pouvait pas dormir. Il se tournait, il se retournait.

— Il fait un clair de toute beauté, se disait-il.

Il n'avait jamais vu ça.

Le ciel tremblait comme un ciel de métal. On ne savait pas de quoi, puisque tout était immobile, même le plus petit pompon ~~de frêne~~ d'osier. Ça n'était pas le vent. C'était tout simplement le ciel qui descendait jusqu'à toucher la terre, racler les plaines, palper les montagnes et faire sonner les cordons des forêts. Après, il remontait au fond des hauteurs.

Jourdan essaya de réveiller sa femme. Il avait une idée. Ça vous saoulait un tout petit peu. Ce tambour du ciel et puis cette couleur de la nuit.

The Elegant Districts

Louis Aragon, 1936

The writers who allied themselves with Surrealism, and especially those who, like André Breton and Aragon, associated with the movement from the start, never made a mystery of their utter contempt for the novel, in their eyes an outdated, bourgeois genre. Nonetheless, with superb indifference to the contradiction—but then, they held paradox to be a form of genius—they eventually succumbed to its charms (sometimes surreptitiously, like Breton with *Nadja*), realizing that it could serve their purposes.

It is to this very forgivable about-face that we owe a considerable portion of Aragon's production: ten novels that could eclipse his poetry, which can be facile, even dutiful. It might be the judgment of history that Aragon, despite his occasionally inspired poems, his eclectic corpus of essays, his conscientious historical writing, and his sectarian militancy, was preeminently a great novelist, which is to say a writer capable of drawing on reality to create dreams, and vice versa.

Admittedly, his relationship to the novel remains ambiguous, even conflicted, as evidenced by a text from his Dada period, *Anicet ou le Panorama, Novel* (*Anicet or the Panorama, Novel*), which incorporates the name of the genre in the title the better to subvert it by its content, and by *Blanche ou l'Oubli* (*Blanche or Oblivion*), a late work that gives us access to the mysterious laboratory of the creative imagination.

As does the pseudo-realist interlude of *Le Monde Réel* (*The Real World*), a five-novel cycle of which *Les Beaux Quartiers* (*The Elegant Districts*) is the second. Despite its title, this saga, more than 4,000 pages long and spanning more than half a century, plunges us into dream, juxtaposing love songs, political fables, hymns to happiness, and utopian exaltation. Doubtless we should construe this work as an illustration of the oxymoronic title of another of Aragon's books: *Le Mentir-Vrai* (*True Lies*). One sentence sums up the project of the novel: "The extraordinary thing about the novel is that, to understand objective reality, it invents." Literature will always be a delicious mystification.

Yves Stalloni

In a small French town, a river dies of heat below a boulevard where, in the evening men play boules, and the jack waltzes to the skillful blows of a conscript in whose hat, folded into a triangle, is one of those illustrated diplomas sold at the door of the mayoralty of brown and authoritarian fairground types.

In a small French town presided over by a pot-bellied sovereign who collects baking trays, blackened and from all centuries, with his wife and three daughters, angelic beauties, it was said, mascots of the paternal chocolate factory, whose workers never failed, when a new snack bar or candy in a modern shape was introduced, to present these young ladies with vigorous mountain of wild flowers, a way of associating them with their hopes for the destiny of a product issuing from their own rough hands for which the walls of the capital were already covered with posters of little schoolgirls wearing woolen socks pulled up high under their very short smocks . . . In a small French town, the blue soap of the hot clothes boiler at the back of a courtyard where a young girl is crying and a middle-aged man is laughing, his moustache strong like his breath, full of garlic, onions, and the radical politics of the better neighborhoods.

A rivulet snaked between the pebble-round paving stones of the narrow, descending street where the old sign of a blacksmith screeched in the summer wind because it felt ill at ease on the slope of the city, full of deserted houses, reminders of the grandeur of an earlier time when the kings of France, once during their reigns, spent an entire day, with their lords and officers of the guard, in the old city where the sun finds it difficult to slip between the roofs toward the bumpy surface of the streets.

But toward the train station, on the plain, was an array of garages where traveling businessmen had just parked their cars, and restaurants full of dusty men who, looking at their plates, hastily swallowed greasy soup and nostalgic stews.

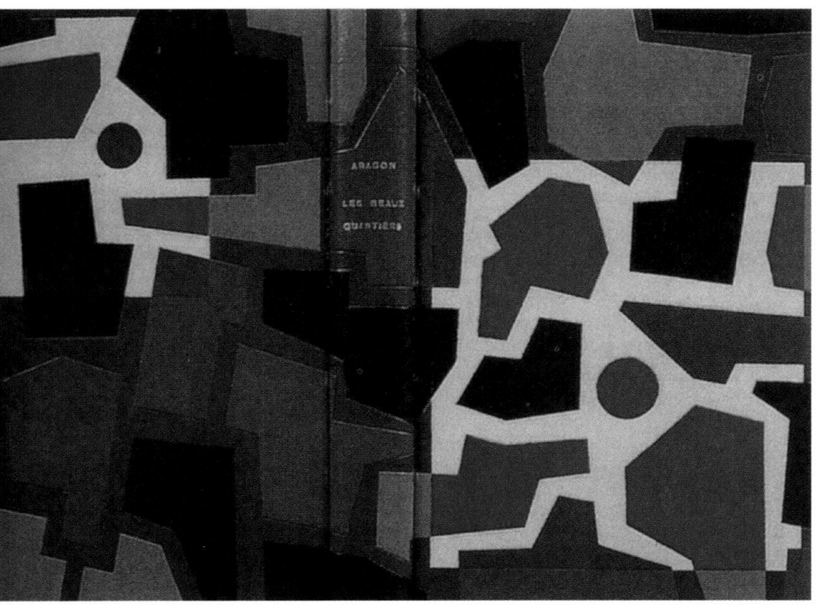

Top left: Photograph of Louis Aragon by Gisèle Freund, 1939.
Left: Binding for *Les Beaux Quartiers* (*The Elegant Districts*) made by Georges Leroux in 1967.
Right: Advertisement for a 1983 French television movie of *Les Beaux Quartiers*.
Opposite: Page from the autograph manuscript of *Les Beaux Quartiers*. Paris, Bibliothèque Nationale de France.

1

I

Dans une petite ville française, une rivière serpente de chaud ~~[illegible]~~ au dessous d'un boulevard, où vers le soir des hommes jouent aux boules, et le cochonnet valse aux coups habiles d'un conscrit ~~qui~~ portant à sa casquette le diplôme illustré, plié en triangle, que vendaient à la porte de la mairie des forains bruns et autoritaires.

Dans une petite ville française où règne un souverain ventru, qui fait collection de plaques de foyer, noires et vernies de tous les siècles, avec sa femme et ses trois ~~[illegible]~~ filles, des anges de beauté dit-on, mascottes de la fabrique de chocolat paternelle, dont les ouvriers ne manquent jamais lors de la sortie d'une nouvelle tablette-régal ou d'un ~~nouveau~~ goûter-au-lait d'une forme moderne de venir offrir à ces demoiselles les fleurs vigoureuses de la montagne, histoire de les associer ~~[illegible]~~ à l'espoir qu'ils fondent en la destinée d'un produit sorti de leurs mains frustes pour lequel déjà les murs de la capitale se couvrent de petites écolières aux ~~[illegible]~~ bien tirés sous la serrant très court... dans une petite ville française, le savon bleu de la lessive bouillonne au fond d'une cour où pleure une jeune femme et rit un homme entre deux âges, à la moustache forte comme son haleine, aliacée, et pleine de la politique radicale des hauts quartiers.

Un petit ruisseau serpente entre les pavés ronds comme des galets qui descendent la rue étroite où crie au vent d'été l'enseigne ancienne d'un maréchal-ferrant. Il est parti pour le Mexique, le maréchal-ferrant, parce qu'il se sentait mal à son aise sur le coteau de la cité, plein de demeures désertées, souvenirs des grandeurs de jadis, quand les rois de France ~~[illegible]~~ une fois dans leur règne s'arrêtaient pour tout un jour avec les seigneurs et les officiers de la garde dans la ville vieille où le soleil trouve difficilement à se glisser entre les toits vers le sol boueux des rues.

Mais vers la garde, dans la plaine, s'échelonnent les ~~pompes~~ garages ~~[illegible]~~ arrivent les voitures des voyageurs de commerce, et des restaurants pleins d'hommes poussiéreux, qui regardent avalant à la hâte une soupe grasse et des ragoûts nostalgiques

Diary of a Country Priest

Georges Bernanos, 1936

Like Bernanos's country priest, the damned characters in his work are the twentieth-century wanderers foreseen by Nietzsche, and of whom he wrote despairingly: "Woe unto him who harbors wildernesses!" The inhabitants of faceless lands, lost below skies deprived of God, in a world without transcendence, have nothing to gnaw on but the dry bones of ideology. Shackled by their freedom, they know not what to do, save to occasionally choose some form of slavery. A Catholic armed with the sword of an archangel or a royal scepter, the great lord Bernanos evokes, in the realm of letters, the name of old knighthoods devoted to redressing wrongs. He made allowances for no one and for nothing, not even the Church of his day. His straight path led to exposing imposture, skewering infamy, and wringing complacency, to making them disgorge their black bile of criminal lies. In an era more hospitable to grandeur, this lyrical writer would have been less militant; he claimed he wrote novels "because that was the only thing he knew how to do." Balzac could have said the same thing. These days, Bernanos's polemical thrusts seems more apposite than ever; we comprehend the prescience of prophets too late. "Idiots!" Bernanos would have lashed out. For prophets are more than lucid charlatans. From their exalted viewpoints, they can discern the seeds of apocalypses to come. They warn man against Satan's sun, an illusion of happiness that glistens temptingly in the dark.

Pierre-Emmanuel Prouvost d'Agostino

My parish is a parish like any other. All parishes are the same—those of today, of course. Yesterday I said to the priest from Norenfontes: "Good and evil ought to balance here, but the center of gravity is low, very low. Or if you prefer, they are superimposed one over the other without mixing, like two liquids of different density." He laughed heartily. He's a good priest, very kind, very paternal, and he's regarded in the archbishop's circle as a freethinker, as a bit dangerous. His jokes are the delight of his parishioners, and he reinforces them with a look that he means to be vivacious but that I find basically so tired, so weary, that it makes me want to cry.

My parish is consumed by boredom, that's the word. Like so many other parishes! Boredom consumes them right before our eyes and we can do nothing about it. Perhaps one day the contagion will infect us, we will discover this cancer within ourselves. One can live quite a long time like that.

This idea came to me yesterday on the road. One of those fine rains was falling that you swallow by the lungful, that descends down to your gut. From the Saint-Vaast hill, the village appeared to me suddenly, wizened and miserable under the hideous November sky. Water streamed from all parts, and it seemed spread out there, in the rustling grass, like some poor exhausted animal. It's so small, a village! And this village was my parish. It was my parish, and I watched it sink sadly into the night and disappear. . . . A few more moments and it would be invisible. Never had I felt its solitude, and my own, so cruelly. I thought about the animals that I could hear coughing in the fog, and that the little herdsman, returning from school, his satchel under his arm, would soon bring through the drenched pastures toward the warm, fragrant stable. . . . And the village, too, seemed to be waiting—without much hope—after so many nights spent in the mud, for a master it could follow towards some unlikely, some unimaginable refuge.

Top left: Georges Bernanos in 1929. *Right:* Watercolor by Maxime Rebière. *Opposite.* Page from the autograph manuscript (fine copy for the printer) of *Journal d'un Curé de Campagne* (*Diary of a Country Priest*). Paris, Bibliothèque Nationale de France.

Ma paroisse est une paroisse comme les autres. Toutes les paroisses se ressemblent. Les paroisses d'aujourd'hui, naturellement. Je le disais hier à M. le curé de Norenfontes: le bien et le mal doivent s'y faire équilibre, seulement le centre de gravité est placé bas, très bas. Ou, si vous aimez mieux, l'un et l'autre s'y superposent sans se mêler, comme deux liquides de densité différente. M. le Curé m'a ri au nez. C'est un bon prêtre, très bienveillant, très paternel et qui passe même à l'archevêché pour un esprit fort, un peu dangereux. Ses boutades font la joie des presbytères, et il les appuie d'un regard qu'il voudrait vif et que je trouve au fond si usé, si las, qu'il me donne envie de pleurer.

Ma paroisse est dévorée par l'ennui, voilà le mot. Comme tant d'autres paroisses! L'ennui les dévore sous nos yeux et nous n'y pouvons rien. Quelque jour peut-être la contagion nous gagnera, nous découvrirons en nous ce cancer. On peut vivre très longtemps avec ça.

Factory Life

Simone Weill, ca. 1937

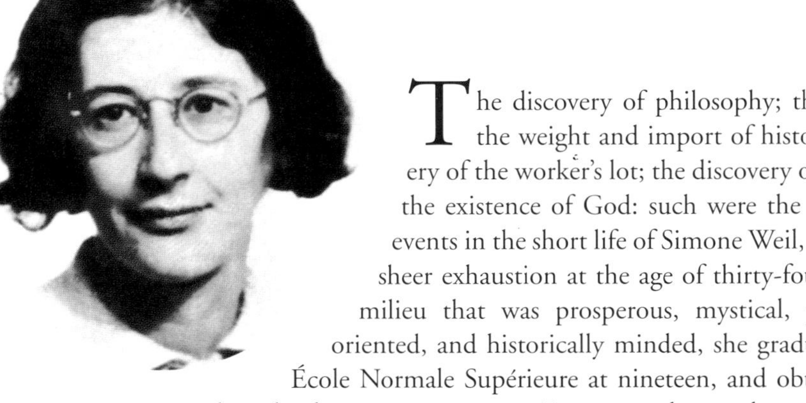

The discovery of philosophy; the discovery of the weight and import of history; the discovery of the worker's lot; the discovery of Christ and of the existence of God: such were the four landmark events in the short life of Simone Weil, who died from sheer exhaustion at the age of thirty-four. Born into a milieu that was prosperous, mystical, philosophically oriented, and historically minded, she graduated from the École Normale Supérieure at nineteen, and obtained her philosophy degree at twenty-two. From an early age, she was an activist for the anarchist and social activist.

In October 1932, her intellectual and political astuteness prompted her to denounce the rise of Hitler and warn of the dangers posed by Nazism: "Hitler means organized massacre, the suppression of liberty and of all culture." "The German middle class will grant him ever increasing power, and finally, perhaps, absolute power," she wrote in 1933, upon his becoming chancellor of Germany. In 1934–35, she took time off from her schooling to acquaint herself with the living conditions of industrial workers, and herself held a job in a factory, during which stint she wrote (February 1935): "In the end, exhaustion makes me forget the real reasons for my sojourn in the factory, making it all but impossible for me to resist the greatest temptation of this life: that of not thinking, the one and only means to avoid suffering from it." After several periods of unemployment, in June 1935 she became a milling-machine operator for Renault, where the work compromised her already fragile health. The next year she supported the Spanish republicans, and in 1943 she returned from the United States to support the cause of Free France in England, but due to her physical condition, her superiors refused to send her on a mission to France. Wasted by tuberculosis, she was hospitalized in 1943 and died in August of that year, having effectively starved herself to death. Her body now rests in the Catholic section of the New Cemetery in Ashford, England.

La Condition Ouvrière (*Working-Class Life*), published in 1937, contains texts that are among the finest and most beautiful ever written about human suffering in the industrial era. Whether she was examining the follies of modern humanity, the distress of those close to her, or the sacrifice of Christ, Simone Weil always evidenced a thirst for the absolute that seems to have been unquenchable.

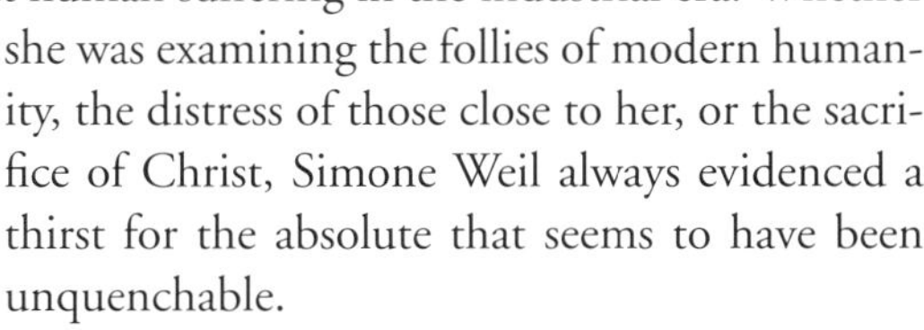

Jean-Pierre Guéno

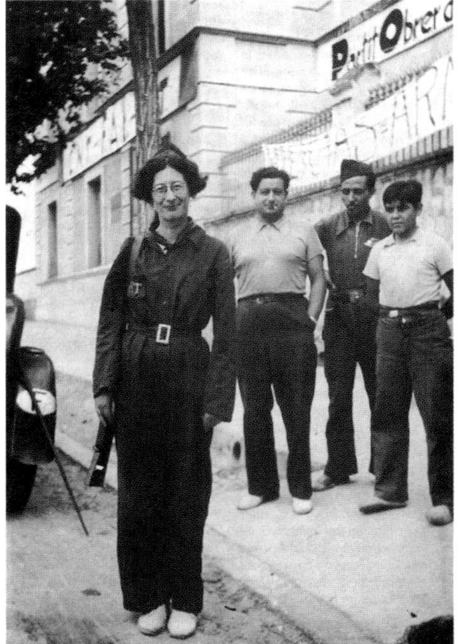

Top left: Simone Weil in New York, 1942.
Left: Simone Weil in Barcelona wearing mechanic's overalls.
Opposite: Page of the incomplete autograph manuscript of *Life in the Factory: An Open Letter to Jules Romains*, 1941. Paris, Bibliothèque Nationale de France.

All the noises have meaning, all are rhythmic, they blend into the great breath of a communal work that is exhilarating. It is all the more exhilarating because the feeling of solitude is not altered by it. There are only metallic sounds, turning wheels, thudding metal; noises that speak neither of nature nor of life, but of the serious, sustained, uninterrupted action of men on things. You get lost in this great clamor, but at the same time you dominate it, because what stands out against this sustained, permanent, and ever changing bass, despite blending into it, is the noise of the machine you're operating yourself. You don't feel tiny, as in a crowd; you feel indispensable. The driving belts, where there are such, make it possible to drink in with your eyes the rhythmic unity experienced by the whole group through the noise and the slight vibration of everything. In the dark hours of the morning, and of winter evenings, when nothing is shining but electric lights, all of the senses participate in a universe where nothing recalls nature, where nothing is gratuitous, where everything is the clank, hard but also conquering, of man against matter. The lamps, belts, and noises, the hard and chilly clatter, everything conspires to transform men into workers.

If factory life were like that, it would be quite beautiful. But it isn't. These joys are the joys of free men; the ones who populate factories don't feel them, except perhaps short, rare spurts, because they are not free men. They can feel them only when they forget that they are not free; but they can rarely forget this, for the pressures of subordination are made apparent to their senses and their bodies by the thousand little details that fill up the minutes which constitute a life.

The first detail that, in the course of the day, makes servitude apparent is the time-clock. The trip from home to the factory is dominated by the fact that you must arrive before a second that is determined mechanically. Even if you arrive five or ten minutes early, the march of time seems pitiless, leaving nothing to chance. In the worker's day, this is only the first effect of a regulatory regime whose brutality dominates the part of life spent among the machines; chance has no legitimacy in the factory. It exists there, of course, as it does everywhere else, but it is not acknowledged. What is allowed, often to the detriment of productivity, is the principle of the barracks: "I don't want to know about it." Fictions are quite powerful in the factory. There are rules that are never observed but are always in force.

rythmés, ils se fondent dans une espèce de grande respiration du travail en commun à laquelle il est enivrant d'avoir part. C'est d'autant plus enivrant que le sentiment de solitude n'en est pas altéré. Il n'y a que des bruits métalliques, des roues qui tournent, des morsures sur le métal; des bruits qui ne parlent pas de nature ni de vie, mais de l'activité sérieuse, soutenue, ininterrompue de l'homme sur les choses. On est perdu dans cette grande rumeur, mais en même temps on la domine, parce que sur cette basse soutenue, permanente et toujours changeante, ce qui ressort, tout en s'y fondant, c'est le bruit de la machine qu'on manie soi-même. On ne se sent pas petit comme dans une foule, on se sent indispensable. Les courroies de transmission, là où il y en a, permettent de boire par les yeux cette unité de rythme que tout le corps ressent par les bruits et par la légère vibration de toutes choses. Aux heures sombres des matinées et des soirées d'hiver, quand ne brille que la lumière électrique, tous les sens participent à un univers où rien ne rappelle la nature, où rien n'est gratuit, où tout est heurt, heurt dur et en même temps conquérant, de l'homme avec la matière. Les lampes, les courroies, les bruits, la dure et froide ferraille, tout concourt à la transmutation de l'homme en ouvrier.

Si c'était cela, la vie d'usine, ce serait trop beau. Mais ce n'est pas cela. Ces joies sont des joies d'hommes libres; ceux qui peuplent les usines ne les sentent pas, sinon en de courts et rares instants, parce qu'ils ne sont pas des hommes libres. Ils ne peuvent les sentir que lorsqu'ils oublient qu'ils ne sont pas libres; mais ils peuvent rarement l'oublier, car l'étau de la subordination leur est rendu sensible à travers les sens, le corps, les mille petits détails qui remplissent les minutes dont est constituée une vie.

Le premier détail qui, dans la journée, rend la servitude sensible, c'est la pendule de pointage. Le chemin de chez soi à l'usine est dominé par le fait qu'il faut être arrivé avant une seconde mécaniquement déterminée. On a beau être de cinq ou dix minutes en avance; l'écoulement du temps apparaît de ce fait comme quelque chose d'impitoyable, qui ne laisse aucun jeu au hasard. C'est, dans une journée d'ouvrier, la première atteinte d'une règle dont la brutalité domine toute la partie de la vie passée parmi les machines; le hasard n'a pas droit de cité à l'usine. Il y existe, bien entendu, comme partout ailleurs, mais il n'y est pas reconnu. Ce qui est admis, souvent au grand détriment de la production, c'est le principe de la caserne: "Je ne veux pas le savoir". Les fictions sont très puissantes à l'usine. Il y a des règles qui ne sont jamais observées, mais qui sont perpétuellement en vigueur.

IV.A

Nausea

Jean-Paul Sartre, 1938

What will survive of the thousands of pages written by Jean-Paul Sartre? What will remain of his fame, for a time as commanding as Picasso's?

No Exit, certainly. This four-character play is premised on a constant existential datum: the inevitability of human conflict. And on Existentialism's core position that man is but the sum total of his actions. A reading of Hegel and a life freely lived in Saint-Germain formed this precisely calibrated theatrical machine. Since its premiere, *No Exit* has been performed almost continuously by amateurs as well as by professionals, always a good sign.

The Words should also survive. It is difficult to discuss autobiography without evoking it. Few writers have described the emergence and evolution of their vocation with such lucidity. More important, Sartre here transcended his particularity to attain universality, as is borne home by the book's final sentence: "A whole man, composed of all men and no better or worse than any."

Nausea is also likely to survive. It was so christened by its original publisher, who objected to the title proposed by Sartre ("Melancholia"). To write a novel about contingency! A daring undertaking. But the gamble paid off, thanks to the book's subtle and ironic blend of genres, and especially to its truly virtuosic prose.

It closes on a note of despair. Roquetin listens to "Some of These Days" and tells himself that it may be possible to justify his existence. At least a little bit. Sartre spent much of his life trying to demonstrate that redemption through art is an illusion.

Paul Desalmand

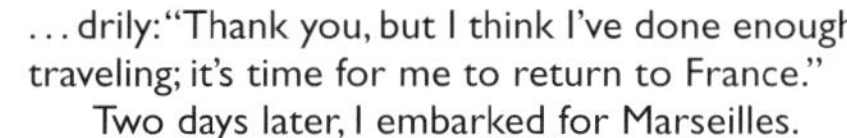

. . . drily: "Thank you, but I think I've done enough traveling; it's time for me to return to France."

Two days later, I embarked for Marseilles.

If I'm not mistaken, if all of the gathering signs indeed point to another upheaval in my life, well, then I'm scared. It's not that my life is rich, or weighty, or precious. But I'm afraid of what might happen, of what might take hold of me—and take me where? Will I have to set off again, drop everything, my research, my book? Will I wake up again in a few months, in a few years, worn out, disappointed, amidst new ruins? I want to get a clear sense of myself before it's too late.

Top left: Jean-Paul Sartre at the Café de Flore, photograph by Brassaï, 1945.
Left: Albrecht Dürer, *Melancholia I*, engraving, 1514. Sartre's original title for *Nausea*, "Melancholia," was inspired by this celebrated print.
Opposite: Page from the autograph manuscript of *Nausea*. Paris, Bibliothèque Nationale de France.

13 bis
10

Sèchement :

"Je vous remercie mais je crois que j'ai assez voyagé : il faut maintenant que je rentre en France."

Le surlendemain, je prenais le bateau pour Marseille.

Si je ne me trompe pas, si tous les signes qui s'amassent sont précurseurs d'un nouveau bouleversement de ma vie, eh bien j'ai peur. Ce n'est pas qu'elle soit riche, ma vie, ni lourde, ni précieuse. Mais j'ai peur de ce qui va naître, s'emparer de moi – et m'entraîner où ? Va-t-il falloir encore que je m'en aille, que je laisse tout en plan, mes recherches, mes livres ? ~~que je m'enfuie comme un voleur, avec un goût de fièvre dans la bouche~~ ? me réveillerai je dans quelques mois, dans quelques années, éreinté, déçu, au milieu de nouvelles ruines ? Je voudrais voir clair en moi avant qu'il ne soit trop tard.

Exile

Saint-John Perse, 1941

Pseudonyms reveal more about personality than given names do. When the civil servant and diplomat Alexis Léger chose Saint-John Perse as his nom de plume, it signaled his affinity with the aristocratic ethos. He himself remarked the "loftiness" of *Éloges* (*Accolades*), his first poetry collection, and his second, *La Gloire des Rois* (*The Glory of Kings*), contains the following avowal (directed towards another): "I saw the sign on your forehead and I considered your role among us." His next volume, entitled *Anabase* (*Anabasis*), is an expedition towards inner heights.

But this aristocrat of letters was above all a lofty dreamer. Saint-John Perse is a poet of elemental nature, of life's fundamental realities, of the vibrant sensuality of odors, sounds, and caresses. He views the world through the microcosm of its luminous islands, especially their rustling vegetation and brilliantly hued flora. Grasping life as a thing of wondrous, spontaneous gushes, he offers his readers nothing less than the cosmos. He sings the praises of a creation that is as much pagan as it is metaphysical.

Exil (*Exile*), his fourth collection, was written in the Summer of 1941, in Long Island Beach, New Jersey, in a summer house overlooking the sea. In a Europe devastated by war, readers of a clandestine edition were astonished by its splendid, meticulously spaced verses (to an exceptional degree, their spacing strengthens their impact). It was a reminder that art has its reasons, and that poets, however haughty their self-image, should make it possible for us to "live better and farther." In the face of evil, gratuitous beauty—beauty with an opaque, mineral perfection—is an encouragement to existence, a noncombative and humanist form of resistance.

There is a word that conveys something of the grandeur, strength, and emotional impact of this poetry. It is a bit outdated, a bit out of sync with the realities of modern life, but it carries within it traces of the purity and exaltation, of the vatic diction and emotive immediacy of its Greek origins. The word is *lyrical.* A beautiful word, and worthy of a prince.

Yves Stalloni

Exile

To Archibald MacLeish

Doors open to the sand, doors open to exile,
The keys are the lighthouse people's, and the monster broken on my well wheel . . .
My host, leave me your house of glass in the sand.
The summer of gypsum sharpens its iron lances in our wounds.
The sky envies me this place blatant and empty like an ossuary of the seasons,
And on all the graves of this world, the spirit of the smoking god abandons its asbestos bed:
The spasms of lightning are for the ravishment of Princes in Taurus.

St. John Perse

A la question toujours posée : "Pourquoi écrivez-vous ?" la réponse du Poète sera toujours la plus brève : "Pour mieux vivre".

Top left: Alexis Léger at Les Vigneaux, his estate in Provence, ca. 1958.
Right: Passage from an autograph manuscript: "To the often asked question: 'Why do you write?' the poet's response will always be brief: 'To live better.'" Fondation Saint-John Perse.
Opposite: Page from the autograph manuscript of *Exile*. Fondation Saint-John Perse.

1

Exil

—

A Archibald MacLeish

Portes ouvertes sur les sables, portes ouvertes sur l'exil,
Les clés aux gens du phare, et le monstre roué vif à la margelle de mon puits...
Mon hôte, laissez-moi votre maison de verre dans les sables.
L'Été de gypse aiguise ses fers de lance dans nos plaies,
Le ciel m'envie un lieu flagrant et nul comme l'ossuaire des saisons
Et, sur toutes grèves de ce monde, l'esprit du dieu fumant déserte sa couche d'amiante:
Les spasmes de l'éclair sont pour le ravissement des Princes en Tauride.

× × ×

The Little Prince

Antoine de Saint-Exupéry, 1942

On May 23, 1940, when he flew over the hell of Arras on a suicide mission from which he miraculously returned, Captain Antoine de Saint-Exupéry witnessed the dreadful spectacle of a France "losing its entrails" on its roads, of a people "trudging wearily towards the threshold of eternity." The anti-aircraft fire—"shooting stars with vicious claws"—and the Dantesque vision of Arras in flames transformed this forty-year-old, melting the wax of his wings of pride, softening a protective carapace he had fashioned for himself through a string of battles, accidents, adventures, disappointments, and fleeting liaisons. Suddenly conscious of the vast scope of human misery and the utter vulnerability of human life, the author of *Southern Mail* and *Night Flight* recovered his faith in humankind and acknowledged his former blindness: "I no longer inhabited the human community as an architect. . . . My status was that of a sacristan or a chair attendant. Thus of a parasite, a defeated man. . . . The gunfire shattered a shell. I was only a grumpy manager. So much for the individual. But a man appeared. He simply took over. . . . It was not a matter of discovery; rather, as if awaking from deep sleep, I simply saw again what I had stopped seeing." He had just discovered that one must "know how to give before receiving, how to build before inhabiting." This epiphany would issue in *Pilote de Guerre* (*War Pilot*) and *The Little Prince*, both written in exile in the United States.

Since adolescence, Saint-Exupéry had traced—on letters, manuscripts, prospectuses, paper tablecloths, and used envelopes—the awkward outline of a solitary and perplexed young hero, a figure that, in the summer of 1942, acquired its definitive features and became the Little Prince.

The book that introduced this character to the world transports us to a realm of universal childhood. Its fresh, clear-sighted vision is consistent with these words, effectively Saint-Exupéry's last, for he wrote them to a friend shortly before leaving on a mission from which he never returned: "If I am shot down, I will have absolutely no regrets. The termite-mound future terrifies me; I hate their robotic ideals. Myself, I was made to be a gardener."

Jean-Pierre Guéno

I remembered that what I had studied most was geography, history, mathematics, and grammar.

"I don't know how to draw!"

"That doesn't matter, draw me a sheep."

Since I had never drawn a sheep, I made him the only drawing that I knew how to make. I was startled to hear the little fellow say to me:

[drawing]

"No, I don't want an elephant in a boa. Boas don't interest me. They [illegible] me. Elephants are better, but they're too cumbersome. What I want is a sheep, I need one. My house is very small."

So I drew.

[drawing]

He looked intently. Then:

"That one's sick, make another one."

I started over.

[drawing]

"That's not a sheep, it's a bull. It has horns."

I started over.

"That one's too old, I want one that will live a long time."

Top left: Photograph of Saint-Exupéry taken by John Philips in Alghero, Sardinia, May 1944. *Right and left:* Some of Saint-Exupéry's original drawings for *The Little Prince*. New York, Pierpont Morgan Library. *Opposite:* Page from an early draft of *The Little Prince*. New York, Pierpont Morgan Library.

(3) 4

me rappelai que j'avais surtout appris la géographie, l'histoire, le calcul et la grammaire.

— Je ne sais pas dessiner!

— Ça ne fait rien. Dessine-moi un mouton.

Comme je n'avais jamais dessiné un mouton je fis pour lui le seul dessin que je savais faire. Je fus stupéfait d'entendre le petit bonhomme me dire :

— Non. Je ne veux pas d'un éléphant dans un boa. Les boas ne m'intéressent pas. Ils sont dangereux, les éléphants trop encombrants. Ce que je veux c'est un mouton. Chez moi c'est tout petit.

Alors je dessinai

Il regarda gravement, puis

— Celui-là est malade. Fais-en un autre.

Je recommençai.

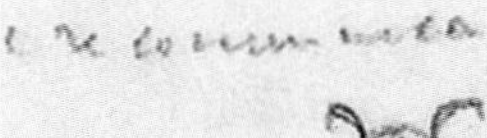

— Ce n'est pas un mouton c'est un bélier. Il a des cornes.

Je recommençai :

— Celui-là est trop vieux. J'en veux un qui vive longtemps.

Henry de Montherlant, 1943

This is the story of a little boy who, at age twelve, after reading the novel *Quo Vadis?*, decided to become, simultaneously, Nero and Petronius. One can imagine worse choices. Still, his parents must have been alarmed upon hearing the boy's answer to the idiotic but unavoidable question "What do you want to be when you grow up?"

Fantasy and art, without bounds or scruples; Montherlant found that his commitment to absolute freedom was not unlike being enslaved by the most demanding of taskmasters. Later, he would distance himself from his years of unbridled adventurism around the Mediterranean basin, writing: "That was the worst of all experiences." The typical crisis of a thirty-year-old? Perhaps. But once he had exhausted his fear of missing out on the limit of experience, of not, in the words of Roland Barthes, "having squeezed things dry like so many lemons to be discarded afterwards," he reverted to a delectably sedentary Parisian existence—and to the craft of writing, which he used to plumb the depths of sensation.

Montherlant sought, and attained, a freedom comparable to that of a Roman emperor. *La Reine Morte* (translated as *Queen After Death, or How to Kill Women*) reflects these aspirations. Although it began as a commissioned work, a mere stylistic exercise, it became a personal confession responsive to the author's deepest impulses. What could be more piercing than this noble and grandiose pavane without a moral? Faithful to his principles, Montherlant here staged a battle between beings who erroneously regard themselves as clear-sighted and superior, with the result that they are destroyed by their own pride and purity. For Montherlant believed that "everyone is always right; everything comes down to circumstances. The only thing that never lies is desire."

Pierre-Emmanuel Prouvost d'Agostino

Act 4, scene 7

Malatesta, Porcellio
At his entrance, Porcellio is accompanied by servants who light torches and then withdraw.

PORCELLIO: My lord, we have just received a letter from the Marquese d'Este. As you asked me to write to him, I thought you should be informed, in case you wanted to change the contents of your own letter.

MALATESTA (after perusing the letter): There's nothing important here; we'll discuss it later. There are weightier matters to consider. (Pause) Men are like children, Porcellio: they can be frightened or secure at will. Which is sad. Myself, I can say that I have lived without anxiety. During these three months in Rome, there hasn't been a single hour of day or night when I wasn't expecting prison, even death. But that hasn't kept me from eating well, or making love, or reading, or sleeping. I've never slept as well as during this time, when I had reason to suspect that assassins were sleeping in the next room. I've never collected as many women as during the six years since I was declared fit for burning at the stake. And if you asked me what one feels on learning of one's own death sentence, I would answer: "One feels nothing."

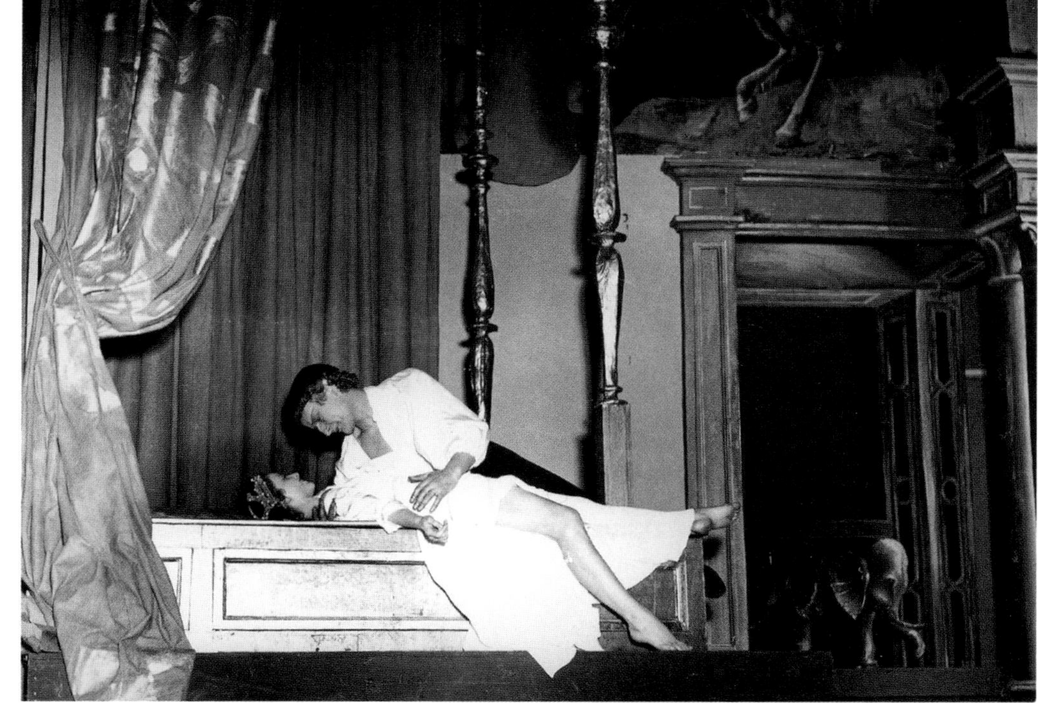

Top left: Henry de Montherlant, phototype of a painting by Mariette Lydis, 1949. Collection T. Bodin. *Left:* Jean-Louis Barrault and Violette Verdy in a scene from a 1950 production of *Malatesta* directed by Barrault (Théâtre Marigny, Paris). *Right:* Page from a working draft of *Malatesta*. Collection Jean-Claude Barat.

20

Scène VII

Malatesta. Porcellio

En même temps que Porcellio, entrent des serviteurs qui allument des flambeaux, puis se retirent.

Porcellio. — Monseigneur, on apporte une lettre du marquis d'Este. Comme vous m'aviez prié de lui écrire, j'ai voulu que vous en ayez connaissance, pendant que ma lettre en serait modifiée, peut-être.

Malatesta, (ayant parcouru la lettre) — Rien d'important : nous en reparlerons. Les choses importantes sont ailleurs. (temps) Les hommes sont comme les enfants, Porcellio : on les effraye et on les rassure à volonté. Cela est triste. Moi, ~~dans l'engeance~~ je puis dire que j'ai été rassuré ! Pendant ces trois mois de Rome, il n'était pas une heure du jour ni de la nuit où je n'attendisse ~~de~~ la prison, sinon la mort. Cela ne m'empêchait ni de bien manger, ni de bien forniquer, ni de bien lever, ni de bien dormir. Je n'ai jamais si bien dormi que durant cette période, quand j'avais l'impression que mes assassins dormaient dans mon antichambre. Je n'ai jamais levé autant de femmes qu'il y a six ans, quand ~~j'étais un condamné à mort.~~ je venais d'être ~~jeté~~ déclaré passible du bûcher. ~~ma tête était mise à prix,~~ Et si tu me demandais ce que l'on ressent au moment où l'on apprend qu'on est condamné à

The Madwoman of Chaillot

Jean Giraudoux, 1945

Giraudoux was a diplomat perpetually on the move for the cause of literature. He entered the Foreign Service through the back door, but through happenstance became a high-ranking state bureaucrat. Luckily for him, the Third Republic downplayed foreign policy, a decision that proved diplomatically disastrous but fostered a peerless generation of French writers. To his colleague Morand, Giraudoux, then a young ambassadorial attaché, quoted one of La Fontaine's *Fables*:

Tied up? said the fox;
So you don't run where you will?

Berthelot, his first boss, nicknamed him "the most detached of my attachés." By the time the actor Louis Jouvet suggested Giraudoux try writing plays, he had already published a refined novel-in-letters with seventeenth-century affinities. His heroines are nubile young women of the 1920s, fantasy figures in whom the Loreleis of German Romantic fiction merge with the emancipated post-war woman in skirts and bobbed hair. Although innocent, they are, with their unnerving grace, capable of anything, notably of torturing the men they love and inevitably leave. Neither happiness nor fulfilled love are to be found in Giraudoux' elegant, precious, and subtly elliptical fictions. Cocktail-party furies dressed in Lanvin and ocean-liner Phaedras stabbing Time to death with their hatpins are more in his line. Giraudoux was a baroque poet through and through, but he knew his classics, and he turned that knowledge to deft, idiosyncratic account.

Pierre-Emmanuel Prouvost d'Agostino

The Madwoman of Chaillot
Act 2

A basement furnished as an apartment in the rue de Chaillot

The madwoman, Irma, the deaf mute

IRMA: There you are, countess. All of the deaf mute's envelopes are done.

MADWOMAN: He should reread his letter.

(The deaf mute, letter in hand, does his pantomime. Irma translates)

IRMA: Mister president, if you should want to convince yourself *de visu* of the presence in Chaillot . . .

MADWOMAN: Why *de visu*? I never dictated *de visu*?

IRMA: He says those words make it sound official. His old boss the bailiff used them.

MADWOMAN: Continue.

IRMA: . . . of the presence in Chaillot of walls of gasoline whose olfactory qualities can be judged by the sample imbibed by the cotton swatch enclosed with this letter . . .

MADWOMAN: Yes, that's much clearer.

IRMA: . . . come immediately, and as quickly as possible, alone or in the company of your advisors, to number twenty-one in the rue de Chaillot. A charming creature, modeled by Clodion and painted by Fragonard . . .

MADWOMAN: What's that all about?

Top left: Jacques-Émile Blanche, *Study for a Portrait of Jean Giraudoux* (detail), 1924. Rouen, Musée des Beaux Arts.
Left: Marguerite Moreno, Louis Jouvet, and Monique Mélinand in the first production of *The Madwoman of Chaillot*, Théâtre de l'Athénée, Paris, December 1945.
Opposite: Page from the autograph manuscript of *The Madwoman of Chaillot*. Paris, Bibliothèque Nationale de France.

La Folle de Chaillot

Acte deuxième

Un sous sol aménagé en appartement dans la rue de Chaillot

La folle. Irma. Le sourd muet

Irma — Il ment, Comtesse. Toutes les enveloppes du sourd muet y ont passé.

La folle — Qu'il relise sa lettre.

Le sourd muet sa lettre à la main fait sa mimique. Irma traduit

Irma — "Monsieur le Président, si vous voulez vous convaincre de visu de la présence dans Chaillot...

La folle — Pourquoi de visu? Je n'ai pas dicté de visu?

Irma — Il dit que cela fait pièce officielle. Ce sont les mots de son ancien patron l'huissier.

La folle — Continue

Irma — " de la présence dans Chaillot de mares de pétrole dont le tampon d'ouate inclus dans cette lettre et imbibé ~~du dit~~ liquide vous permet de juger la qualité de olfactu...

La folle — En effet, c'est plus net.

Irma — "Venez immédiatement et par les moyens les plus rapides, seul ou avec vos conseils, au 21 de la rue de Chaillot. Un être charmant, modelé par Clodion et peint par Fragonard..

La folle — Qu'est ce qu'il lui prend?

The Plague

Albert Camus, 1947

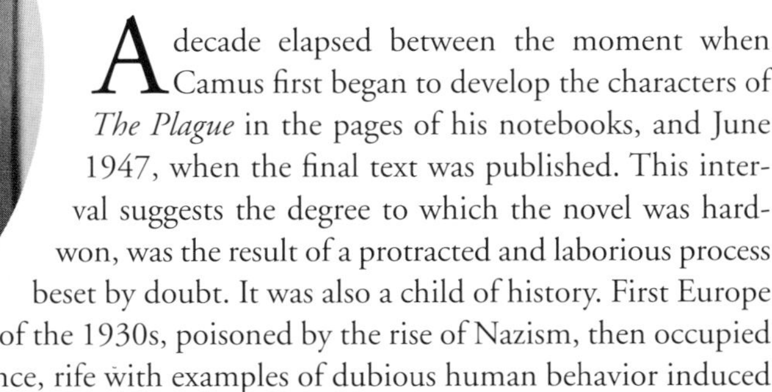

A decade elapsed between the moment when Camus first began to develop the characters of *The Plague* in the pages of his notebooks, and June 1947, when the final text was published. This interval suggests the degree to which the novel was hard-won, was the result of a protracted and laborious process beset by doubt. It was also a child of history. First Europe of the 1930s, poisoned by the rise of Nazism, then occupied France, rife with examples of dubious human behavior induced by trying and claustrophobic circumstances, provided Camus with much material he could use to imbue his subject with additional symbolic power.

But human suffering transcends historical time. It is universal. It also issues from the absurd, itself born of the contradiction between the human mind, an instrument that imparts meaning and clarity, and a world that is hostile, dark, primitive, and irrational. The characters of *The Plague* are constantly rehearsing the myth of Sisyphus. Camus continually restaged the great human *Iliad* and *Odyssey*, the epic of Man imposing meaning on the universe by orienting his revolt and his daily struggle toward the religion of life. He educates us. He teaches us how to live and die, by avoiding the traps of thought and history, which proceed from fascism to collectivism by way of the lure of suicide, cynicism, inquisition, totalitarianism, and destruction.

"I still believe that this world has no ultimate meaning. But I know that there is something in it that has meaning, and that something is man, because he is the only being who requires it," Camus wrote in *Lettres à un Ami Allemand* (*Letters to a German Friend*), published after *The Plague* but written contemporaneously with it. Camus's man remains free because he suffers without trying to ascribe responsibility for his suffering to others. He is not on earth to make accusations, to oppress or manipulate the human community, but rather to help it advance by blending into it: "Compared to *The Stranger*, *The Plague* marks, without any question, a transition from an attitude of solitary revolt to recognition of a community in whose struggles one must participate. Whatever evolution there is from *The Stranger* to *The Plague* moves towards solidarity and participation," he wrote to Roland Barthes five years before rejoining the mysterious brotherhood of the stars.

Jean-Pierre Guéno

Chapter I

On the morning of April 16, Dr. Bernard Rieux left his office and stumbled over a dead rat on the first-floor landing. At first, he kicked it to one side without a second thought and continued down the stairs. But after reaching the street, he retraced his steps and told the concierge to deal with the offender. Only on seeing old M. Michel's reaction did he realize how out of the ordinary his discovery was. Personally, he found the presence of this dead rat merely odd. For the concierge, it was a scandal. M. Michel was categorical; there were no rats in the building. The Doctor assured him that there was at least one, a dead one, on the landing. But the concierge held his ground. There were no rats in the building. It must have been brought in from outside.

That evening, Bernard Rieux was standing in the hallway searching for his latchkey before starting up to his apartment when he saw a large rat emerge from the darkness. The creature was a bit unsteady on its feet. It stopped, tried to regain its balance, continued towards the doctor, stopped again, dropped with a squeal, and fell over throwing up blood. The doctor gazed at it a moment and entered his apartment. The next day the concierge buttonholed him on his way out and accused practical jokers of having left three dead rats in the middle of the hallway the previous night. They must have been caught with big traps, for they were very bloody. Leaving Monsieur Michel, the doctor decided to begin his rounds in the outer neighborhoods where the poorest of his clients lived. Garbage was collected here much later than elsewhere, and the cars driving down the neighborhood's long, straight streets grazed boxes of junk left by the edge of the sidewalk. In the street he was crossing, the doctor counted some ten rats perched on the remains of vegetables and dirty rubbish.

He found his first sick patient in a room on the street doubling as a bedroom and a dining room. There were two heavy pots in front of him and, half undressed on the bed, an old asthmatic man who was throwing himself backwards, gasping, in an attempt to recover his breath. "Yes," said the woman. "The next-door neighbor collected three of them." The old man rubbed his hands: "They're coming out, the garbage cans are full of them. They're hungry." Rieux had no trouble determining that the whole quarter was talking about it.

Albert Camus

Top left: Photograph of Albert Camus by Yousuf Karsh, 1943. Paris, Bibliothèque Nationale de France.
Left: Philippe Zilcken, *View of Algiers*. Paris, Musée d'Orsay.
Opposite: Page from a draft of *The Plague*. Paris, Bibliothèque Nationale de France.

1re version
1er exemplaire

~~[illegible]~~

3

Chapitre premier

I

Le matin du 16 avril, le docteur Bernard Rieux sortit de son cabinet et buta sur un rat mort au palier du premier étage. Sur le moment, il écarta la bête sans y prendre garde et descendit l'escalier. Mais arrivé dans la rue, il revint sur ses pas pour en avertir le concierge et se mettre en règle avec l'autorité. Devant la réaction du vieux M. Michel, il sentit mieux ce que sa découverte avait d'extraordinaire. La présence de ce rat mort lui avait paru seulement surprenante. Pour le concierge elle constituait un scandale. La position de M. Michel était d'ailleurs catégorique : il n'y avait pas de rats ~~[illegible]~~ dans la maison. Le docteur l'assura cependant que sur le palier du premier étage, il y en avait au moins un, et probablement mort. Mais la conviction du principal restait entière. Il n'y avait pas de rats dans la maison. Il fallait donc que celui-ci eût été apporté de l'extérieur. Il s'agissait d'une farce.

Le soir même, Bernard Rieux, debout dans le couloir, cherchait ses clés avant de monter chez lui lorsqu'il vit surgir du fond obscur du couloir un gros rat à la démarche incertaine. La bête s'arrêta, sembla chercher son équilibre, prit sa course vers le docteur, s'arrêta encore, tourna sur elle-même avec un petit cri et tomba enfin en rejetant du sang. Le docteur la contempla un moment et remonta chez lui. Le lendemain, le concierge l'arrêta au passage et accusa de mauvais plaisants d'avoir déposé dans la nuit trois rats morts au milieu du couloir. On avait dû les prendre avec de gros pièges car ils étaient pleins de sang. En quittant ~~[illegible]~~ M. Michel, le docteur décida de commencer sa tournée par les quartiers extérieurs où habitaient les plus pauvres de ses ~~[illegible]~~ clients. La collecte des ordures s'y faisait beaucoup plus tard et l'auto qui roulait le long des rues droites et poussiéreuses de ce quartier frôlait les boîtes de détritus laissés au bord du trottoir. Dans la rue qu'il traversait le docteur compta une douzaine de rats couchés sur les débris de légumes et les chiffons sales.

Il trouva son premier malade ~~[illegible]~~ dans une pièce sur la rue qui servait de chambre à coucher et de salle à manger. Il avait deux marmites de pois devant lui et, à demi dressé dans le lit, se renversait en arrière pour tenter de retrouver son souffle caillouteux de vieil asthmatique. « Hein docteur, dit-il, ils sortent, vous avez vu ? » « Oui, dit la femme, le voisin en a ramassé trois. » Le vieux se frottait les mains. « Ils sortent, les poubelles sont pleines, c'est la faim. » Rieux n'eut pas de peine ensuite à constater que tout le quartier en parlait.

Le soir du 18 avril, le docteur rentrait à pied, fatigué par une journée chargée, quand il trouva M. Michel devant la maison, avec une expression de ~~[illegible]~~ fatigue sur le visage. « Tantôt eux, tantôt moi, tous les matins » répondit-il

The Friendship of Georges Braque

René Char, 1947

Georges Mounin, a noted linguist from Aix-en-Provence, posed a question more than fifty years ago: "Have you read Char?" He was curious about another's response to the poetry of his neighbor (Isle-sur-la-Sorgue, Char's birthplace, is less than an hour from Aix) because it puzzled him. "I feel as though I were encountering a strange language," Mounin wrote, adding that even after repeated encounters he found much of the poet's work impenetrable.

Since then, things have changed considerably. We now understand that it is pointless to require poets to think clearly; we ask only that they contrive language that is strong, apt, and beautiful. In this regard, Char is incomparable. His poetry makes no concessions because it is a perpetual combat with human beings, with misfortune, with life. "Poetry is of all clear waters the one that tarries least before the reflections of its bridges." Char penned this aphorism—he expressed himself with the compact but quizzical diction of an oriental sage—during the French occupation, when he had decided that a poet's proper place was in the Resistance. Was risking one's life in the Maquis that much more heroic than taming language?

Char was rebellious, contrary, angry, but he was so because he suffered from an exigent and unsatisfied love of the true word. "The poet, susceptible to exaggeration, evaluates correctly under punishment." When language comes into the world painfully, it demands close reading. Entering Char's universe requires not only time but patience, empathy, and an open mind. The opacity of his work will discourage the timid and the easily distracted. But once a certain threshold is passed—once his novel rhythms have been mastered, his luminous language conquered—the reward is a boundless joy, that of escaping the commonplace world to enter a realm of infinite Beauty: "The key remains quicksilver." To "read Char," one must set aside conventional reason and surrender to poetic alchemy.

Yves Stalloni

G Braque

Nous ne jalousons pas les dieux, nous ne les servons pas, ne les craignons pas, mais au péril de notre vie nous attestons leur existence multiple, et nous nous émouvons d'être de leur élevage aventureux lorsque cesse leur souvenir.

René Char

Top left: Victor Brauner, *Portrait of René Char*, 1934. Paris, Bibliothèque Littéraire Jacques-Doucet.
Left and opposite: Two pages from the autograph manuscript of *L'Amitié de Georges Braque* (*The Friendship of Georges Braque*), decorated by Char with tracings etc. after Braque. Left: "Nous ne jalousons pas les dieux" (We do not envy the gods). Right: "Le Thor." Paris, Bibliothèque Nationale de France.

Le Thor

On the path of numbed grass where we were astonished, children, that night should venture to pass, wasps no longer went to the blackberry bushes or birds to the branches. The air opened to the guests of morning its turbulent immensity. There were only filaments of wings, the temptation to scream, flutterings between light and transparency. Le Thor exalted itself on the lyre of its stones. Mount Ventoux, mirror of eagles, was in view.

On the numbed grass path, the chimera of a lost age smiled at our young tears.

Le Thor, Vaucluse

September 15, 1947

Le Thor

Dans le sentier aux herbes engourdies où nous nous étonnions, enfants, que la nuit se risquât à passer, les guêpes n'allaient plus aux ronces et les oiseaux aux branches. L'air ouvrait aux hôtes de la matinée sa turbulente immensité. Ce n'étaient que filaments d'ailes, tentation de crier, voltige entre lumière et transparence. Le Thor s'exaltait sur la lyre de ses pierres. Le Mont Ventoux, miroir des aigles, était en vue.

Dans le sentier aux herbes engourdies, la chimère d'un âge perdu souriait à nos jeunes larmes.

René Char

Le Thor, Vaucluse
15 Septembre 1947

Mood Indigo

Boris Vian, 1947

In the aftermath of the festive chaos of May 1968, young French students who had missed this laughing revolution, and thus found themselves reduced to more symbolic forms of transgression, rallied in large numbers around a book that, although it had been published some twenty years before, was destined to become a Bible of adolescent anguish: *L'Écume des Jours*, translated as *Mood Indigo*.

The book could scarcely have been more precisely pitched to appeal to the youth of that uncertain moment. First, its author personified contradictions that are the stuff of legend: a brilliant student (he was a graduate of the prestigious École Normale Centrale), he cultivated a profile that was bohemian (he played trumpet in jazz clubs), iconoclastic (he wrote a scandalous song entitled "The Deserter" as well as violent novels, which he published under a pseudonym), and given to hoaxes (various parodic works). Immensely gifted (and blessed with an appealingly exotic Slavic first name, despite his being born in Ville-d'Avray), he was sufficiently elegant to leave this earth at thirty-nine, an age at which election to the Académie Française must remain a distant dream. *Mood Indigo* is of a piece with its author: brilliant, irreverent, desperate, and droll. Combining elements drawn from Alfred Jarry, the Surrealists, and Sartre, Vian contrived a fantastic universe in which time is elastic, pianos prepare mixed drinks, ice-skating is a murderous sport, mice dissect human motivations, neckties are intractable animals, and deadly water lilies devour blooming young girls.

All of this would be amusing enough but a bit gratuitous if this strange world were not the backdrop for a story of love and death reminiscent of the Tristan legend unfolding between the characters of Colin and Chloe. Their passion, utterly pure but contrary to bourgeois propriety and the designs of fate, is mercilessly condemned. It is not surprising that a young generation given to idealism, generosity, and nonconformity should have embraced this book, which Raymond Queneau called "the most poignant of contemporary novels of love."

Yves Stalloni

Colin finished his daily grooming. Leaving the shower, he wrapped himself in a large bath towel such that only his legs and torso emerged. From the glass shelves, he took down a vaporizer and sprayed perfumed oil onto his light hair. His amber comb divided the silky mass into long orange strands that resembled furrows ploughed with a fork by a happy ploughman in apricot jam. Colin put down the comb and, arming himself with a nail clipper, beveled the corners of his flat eyelashes to give his gaze an air of mystery. He had to begin again several times, for they grew back quickly. He switched on the small light of the expanding mirror and moved closer to assess the state of his skin. A few blackheads were popping out around the base of his nose. On seeing themselves so ugly in the expanding mirror, they quickly receded into the skin, and Colin, satisfied, switched off the light. He removed the towel from around his hips and used one of its corners to absorb the last traces of dampness between his toes.

au sortir du bain, d'une ample serviette de tissu bouclé dont
seules ses jambes et son torse dépassaient. Il prit
à l'étagère, de verre, le vaporisateur, et pulvérisa
l'huile et odorante sur les cheveux clairs.
Son peigne d'ambre divisa. la masse soyeuse
en longs filets orange pareils aux sillons
que le gai laboureur trace à l'aide d'une
fourchette dans de la confiture d'abricot.
et s'armant

Top left: Boris Vian in 1948.
Right and opposite: Page (and detail) from the autograph manuscript of *Mood Indigo*. Paris, Bibliothèque Nationale de France.

I

Colin terminait sa toilette. Il s'était enveloppé, au sortir du bain, d'une ample serviette de ~~[illegible]~~ tissu bouclé dont seules ses jambes et son torse dépassaient. Il prit ~~sur~~ à l'étagère, de verre, le vaporisateur, et pulvérisa l'huile ~~fluide~~ et odorante sur ses cheveux clairs. Son peigne d'ambre divisa la masse soyeuse en longs filets orange ~~[illegible]~~ pareils aux sillons que le gai laboureur trace à l'aide d'une fourchette dans de la confiture d'abricot. Colin reposa le peigne ~~[illegible]~~ et s'armant du coupe-ongles, tailla en biseau les coins de ses paupières mates ~~[illegible]~~ pour donner du mystère à son regard. Il devait recommencer souvent car elles repoussaient vite. Il alluma la petite lampe du miroir grossissant et s'en rapprocha pour vérifier l'état de sa peau. Quelques comédons saillaient aux alentours des ailes du nez. En se voyant si laids dans le miroir grossissant, ils rentrèrent prestement sous la peau et, satisfait, Colin ~~[illegible]~~ éteignit la lampe. Il détacha la serviette qui lui ceignait les reins et passa l'un des coins entre ses doigts de pied pour absorber les dernières traces d'humidité.

There Is Evil Abroad

Jacques Audiberti, 1947

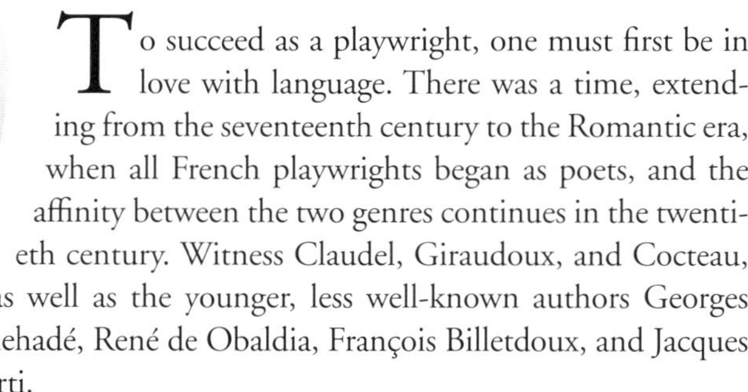

To succeed as a playwright, one must first be in love with language. There was a time, extending from the seventeenth century to the Romantic era, when all French playwrights began as poets, and the affinity between the two genres continues in the twentieth century. Witness Claudel, Giraudoux, and Cocteau, as well as the younger, less well-known authors Georges Schehadé, René de Obaldia, François Billetdoux, and Jacques Audiberti.

Our subject here is the last-mentioned, a mischievous fellow from Antibes who came to Paris to try his luck in literature. Although he produced work in many genres (novels, essays, poetry, autobiography), posterity, capricious and selective, has opted to favor his plays. Admittedly, the 1950s were a period rich in theatrical innovation, much of it focused on the problematic of language. On one side were iconoclasts such as Ionesco, Beckett, and Tardieu, who aggressively, and mockingly, put verbal communication on trial. On the other side were conjurers such as Vian, Ghelderode, and Vauthier, who, like the above-mentioned poet-playwrights, probed the relationship between language and dream. Audiberti—who once claimed that, as a writer, he saw himself as "a manipulator of those objects that are words"—belonged to this last group.

Although extravagant and poetic, his fifteen or so plays (*Quoat-Quoat, Le Mal Court* [*There is Evil Abroad*], *Le Cavalier Seul*, and *La Hobereaute*) steer clear of both sterile logorrhoea and a dubious militancy. They offer enlightenment about the mystery of life and the disturbing prevalence of evil, reminding us that, in the face of the world's horror and disorder, metaphysical and political solutions are powerless. We must place our hopes in dreams and the imagination, which can transport us to a mythical moment before the fall when man, innocent and at one with a benevolent nature, knew happiness. Such a blend of lucidity and fantasy, enabled by a passion for language, is the exclusive province of poets.

Yves Stalloni

From Act 3

GOVERNESS: What's bothering you? Is it worthy of you, my sweet, to be so irritated about this throne's having slipped through your fingers? There are other princes, for god's sake.

ALARICA: We're talking about the throne, for god's sake! It's a lie, an evil, to which I will never accommodate myself. It's no good! It's no good! Every word is a trap. Every helping hand breaks at the touch. (To the governess) They even rigged the wheels of my carriage.

GOVERNESS (to F.): You told her? Swine!

F: Carrion!

GOVERNESS: I'll report you.

F: I spit on your ass.

GOVERNESS: Trash!

F: Whore.

GOVERNESS: You know the cost of forfeiture! All you have to do is disappear. Why are you still here? To torture her? To ruin everything?

F: She kept me here. And you haven't done anything to encourage me to leave.

GOVERNESS: What could I do? She got into it up to her neck, and even deeper. She's only nineteen. A mere girl. Their nipples are as hard as marble, but their brains! Chicken! Lavender! I would have tried to prevent her from . . . well, with you there . . . she would have gotten suspicious . . .

F: And all that time, you weren't angry about being outwitted by this Pulcinella?

Top left: Jacques Audiberti in 1950.
Left: Photographs taken on the occasion of the first production of *Le Mal Court* (*There is Evil Abroad*) at the Théâtre de Poche, Paris, June 1947, starring Suzanne Plon and Georges Vitaly, who also directed.
Opposite: Page from the autograph manuscript of *Le Mal Court*. Paris, Bibliothèque Nationale de France.

A. Il s'agit bien du trône, du boulgre, du valaque. C'est au mensonge, c'est au mal que jamais je ne me ferai. Rien ne tient. Rien ne vaut. Chaque bouche est un piège. Tous les bras se cassent en deux dès qu'on les touche. (A la G.) On a même truqué les roues de ma voiture. 16

G. (à F.) Vous avez parlé? Salaud!

F. Charogne!

G. Je vous signalerai.

F. Je vous crache aux fesses.

G. ~~Vous avez forfait.~~

~~G. La forfaiture, vous savez ce que ça coûte~~

G. Voyou!

F. Maquerelle.

G. La forfaiture, vous savez ce que ça coûte. Vous n'aviez qu'à disparaître. Pourquoi êtes-vous resté? Pour la torturer? Pour tout démolir?

F. C'est elle qui m'a retenu. Et vous n'avez rien fait pour que je parte.

G. Que pouvais-je faire? Elle entrait

A Short History of Decay

Cioran, 1949

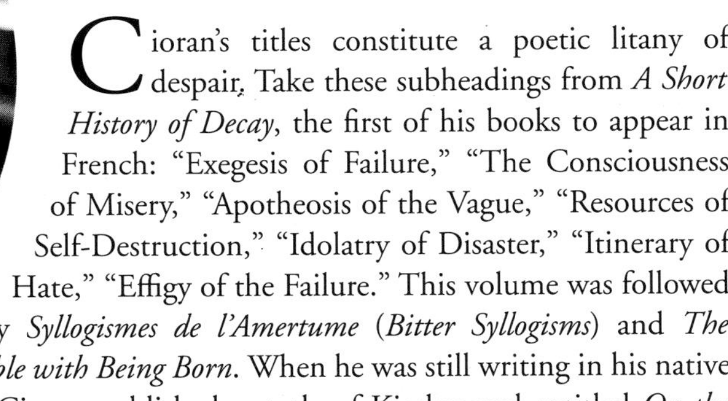

Cioran's titles constitute a poetic litany of despair. Take these subheadings from *A Short History of Decay*, the first of his books to appear in French: "Exegesis of Failure," "The Consciousness of Misery," "Apotheosis of the Vague," "Resources of Self-Destruction," "Idolatry of Disaster," "Itinerary of Hate," "Effigy of the Failure." This volume was followed by *Syllogismes de l'Amertume* (*Bitter Syllogisms*) and *The Trouble with Being Born*. When he was still writing in his native Rumanian, Cioran published a study of Kierkegaard entitled *On the Heights of Despair*. It is, then, on the peaks of misfortune that we are most likely to encounter Cioran, a pessimistic moralist who, like his seventeenth-century models, demonstrates that the pairing of these words is redundant. The close study of human behavior breeds uneasiness, just as the contemplation of existence fosters melancholy. In their own day, Montaigne, Pascal, La Rochefoucauld, and Nietzsche variously illuminated our lamentable human condition. Cioran begins where they leave off. But he eschews brutality and superficial brilliance, delivering his bleak message with the detachment of a lepidopterist observing the gesticulations of a butterfly.

A case in point is this portrait of fanaticism, composed of little touches, of finely honed aphoristic sentences: "Periods of fervor excel in bloody exploits." A voice is constituting itself, acquired only at the cost of ascetic sacrifice and difficulties surmounted. Every word is weighed on Mallarmean scales, and syntax is corseted by the spatial constraints of the fragment, the form of writing closest to silence, and one embraced by Maurice Blanchot ("Free me from the overextended word").

This linguistic "limit-experience" inevitably leads to an interrogation of the unique subject of all reflection: man. Rejecting both humanist illusions and the anathema of nihilism, Cioran, a contemporary sage stripped bare, like Job, of literary superfluities, ponders us with a gaze that is precise, measured, full of a lucid severity moderated by boundless tenderness and irrepressible humor.

Yves Stalloni

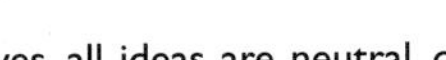

Genealogy of Fanaticism

In themselves, all ideas are neutral, or ought to be; but man animates them, projects onto them his ardor and his madness. Rendered impure, transformed into beliefs, they are inserted into time, acquire the status of *events:* a transition from logic to epilepsy is consummated. . . . Thus are born ideologies, doctrines, bloody farces.

Idolatrous by instinct, we convert the objects of our dreams and interests into constants. History is nothing but a procession of false absolutes, a series of temples erected to pretexts, a debasement of the mind before the improbable. Even when he distances himself from religion, man remains subject to it; wearing himself out forging simulacra of the gods, he then embraces them feverishly: his need for fiction, for mythology, triumphs over evidence and irony. His power to adore is responsible for all crimes: those who love a god without justification compel others to love it, and exterminate them if they refuse. All intolerance, all ideological intransigence and proselytism is rooted in bestial enthusiasm. Whenever man loses his faculty of indifference, he becomes a virtual assassin; whenever he transforms *his* idea into a god, the consequences are incalculable.

Top left: Photograph of Cioran by Louis Monier, 1977.
Below: Hieronymous Bosch, *The Garden of Earthly Delights*, "Musical Hell" panel (details). Madrid, Museo del Prado.
Opposite: Page from the autograph manuscript of *A Short History of Decay*. Paris, Bibliothèque Nationale de France.

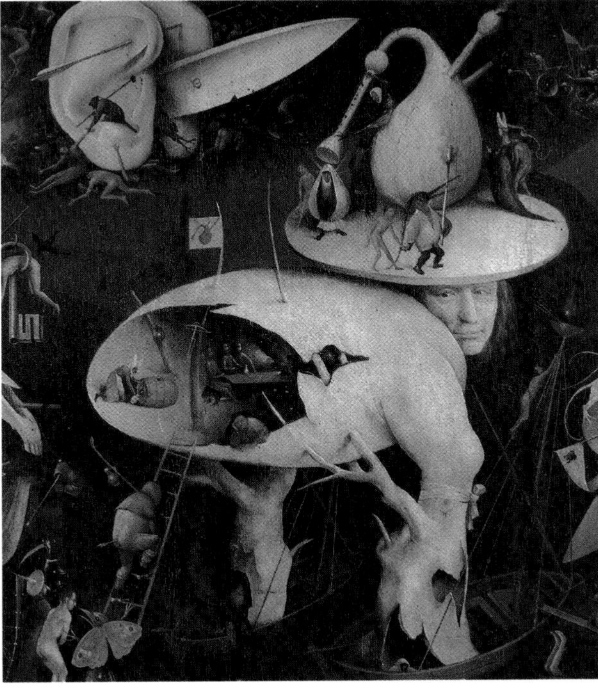

Généalogie du fanatisme

En elle même toute idée est neutre, ou devrait l'être; mais l'homme l'anime, y projette ses flammes et ses démences; impure, transformée en croyance, elle s'insère dans le temps, prend figure d'<u>événement</u>: le passage de la logique à l'épilepsie est consommé... Ainsi naissent les idéologies, les doctrines, les farces sanglantes.

Idolâtres par instinct, nous convertissons en inconditionné les objets de nos songes et de nos intérêts. L'Histoire n'est qu'un défilé de faux Absolus, une succession de temples élevés à des prétextes, un avilissement de l'esprit devant l'Improbable. Lors même qu'il s'éloigne de la religion, l'homme y demeure assujetti; s'épuisant à forger des simulacres de dieux, il les adopte ensuite fiévreusement: son besoin de fiction, de mythologie triomphe de l'évidence et de l'ironie. Sa puissance d'adorer est responsable de tous ses crimes: celui qui aime indûment un dieu, contraint les autres à l'aimer, en attendant qu'il les extermine s'ils s'y refusent. Point d'intolérance, d'intransigeance idéologique ou de prosélytisme qui ne révèlent le fond bestial de l'enthousiasme. Que l'homme perde sa <u>faculté d'indifférence</u>: il devient assassin virtuel; qu'il transforme <u>son</u> idée en dieu: les conséquences sont incalculables.

The Bald Soprano

Eugène Ionesco, 1950

Ionesco, with his verve, theatricality, and wit, never disappoints one. His work was born of the feeling that something about the bourgeois theater of his day was false. Why rest content with removing the fourth wall to reveal a laborious imitation of reality? Ionesco opted instead to open all the floodgates of his fantasy, rendering visual what previously had been discursive and imitating the extravagance of clowns. And if you're going to exaggerate along such lines, why stop halfway?

Ionesco turned on life the same withering gaze with which he dissolved theatrical conventions. Theater of the Absurd, they called it. The formula is apt. We live protected by a cocoon of habit, so intent on our actions that we never question their meaning, much less the meaning of our place in the world. But when the machinery goes awry, illusions crumble. Since nothing has any meaning, we must laugh about this to avoid hanging ourselves. For Ionesco, writing was truly a defense against suicide.

His first play went right to the heart of things. *The Bald Soprano* takes on two inseparable problems, interpersonal communication and the inadequacy of language. Every word is prejudicial. We find ourselves trapped in commonplaces and grammatical structures. To cite the title of one of Ionesco's essays, *The Bald Soprano* illustrates the "tragedy of language." Because of the inability of language to express the essential, each of us remains an island.

Giving tangible form to the confusion of modern man, profoundly reshaping theatrical expectations, Ionesco's plays have rapidly come to be regarded as classics of French literature.

Paul Desalmand

MRS. SMITH: . . . (she screams, stamps her foot, raises her fists.) Leave me alone, leave me alone, leave me alone! (she plops down into her armchair.) Open it if you like! Me, I'm not going to anymore! Go ahead! There won't be anyone there!

MR. SMITH (imperturbable; ironic; an air of slight contempt; without answering, he walks to the door and opens it. On the threshold, the town fire chief).

Scene II

(the same; the fire chief, aged between 40 and 50, in uniform and wearing a dazzling helmet)

MR. SMITH: Good day, Mr. Fireman! (to Mrs. Smith, victoriously) You see, there *was* someone there. (Mrs. Smith doesn't respond; she is caught up in her darning) I was right!

FIRE CHIEF: What did you say, Mr. Smith?

MR.SMITH: I wasn't talking to you. I was talking to my wife. She told me not to open the door because she didn't think anyone was there.

FIRE CHIEF: Ah! Ah! Ah! Ah! That's a good one, that is!

MRS. SMITH (annoyed, she rises and approaches the two others; to her husband): Please, don't get strangers mixed up in our private quarrels!

FIRE CHIEF (confused): Excuse me! . . .

Top left: Eugène Ionesco at home. On his desk is the inkwell illustrated at left. Collection Eugène Ionesco. *Right:* Saul Steinberg, drawing inspired by *The Bald Soprano*, 1958. Collection Eugène Ionesco. *Opposite:* Page from the autograph manuscript of *The Bald Soprano*. Collection Eugène Ionesco.

(elle crie, tape du pied, montre les poings) : Fiche moi la paix, fiche-moi la paix, fiche-moi la paix ! (elle se laisse choir dans son fauteuil) Va ouvrir si tu veux ! Moi je n'y vais plus ! Vas-y ! Il n'y aura personne !

<u>Monsieur Smith</u>

(imperturbable ; ironique ; l'air ~~ne~~ légèrement méprisant ; sans répondre, il va vers la porte et l'ouvre. Sur le seuil, le capitaine des pompiers de la ville).

Scène <u>II</u>

(les mêmes ; le capitaine des pompiers ; celui-ci, âgé de 40 à 50 ans, coiffé d'un casque éblouissant, en uniforme)

<u>Monsieur Smith</u>

Bonjour, monsieur le pompier ! (à Madame Smith, victorieusement) Tu vois qu'il y avait quelqu'un ? (Madame Smith ne répond pas ; elle est confondue dans son travail de raccomodage). J'avais raison !

<u>Le Capitaine des Pompiers</u>

Vous dites, monsieur Smith ?

<u>Monsieur Smith</u>

Ce n'est pas à vous que je m'adressais. Je parlais à ma femme. Elle me disait de ne pas ouvrir la porte car elle prétendait qu'il n'y avait personne.

<u>Le Capitaine des Pompiers</u>

~~He~~ Ah ! Ah ! Ah ! Ah ! Elle est bien bonne, celle-là !

<u>Madame Smith</u>

(vexée, se lève, s'approche des deux autres, ~~interrompt~~ à son mari :) ~~Son~~ Je t'en prie de ne pas mêler les étrangers à nos conflits intimes !

<u>Le Capitaine des Pompiers</u> (confus)

Excusez-moi ! . . .

"Olives"

Francis Ponge, 1950

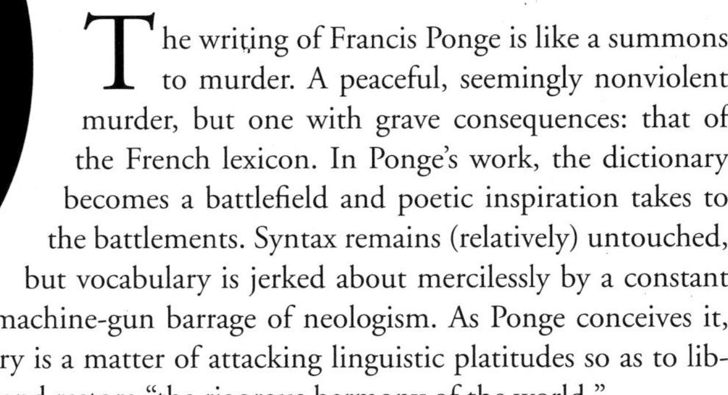

The writing of Francis Ponge is like a summons to murder. A peaceful, seemingly nonviolent murder, but one with grave consequences: that of the French lexicon. In Ponge's work, the dictionary becomes a battlefield and poetic inspiration takes to the battlements. Syntax remains (relatively) untouched, but vocabulary is jerked about mercilessly by a constant machine-gun barrage of neologism. As Ponge conceives it, poetry is a matter of attacking linguistic platitudes so as to liberate words and restore "the rigorous harmony of the world."

The collection *Cinq Sapates*, for example, which includes the poem "Olives," exemplifies these bellicose intentions. Likewise the collection *Pièces*, in which the same prose poem appears. Only a single consonant distinguishes *pièce* from *piège* (trap), which can serve to remind us that conventional modes of analysis are not of much use here. How are we to take seriously prose poems expostulating on potatoes, spiders, jugs, factory smokestacks, dung, and . . . olives? The accused pleads guilty: "I don't think of myself as a poet. . . . I use poetic magma, but only to dispense with it." Is he, then, less a sanguinary general than a humble wordsmith, a craftsman who manipulates linguistic material, wading through Baudelairean mud in the hope of rehabilitating objects and realities that we tend to regard with unwarranted contempt?

Perhaps, for his notion of poetic writing is premised on striking a delicate balance between coarse realism and a shimmering lyricism. Careless readers tend to reduce his poems to one extreme or the other, either to a Sartrean wallowing in things base, trivial, and commonplace, or to a euphoric exaltation of the overlooked. But Ponge manages to steer a course between the two, thanks to the *objeu*, a term he coined to designate playful "word-objects," or lexical sites, in which feeling and language, meaning and sensation, rhetoric and freedom can cohabit, places where language is reconquered with a kind of tender exertion. An exertion such as we find, in fact, in olives.

Yves Stalloni

Olives

Olives green, *vâtre*, black: the *olivâtre* between green and black on the way to carbonization. A gentle carbonization, in oil, perhaps imbued with a hint of rancidity.

But . . . is this accurate?

Does every olive, between green and black, pass through *olivâtre*? Or isn't it rather a case, in some, of sickness?

It seems to come from the pit, which rather ignobly tries to trade a bit of its hardness for the tenderness of the pulp . . . Instead of fulfilling its obligation: which is, conversely, not to harden the pulp (under any pretext!), but, up against it, to become harder and harder . . . So as to discourage it to the point that it decomposes, allowing it to reach the ground . . . And to sink into it. Free (if only for the moment) to relax; to open and germinate . . .

However that may be, the circumflex in *olivâtre* gives pleasure. It is shaped like a large black eyebrow, below which something instantly swoons, while decomposition impends.

But when the olive has turned black, nothing could be so more brilliantly. How marvelous, these puckered shapes! But as tasty as possible, and polished, and not excessive, with no hint of strain.

Better even than prunes for deposit in the mouth.

After these ramblings about the color of the pulp and its shape, let us turn to the main thing—most apparent when one sucks the seeds—which is the kinship of olives to ovals.

Here's a kinship that's right on the money, and almost naive.

What could be more naive than an olive,
Gracious and nimble in the handling.

. . . All the same, they are not sweet like those other young girls, sugared almonds, precious little things . . .

Rather bitter, in fact. And perhaps they must be treated in a certain way to sweeten them: left to marinate a bit.

But otherwise, what one ultimately finds at the core is not an almond! It's a little ball, a little torpedo made of wood that's very hard, that could easily penetrate as far as one's heart.

No; let's not exaggerate. Instead, let's smile over it—at least on one side of our mouths—and then place it on the edge of our plates.

All in all, quite simple. Neither too good a taste, nor too bad.

. . . One that doesn't lay claim to any more perfection than I have just attributed to it . . . and yet still can give pleasure, and often does, as an hors-d'oeuvre.

Francis Ponge

Top left: Photograph of Francis Ponge by Louis Monier.
Left: Watercolor by Maxime Rebière.
Opposite: Autograph manuscript of "Olives." Paris, Bibliothèque Nationale de France.

6

Les Olives

Olives vertes, vâtres, noires : l'olivâtre entre la verte et la noire sur le chemin de la carbonisation. Une carbonisation en douce, dans l'huile, où s'immisce alors peut-être une idée de rancissement.

Mais,... est-ce juste ?

Chaque olive, du vert au noir, passe-t-elle par l'olivâtre ? Ou ne s'agit-il, chez d'aucunes, plutôt d'une maladie ?

Cela semble venir du noyau, qui tenterait assez ignoblement alors d'échanger un peu de sa dureté contre la tendresse de la pulpe... Au lieu de s'en tenir à son devoir : qui est, tout au contraire, non de durcir la pulpe (sous aucun prétexte !), mais, contre elle, de se faire de plus en plus dur... Afin de la décourager, au point qu'elle se décompose et lui permette,

7

à lui, de gagner le sol... Et de s'y enfoncer. Libre à lui, alors (mais alors seulement), de se détendre ; s'entrouvrir et germer...

Quoiqu'il en soit, l'accent circonflexe se lit avec satisfaction sur olivâtre. Il s'y forme comme un gros sourcil noir, sous lequel quelque chose aussitôt se pâme, tandis que la décomposition se prépare.

Mais quand l'olive est devenue noire, rien ne l'est plus brillamment. Quelle merveille, ce côté flétri dans la forme ! Mais savoureuse au possible, et polie mais non trop, sans rien de tendu.

Meilleur suppositoire de bouche encore que le pruneau.

Après en avoir fini, de ces radotages sur la couleur de la pulpe et sa forme, venons-en au principal, -plus sensible à sucer le noyau, – qui est la proximité

8

d'olive et d'ovale.

Voila une proximité fort bien jouée, et comme naïve.

Quoi de plus naïf au fond qu'une olive,

Gracieuse et preste dans l'entregent.

...Elles ne font pas pour autant les sucrées, comme ces autres jeunes filles : les dragées, ces précieuses...

Plutôt amères, à vrai dire. Et peut-être faut-il les traiter d'une certaine façon pour les adoucir : les laisser mariner un peu.

Mais d'ailleurs, ce qu'on trouve enfin au noyau, ce n'est pas une amande ! Une petite balle, une petite torpille d'un bois très dur, qui peut à l'occasion pénétrer facilement jusqu'au cœur.

Non ; n'exagérons rien. Sourions-en plutôt, – d'un côté du moins de la bouche – pour la poser bientôt sur le bord

9

de l'assiette.

×

Voila qui est tout simple. Ni de trop bon, ni de trop mauvais goût.

... Qui n'exige pas plus de perfection que je ne viens d'y mettre... Et peut plaire pourtant, plait d'habitude à tout le monde, comme hors d'œuvre.

=

"Those who happen to enter"

René-Guy Cadou, 1950

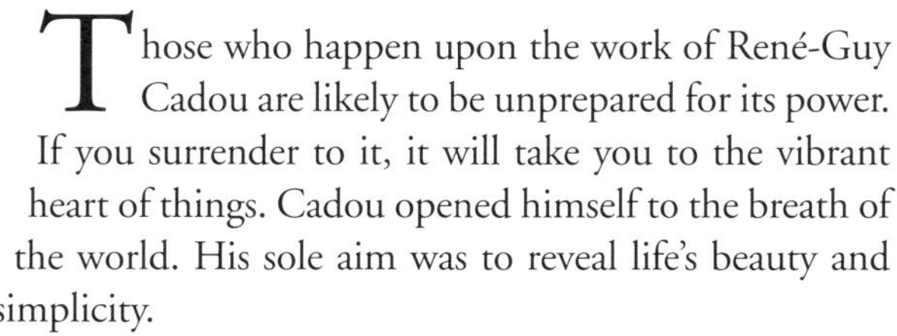

Those who happen upon the work of René-Guy Cadou are likely to be unprepared for its power. If you surrender to it, it will take you to the vibrant heart of things. Cadou opened himself to the breath of the world. His sole aim was to reveal life's beauty and simplicity.

Death awaits. Who is unaware of this? Who is unaware that one day the winds of time will sweep everything away? But life awaits, too. And with it friends, the world of childhood too soon abandoned, if never forgotten, the smell of fresh bread, of flowering cherry trees. As a poet, he was not a perfectionist, for he felt that many readers would find its human imperfections moving and revealing. Nonetheless, he produced a few poems that may be deemed perfect: "*Antonin Artaud*," "*Art poétique*," "*Aller simple*" ("One-Way Ticket"), and *"Celui qui entre par hasard"* ("Those who Happen to Enter"). They are miraculous: mysterious arrangements of words, intangible architectural structures that, once encountered, are hard to forget.

Death claimed this provincial teacher when he was barely thirty. It did not surprise him. All his life, he sensed it lurking behind the splendor of this world. But in the end, the Grim Reaper emerged the loser, for thousands of words written across hundreds of pages attest to the brief existence of a discreet but warm-hearted poet who was called René-Guy Cadou.

Do not call out.
But hear this numberless cortège of steps.

Paul Desalmand

Those who happen to enter the house of a poet
Know not that the furniture has power over
them,
That every knot in the wood contains more
Bird cries than the whole heart of the forest
A lamp need only place its female neck
At nightfall against a varnished corner
To deliver suddenly whole populations of bees
And the smell of fresh bread, of flowering
cherry,
For such is the beauty of this solitude
That a mere caress of the hand
Restores to these large and taciturn black pieces
The lightness of a tree in the morning.

Louisfert, September 1950

rené guy cadou.

Top left: René-Guy Cadou in 1949.
Right: The poet's house at Louisfert, in Loire-Atlantique.
Opposite: Autograph manuscript of "Those who Happen to Enter."

Celui qui entre par hasard dans la
demeure d'un poète
Ne sait pas que les meubles ont
pouvoir sur lui
Que chaque noeud du bois renferme
davantage
De cris d'oiseaux que tout le coeur
de la forêt
Il suffit qu'une lampe pose son cou
de femme
A la tombée du soir contre un angle
verni
Pour délivrer soudain mille peuples d'
abeilles
Et l'odeur de pain frais des cerisiers
fleuris
Car tel est le bonheur de cette solitude
Qu'une caresse toute plate de la main
Redonne à ces grands ~~[illegible]~~ meubles noirs et
taciturnes
La légèreté d'un arbre dans le matin.

Louisfert, 6 sept. 1950

René Guy Cadou.

"Here, there, everywhere"

Paul Éluard, 1953

Some readers have sought to isolate two strains within the work of Paul Éluard: that of the love poet, a celebrant at the altar of female beauty who, like a modern Petrarch, rediscovered the language of courtly love; and that of the revolutionary bard, a Surrealist who used his verse to advance the cause of communism and the humble working man. In the end, however, such attempts are misguided. Éluard indeed expressed himself in various and seemingly contradictory ways, but all of his poetry springs from a common source: a boundless faith in the brotherhood of man fueled by a generous creative energy.

This warm-hearted empathy can seem naive. We have many reasons to dismiss those who focus on the angelic side of our natures as blind. In the course of the last century, humanity seemed hell-bent on spreading evil and distress. Mars killed Orpheus. And a beautiful alexandrine has never stilled a cannon. But this makes it all the more urgent for us to read Éluard. His tender voice and straightforward diction summon us, if not to belief, then at least to hope. Every line of *Poésie Ininterrompue II* (1953), his final collection, published posthumously, is a hymn to love, mutual understanding, and openness to life:

To open truly a larger door to man.

Perhaps Éluard exemplifies the "popular poet": one who, in accessible language, praises happiness when reality is dark and exalts love when cynicism stalks. But we should take care: almost half a century after his death, Éluard, so greatly admired by our fathers and our grandfathers, is slipping from view. This does not bode well for peace—or for poetry.

Yves Stalloni

There are the thousand walls
Of our well-aging houses
And mothers of a thousand houses
There sleep waves of tiles
Renewed by the sun
And bearing the shadows of birds
Like the water bears fish.

There all work is easy
And objects caress the hand
Hands know only promises
Life stimulates all eyes
The body has happy fevers
Named the Pearl of noon
Or the Rumblings of light.

There I see both near and far
There I hurl myself into space
Day and night are my trampolines
There I return to the world entire
To rebound towards every thing
Towards every instant and always
And I rediscover my kind.

I speak of a time delivered
From the gravediggers of reason
I speak of liberty
Which in the end will convince us
No one will fear tomorrow
Hope raises no dust
Nothing will ever be in vain.

Top left: Max Ernst, *Portrait of Paul Éluard.* Private collection.
Below: Fernand Léger, *Liberty,* tapestry incorporating a poem by Paul Éluard. Biot, Musée Fernand-Léger.
Opposite: Page from the autograph manuscript of *"Ailleurs, ici, partout"* (*"Here, There, Everywhere"*), published in *Poésie Ininterrompue II* (1953).

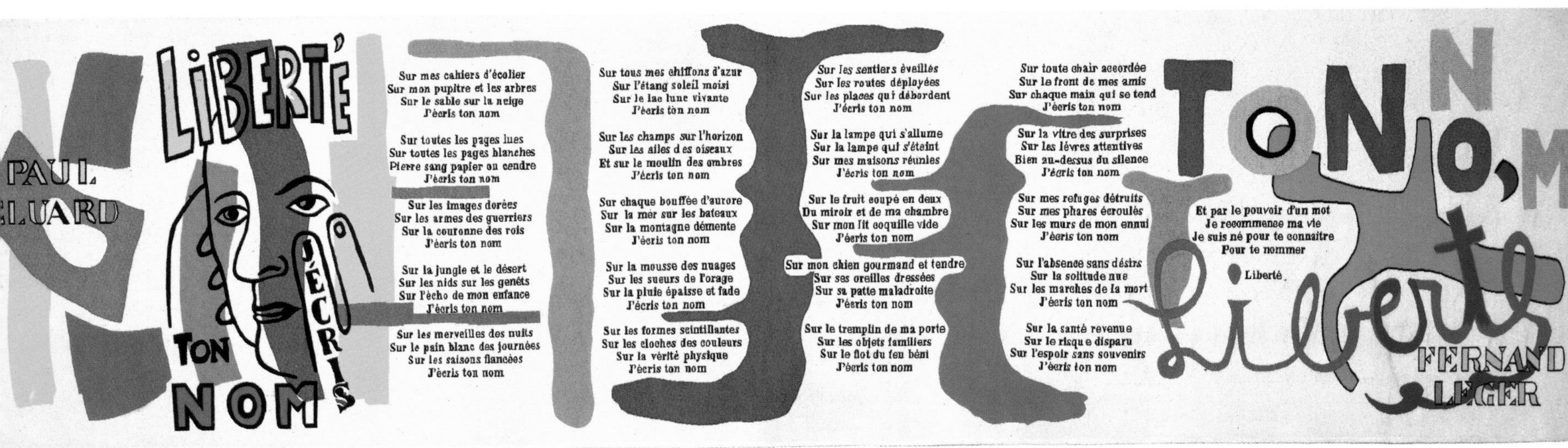

13

Là se dressent les mille murs
De nos maisons vieillissant bien
Et mères de mille maisons
Là dorment des vagues de tuiles
Renouvelées par le soleil
Et portant l'ombre des oiseaux
Comme l'eau porte les poissons

Ⓓ Là tous les travaux sont faciles
Et l'objet caresse la main
La main ne connaît que promesses
La vie éveille tous les yeux
Le corps a des fièvres heureuses
Nommées la Perle de midi
Ou la Rumeur de la lumière

Là je vois de près ~~ou~~ et de loin
Là je m'élance dans l'espace
Le jour la nuit sont mes tremplins
Là je reviens au monde entier
Pour rebondir vers chaque chose

Passage from Milan

Michel Butor, 1954

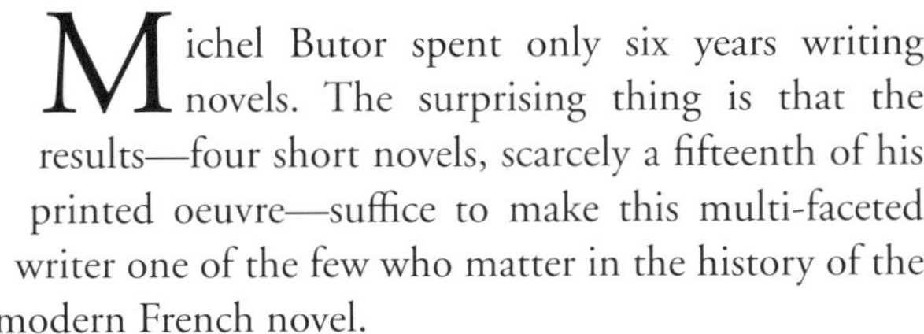

Michel Butor spent only six years writing novels. The surprising thing is that the results—four short novels, scarcely a fifteenth of his printed oeuvre—suffice to make this multi-faceted writer one of the few who matter in the history of the modern French novel.

Timing plays an important role here. The decade between 1953 and 1962, during which all of Butor's novels appeared, saw the emergence of a small group of young writers, all affiliated with the same publisher (Éditions de Minuit), whose novels sidestepped the conventions of the genre to embrace an array of radical strategies, eschewing anthropocentrism, transforming objects into obsessive presences, avoiding narrative suspense, willfully manipulating space and time, and replacing the palette of "style" with a neutral "white writing." Academics and critics hastened to christen the results the "Nouveau Roman," or New Novel. With Alain Robbe-Grillet, Claude Simon, Nathalie Sarraute, Robert Pinget, Jean Ricardou, and a few others, Michel Butor became, unwittingly, a standard-bearer of the new school.

Passage de Milan (*Passage from Milan*) appeared in 1954, one year after Robbe-Grillet's *The Erasers*, which is generally credited with having launched the new tendency. *Passage from Milan* is characterized by a number of innovative techniques: complex narrative structure, spatial consistency (the book tells the story of a Parisian tenement building), a profusion of mythological and cultural references, and idiosyncratic symbolic coding.

Using these tools, Butor interrogated what he called "representational techniques," or the ways of "recounting things," of depicting reality. An approach in which the choice of narrative voice plays a key role: a diffuse third person in *Passage de Milan*, an unequivocal first person in *Passing Time*, an enigmatic third person in *A Change of Heart*. In Butor's hands, the novel is not simply an esthetic diversion; it becomes a meditation on the nature of writing. Art that seeks to understand art is still art.

Yves Stalloni

At the bank where Frédéric Magne is employed, they say that he is a man of forty who looks sixty, but in fact he is fifty-five. He married late, because of the 1914 war, a woman much younger than he. He has no hope of promotion, his job doesn't interest him, and he is haunted by the idea of retirement. He retains a certain vehemence that he uses as a mask and that is inconsistent with his facial features and his sparse hair, already gray, which is what confuses people about his age, but in fact when he returns home, he abandons this posture like an awkward piece of clothing, and it is a weary, draggy man who looks in the concierge's lodge to see if he has any mail, although he isn't expecting any and he knows that it would already have been brought up by his family. If he takes the elevator, it isn't to save time but to spare himself, the breath of the machine does his complaining for him and he tries to slow down when he opens the doors, closes them again, presses the button, watches the contraption descend, turns on the lights, looks for his key. The building in which he lives is narrow. At times, there are so many people jammed into it that there's no room to look at them. You come home, you eat dinner, you avoid others, you don't complain, you go to bed while everyone else is still up; and the next day you must return to the bank. In short, life doesn't add up to much. He hangs up his hat, drops his cane into the old umbrella stand. The house is full but no one is there to greet him. A young girl's voice shouts: "Mama, papa is home." He goes to his bedroom, turns on the light, sits on his bed, removes his damp socks, [illegible] his feet, opens the large black armoire that contains all of the house's linen and that leaves just enough room for the large bed. He never knows where his things are, the piles of sheets are crowned by [illegible]. It's an old shoe box, here's a little soft egg of black tissue paper that he unfolds and divides into two irregular bands that open under his fingers and that he conscientiously folds back one after the other. He pulls out his slippers, puts them on, turns out the light, and sits down in the living room close to the small table where his son Felix usually does his homework. Felix is reading something furtively, and looks up a bit uneasily when his father arrives.

Top left: Michel Butor in 1980.
Left: Max Ernst, *The Hat Makes The Man*, 1920.
Opposite: Page from a draft of *Passage from Milan*. This page was substantially recast prior to publication. Paris, Bibliothèque Nationale de France.

On dit à la banque de Frédéric Mogne que c'est un homme de quarante ans qui en paraît soixante, mais en réalité c'est qu'il a cinquante-cinq. Il s'est marié tard, à cause de la guerre de 1914 avec une femme nettement plus jeune que lui. Il est sans espoir d'avancement, son métier ne l'intéresse pas et l'idée de la retraite le travaille. Il a gardé une certaine sévérité dont il se sert comme d'un masque et qui contraste avec les traits de son visage et ses cheveux déjà gris, c'est ce qui rend ceux qui l'abordent incertains sur son âge, mais en réalité quand il rentre chez lui, il abandonne ce rôle comme un vêtement trop lourd, et c'est un homme usé, traînant qui regarde dans la loge du concierge s'il y a du courrier pour lui, alors qu'il n'attend rien et qu'il sait bien que tout aura déjà été monté par l'un des membres de sa smala. S'il prend l'ascenseur ce n'est pas pour gagner du temps, mais pour se reposer, le souffle de la machine se plaint pour lui et il fait effort de lenteur pour ouvrir les portes les refermer, presser sur le bouton, quitter à la descente de l'engin, rallumer, chercher sa clé. La maison dans laquelle il rentre est étroite. Tant de personnes s'y côtoient sans nonchalance, qui n'ont pas la place de se regarder. On rentre on dîne, on s'évite on ne sait rien se dire on s'endort tandis que tout continue à s'agiter et le lendemain il faut bien retourner à la banque. Tout cela n'est rien. Il accroche son chapeau, jette sa canne dans le vieux porte parapluie. La maison est pleine, mais personne n'est là pour l'accueillir. On entend une voix de jeune fille crier : "Maman papa est rentré". Il va jusqu'à sa chambre allume, s'assied sur le lit dénoue les cordons de ses chaussures, enlève ses chaussettes humides, va se laver les pieds ouvre la grande armoire noire, où est tout le linge de la maison, et qui laisse juste assez de place pour le grand lit à. Il ne sait jamais où sont ses affaires les piles de draps sont couronnées chacune par un sachet de lavande. C'est un vieux carton à chaussures, voilà un petit [illegible] qu'il déplie et divise en deux bandes irrégulières qui s'enroulent sous ses doigts et qu'il enfile l'une après l'autre consciencieusement. Il tire ses pantoufles s'installe dedans, éteint et va s'asseoir au salon près de la petite table où son fils Félix a l'habitude de faire ses devoirs. Il lit quelque chose maintenant qu'il cache, et il lève un regard un peu inquiet à l'arrivée

The Voyage

Georges Schehadé, 1961

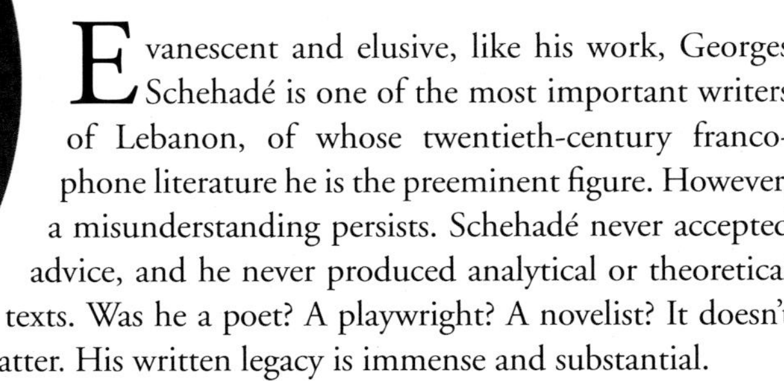

Evanescent and elusive, like his work, Georges Schehadé is one of the most important writers of Lebanon, of whose twentieth-century francophone literature he is the preeminent figure. However, a misunderstanding persists. Schehadé never accepted advice, and he never produced analytical or theoretical texts. Was he a poet? A playwright? A novelist? It doesn't matter. His written legacy is immense and substantial.

Born in Alexandria, Egypt, on November 2, 1905, into an emigré Lebanese family of Christian faith that had gone there in search of fortune, he arrived in Beirut at age fifteen and lived in the Sursock quarter, where the prosperity of the great Greek Orthodox families that succeeded brilliantly in business and in the upper administrative echelons of the Ottoman Empire was much in evidence. In this world, Schehadé was a poor relative who was kept lightly under wraps. Encouraged by his family, he began to study business, a path that he soon abandoned, deciding to study law instead. It was perhaps at this time that he began to write the early poems that he later destroyed.

In 1938, when his collection *Poésies I* finally appeared, Schehadé tried his hand at writing plays. Although he did not abandon other genres, he found writing for the theater congenial. Witness *The Voyage*, mounted in 1961 at the Théâtre de l'Odéon in Paris, in a production directed by Jean-Louis Barrault. He had begun to draft it in February of 1960 under the working title "Christopher and The Voyage." After being informed of the project, Barrault quickly wrote him: "Of course I'm interested in *The Voyage*. I told you without qualification that everything you do interests me." In his review of the opening night (February 1961), Claude Sarraute was enthusiastic: "Never . . . has Georges Schehadé been more inspired. This *Voyage* is a complex and accomplished piece of work. The poet has realized that he is also a playwright. . . . A bird catcher with deft fingers, he has never caught in his nets images that are more agile, more vigorous. They command attention and stick in the mind. They are hard to forget."

Roselyne de Ayala

QUARTERMASTER ALEXANDER: Tell me, Christopher, are you reading anything interesting these days? A little knowledge improves the wine and might advance the career of a first quartermaster.

CHRISTOPHER: A history of the Northern Islands and their mysteries.

QUARTERMASTER: And what's so interesting about these islands where you have to light candles beginning at noon?

CHRISTOPHER: Ah, well! . . . They have orchards.

QUARTERMASTER: What season?

CHRISTOPHER: In mid-winter! While everything around them is walls of ice, gusts of wind, and terror. There are strips of land several leagues long that, for some mysterious reason, the cold can't reach. They have running streams and ferns.

Below: Poster announcing the first production of *The Voyage*.
Opposite: Page from the autograph manuscript of *The Voyage*.
Schehadé-IMEC Archive.

Below left: Drawing by Georges Schehadé in the margin of the autograph manuscript of *The Voyage;*
Right: a set design by Jean-Denis Malclès for the play's first scene.
Top left: Fernand Desnos, *Portrait of Georges Schehadé*, ca. 1960. Schehadé-IMEC Archive.

(130)

Quartier Maître Alexandre

Dites, Christopher, que lisez-vous d'intéressant ces temps-ci?... Un peu de savoir agrémente la vie et peut aider la carrière d'un premier quartier-maître.

Christopher

Une histoire des îles du Nord et de leurs mystères.

Quartier-Maître Alexandre

Et qu'ont-elles de si ~~[illegible]~~ séduisant ces îles où il faut s'éclairer à la chandelle à partir de midi?

Christopher

Ah, voilà-!... Elles ont des vergers.

Quartier-Maître Alexandre

~~[illegible]~~ A quelle époque?

Christopher

En plein hiver! alors que tout est ~~[illegible]~~ muraille de glace autour d'elles, rafales de vent et terreur. Il existe des bandes de terres longues de plusieurs lieues et imprenables par le froid, à cause de je ne sais quel mystère. Là coulent les ruisseaux et poussent les fougères.

("Le Voyage")

Manon of the Springs

Marcel Pagnol, 1964

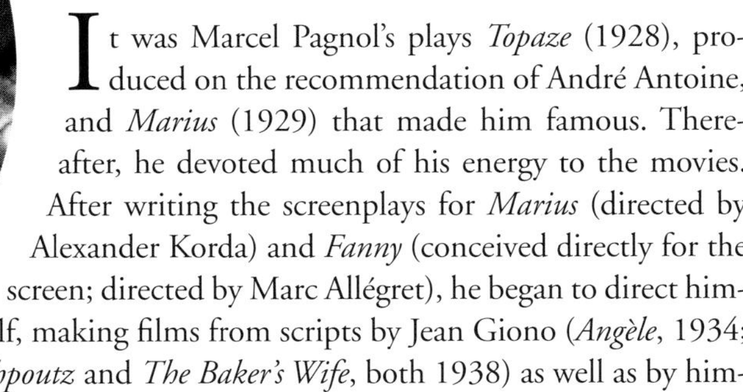

It was Marcel Pagnol's plays *Topaze* (1928), produced on the recommendation of André Antoine, and *Marius* (1929) that made him famous. Thereafter, he devoted much of his energy to the movies. After writing the screenplays for *Marius* (directed by Alexander Korda) and *Fanny* (conceived directly for the screen; directed by Marc Allégret), he began to direct himself, making films from scripts by Jean Giono (*Angèle*, 1934; *Le Schpoutz* and *The Baker's Wife*, both 1938) as well as by himself (*César*, 1935; *Harvest*, 1937; *Topaze*, 1950; *Manon des Sources*, 1952). It is probably true that, as Bernard de Fallois has claimed, "thanks to the movies," Pagnol "is better known to many of his fellow citizens than any writer of his country has ever been." But this remark also signals the limit of his reputation.

His four-volume autobiography—the first half of which has been translated as *The Days Were Too Short*—is not as well known as his films. In his preface, Pagnol noted: "Here, for the first time—apart from a few modest essays—I write in prose. It is no longer [the actor] Raimu who speaks; it is I myself." In these books, he reveals himself to be a wonderful storyteller and portraitist, possessed of a clear and vivid style in the tradition of Rabelais, La Fontaine, and Voltaire, combining lightness of touch with moral seriousness, fashioning colloquial barbs that have become famous ("You're not a good-for-nothing, you're bad at everything"; "You're breaking my heart"; "When they make imbeciles dance, you won't be in the orchestra").

Although he advocated—not altogether seriously—comfortable mediocrity, submission to destiny, love of one's own, and tolerance of others, his achievement is substantial, various, and largely underestimated. In addition to his films and his autobiography, he left behind several remarkable novels (*Pirouettes*, *Jean de Florette*, *Manon of the Springs*), translations of Shakespeare and Virgil (*Hamlet*, *The Bucolics*), and a fascinating book about the so-called Man in the Iron Mask.

Pierre Chalmin

Around 1925, Bastides Blanches was a village of one hundred inhabitants perched on a hill in Provence. In front of it, barely five or six kilometers away, began the suburbs of Marseilles, and in the distance, at the end of the green valley of the Huveaune, one could see the red sun sink into the sea.

Behind the village, a desert of scrub land spotted with pine groves rose toward rocky summits whose half-circle extended from Sainte-Baume as far as the long chain of the Étoile.

The Bastidians were rather tall, dark, thin, and muscular. They lived at the edge of a large city, but it was quite obvious that they didn't come from there, that they were born in their hills.

Top left: Marcel Pagnol with his daughter Estelle in 1952.
Left: Pagnol's inkwell and reed pen.
Right and Opposite: Pages from the autograph manuscript of *Manon of the Springs*. Archives Jacqueline Pagnol.

je l'ai connue quand elle avait dix ou onze ans... Elle 2
me détestait, j'ai jamais su pourquoi. Alors moi,
elle me plaisait pas du tout; et puis maintenant,
tout ce que je regarde, elle est devant. C'est comme
si elle était peinte sur une vitre... Quand j'arrose
les œillets, l'eau traverse sa figure. Et quand
je ferme les yeux, je la vois encore mieux...
D'une voix lugubre, et comme effrayée, la vieille
chuchota :
– Surtout la nuit...
– Oh pour ça, je la rêve toutes les nuits... Et même je
fais exprès de me coucher de bonne heure pour être
plus vite au rendez-vous. Oh! C'est pas qu'elle me
parle gentiment, au contraire... Mais enfin, elle est
là, je la vois, je l'entends... Souvent, elle se
moque de moi, et elle a
raison, parceque je fais des choses bêtes... Des

choses risibles, tellement que c'est pas croyable... D'abord,
il y a cette poupée que j'ai trouvée au grenier...
Parceque, avant, elle habitait dans cette maison...
Une mauvaise poupée de chiffons, avec les yeux marqués
à la peinture bleue, et une petite bouche rouge...
quand je mange seul à la maison, je la mets à
côté de moi, assise sur la table, avec son verre et
son assiette; et puis le soir, je la couche sur mon
traversin, je lui fais la bise, et elle dort avec moi.
J'ai honte de le dire, mais c'est comme ça...
Il se tût quelques secondes, ouvrit les yeux,
les referma, et reprit :
– Dans le gros olivier, devant la maison, il reste deux
anneaux en fil de fer, autour d'une branche, et le
fil de fer a fait comme une rigole dans l'écorce.
c'était pour accrocher sa balançoire quand elle

Manon des Sources

—

Les Bastides Blanches, vers 1925, c'était un village de cent habitants perché sur une colline de Provence. Devant lui, à cinq ou six kilomètres à peine, commençait la banlieue de Marseille, et l'on voyait au loin, au bout de la verte vallée de l'Huveaune, le soleil rouge se coucher sur la mer.

MP

Derrière le village, un désert de garrigues, coupé de pinèdes, montait vers des sommets rocheux dont le demi cercle s'étendait de la Sainte Baume jusqu'à la longue chaîne de l'Etoile.

Les Bastidiens étaient plutôt grands, bruns, maigres et musclés. Ils vivaient au bord de la grande ville, mais on voyait bien qu'ils n'en venaient pas, et qu'ils étaient nés de leurs collines,

The Abyss

Marguerite Yourcenar, 1968

Sometimes literary achievement is like vinticulture: success is measured more in terms of quality than of quantity. A few superb wines are produced only on properties of very limited extent, just as some authors become classics on the basis of very few titles. A case in point is Marguerite Yourcenar. Apart from her critical and autobiographical work, she owes her entry into the French literary pantheon—and into the prestigious Académie Française, where she broke a long-standing gender barrier—to only three or four novels. The ambition and depth of these works compensate for their rarity.

Her principal aim in these novels is to evoke successfully the texture of lived experience. One of her preferred strategies for doing this is to root her fiction in historical reality. History can provide much useful material, and characters can be "singularly enriched by fidelity to the facts." Despite such statements, Yourcenar's subtle reconstructions must not be confused with realist illusionism; indeed, the two approaches are almost diametrically opposed. Her meticulous documentation, born of "sympathetic magic," serves in part to mask her work's deeply personal character.

Take Zeno, the central character of *L'Oeuvre au Noir* (*The Abyss*). He could be straight out of an engraving by Dürer or the library of a Renaissance monastery. He is a brother of Erasmus, a cousin of Jean Myers, a disciple of Rabelais, an intimate of Étienne Dolet, a descendent of Nicolas Flamel. But this erudite mystic tempted to crack the Great Code is a timeless, disillusioned brother of ourselves. "Man is an ongoing project. . . . Few bipeds since Adam have been worthy of the name 'man'." The Emperor Hadrian, as conjured by Yourcenar in her most famous novel, *Memoirs of Hadrian*, likewise sought absolute wisdom through ascetic self-transcendence.

Each of Yourcenar's main characters embarks on a quest that is analogous to her own creative adventure. This can lead to a dizzying confusion between objectivity and subjectivity, but such effects are intentional, the result of finely honed craft. Yourcenar's books are by turns shimmering and severe, full-bodied and sere, heady and austere. By any measure, a great vintage.

Yves Stalloni

. . . a hateful silence. From that day forward, he prolonged his absences. Jacqueline thought he must be having a little fling with a farm girl.

Once, he took enough bread with him to last several days and ventured as far as the forest of Hauthuist. This was all that remained of the great forests of pagan times, and strange counsels fell from its leaves. Head upraised, contemplating the thick foliage and needles from below, Zeno again pondered strange alchemical speculations such as had been discussed at school, or were at odds with its teachings; he discerned in each of these vegetal pyramids a hermetic hieroglyph of ascendent forces, a sign of the air that bathes and nourishes these beautiful sylvan entities; or of the fire that they harbored within them as a virtuality, and that might one day destroy them. But these upward movements were balanced by a descent: beneath his feet, the blind and sentient root people imitated in darkness the infinite division of twigs in the sky, tentatively heading towards some unknown nadir. Here and there, a prematurely yellow leaf betrayed the presence below the green of metals from which it had drawn its substance and which it was in the process of transmuting. The force of the wind twisted the tall trunks much as men were tossed about by destiny. The cleric felt as free as a wild animal, and as threatened, suspended like a tree between the lower world and the upper world, and likewise subject to pressures that would cease only with death. But for this twenty-year-old the word death remained a mere word.

At twilight, he noticed on the moss the tracks of a cart. . . .

Top left: Marguerite Yourcenar.
Right: Pieter Bruegel the Elder, *Hunters in the Snow (January)* (detail), 1565. Vienna, Kunsthistorisches Museum.
Opposite: Page from typed manuscript of *L'Oeuvre au Noir* (*The Abyss*) with autograph revisions. Paris, Bibliothèque Nationale de France.

41

un silence haineux. A partir de ce jour-là, il prolongea ses absences. Jacqueline croyait à quelque amourette avec une fille de ferme.

Une fois, emportant avec lui son pain pour plusieurs jours, il s'aventura jusqu'à la forêt d'Houthulst. Ces bois étaient le reste des grandes futaies du temps paien : d'étranges conseils tombaient de leurs feuilles. La tête levée, contemplant d'en bas ces épaisseurs de verdure et d'aiguilles, Zénon se rengageait dans les spéculations alchimiques abordées à l'école, ou en dépit de l'école; il retrouvait dans chacune de ces pyramides végétales le hiéroglyphe hermétique des forces ascendantes, le signe de l'air, qui baigne et nourrit ces belles entités sylvestres, du feu, dont elles portent en soi la virtualité, et qui peut-être les détruira un jour. Mais ces montées s'équilibraient d'une descente: sous ses pieds, le peuple aveugle et sentient des racines imitait dans le noir l'infinie division des brindilles dans le ciel, s'orientait précautionneusement vers on ne sait quel nadir. Ça et là, une feuille trop tôt jaunie trahissait sous le vert la présence des métaux dont elle avait formé sa substance et dont elle opérait la transmutation. La poussée du vent déjetait les grands fûts comme un homme son destin. Le clerc se sentait libre comme la bête et menacé comme elle, équilibré comme l'arbre entre le monde d'en bas et le monde d'en haut, ployé lui aussi par des pressions s'exerçant sur lui et qui ne cesseraient qu'à sa mort. Mais le mot mort n'était encore qu'un mot pour cet homme de vingt ans.

Au crépuscule, il remarqua sur la mousse la trace d'un charroi

ch. III Les Loisirs de l'été (L'Oeuvre au Noir) Le mot condamné à l'allelage I.

[handwritten in right margin:] ... been doing. So you will probably redo all this page # 45 by your typing

Life: A User's Manual

Georges Perec, 1972

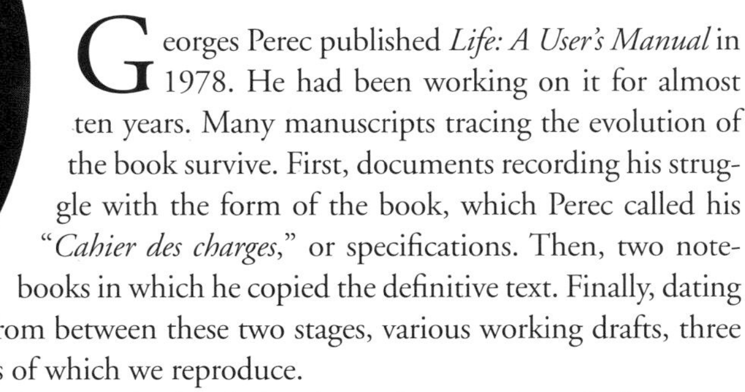

Georges Perec published *Life: A User's Manual* in 1978. He had been working on it for almost ten years. Many manuscripts tracing the evolution of the book survive. First, documents recording his struggle with the form of the book, which Perec called his "*Cahier des charges*," or specifications. Then, two notebooks in which he copied the definitive text. Finally, dating from between these two stages, various working drafts, three pages of which we reproduce.

The first (opposite), dated October 26, 1972, is a draft for the opening. Two days earlier, he had written a first draft of the same passage. These are the earliest known manuscripts, but they are very clean, suggesting the existence of earlier drafts that have since been lost. Some elements, like the indication "between the 3rd and 4th floors," would be retained, but the description of the female character would change considerably, becoming more and more precise.

The second sheet (below left) is from a draft of Chapter LXV, which tells the story of "the woman who made the devil appear eighty-three times." The narrative is present only in broad outline, but all of the essential elements (characters, conclusion) are in place, along with certain details (the flowers, the Pontiac). Nonetheless, this is very much a working draft, and Perec scribbled drawings in the margin: abstract shapes and the bust of a man, all seemingly unrelated to the story. They are not illustrations but record moments of rest or hesitation in the creative process.

There are even more such doodles on the third sheet (below right), from a draft of chapter LXXX, where they occupy the entire lower half of the page. Here, too, they have no discernible connection to the paragraphs above. On the other hand, the words in capital letters (CONSOBRINIA, COLUMBIA, etc.) indeed pertain to the text, part of which concerns a "Spanish archivist" who discovers a map of North America bearing inscriptions that have been partly effaced.

These drafts reveal that, during the protracted period of revision, Perec found release and even creative stimulus in such graphic distractions, a discovery that adds a new facet to the creative profile of a fascinating and surprising writer.

Bernard Magné

26.X.72
We can begin like this: Between the 3rd and 4th floors, a woman is on her way up the stairs; she wears a Bordeaux tweed suit and a large, light beige canvas handbag decorated with a gray, repeated motif that is nothing other than the interlaced initials of the manufacturer; she holds in her left hand a sheet of paper on which has been drawn carefully, even professionally, in addition to the precise measurements of the apartment she is about to visit, a plan with lines of varying thickness indicating its inner and outer walls, as well as half-circles with arrows indicating the direction in which the various doors open.

27.X.72
Several days earlier, the apartment had been for sale. An employee of the real estate agency with which the property had been listed had come to measure it and to make a preliminary assessment of its value, and the agency's female director had visited it to size it up prior to making her decision....

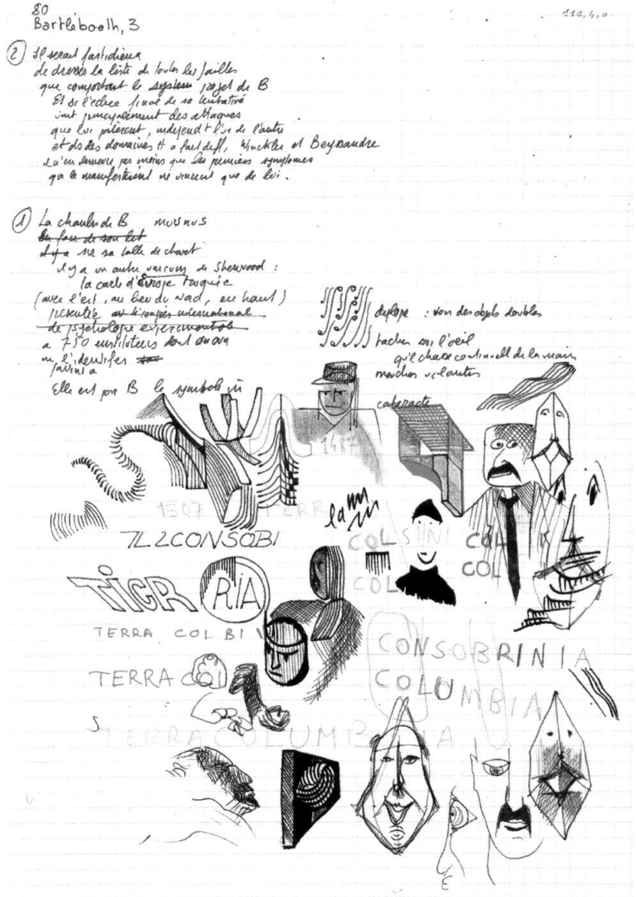

Top left: Photograph of Georges Perec by Louis Monier.
Left and right: Pages from the *"Cahiers des charges"* for *Life: A User's Manual.* Paris, Bibliothèque de l'Arsenal.
Opposite: Draft for the opening lines of *Life: A User's Manual.* Paris, Bibliothèque de l'Arsenal.

1

26.X.72

— On peut commencer comme cela : Entre le 3e et le 4e étage, une femme est en train de monter les escaliers ; elle porte un ensemble de tweed bordeaux, et un grand sac de toile ~~couleur sable~~ [marron clair] orné d'un motif ~~stylisé~~ [gris] apparemment [illegible] et qui n'est autre que les deux initiales entrelacées du fabricant. Elle tient dans la main gauche une feuille de papier sur laquelle a été dessiné soigneusement, professionnellement pourrait-on dire, non seulement avec des mensurations précises, mais avec, par exemple, des traits plus épais pour distinguer les murs des cloisons, avec, également, des demi-cercles fléchés indiquant dans quel sens s'ouvrent les portes, le plan de l'appartement qu'elle va visiter.

27.X.72

Quelques jours auparavant, l'appartement a été mis en vente. Un employé de l'agence immobilière à laquelle cette opération a été confiée est venu le métrer, en a fait une première estimation et la directrice de l'agence vient sur place se rendre compte de l'état des locaux avant de prendre sa décision ; on peut le

The Lover

Marguerite Duras, 1984

Marguerite Duras always refused to accept the view that familiarity with an author's biography sheds light on his or her work. It is nonetheless true that much of her own writing is autobiographical—indeed, that it rehashes the same story. From *The Sea Wall* (1950) to *The Lover* (1984) and *The North China Lover* (1991), Marguerite Duras repeatedly tells the story of her tormented life as an ill-loved adolescent in colonial Indochina.

Paradox of paradoxes: despite all this storytelling, the young girl never becomes fully present to us. One indication of this is that, prior to the appearance of *The Lover*, Duras was dismissive of all her work: "I have never written; that's what I thought I was doing, but all I've ever done is wait in front of the closed door." Conceits, dissimulations, and ellipses always managed to obscure the truth. But in *The Lover*, the veil of lies is shredded. That is why this short book, surely not the author's best, won the Goncourt Prize and became a huge success in France. Here, the misleading fictional surrogates of her earlier fictions—Suzanne, Aurélia, Lol, Anne-Marie—are replaced by an amorous young girl who transgresses against the moral code of her day. Result: notoriety and commercial success, but also a serious misprision.

For it is not the old saws of an earlier literature—theme, plot, character—that matter in the work of Duras. What matters is the writing, or, to use a more specifically Durasian term, the music: "If a book lacks music, then there is no book." Some of the author's titles underscore this musical ambition: *Moderato Cantabile, India Song, La Musica*. Duras's musicality is obtained by dint of scales, exercises, and all manner of exhausting work. In short, it is the result of a tenacious struggle with words to determine what should be said and what left unsaid: exploratory efforts that issue in fragmented texts pocketed with blanks and punctuated with repetitions. Undergirding all of these studied encounters between garrulity and taciturnity is desire, the key word in a literary career devoted to an exploration of corporeal mystery and arcana of the soul: to comparing the relative merits of avowal and silence, of transgression and appeasement, of the drive towards the absolute and the temptation of failure. Desire is sometimes said to be "revolutionary." The work of Marguerite Duras is revolutionary.

Yves Stalloni

The desert, that is not immortality, which passed through it but then proceeded on its way; it is what remains after it has left. The moving sands along the seashore have likewise replaced it.

In the little brother, it simply merged echoless with death, an immortality without caption, without words. During his lifetime, he had nothing to shout, nothing to say, he was completely untutored; he didn't even know enough to suffer so that others would notice his pain. Nothing. He was useless. He was a child. It was from the outside and despite himself that others perceived him. One might have thought, in this very moment in which I speak of him, that what's happening in the park here might testify to the immortality of this little brother, this child. Since the beginning of the world, people have thought that light makes no shadows when it rains. But not the poem or the song, but when to say so? Where is this place in the pain? Where this pause in the wind when there's not the slightest breath and the birds cry, this presence of birds that sharpen their beaks against the cold air, making a sound heard far and wide so that it is almost deafening, might make one think that this adorable violence of life will remain always, a sign in the centuries to come. To write about this, too: about a memory of the same thing.

Marguerite Duras

Top left: Photograph of Marguerite Duras taken by Louis Monier during an appearance on the television program "Apostrophes" (October 1984).
Left and below: watercolors by Maxime Rebière.
Opposite: Page from an early draft of *The Lover*.

(0) ~~Ce n'est pas parce que~~

C'est ce qui a fait sa santé admirable c'est que rien n'avait été commencé alors que c'était [illegible]

Le désert ce n'est pas l'immortalité, elle est passée par là et elle a quitté les lieux, c'est ce qui reste après qu'elle soit partie.

Le sable mouvant au bord des mers l'est de même remplacé

~~Et le petit frère mort s'est~~ [illegible] la mort, l'immortalité sans défense, sans mots, De son vivant, il n'avait rien à cacher, rien à dire, il était sans aucune instruction, il ne savait même pas sa douleur. [illegible] afin qu'on [illegible] c'était un effort. C'était [illegible] Rien. C'était de l'extérieur de lui et malgré lui qu'on le percevait. On pouvait croire qu'en ce moment même où je parle de lui, que ce qui se passe dans le [illegible] fait témoigner de cette immortalité de lui, ~~de l'enfant~~. Depuis que le monde est le monde on croit ~~que~~ c'est lumière sans ombre [illegible] Mais [illegible] de pluie [illegible] mais quand le [illegible] cet arrêt du vent lorsque les oiseaux crient, que et que les [illegible] et cette présence du souffle [illegible] et qui [illegible] les oiseaux qui s'aiguisent le bec contre l'air froid, le faisant sonner dans toute son étendue alentour, [illegible] de façon assourdissante [illegible] pouvait appeler à penser que de cette violence adorable de la vie il retiendra toujours signe dans les siècles à venir. D'en écrire aussi: D'en mourir de même Et etc etc etc.

"Stroll through the Centuries"

Andrée Chedid, 1987

Andrée Chedid is a poet, a playwright, and, especially, a novelist. Born in Cairo in 1902, to Lebanese parents, she has lived in Paris since 1946, and she lays claim to both her Lebanese and her Egyptian heritage.

She is prolific, and her writing quickly won her international recognition. Two of her novels have been made into films (*The Sixth Day*, *L'Autre*); like most of her work, they are informed by her double perspective on the intense feelings that have shaped the cruel destiny of the Middle East. Nonetheless, she is interested in far more than exoticism and political agendas. She is deeply committed to humanist values, and her fiction tends to adhere to a rigorous but recurrent structure: in a tragic context of war or natural catastrophe, two characters of different generations overcome the years that separate them to achieve genuine communication. Despite varying narrative particulars, each of these encounters follows a similar pattern. The child (or young man) is a victim of violence, but his or her suffering proves redemptive, effecting a purification that justifies the world's existence. In these dialogues, the older characters recover their original purity by returning, through their younger interlocutors, to their own childhoods.

This page from a working draft of the vignette "*La Balade des Siècles*" (*Stroll through the Centuries*) reveals the rigor with which Chedid revises her work. The typed manuscript is meticulously corrected in four different colors, each of which signifies something different. Published in *Mondes, Miroirs, Magie* (*Worlds, Mirrors, Magic*), this short text was inspired by the excavation of a solar bark near the Pyramid of Khufu in October of 1987.

Roselyne de Ayala

Stroll through the Centuries

You wouldn't have believed how they screamed with joy when, three days ago, through a hole pierced in the rock, they glimpsed my Solar Bark! In anticipation of this moment, they had been excavating for days and days at the foot of the southern face of the Pyramid of Khufu.

Followed by a group of whites and a few darkies, these little yellow men, used to feats and exploits, managed to discover it first. Thanks to their sonic probe, the bark appeared to them half-intact; the mast, the joists, all the other elements that they would need to complete it—after discovering the meticulous plans inscribed on papyrus scrolls—were piled in various other parts of the cavity.

2nd draft 29/X/87

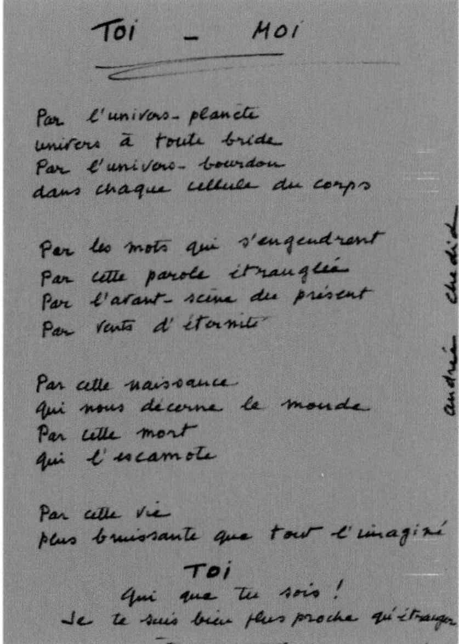

TOI — MOI

Par l'univers-planète
univers à toute bride
Par l'univers-bourdon
dans chaque cellule du corps

Par les mots qui s'engendrent
Par cette parole étranglée
Par l'avant-scène du présent
Par vents d'éternité

Par cette naissance
qui nous décerne le monde
Par cette mort
qui l'escamote

Par cette vie
plus bruissante que tout l'imaginé
TOI
qui que tu sois!
Je te suis bien plus proche qu'étranger

Andrée Chedid

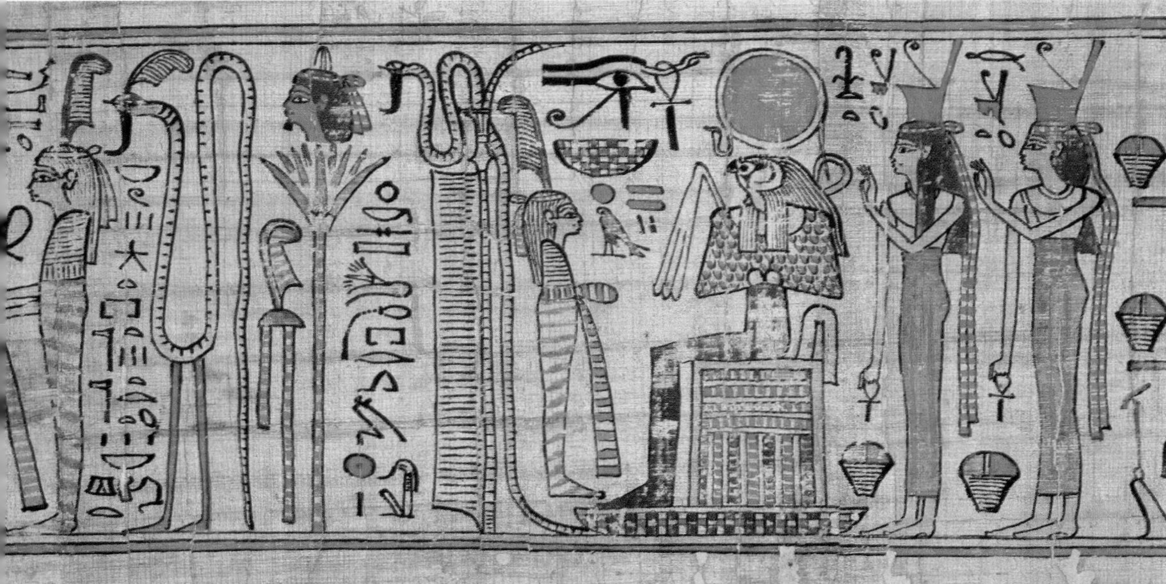

Top left: Andrée Chedid.
Left: Detail of a papyrus scroll with painting of a solar bark. Third Intermediate Period. Paris, Musée du Louvre.
Above: Autograph manuscript of the poem "You—Me."
Opposite: Second draft of "Stroll through the Centuries," typed manuscript with autograph revisions.

LA BALADE DES SIÈCLES SOLAIRES (1)

Il aurait fallu les entendre hurler de joie, quand par le trou taillé dans le roc, ils découvrirent ma barque solaire. cela faisait des jours et des jours qu'ils creusaient cette cavité au pied et sur la face sud de la pyramide de Kheops.

Ce sont de petits hommes jaunes habitués aux exploits aux prouesses, qui sont parvenus les premiers. Suivis d'un groupe de blancs, puis de quelques basanés. Avec des plus grands soins minutieux et leur camera-sonde, ils ont pris la dimension de cette barque à moitié construite, et dont les plans comme celle déjà trovée se trouve inscrite sur des papyrus avec tous les éléments

Il aurait fallu les entendre hurler de joie quand, à travers le trou taillé dans le roc, ils ont découvert, pour la première fois ma Barque Solaire. Avant cela, ils avaient creusé des jours et des jours au pied de la Pyramide de Kheops. sur sa face sud.

Suivis d'un groupe de blancs et de quelques basanés, ces petits hommes jaunes, habitués aux exploits, aux prouesses, qui sont parvenus les premiers, à cette découverte. Grâce à leur camera-sonde, la barque leur est apparue à moitié construite; ils ont également repérés d'autres éléments, qui serviront à la compléter une fois qu'ils auront retrouvé les plans minutieux inscrits sur des rouleaux de papyrus, entassés en divers coins de la cavité.

2e version

29/X/87

BIBLIOGRAPHY

We provide a single title for each of the authors discussed, when possible in English translation. They are arranged by author. For a handy bilingual compilation of French poetry from Lamartine to Char, see *French Poetry 1820–1950*, edited and translated by William Rees (London and New York: Penguin Books, 1990).

N.B.: Unless otherwise noted, all translations of the illustrated manuscript texts in the body of the book are by John Goodman.

Alain-Fournier (Henri Alban Fournier). *Meaulnes: The Lost Domain*, translated by Sandra Morris. London and Glasgow: Blackie [1966].

Apollinaire, Guillaume. *Selected Writings of Guillaume Apollinaire*, edited and translated by Roger Shattuck. New York: New Directions, 1971.

Aragon, Louis. *Les Beaux Quartiers*. Paris: Gallimard (collection Blanche).

Audiberti, Jacques. *Le Mal Court*. Paris: Gallimard (collection Folio/Théâtre).

Aymé, Marcel. *The Green Mare*, translated by Norman Denny. London: The Bodley Head [1955].

Balzac, Honoré de. *Père Goriot*, edited by Peter Brooks, translated by Burton Raffel. New York: W.W. Norton & Co. [1998]. Norton Critical Edition.

Barbey d'Aurevilly, Jules. *The She-Devils*, translated by Jean Kimber. London and New York: Oxford University Press, 1964.

Baudelaire, Charles. *My Heart Laid Bare, and Other Prose Writings*, edited by Peter Quennell, translated by Norman Cameron. New York: Vanguard Press [1951].

Beaumarchais, Pierre-Augustin Caron de. *Three Plays*, translated by Graham Anderson. Bath, England: Absolute Press, 1993.

Bernanos, Georges. *The Diary of a Country Priest*, translated by Pamela Morris. New York: The Macmillan Company, 1937.

Bernardin de Saint-Pierre, Jacques-Henri. *Paul and Virginia*, translated by John Donovan. London and Boston: P. Owen, 1982.

Bloy, Léon. *Pilgrim of the Absolute*, edited by Raïssa Maritain, introduction by Jacques Maritain, translated by John Coleman and Harry Lorin Binsse. New York: Pantheon Books [1947].

Breton, André and Philippe Soupault. *The Magnetic Fields*, translated by David Gascoyne. London: Atlas Press, 1985.

Butor, Michel. *Passage de Milan*. Paris: Éditions de Minuit [1954].

Cadou, René-Guy. *Oeuvres Poétiques Complètes*. Paris: Seghers.

Camus, Albert. *The Plague*, translated by Stuart Gilbert. New York: Knopf, 1964.

Cendrars, Blaise. *Modernities and Other Writings*, edited by Monique Chefdor, translated by Esther Allen with Monique Chefdor. Lincoln: University of Nebraska Press, 1992.

Char, René. *Selected Poems of René Char*, edited and translated by Mary Ann Caws and Tina Jolas. Bilingual edition.

Chateaubriand, François-Auguste-René, Vicomte de. *Memoirs*, selected and translated by Robert Baldick. London: H. Hamilton [1961].

Chedid, Andrée. *The Prose and Poetry of André Chedid: Selected Poems, Short Stories, and Essays*, translated by Renée Linkhorn. Birmingham, AL: Summa Publications, 1990.

Cioran, E. M. *A Short History of Decay*, translated by Richard Howard. New York: Viking Press, 1975.

Claudel, Paul. *Le Partage de Midi*. Paris: Gallimard (collection Folio).

Cocteau, Jean. *Oeuvres*. Paris: Gallimard (Bibliothèque de la Pléiade).

Colette, Sidonie-Gabrielle. *The Collected Stories of Colette*, edited by Robert Phelps, translated by Matthew Ward et al. New York: Farrar, Straus, Giroux, 1984.

Corbière, Tristan. *These Jaundiced Loves*, translated by Christopher Pillings. Calstock, Cornwall: Peterloo Poets, 1995.

Corneille, Pierre. *Seven Plays*, translated by Samuel Solomon. New York: Random House [1969].

Daudet, Alphonse. *Jack*, 2 volumes, translated by Marian McIntyre. Boston: Little, Brown [1900].

Descartes, René. *Correspondence of Descartes and Constatyn Huygens, 1635–1647*, edited by Leon Roth. Oxford: The Clarendon Press, 1926. The authoritative scholarly edition (letters in French).

Desnos, Robert. *The Selected Poems of Robert Desnos*, edited by William Kulik, translated by Carolyn Forché and William Kulik. New York: Ecco Press, 1991.

Diderot, Denis. *The Nun*, translated by Leonard Tancock. Harmondsworth and New York: Penguin Books, 1972.

Drieu La Rochelle, Pierre. *Will-o'-the-Wisp: A Novel*, translated by Martin Robinson. London: Marion Boyars, 1998.

Dumas, Alexandre. *The Count of Monte Cristo*, translated by Robin Buss. New York: Viking Penguin, 1997.

Dumas the Younger, Alexandre. *Camille*, translated by Edmund Gosse. London: Printed for the Limited Editions Club at the Curwen Press, 1937.

Duras, Marguerite. *The Lover*, translated by Barbara Bray. New York: Pantheon Books, 1985.

Éluard, Paul. *Selected Poems*, edited and translated by Gilbert Bowen, introduction by Max Adereth. London: Calder; New York: Riverrun Press, 1988. Bilingual edition.

Fénelon (François de Solignac de La Mothe-Fénelon), *The Adventures of Telemachus, the Son of Ulysses*, translated by John Hawkesworth with revisions by G. Gregory, 2 volumes. London: John Manson, 1797.

Feydeau, Georges. *A Flea in Her Ear*, translated by Graham Anderson. London: Oberon Books, 1993.

Flaubert, Gustave. *A Sentimental Education*, translated by Robert Baldick. Baltimore: Penguin Books, 1964.

Gautier, Théophile. *The Works of Théophile Gautier*, 24 volumes, translated and edited by F. C. de Sumichrist. New York: published for subscribers only by G. D. Sproul, 1900–1903. *Captain Fracasse* is in volumes 17–19.

Gide, André. *Strait is the Gate*, translated by Dorothy Bussy. New York: Vintage Books, 1956.

Giono, Jean. *Joy of Man's Desiring*, translated by Katherine Allen Clarke. San Francisco: North Point Press, 1980.

Giraudoux, Jean. *The Madwoman of Chaillot*, translated and adapted by Maurice Valency. New York: Random House, 1947.

Goncourt, Edmond and Jules de. *Paris and the Arts, 1851–1896; from the Goncourt Journal*, edited and translated by George J. Becker and Edith Philips. Ithaca, NY: Cornell University Press [1971].

Hugo, Victor. *The Novels and Poems of Victor-Marie Hugo*, 16 volumes. New York: Dumont, 1887–1896.

Huysmans, Joris-Karl. *Against Nature*, edited by Nicholas White, translated by Margaret Mauldon. Oxford and New York: Oxford University Press, 1998.

Ionesco, Eugène. *Four Plays*, translated by Donald M. Allen. New York: Grove Press [1958].

Jacob, Max. *The Dice Cup: Selected Prose Poems*, edited by Michael Brownstein, translated by John Ashbery et al. New York: SUN, 1979.

Jarry, Alfred. *The Ubu Plays*. translated by C. Connolly and S.W. Taylor. London: Methuen [1968].

Laclos, Pierre-Ambroise-François Choderlos de. *Les Liaisons Dangereuses*, translated by P.W. K. Stone. Harmondsworth and New York: Penguin Books, 1961.

Lacy, Norris J., editor. *Lancelot-Grail: The Old French Arthurian Vulgate and Post-Vulgate in Translation*. New York: Garland Publishing, 1993.

La Fontaine, Jean de. *Selected Fables*, bilingual edition with translations by Christopher Wood. Oxford and New York: Oxford University Press, 1995.

Lamartine, Alphonse de. *Selected Poems from Premières et Nouvelles Méditations*, edited by George O. Curme. Boston: D. C. Heath & Company, 1903.

Lorris, Guillaume de, and Jean de Meun. *The Romance of the Rose*, translated by Charles Dahlberg. Princeton, N. J.: Princeton University Press, 1971. A prose translation.

Loti, Pierre. *A Tale of the Pyrenees*, translated by W. P. Baines. London: T. W. Laurie, Ltd. [1923].

Malherbe, François de. *Oeuvres*. Paris: Gallimard (Bibliothèque de la Pléiade).

Mallarmé, Stéphane. *The Meaning of Mallarmé: A Bilingual Edition of his Poésies and Un Coup de Dés*, translated by Charles Chadwick. Aberdeen: Scottish Cultural Press, 1996.

Malraux, André. *Man's Fate*, translated by Haakon M. Chevalier. New York: Modern Library, 1961.

Marivaux, Pierre Carlet de Chamblain de. *Plays*, various translators. London: Methuen, 1988.

Maupassant, Guy de. *The Dark Side of Guy de Maupassant*, edited and translated by Arnold Kellett. New York: Carroll & Graf, 1989.

Mauriac, François. *Vipers' Tangle*, translated by Warren B. Wells. London: V. Gollancz, Ltd., 1933.

Mérimée, Prosper. *The Novels, Tales and Letters of Prosper Mérimée*, 8 volumes, edited by George Saintsbury, translated by Emily Mary Waller et al. Magnolia, Mass.: Himebaugh & Browne, 1915.

Michelet, Jules. *Michelet*, edited by Roland Barthes, translated by Richard Howard. New York: Hill and Wang, 1987.

Mirbeau, Octave. *The Diary of a Chambermaid*, translated by Douglas Garman. London: Elek [1966].

Montaigne, Michel de. *The Complete Essays of Montaigne*, translated by Donald M. Frame. Stanford, CA: Stanford University Press, 1958.

Montesquieu, Baron (Charles-Louis de Secondat). *The Spirit of the Laws*, translated and edited by Anne M. Cohler, Basia Carolyn Miller, and Harold Samuel Stone. Cambridge and New York: Cambridge University Press, 1989.

Musset, Alfred de. *The Complete Writings of Alfred de Musset*, 10 volumes, translated by Andrew Lang et al, revised edition. New York: Edwin C. Hill Company, 1907.

Nerval, Gérard de. *Aurélia and Other Writings*, translated by Geoffrey Wagner et al. Boston: Exact Exchange, 1996.

Noailles, Anna-Elisabeth Mathieu, Comtesse de. *Le Coeur Innombrable*. Paris: Grasset.

Orléans, Charles d' et al. *Formal Spring: French Renaissance Poems of Charles d'Orléans & Others*, translations by R. N. Currey. Freeport, N.Y.: Books for Libraries Press [1969].

Pagnol, Marcel. *The Water of the Hills: Two Novels*, translated by W. E. van Heyningen. San Francisco: North Point Press, 1988. Contains *Jean de Florette* and *Manon of the Springs*.

Pascal, Blaise. *Pensées*, translated by A. J. Krailsheimer. London and New York: Penguin Books, 1966.

Péguy, Charles. *God Speaks: Religious Poetry [by] Charles Péguy*, translated by Julian Green. New York: Pantheon [1945].

Perec, Georges. *Life: A User's Manual*, translated by David Bellos. Boston: D. R. Godine, 1987.

Perse, Saint-John. *Collected Poems*, translated by W. H. Auden et al. Princeton, NJ: Princeton University Press [1971].

Pizan, Christine de. *The Book of the City of Ladies*, translated by Earl Jeffrey Richards. New York: Persea Books, 1998.

Ponge, Francis. *Selected Poems*, translated by C.K. Williams, John Montague, and Margaret Guiton. Winston-Salem, NC: Wake Forest University Press, 1994. Bilingual edition.

Proust, Marcel. *In Search of Lost Time*, 6 volumes, translated by C. K. Scott Moncrieff & Terrence Kilmartin, revised by D. J. Enright. New York: Modern Library, 1982.

Rabutin-Chantal, Marie de, Marquise de Sévigné. *Selected Letters*, translated by Leonard Tancock. Harmondsworth, England, and New York: Penguin Books, 1982.

Racine, Jean. *Complete Plays*, translated by Samuel Solomon. New York: The Modern Library [1969].

Radiguet, Raymond. *Count d'Orgel's Ball*, translated by Annapaola Cancogni. Hygiene, CO: Eridanos Press; New York: distributed by Rizzoli International, 1989.

Renan, Ernest. *The Memoirs of Ernest Renan*, translated by J. Lewis May. London: G. Bles [1935].

Renard, Jules. *Poil de Carotte*. Paris: Livre de Poche (collection Classiques).

Retz, Cardinal de (Jean-François-Paul de Gondi). *Memoirs of the Cardinal de Retz*, translated by Peter Davall, 4 vols. London: Jacob Tonson, 1723.

Rimbaud, Arthur. *Complete Works*, translated by Paul Schmidt. New York: Harper & Row [1975].

Romains, Jules. *Doctor Knock: A Comedy in Three Acts*, translated and adapted by Harley Granville-Barker. London: Ernest Benn, 1925.

Ronsard, Pierre de. *Poems of Pierre de Ronsard*, translated and edited by Nicolas Kilmer. Berkeley: University of California Press, 1979.

Rostand, Edmond. *Cyrano de Bergerac: A Heroic Comedy in Five Acts*, translated by Christopher Fry. Oxford and New York: Oxford University Press, 1996.

Rousseau, Jean-Jacques. *The Confessions; and Correspondence, Including the Letters to Malesherbes*, edited by Christopher Kelly, Roger D. Masters, and Peter G. Stillman; translated by Christopher Kelly. Hanover: Published by University Press of New England [for] Dartmouth College, 1995.

Rouvroy, Louis de, Duc de Saint-Simon. *Historical Memoirs of the Duc de Saint-Simon: A Shortened Version*, edited and translated by Lucy Norton. London: H. Hamilton, 1967. Contains texts pertaining only to 1691–1709.

Sade, Donation-Alphonse-François, Marquis de. *The Marquis de Sade: The Complete Justine, Philosophy in the Bedroom and Other Writings*, compiled and translated by Richard Seaver and Austryn Wainhouse, with introduction by Jean Paulhan and Maurice Blanchot. New York: Grove Press [1966].

Saint-Exupéry Antoine-Marie-Roger de. *The Little Prince*, translated by Richard Howard. New York: Harcourt Brace, 2000.

Sand, George (Amandine-Aurore-Lucile Dudevant). *The Devil's Pool*, translated by Antonia Cowan. London and Glasgow: Blackie, 1966.

Sartre, Jean-Paul. *Nausea*, translated by Lloyd Alexander. Norfolk, CN: New Directions, 1959.

Schehadé, Georges. *Le Voyage*. Paris: Gallimard (collection Le Manteau d'Arlequin).

Segalen, Victor. *Steles*, translated by Michael Taylor. Santa Monica: Lapis Press, 1987.

Ségur, Sophie, Comtesse de. *Memoirs of a Donkey*, translated by Marguerite Fellows Melcher. New York: the Macmillan Company, 1926.

Stendhal (Henri Beyle). *Lucien Leuwen*, translated by H. L. R. Edwards. Woodbridge, Suffolk: Boydell Press, 1984.

Vallès, Jules. *The Insurrectionist*, translated by Sandy Petry. Englewood Cliffs, N. J.: Prentice-Hall [1971].

Verlaine, Paul. *One Hundred and One Poems by Paul Verlaine: A Bilingual Edition*, translated by Norman R. Shapiro. Chicago: The University of Chicago Press, 1999.

Verne, Jules. *Around the World in Eighty Days*, translated by Butcher Williams. New York and Oxford: Oxford University Press, 1995.

Vian, Boris. *Mood Indigo*. New York: Grove Press [1968].

Vigny, Alfred de. *Poèmes Antiques et Modernes. Les Destinées*. Paris: Gallimard (collection Poésie).

Villiers de L'Isle-Adam, Auguste, Comte de. *Cruel Tales*, translated by Robert Baldick. London and New York: Oxford University Press, 1963.

Voltaire (François-Marie Arouet). *Select Letters*, translated and edited by Theodore Besterman. London, New York: T. Nelson [1963].

Weil, Simone. *Formative Writings, 1929–1941*, edited and translated by Dorothy Tuck McFarland and Wilhelmina Van Ness. Amherst: University of Massachusetts Press, 1987.

Yourcenar, Marguerite. *L'Oeuvre au Noir*. Paris: Gallimard (collection Folio).

Zola, Émile. *The Ladies' Paradise*. Berkeley: University of California Press, 1992.

LIST OF ILLUSTRATIONS AND PHOTO CREDITS

Abbreviations
BNF Bibliothèque Nationale de France
RMN Réunion des Musées Nationaux

p. 12: *Le Roman de la Rose*. Paris, Bibliothèque Nationale de France, Département des Manuscrits, Fr 380, page de garde and fol. 2. Photo: BNF.

p. 13: *Le Roman de la Rose*. Paris, Bibliothèque Nationale de France, Département des Manuscrits, Fr 378, fol. 1. Photo: BNF.

p. 14: *Lancelot*. Paris, Bibliothèque Nationale de France, Département des Manuscrits, Fr 116, fol. 610 v. (detail). Photo: BNF.

p. 15: *Lancelot du Lac*. Paris, Bibliothèque Nationale de France, Département des Manuscrits, Fr 111, fol. 1. Photo: BNF.

p. 16: Christine de Pizan, *Le Livre de la Cité des Dames*, illuminated manuscript. Paris, Bibliothèque Nationale de France, Département des Manuscrits, Fr 607 fol. 31 v. Photo: BNF.

p. 17: Christine de Pizan, *Le Livre de la Cité des Dames*, illuminated manuscript. Paris, Bibliothèque Nationale de France, Département des Manuscrits, Fr 607, fol. 2 recto. Photo: BNF.

p. 18: Charles d'Orléans, *Rondeaux*. Paris, Bibliothèque Nationale de France, Département des Manuscrits, Fr 25458, p. 366 (detail). Photo: BNF.

p. 19: Charles d'Orléans, *Rondeaux*. Paris, Bibliothèque Nationale de France, Département des Manuscrits, Fr 25458, p. 366. Photo: BNF.

p. 20: Top: Anonymous, *Pierre de Ronsard*. Blois, Musée des Beaux-Arts. Photo: Roger-Viollet. Bottom: Detail of a page from a translation of Psalm 113 by Pierre de Ronsard. Photo: Harlingue Viollet.

p 21: Pierre de Ronsard, *Discours de la Joie et de la Tristesse*. Paris, Bibliothèque Nationale de France, Département des Manuscrits, Autographe Rothschild 164, fol. 1. Photo: BNF.

p. 22: French school (sixteenth century), *Portrait of Michel de Montaigne*.

p. 23: Michel de Montaigne, *Essais*, 1588, chapter 28, "De l'Amitié," with autograph revisions. Bordeaux, Bibliothèque Municipale. Photo: © Montaigne Club, Dallas, Texas.

p. 24: Top: Briot and Jollain, *François de Malherbe, Gentleman of the King's Chamber*, 1658. Photo: Viollet. Bottom: Giovanni Battista di Jacopo, *View of the Château de Fontainebleau*, fresco, c. 1540. Château de Fontainebleau. Photo: RMN - Gérard Blot.

p. 25: Autograph of two sonnets by Malherbe. Paris, Bibliothèque Nationale de France, Département des Manuscrits, Fr 9535, fol. 68. Photo: BNF.

p. 26: Top: French school (seventeenth century), *Portrait of Paul-François de Gondi, Cardinal de Retz*. Blois, Musée des Beaux-Arts Louis XII. Photo: museum. Bottom: *Episode from the Fronde (1648–52): Two Knights on Horseback Engage below the Fortifications of the Bastille*. Châteaux de Versailles et de Trianon. Photo: RMN.

p. 27: Page from the autograph of Cardinal de Retz, *Mémoirs*. Paris, Bibliothèque Nationale de France, Département des Manuscrits, Fr 110325, fol. 273. Photo: BNF.

p. 28: Top: Anonymous (seventeenth century), *Portrait of Descartes* (detail). Toulouse, Musée des Augustins. Photo: museum. Bottom: Thomas de Keyser, *Portrait of Constantijn Huygens and His Clerk*, 1627. London, The National Gallery. Photo: museum.

p. 29: Page from autograph of letter from René Descartes to Constantijn Huygens. Paris, Bibliothèque Nationale de France, Département des Manuscrits, Fr 23084, fol. 152 recto and verso. Photo: BNF.

p. 30: Top: Jean Domat, *Portrait of Blaise Pascal*, fixed to the cover of a manuscript of Justinian, *Corpus Juris Civilis*, dating from 1583. Paris, Bibliothèque Nationale de France, Département des Imprimés, Réserve. Photo: BNF. Bottom: Detail of illustration on page 31.

p. 31: Autograph of Pascal's "Mémorial." Paris, Bibliothèque Nationale de France, Département des Manuscrits, Fr 9902, fol. D. Photo: BNF.

p. 32: Top: Hyacinth Rigaud, *Portrait of Jean de La Fontaine* (detail). Paris, Musée Carnavalet. Bottom left: French school (seventeenth century), *Portrait of the Comtesse de La Fayette*. Private collection. Bottom right: Antoine Trouvain, *Louis XIV Playing Billiards*. Châteaux de Versailles et de Trianon. Photo: RMN - Gérard Blot.

p. 33: Page from an autograph of La Fontaine's poem for Madame de Coulanges, sent by him to Madame de La Fayette. Collection Bernard and Stéphane Calvreuil. All rights reserved.

p. 34: Top: Charles Le Brun (copy after), *Portrait of Pierre Corneille*. Châteaux de Versailles et Trianon. Photo: RMN. Bottom: Abraham Bosse, *Theater in a Tennis Court*, 1630. Paris, Bibliothèque Nationale de France. Photo: BNF.

p. 35: Autograph letter from Pierre Corneille to Monsieur l'abbé de Pure, 1660. Paris, Bibliothèque Nationale de France, Département des Manuscrits, Fr 12763, fol. 157 v. and 158 r. Photo: BNF.

p. 36: Top: Jean Baptiste Racine, *Portrait of Jean Racine*, after 1714. Bottom left: Jean Jouvenet, *The Sacrifice of Iphigenia*, oil on canvas, 1685. Troyes, Musée des Beaux-Arts. Photo: RMN - Hervé Lewandowski. Bottom right: Jean-Auguste Ingres, *Studies for the Apotheosis of Homer: Profile of Raphael; Hands of Apelles, Raphael, and Racine*, c. 1827. Paris, Musée du Louvre. Photo: RMN - Gérard Blot.

p. 37: Autograph by Jean Racine, beginning of a prose summary of a projected play, "Iphigénie en Tauride." Bibliothèque Nationale de France, Département des Manuscrits, Fr 12887, fol. 95. Photo: BNF.

p. 38: Top: Claude Lefebvre, *Portrait of Madame de Sévigné* (detail). Paris, Musée Carnavalet. Photo: museum. Bottom left: Desk of the Marquise de Sévigné. Private collection. All rights reserved. Bottom right: Pierre Mignard (after), *Portrait of the Comtesse de Grignan*. Private collection. All rights reserved.

p. 39: Part of an autograph letter from the Marquise de Sévigné to her daughter, Madame de Grignan, dated September 18, 1684. Bibliothèque Nationale de France, Département des Manuscrits, Autographe Rothschild XVII-803, fol. 1 verso and fol. 2 recto. Photo: BNF.

p. 40: Top: Anonymous, detail of a portrait on vellum of François de Salignac de La Mothe-Fénelon, situated at the head of the autograph of *Les Aventures de Télémaque*. Bibliothèque Nationale de France, Département des Manuscrits, Fr 14944. Bottom: Jean Raoux, *Telemachus Recounting His Adventures to Calypso*, oil on canvas. Paris, Musée du Louvre. Photo: RMN - J.G. Berizzi.

p. 41: Page from the autograph of *Les Aventures de Télémaque*. Bibliothèque Nationale de France, Département des Manuscrits, Fr 14944. Photo: BNF.

p. 42. Top: Perrine Viger Duringeau, *Portrait of Saint-Simon* (detail), second half of the eighteenth century. Châteaux de Versailles et de Trianon. Bottom: Arnoult, colored prints from the series *La Vie à Versailles sous Louis XIV*, eighteenth century. Private collection.

p. 43: Duc de Saint-Simon, *Mémoires*, page from the autograph manuscript. Bibliothèque Nationale de France, Département des Manuscrits, NAF 23096, fol. 106. Photo: BNF.

p. 44: Van Loo, *Portrait of Marivaux* (detail), 1753. Paris, Comédie Française. Bottom: *Characters from the Plays of Marivaux*, watercolor by Maxime Rebière, 2000.

p. 45: Page from a manuscript of Marivaux's *Le Legs*; not an autograph, but a copy made ca. 1750, with many cuts indicated for a performance at the private theater of the Comte de Clermont at Berny. Paris, Bibliothèque de l'Arsenal, ms. 3113, fol. 457 verso. Photo: BA. Apart from a single letter and a prompter's copy of *Le Legs* on which are inscribed a few autograph revisions (Paris, Académie Française), all of Marivaux' autographs are lost.

p. 46: Top: French school (eighteenth century), *Portrait of Montesquieu*. Châteaux de Versailles et de Trianon. Bottom: portable desk dating from the eighteenth century. Bayonne, Musée Bonnat. Photo: RMN - R.G. Ojeda.

p. 47: Page (recto and verso: the beginning of chapter 1) from an incomplete early draft of Montesquieu, *De l'Esprit des Lois*, with autograph revisions. Bibliothèque Nationale de France, Département des Manuscrits, NAF 12832, fol. 2 recto and verso. Photo: BNF. The first page is inscribed at the top: "*Matériaux pour servir à l'espirt des Lois de la main de Montesquieu en grande partie.*"

p. 48: Top: Louis-Michel Van Loo, *Portrait of Denis Diderot* (detail), oil on canvas, 1767. Paris, Musée du Louvre. Bottom: Fleury-François Richard, *Gallery in a Convent*, oil on canvas. Lyon, Musée des Beaux-Arts. Photo: RMN - R.G. Ojeda.

p. 49: Page from an autograph of *La Religieuse*. Bibliothèque Nationale de France, Département des Manuscrits, NAF 13726, fol. 45 v. Photo: BNF.

p. 50: Top: *Portrait of Voltaire at His Desk* (detail). Paris, Musée Carnavalet. Bottom: Gabriel de Saint-Aubin, *The Crowning of Voltaire at the Théâtre Français* (detail). Paris, Musée du Louvre, Cabinet des Arts Graphiques. Photos: RMN - Michèle Bellot.

p. 51: Beginning of a letter from Voltaire to d'Alembert dating from June 17, 1762 or 1763. Paris, Bibliothèque Nationale de France, Département des Manuscrits, NAF 24330, fol. 47. Photo: BNF.

p. 52: Top: Joseph Ducreux (attributed to), *Choderlos de Laclos* (detail), pastel. Châteaux de Versailles et de Trianon. Photo: RMN - Gérard Blot. Bottom: detail of mansucript page illustrated on page 53.

p. 53: Choderlos de Laclos, *Les Liaisons Dangereuses*, autograph manuscript, beginning of Letter 1. Paris, Bibliothèque Nationale de France, Département des Manuscrits, Fr 12845, fol. 40 recto. Photo: BNF.

p. 54: Top: Charron, *Jean-Jacques Rousseau in Switzerland, Persecuted and Without Refuge* (detail), colored print. Paris, Musée Carnavalet. Bottom: John-Claude Nattes, *View of the Park at Montmorency, with Lodging of Jean-Jacques Rousseau*, colored print. Châteaux de Versailles et de Trianon. Photo: RMN - Arnaudet.

p. 55: Page from the autograph of Jean-Jacques Rousseau, *Confessions* (book four). Paris, Bibliothèque de l'Assemblée Nationale. Photo: library.

p. 56: Top: Jean-Marc Nattier (copy after), *Portrait of Pierre-Augustin Caron de Beaumarchais* (detail), oil on canvas. Paris, Comédie Française. Bottom: *The Marriage of Figaro*, watercolor by Maxime Rebière, 2000.

p. 57: Page from a manuscript of *Le Mariage de Figaro, ou la Folle Journée* (Act 2, scene 1). Paris, Bibliothèque Nationale de France, Département des Manuscrits, Fr 12544, fol. 33. Photo: BNF.

p. 58: Top: Paul Carpentier after Elisabeth Hervey, *Portrait of Jacques-Henri Bernardin de Saint-Pierre*, oil on canvas. Châteaux de Versailles et de Trianon. Photo: RMN - Gérard Blot. Bottom left: *Paul and Virginia*, watercolor by Maxime Rebière, 2000. Bottom right: Morocco binding (signed "Purgold") of a working draft of *Paul et Virginie* dating from 1777-1785. Paris, Bibliothèque de la Sorbonne, fonds Victor Cousin, ms. 8, fol. 1 recto. Photo: J.-L. Charmet. In 1825, the manuscript was sold by Louis-Aimé Martin, who had married the widow of Bernardin de Saint-Pierre, to Antoine-Auguste Renouard, who commissioned this binding. At the auction of the Renouard collection in 1854, it was acquired for 700 francs by Gassicourt, who in turn sold it, for the same price, to Victor Cousin. The original title of the novel was *Histoire de Mlle Virginie de la Tour*.

p. 59: Page from an autograph manuscript (first draft) of *Paul et Virginie*, written between 1777 and 1785. Bibliothèque de la Sorbonne, fonds Victor Cousin, ms. 8, fol. 20 recto. Photo: J.-L. Charmet.

p. 60: Top: Man Ray, *Imaginary Portrait of the Marquis de Sade*, Houston, Ménil Collection. Photo: Roger-Viollet. © ADAGP, Paris 2000. Bottom: Léopold Boilly (or Marguerite Gérard), *The Hasty Departure*, oil on wood, c.1788-1791. Paris, Musée Cognac-Jay. Photo: Roger-Viollet.

p. 61: Page from the autograph of *Les Infortunes de la Vertu*, an early version of *Justine, ou les Malheurs de la Vertu*. Paris, Bibliothèque Nationale de France, Département des Manuscrits, NAF 4010, fol. 249. Photo: BNF.

p. 62: Top: Anne-Louis Girodet-Trioson, *Portrait of Chateaubriand* (detail), oil on canvas, 1811. Châteaux de Versailles et de Trianon. Louis-Gabriel-Eugène Isabey, *The Tomb of Chateaubriand*, watercolor and gouache. Paris, Musée du Louvre. Photo: RMN - J. G. Berizzi.

p. 63: René de Chateaubriand, *Mémoires de Ma Vie* (an autobiographical text later incorporated into *Mémoires d'Outre-Tombe*), three pages from a manuscript copy made by Juliette Récamier, with the assistance of Charles Lenormand, at Vallée-aux-Loups in 1826. Paris, Bibliothèque Nationale de France, Département des Manuscrits, NAF 12966, fol. 323, 324, 325. Photo: BNF.

p. 64: Top: Madame de Lamartine, *Portrait of Alphonse de Lamartine* (detail). Paris, Musée de la Vie Romantique. Photo: Roger-Viollet. Bottom: Achille Devéria, *Dozing Young Ladies*, oil on canvas. Paris, Musée du Louvre. Photo: RMN - G. Blot/C. Jean.

p. 65: Autograph of the first poem from Lamartine's *Méditations*, inscribed "à Julie." Paris, Bibliothèque Nationale de France, Département des Manuscrits, NAF 14013, fol. 16 recto and verso. Photo: BNF.

p. 66: Top: Pollet after Landelle (nineteenth century), *Alfred de Musset* (detail), pastel on paper. Paris, Comédie Française. Bottom: *Lorenzaccio*, watercolor by Maxime Rebière, 2000.

p. 67: Page from the autograph of *Lorenzaccio* (Act II, scene 2) used for the original edition of 1833. Paris, Bibliothèque de la Comédie-Française.

p. 68: Top: J.-A.-G. Seguin, *Portrait of Balzac* (detail). Tours, Musée des Beaux-Arts. Bottom left: Autograph of Balzac's *Père Goriot*, cover page with autograph computations relating to Balzac's ever-perilous finances. Paris, Bibliothèque de l'Institut. Fonds Lovenjoul A 183, fol. A. Photo: J.-L. Charmet. Bottom right: An arrangement of books, manuscripts, and coffeepot at the Maison de Balzac in Paris, now a museum. Photo: Photothèque des Musées de la Ville de Paris. Photo by Lifermann.

p. 69: Page (with heading "La Mort du Père") from the autograph of Balzac's *Père Goriot*. Paris, Bibliothèque de L'Institut, Fonds Lovenjoul A 183, fol. 135. Photo: J.-L. Charmet.

p. 70: Top: Simon Rochard, *Portrait of Prosper Mérimée in 1852* (detail), pastel. Paris, Musée Carnavalet. Photo: Roger-Viollet. Bottom: *Aphrodite*, bronze with eyes of inset silver, Hellenistic period (300–250 B.C.). Paris, Musée du Louvre. Photo: RMN - Hervé Lewandowski.

p. 71: Four pages from the autograph of Mérimée's "Le Vénus d'Ille." Paris, Bibliothèque Nationale de France, Département des Manuscrits, NAF 25740, folios 18 recto and verso, 19 recto and verso. Photos: BNF.

p. 72: Top: Alfred de Vigny, *Self-Portrait* (detail), 1825. Paris, Comédie-Française. Jean-Baptiste Oudry, *Wolf Hunt*, oil on canvas, 1725. Chantilly, Musée Condé. Photo: RMN - Harry Bréjat.

p. 73: First page of an autograph of "La Mort du Loup" by Alfred de Vigny. Paris, Bibliothèque de l'Institut, Fonds Lovenjoul, D631, fol. 64 recto. Photo: J.-L. Charmet.

p. 74: Henri Lehmann, *Portrait of Stendhal* (detail), graphite, 1841. Grenoble, Bibliothèque Municipal. Photo: library. Bottom: Three autograph pages pertaining to Stendhal's unfinished novel *Lucien Leuwen*. Grenoble, Bibliothèque Municipale. Photos: library.

p. 75: Page from the working draft of Stendhal's *Lucien Leuwen*. Grenoble, Bibliothèque Municipale. Photo: library.

p. 76: Top: Louis Gauffier (attributed to), *Portrait of Alexandre Dumas in Hunting Garb*. Bayonne, Musée Bonnat. Photo: RMN - Arnaudet. Bottom: Page of the autograph first draft of Alexandre Dumas' *Le Comte de Monte-Cristo*. Villers-Cotterets, Musée Alexandre-Dumas. Photo: Racault.

p. 77: First page, autograph manuscript, first draft of *Le Comte de Monte-Cristo*. Villers-Cotterets, Musée Alexandre-Dumas. Photo: Racault.

p. 78: Top: Thomas Couture, *Portrait of George Sand* (detail). Paris, Musée de la Vie Romantique. Bottom left: George Sand, *Marsh with Waterlilies* (*"The Devil's Pool"*), dendritic drawing. Private collection. Bottom right: George Sand's inkwell. Collection Christiane Sand. Photo: Jean-Pierre Guéno.

p. 79: Page (with heading "Ch 4 / sous les grands chênes") from the autograph of George Sand's *La Mare au Diable*. Paris, Bibliothèque Nationale de France, Département des Manuscrits, NAF 12231, fol. 54. In the final version of the novel, these lines appear at the beginning of chapter 7.

p. 80: Top: Nicolas-François Chifflart, *Portrait of Victor Hugo* (detail), c.1868. Paris, Maison de Victor Hugo. Photo: Photothèque des Musées de la Ville de Paris. Photo by Trocaz. Bottom: Chatillon, *Portrait of Léopoldine Hugo with a Book of Hours*. Paris, Maison de Victor Hugo. Photo: Photothèque des Musées de la Ville de Paris, photo by Trocaz.

p. 81: Autograph of "Demain, dès l'aube," poem by Victor Hugo published in *Contemplations* (1847). Paris, Bibliothèque Nationale de France, Département des Manuscrits, NAF, 13363, fol. 265.

p. 82: Top: Léon Bonnat, *Portrait of Alexandre Dumas the Younger* (detail). Châteaux de Versailles et de Trianon. Photo: RMN - Arnaudet. Bottom: *Camille*, watercolor by Maxime Rebière.

p. 83: Two pages from the autograph of Alexandre Dumas the Younger's dramatization of his novel *La Dame aux Camélias* (Act II, scene 8). Paris, Bibliothèque Nationale de France, Département des Manuscrits, NAF 24643, folios 51 and 52. Photos: BNF.

p. 84: Top: Adolphe Legros, daguerreotype of Gérard de Nerval, 1853–54. Bottom: *A Mid-Nineteenth-Century Theater Box*, watercolor by Maxime Rebière, 2000.

p. 85: Beginning of an early draft of what later became *Aurélia*. Paris, Bibliothèque Nationale de France, Département des Manuscrits, NAF 14481, fol. 2. Photo: BNF.

p. 86: Top: Gaston de Ségur, *The Comtesse de Ségur at the Age of Forty-Two*, watercolor. *Sophie's Misfortunes*, watercolors by Maxime Rebière, 2000.

p. 87: Page from the autograph of *Les Malheurs de Sophie* by the Comtesse de Ségur. Paris, Bibliothèque Labadens. Photo: Art-Go.

p. 88: Top: Nadar, photograph of Edmond and Jules de Goncourt. Private collection. Bottom: Detail of illustration on page 89.

p. 89: Page from the autograph of the *Journal de la vie littéraire*, by Edmond and Jules de Goncourt, with entries in both their hands (April 25 and April 28, 1858). Paris, Bibliothèque Nationale de France, Département des Manuscrits, NAF 22 440, fol. 94. Photo: BNF.

p. 90: Top: Charles Baudelaire, *Self-Portrait* (detail), brown ink and red crayon. Paris, Musée du Louvre, Département des Arts Graphiques (fonds Orsay). Photo: RMN - Michèle Bellot. Bottom: Detail of manuscript page illustrated on page 91.

p. 91: Page from autograph of *Mon Coeur Mis à Nu*. Paris, Bibliothèque Nationale de France, Département des Manuscrits, NAF 19800, fol. 21. Photo: BNF. This manuscript consists of 93 loose sheets of various dimensions mounted on 54 larger sheets of uniform dimensions (365 x 235 mm). Brown morocco binding. Ex-libris of Auguste Poulet-Malassis.

p. 92: Top: Antoine Bourdelle, *Édouard and Tristan Corbière* (detail). Collection Viollet. Bottom: Jules-Achille Noël, *A Street in Morlaix in 1830*, oil on canvas. Quimper, Musée des Beaux-Arts. Photo: Roger-Viollet.

p. 93: Last page, autograph of "La Complaincte Morlaisienne" by Tristan Corbière. Morlaix, Bibliothèque Municipale.

p. 94: Top: Jean-Baptiste Clesinger, *Portrait of Théophile Gautier* (detail), pastel and charcoal. Châteaux de Versailles et de Trianon. Bottom: Nicolas-Antoine Taunay, *Itinerant Players*, pen and wash. Reims, Musée des Beaux-Arts. Photos: RMN.

p. 95: First page, autograph of *Le Capitaine Fracasse* by Théophile Gautier. Paris, Bibliothèque de l'Institut, fonds Lovenjoul, C 415, fol. 3. Photo: J.-L. Charmet.

p. 96: Top: Iphigénie Cupont-Zipcy, *Portrait of Jules Michelet* (detail), oil on canvas. Châteaux de Versailles et de Trianon. Photo: RMN - Gérard Blot. Bottom: Page from the autograph of Michelet's *Journal*. Paris, Bibliothèque de l'Institut de France, ms 2201, fol. 133. Photo: J.-L. Charmet.

p. 97: Page from the autograph of Michelet's *Journal*. Bibliothèque de l'Institut de France, ms. 2201, fol. 593. Photo: J.-L. Charmet.

p. 98: Top: Eugène Giraud, *Portrait of Gustave Flaubert* (detail), c.1866. Châteaux de Versailles et de Trianon. Photo: RMN-Gérard Blot. Bottom: detail of manuscript page reproduced on page 99.

p. 99: Page from a partly unpublished autograph draft of *L'Éducation Sentimentale* by Gustave Flaubert. Paris, Bibliothèque Nationale de France, Département des Manuscrits, NAF 17599, fol. 88 verso. Photo: BNF.

p. 100: Top: Henri Fantin-Latour, portrait of Rimbaud, detail of *Still Life: Corner of a Table*, oil on canvas, 1872. Paris, Musée d'Orsay. Bottom: Another page from the autograph letter reproduced on page 101. Photo: BNF.

p. 101: Page from autograph of letter from Rimbaud to Paul Demeny dated May 15, 1871 (so-called "lettre du voyant"), with poem "Chant de Guerre Parisien." Paris, Bibliothèque Nationale de France, Département des Manuscrits, manuscripts without classification numbers. Photo: BNF.

p. 102: Top: Photograph of Jules Verne by Nadar. Bottom: Poster for a dramatization of *Around the World in Eighty Days* produced at the Théâtre du Châtelet in Paris. Nantes, Musée Jules-Verne. Photo: museum.

p. 103: Beginning of an autograph manuscript of *Le Tour du Monde en Quatre-Vingts Jours*. Paris, Bibliothèque Nationale de France, Département des Manuscrits, NAF 16998, fol. 1. Photo: BNF.

p. 104: Top: Joseph Delteil, *Portrait of Auguste de Villiers de L'Isle-Adam*, 1896. Photo: Roger-Viollet. Bottom: James Ensor, *Christ's Entry into Brussels in 1889*, oil on canvas, 1888. Los Angeles, J. Paul Getty Museum. Photo: ADAGP, Paris 2000.

p. 105: First page, autograph draft of "La Machine à Gloire," published (much revised) in *Contes Cruels*. Paris, Bibliothèque Nationale de France, Département des Manuscrits, fonds Villiers de L'Isle-Adam.

p. 106: Top: F.-A. Cazals, *Portrait of Paul Verlaine* detail). Paris, Musée de la Vie Romantique. Photo: Roger-Viollet. Bottom: William Samuel Horton, *The Tuileries*, oil on cardboard. Paris, Musée d'Orsay. Photo: RMN - C. Jean.

p. 107: Autograph of "Il pleure dans mon Coeur" by Paul Verlaine, published in *Romances sans Paroles*. Paris, Bibliothèque Littéraire Jacques-Doucet, B.VI 23. Photo: J.-L. Charmet.

p. 108: Top: Émile Lévy, *Portrait of Jules Barbey d'Aurevilly* (detail), 1881. Châteaux de Versailles et de Trianon. Photo: RMN - Jean Lewandowski. Bottom: Félicien Rops, frontispiece for *Les Diaboliques* by Barbey d'Aurevilly. Paris, Musée du Louvre, Département des Arts Graphiques. Photo: RMN - J. G. Berizzi.

p. 109: Page from an autograph of "Le Bonheur dans le Crime," a story published in *Les Diaboliques* by Jules Barbey d'Aurevilly. Paris, Bibliothèque Nationale de France, Département des Manuscrits, NAF 17372, fol. 54.

p. 110: Top: Eugène Carrière, *Alphonse Daudet and His Daughter Edmée* (detail). Paris, Musée d'Orsay. Photo: RMN - Jean Schormans. Bottom: Two facing pages from the autograph manuscript of *Le Doulou* by Alphonse Daudet. Private collection.

p. 111: Page from autograph draft of *Jack* by Alphonse Daudet. Private collection.

p. 112: Top: Édouard Manet, *Portrait of Stéphane Mallarmé* (detail), 1876. Paris, Musée d'Orsay. Bottom left: Paul Gauguin, *Afternoon of a Faun*, tamanu wood. Vulaines, Musée Stéphane Mallarmé. Photo: RMN - M. Bellot. Bottom right: Binding, autograph of *Monologue d'un Faune* by Stéphane Mallarmé. Paris, Bibliothèque Littéraire Jacques-Doucet, ms. 1161. Photo: J.-L. Charmet.

p. 113: First page, autograph of *Monologue d'un Faune*. Paris, Bibliothèque Littéraire Jacques-Doucet, ms. 1161. Photo: J.-L. Charmet.

p. 114: Top: Gustave Courbet, *Portrait of Jules Vallès* (detail), c.1861. Bottom: Detail of illustration on page 115.

p. 115: Page from autograph of *Le Bachelier* by Jules Vallès. Paris, Bibliothèque Nationale de France, Département des Manuscrits, fonds Vallès, vol. II, fol. 125. Photo: BNF.

p. 116: Top: Émile Cohl, *Caricature of Ernest Renan* (detail). Photo: Roger-Viollet. Bottom: Gabriel Prieur, *The Statue of Demosthenes in Athens*, 1847. Photo: Roger-Viollet.

p. 117: Page from the autograph of *Souvenirs d'Enfance et de Jeunesse* by Ernest Renan. Paris, Bibliothèque Nationale de France, Département des Manuscrits, NAF 11477, fol. 50. Photo: BNF.

p. 118: Top: François-Nicolas Feyen-Perrin, *Portrait of Guy de Maupassant* (detail), oil on wood, 1876. Châteaux de Versailles et de Trianon. Photo: RMN. Bottom: Edvard Munch, *The Scream*, 1893. Oslo, Nasjonalgalleriet. Photo © ADAGP, Paris 2000.

p. 119: First page, autograph of "La Horla" by Guy de Maupassant. Paris, Bibliothèque Nationale de France, Département des Manuscrits, NAF 23283, fol. 1. Photo: BNF.

p. 120: Top: Jean-Louis Forain, *Portrait of Georges-Charles, known as Joris-Karl Huysmans* (detail), pastel. Châteaux de Versailles et de Trianon. Photo: RMN. Bottom: Photograph of Robert de Montesquieu by Nadar. Huysmans's character Des Esseintes was largely inspired by Robert de Montesquieu. Private collection.

p. 121: Page from the autograph of *À Rebours* by Joris-Karl Huysmans. Paris, Bibliothèque Nationale de France, Département des Manuscrits, NAF 15761, fol. 38. Photo: BNF.

p. 122: Top: Jean-François Raffaëlli, *Portrait of Émile Zola* (detail), 1892, attached to the cover of a parchment binding of a copy of the first edition of *L'Assommoir*. Paris, Bibliothèque Nationale de France. Photo: BNF. Bottom: Watercolor by Maxime Rebière, 2000.

p. 123: Cover pages, autograph copies of four novels in the Rougon-Macquart series by Émile Zola: *Au Bonheur des Dames*, *Germinal*, *L'Assommoir*, and *La Terre*. The cover page of the *La Terre* manuscript was reconstituted by Alexandrine Zola, the author's wife, on June 9, 1904, the original having been mislaid in the meantime (Émile Zola died in 1901). Paris, Bibliothèque Nationale de France, Département des Manuscrits: NAF 10275, fol. 1; NAF 10305, fol. 1; NAF 10270 fol. 1; NAF 10335, fol. 1.

p. 124: Top: Photograph of Jules Renard by Ph. Bert. Photo: Archives Larousse-Giraudon. Bottom: Table of contents page and text page, autograph of *Poil de Carotte* by Jules Renard. Nevers, Archives Départementales de la Nièvre, cote AD Nièvre, manuscrit 136. Photo: archives.

p. 125: Page from the autograph of *Poil de Carotte* by Jules Renard. Nevers, Archives Départementales de la Nièvre, cote AD Nièvre, manuscrit 136. Photo: archives.

p. 126: Top: Léon Bloy, *Self-Portrait*, November 1863. Private collection. Bottom: Detail of maunscript page illustrated on page 127.

p. 127: Page from the autograph of *Mon Journal* by Léon Bloy. La Rochelle, Bibliothèque Municipale, ms. 2946. Photo: J + M.

p. 128: Top: M. Amilly, *Pierre Loti in Oriental Costume* (detail), 1912. Private collection. Photo: Roger-Viollet. Bottom: Edmond Hedouin, *The Pig Market at Saint-Jean-de-Luz*, oil on canvas. Bayonne, Musée Bonnat. Photo: RMN - R.G. Ojeda.

p. 129: Page from autograph of *Ramuntcho* by Pierre Loti. Paris, Bibliothèque Nationale de France, Département des Manuscrits, NAF 18188, fol. 26. Photo: BNF.

p. 130: Top: Photograph by Van Bosh of Edmond Rostand in academic garb (detail), 1901. Paris, Bibliothèque Nationale de France, Département des Arts du Spectacle. Photo: BNF. Bottom: *Cyrano de Bergerac*, watercolor by Maxime Rebière, 2000.

p. 131: There are no known autographs of *Cyrano de Bergerac*. All that survives is this excerpt from Cyrano's speech in Act 2, scene 7, which Rostand copied into a guest book at his host's request. His wife also inscribed a few lines. Private collection.

p. 132: Top: Photograph of Octave Mirbeau. Paris, Bibliothèque Nationale de France, Cabinet des Estampes. Photo: BNF. Bottom: Proposed cover design by Octave Mirbeau for *Le Journal d'une Femme de Chambre*. Paris, Bibliothèque Labadens. Photo: Art-Go.

p. 133: First page, autograph of *Le Journal d'une Femme de Chambre* by Octave Mirbeau. Paris, Bibliothèque Labadens. Photo: Art-Go.

p. 134: Top: Philip Alexis de Laszlo, *Portrait of Anna, Comtesse de Noailles* (detail), oil on canvas. Paris, Musée d'Orsay. Photo: RMN - C. Jean. Bottom: Photograph of Maurice Barrès by Nadar.

p. 135: Autograph of "L'Empreinte" by Anna, Comtesse de Noailles, published in *Le Coeur Innombrable*, which she dedicated to Maurice Barrès. Paris, Bibliothèque Nationale de France, Département des Manuscrits, NAF 23730, fol. 13. Photo: BNF.

p. 136: Top: Hermann-Paul, *Portrait of Alfred Jarry* (detail). Crayon, ink, and gouache. Paris, Musée Picasso. Photo: RMN - J.G. Berizzi. Bottom left: Edmond Heuzé, lithograph illustration for an edition of *Ubu Roi* published by Tériade in 1966. Laval, Bibliothèque Municipal. Photo: Bertrand Boufflet © ADAGP, Paris 2000. Rottom right: Alfred Jarry, *True Portrait of King Ubu*, woodcut for the first edition of *Ubu Roi*, 1896.

p. 137: Page from the autograph of *Ubu sur la Butte* by Alfred Jarry. Laval, Bibliothèque Municipale. Photo: Bertrand Boufflet.

p. 138: Top: Daniel de Monfreid, *Portrait of Victor Segalen* (detail). Bottom: Page from the *Journal des Îles*, kept by Victor Segalen during his Polynesian sojourn of 1903–04. Paris, Bibliothèque Nationale de France, Département des Manuscrits, NAF 25786, fol. 56 recto. Photo: BNF.

p. 139: Page from the autograph of *Les Immémoriaux* by Victor Segalen. Paris, Bibliothèque Nationale de France, Département des Manuscrits, NAF 25789, fol. 1 bis. Photo: BNF.

p. 140: Top: Photograph of Paul Claudel by Bernand, 1953. Bottom: Félix Labisse, set design (gouache) for the 1948 production of *Le Partage de Midi* by Paul Claudel, directed by Jean-Louis Barrault. Photo: © ADAGP, Paris 2000.

p. 141: Page from an autograph early draft of *Partage de Midi* by Paul Claudel. Paris, Bibliothèque Nationale de France, Département des Manuscrits, Fonds Claudel, Fol. 62 verso. Photo: BNF.

p. 142: Top: Photograph of Colette c.1900. Private collection. Bottom left: A mandarin yellow Parker U.S.A Duofold Senior pen like the one with which Colette wrote. All rights reserved. Bottom right: *The Tendrils of the Vine*, watercolor by Maxime Rebière, 2000.

p. 143: Three pages from the autograph of "Les Vrilles de la Vigne" by Colette (first version). Paris, Bibliothèque Nationale de France, Département des Manuscrits, NAF 18640, fols. 35, 36, 37. Photos: BNF.

p. 144: Top: Paul Albert Laurens, *Portrait of André Gide* (detail), 1924. Paris, Musée d'Orsay. Photo: RMN - Jean Schormans. Bottom: "Cross of Alisa" necklace with emerald cross. It belonged to Madeleine Rondeaux, André Gide's cousin, and inspired the necklace worn by the heroine of Gide's *La Porte Étroite*. Paris, Bibliothèque Littéraire Jacques-Doucet. Photo: J.-L. Charmet.

p. 145: Page from an early draft of *La Porte Étroite* by André Gide. Gide went through several drafts prior to publication, so this version differs considerably from the final text. Paris, Bibliothèque Nationale de France, Département des Manuscrits, NAF 25174, fol. 116 recto. Photo: BNF.

p. 146: Top: Charles-Émile Carolus-Duran, *Georges Feydeau Reading* (detail), oil on canvas. Lille, Musée des Beaux-Arts. Photo: RMN - P. Bernard. Bottom: scene from a 1967 production of *La Puce à l'Oreille*, Paris, Théâtre Marigny. Photo: Lipnitzki-Viollet.

p. 147: Page from an autograph draft of *La Puce à l'Oreille*. It differs slightly from the final text. Paris, Bibliothèque Nationale de France, Département des Manuscrits, NAF 16256, fol. 12. Photo: BNF.

p. 148: Top: Léon Deshairs, *Portrait of Charles Péguy*, crayon, 1894. Orléans, Centre Charles-Péguy. Bottom: Jean-Baptiste Corot, *Chartres Cathedral*, oil on canvas, 1830 (retouched 1872). Paris, Musée du Louvre. Photos: RMN - C. Jean.

p. 149: Four pages, autograph of "La Présentation de La Beauce à Notre-Dame de Chartres" by Charles Péguy, 1912. Orléans, Centre Charles-Péguy. Photo: RMN.

p. 150: Top: Marie-Louise-Clémentine Breslau, *Portrait of Anatole-François Thibault, known as Anatole France*, pastel on card. Châteaux de Versailles et de Trianon. Photo: RMN - Gérard Blot. Bottom: Charles Louis Muller, *Summons of the Last Victims of the Terror*, oil sketch for the large painting now in the Musée de la Révolution Française in Vizille, c.1850. Paris, Musée du Louvre. Photo: RMN - Gérard Blot.

p. 151: Page from an incomplete autograph of *Les Dieux Ont Soif* by Anatole France. Paris, Bibliothèque Nationale de France, Département des Manuscrits, NAF 15388, fol. 52. Photo: BNF.

p. 152: Top: Giorgio De Chirico, *Premonitory Portrait of Apollinaire*, 1914. Paris, Musée National d'Art Moderne. Photo: © ADAGP, Paris 2000. Bottom: Autograph of "Tristesse d'une Étoile" by Guillaume Apollinaire, later published in *Calligrammes*. Paris, Bibliothèque Nationale de France, Département des Manuscrits, NAF 25609, fol. 4. Photo: BNF.

p. 153: Autograph of "Le Pont Mirabeau" by Guillaume Apollinaire, later published in *Alcools*. Paris, Bibliothèque Nationale de France, Département des Manuscrits, NAF 25608, fol. 1. Photo: BNF.

p. 154: Top: Jacques-Émile Blanche, *Portrait of Marcel Proust* (detail), c. 1895. Photo: © ADAGP, Paris 2000. Bottom: Facing pages from notebook autograph of *Le Temps Retrouvé* by Marcel Proust, with attached sheets of revisions. Paris, Bibliothèque Nationale de France, Département des Manuscrits. Photo: BNF.

p. 155: Page from autograph draft of *Du Coté de Chez Swann* ("Ouverture"). Paris, Bibliothèque Nationale de France, Département des Manuscrits, NAF 16725, fol. 103. Photo: BNF.

p. 156: Top: Photograph of Alain-Fournier. Archives Alain Rivière. Right: Three pages from a draft of *Le Grand Meaulnes* by Alain-Fournier. Archives Alain Rivière. Photos: Jean-Pierre Guéno. Bottom left: *"Le Grand Meaulnes,"* watercolor by Maxine Rebière, 2000.

p. 157: Page from a draft of *Le Grand Meaulnes*. Archives Alain Rivière. Photo: Jean-Pierre Guéno.

p. 158: Top: Jacques-Émile Blanche, *Study for a Portrait of Jean Cocteau* (detail). Rouen, Musée des Beaux-Arts. Photo: Roger-Viollet. © ADAGP, Paris 2000. Bottom: Self-portrait by Jean Cocteau from a letter to Paul Valéry, October 1924. Paris, Bibliothèque Nationale de France, Département des Manuscrits, NAF 14064, fol. 13. Photo: BNF.

p. 159: Autograph of "La forêt qui marche" by Jean Cocteau, 1914. Paris, Bibliothèque Historique de la Ville de Paris. Photo: library.

p. 160: Top: Marie Laurencin, *Portrait of Max Jacob*, 1907. Orléans, Musée des Beaux-Arts. Photo: RMN. © ADAGP, Paris 2000. Bottom: Illustration by Max Jacob for *Le Cornet à Dés*. Orléans, Bibliothèque Municipale, manuscrit 2535. Photo: Camara.

p. 161: Autograph sheet with illustrations and three poems later published in *Le Cornet à Dés* by Max Jacob. Orléans, Bibliothèque Municipale, manuscrit 2535. Photo: Camara.

p. 162: Top: Photograph of Blaise Cendrars, c. 1919. Bottom left: Blaise Cendrars, cover design for *Poèmes Élastiques*. Paris, Bibliothèque Nationale de France, Département des Manuscrits, NAF 18524. Photo: BNF. Bottom right: detail of illustration on page 163.

p. 163: Autograph (with illustrations) of "Journal" by Blaise Cendrars, later published in *Poèmes Élastiques*. Paris, Bibliothèque Nationale de France, Département des Manuscrits, NAF 18524, fol. 4. Photo: BNF.

p. 164: Left: Francis Picabia, *Portrait of André Breton*, drawing, 1920. Photo: © ADAGP, Paris 2000. Right: Autograph by André Breton for *Les Champs Magnétiques* (beginning of "II. Saisons"). Paris, Bibliothèque Nationale de France, Département des Manuscrits, NAF 18303, fol. 1. Photo: BNF.

p. 165: Left: Autograph by Philippe Soupault for *Les Champs Magnétiques* (beginning of "La Glace sans Tain"). Paris, Bibliothèque Nationale de France, Département des Manuscrits, NAF 18303, fol. 14. Photo: BNF. Right: Francis Picabia, *Portrait of Philippe Soupault*, drawing, 1920. Photo: © ADAGP, Paris 2000.

p. 166: Top: Photograph of Robert Desnos by Man Ray incorporated into the autograph of "Amour des Homonyms" and published in *Corps et Biens*. Paris, Bibliothèque Nationale de France, Département des Manuscrits, NAF 25096, fol. 2. Photo: © ADAGP, Paris 2000. Bottom: Facing pages from the autograph of "Amour des Homonyms" by Robert Desnos. Paris, Bibliothèque Nationale de France, Département des Manuscrits, NAF 25096. Photo: BNF.

p. 167: First page, autograph of "Amour des Homonyms" by Robert Desnos. Paris, Bibliothèque Nationale de France, Département des Manuscrits, NAF 25096, fol. 35. Photo: BNF.

p. 168: Top: Jacques-Émile Blanche, *Study for Full-Length Portrait of Raymond Radiguet* (detail), oil on canvas. Rouen, Musée des Beaux-Arts. Photo: Roger-Viollet. © ADAGP, Paris 2000. Bottom left: Kees Van Dongen, *The Archangel's Tango*, 1930. Nice, Musée des Beaux-Arts Jules-Chéret. © ADAGP, Paris 2000. Bottom right: Kees Van Dongen, *The Revelers*, oil on canvas. Troyes, Musée d'Art Moderne. Photo: RMN - Gérard Blot. © ADAGP, Paris 2000.

p. 169: First page of a draft of *Le Bal du Comte d'Orgel* by Raymond Radiguet. The text was much revised prior to publication. Paris, Bibliothèque Nationale de France, Département des Manuscrits, NAF 18778, fol. 1.

p. 170: Top: Photograph (detail) of Jules Romains with Louis Jouvet and Pierre Renoir, taken on the occasion of a revival of *Knock* in October of 1947. Photo: Lipnitzky-Viollet. Bottom left: Louis Jouvet and Guy Favières in the first production of *Knock*, December 1923. Photo: Harlingue-Viollet. Bottom right: Poster for *Knock* by Becan, known as Cahn. Paris, Bibliothèque Nationale de France, Département des Arts du Spectacle, collection Louis Jouvet. Photo: © ADAGP, Paris 2000.

p. 171: Page from the autograph of *Knock* (Act II) by Jules Romains. Paris, Bibliothèque Nationale de France, Département des Manuscrits, fonds Jules Romains, fol. 74. Photo: BNF.

p. 172: Top: Photograph of Pierre Drieu La Rochelle. Collection Mme Jean Drieu La Rochelle. Photo: Cliché Art-Go. Bottom: Writing implements of Pierre Drieu La Rochelle. Photo: Cliché Art-Go.

p. 173: Page from the autograph of *Feu Follet* by Pierre Drieu La Rochelle. Photo: Cliché Art-Go.

p. 174: Top: Jacques-Émile Blanche, *Study for the Portrait of François Mauriac* (detail). Rouen, Musée des Beaux-Arts. Photo: Roger-Viollet. © ADAGP, Paris 2000. Bottom left: Title page with drawing of a viper, autograph of *Noeud de Vipères* by François Mauriac. Paris, Bibliothèque Littéraire Jacques-Doucet, MRC 34, fol. 1. Photo: K.-L. Charmet. Bottom right: Gustave Moreau, *Studies of Snakes (after Johann Wagler, "Descriptiones et Icones Amphibiorum") for "Hercules and the Lernaean Hydra,"* watercolor. Paris, Musée Gustave Moreau. Photo: RMN - R.G. Ojeda.

p. 175: Page from the autograph of *Noeud de Vipères* by François Mauriac. Paris, Bibliothèque Littéraire Jacques-Doucet, MRC rol. 1. Photo: J.-L. Charmet.

p. 176: Top: Photograph of André Malraux in April 1945. Photo: Rapho - Le Cluziat. Bottom: Detail from another page of the autograph of *La Condition Humaine* by André Malraux. Paris, Bibliothèque Nationale de France, Département des Manuscrits, NAF 16587, fol. 409. Photo: BNF.

p. 177: Page from the autograph of *La Condition Humaine* by André Malraux. Paris, Bibliothèque Nationale de France, Département des Manuscrits, NAF 16587, fol. 1.

p. 178: Top: Photograph of Marcel Aymé, 1933. Collection Mme Françoise Arnaud. Photo: Cliché Art-Go. Bottom: Mare made of green glass that sat on Marcel Aymé's desk until the end of his life. Collection Mme Françoise Arnaud. Photo: Cliché Art-Go.

p. 179: First page, autograph of *La Jument Verte*. Collection Mme Colette Magne and Mme Françoise Arnaud. Photo: Cliché Art-Go.

p. 180: Top: Photograph of Jean Giono by Gisèle Freund, 1968. Bottom: First pages of an autograph of *Que Ma Joie Demeure* by Jean Giono. Avignon, Bibliothèque Municipale Classée, ms. 6720. Photo: F. Lepeltier.

p. 181: Page from the autograph of *Que Ma Joie Demeure* by Jean Giono. Avignon, Bibliothèque Municipale Classée, ms. 6720. Photo: F. Lepeltier.

p. 182: Top: Photograph of Louis Aragon by Gisèle Freund, 1939. Bottom left: Binding for Louis Aragon's *Les Beaux-Quartiers* made by Georges Leroux in 1967. Photo: © ADAGP, Paris 2000. Bottom right: Poster for a television film of Aragon's *Les Beaux-Quartiers*, 1983. Private collection.

p. 183: First page, autograph of *Les Beaux Quartiers* by Louis Aragon. Paris, Bibliothèque Nationale de France, Département des Manuscrits, NAF 18171, fol. 1. Photo: BNF.

p. 184: Top: Photograph of Georges Bernanos, 1929. Photo: Photothèque Plon. Bottom: *"Journal d'un Curé de Campagne,"* watercolor by Maxime Rebière, 2000.

p. 185: First page, autograph fine copy for the printer, *Journal d'un Curé de Campagne* by Georges Bernanos. Paris, Bibliothèque Nationale de France, Département des Manuscrits, fonds Bernanos, fol. 1. Photo: BNF.

p. 186: Top: Photograph of Simone Weil in New York in 1942 (detail). Bottom: Simone Weil wearing mechanic's overalls in Barcelona, photograph. Paris, Bibliothèque Nationale de France, Département des Manuscrits. Photos: BNF.

p. 187: Page from a partial autograph of "Expérience de la vie d'usine, lettre ouverte à Jules Romains." Paris, Bibliothèque Nationale de France, Département des Manuscrits, fonds Simone Weil, fol. 257. Photo: BNF.

p. 188: Top: Photograph of Jean-Paul Sartre by Brassaï, 1945. Bottom: Albrecht Dürer, *Melancholia I*, engraving, 1514. Sartre's original title for *La Nausée*, "La Mélancholie," was inspired by this celebrated image.

p. 189: Page from the autograph of *La Nausée* by Jean-Paul Sartre. Paris, Bibliothèque Nationale de France, Département des Manuscrits, NAF 17900, fol. 10. Photo: BNF.

p. 190: Top: Alexis Léger (Saint-John Perse) on his property in Provence, Les Vigneaux, c. 1958. Archives de la Fondation Saint-John Perse. Bottom: Passage from an autograph manuscript: "To the often asked question: 'Why do you write?' the poet's response will always be brief: 'To live better.'" Archives de la Fondation Saint-John Perse. Photo: Jean-Bernard.

p. 191: Page from an early draft of *Exil* by Saint-John Perse. Archives de la Fondation Saint-John Perse. Photo: Jean-Bernard.

p. 192: Top: Photograph of Antoine de Saint-Exupéry by John Phillips, May 1944. Bottom, left and right: Drawings by Saint-Exupéry from the illustrated manuscript of *Le Petit Prince*. Photos: © Pierpont Morgan Library and Estate of Antoine de Saint-Exupéry.

p. 193: Page from the illustrated manuscript of *Le Petit Prince*. New York, Pierpont Morgan Library. Photo: © Pierpont Morgan Library and Estate of Antoine de Saint-Exupéry.

p. 194: Top: *Henry de Montherlant*, phototype of the painting by Mariette Lydis, 1949. Collection T. Bodin. Photo © ADAGP, Paris, 2000. Bottom: Jean-Louis Barrault and Violette Verdy in the 1950 production of *Malatesta* at the Théâtre Marigny, Paris, directed by Barrault. Photo: Lipnitzki-Viollet.

p. 195: Page from a draft of Malatesta by Henry de Montherlant. Collection Jean-Claude Barat.

p. 196: Top: Jacques-Émile Blanche, *Study for a Portrait of Jean Giraudoux* (detail), 1924. Rouen, Musée des Beaux-Arts. Photo: Roger-Viollet. © ADAGP, Paris 2000. Bottom: Marguerite Moreno, Louis Jouvet, and Monique Mélinand in *La Folle de Chaillot*, Théâtre de l'Athénée, Paris, December 1945. Photo: Roger-Viollet.

p. 197: Page from autograph of *La Folle de Chaillot* (beginning of Act II). Paris, Bibliothèque Nationale de France, Département des Manuscrits, NAF 25379, fol. 73. Photo: BNF.

p. 198: Top: Photograph of Albert Camus by Yousuf Karsh. Paris, Bibliothèque Nationale de France, Département des Estampes. Photo: BNF. Bottom: Philippe Zilcken, *View of Algiers*, oil on canvas. Paris, Musée d'Orsay. Photo: RMN - H. Lewandowski.

p. 199: First page, autograph draft of *La Peste* by Albert Camus. Paris, Bibliothèque Nationale de France, Département des Manuscrits, NAF 25248, fol. 1. Photo: BNF.

p. 200: Top: Victor Brauner, *Portrait of René Char*, oil on canvas, 1934. Paris, Bibliothèque Littéraire Jacques-Doucet. Photo: J.-L. Charmet. © ADAGP, Paris 2000. Bottom: Autograph of "Nous ne jalousons pas les dieux," poem by René Char published in *L'Amitié de Georges Braque*. Paris, Bibliothèque Nationale de France, Département des Manuscrits, fonds René Char. For works of Georges Braque: © ADAGP, Paris 2000.

p. 201: Autograph (detail) of "Le Thor," poem by René Char published in *L'Amitié de Georges Braque*. Paris, Bibliothèque Nationale de France, Département des Manuscrits, fonds René Char. For works of Georges Braque: © ADAGP, Paris 2000.

p. 202: Top: Photograph of Boris Vian, 1948. Photo: Lipnitzki-Viollet. Bottom: Detail of page illustrated on page 203.

p. 203: First page, autograph of *L'Écume des Jours* by Boris Vian. Paris, Bibliothèque Nationale de France, Département des Manuscrits, fonds Boris Vian, fol. 1. Photo: BNF.

p. 204: Top: Jacques Audibert in 1950. Photo: Lipnitzki-Viollet. Bottom: Two scenes from the first production of *Le Mal Court* in 1947, starring Suzanne Flon and Georges Vitaly and directed by Vitaly. Photos: Lipnitzki-Viollet.

p. 205: Page from the autograph of *Le Mal Court* (Act III) by Jacques Audiberti, which premiered at the Théâtre de la Poche, Paris, on June 17, 1947. Paris, Bibliothèque Nationale de France, Département des Manuscrits, n.c., fol. 16. Paris, BNF.

p. 206: Top: Photograph of Cioran. Photo: Louis Monier/Gamma. Bottom: Hieronymous Bosch, *The Garden of Earthly Delights*, "Musical Hell" panel (details). Madrid, Museo del Prado. Photo: museum.

p. 207: Page from the autograph of *Précis de Décomposition* ("Généologie du fanatisme") by Cioran. Paris, Bibliothèque Nationale de France, Département des Manuscrits, NAF 18721, fol. 3. Photo: BNF.

p. 208: Top: Photograph of Eugène Ionesco at his desk. Collection Eugène Ionesco. Photo: Art-Go. Bottom left: Inkwell of Eugène Ionesco. Photo: Art-Go. Bottom right: Drawing by Saul Steinberg inspired by *La Cantatrice Chauve* by Eugène Ionesco, signed "à Eugène Ionesco amicalement / New York 1958." Photo: Art-Go.

p. 209: Page from the autograph of *La Cantatrice Chauve* by Eugène Ionesco. Collection Eugène Ionesco. Photo: Art-Go.

p. 210: Top: Photograph of Francis Ponge by Louis Monier. Photo: Louis Monier/Gamma. Bottom: "*Les Olives*," watercolor by Maxime Rebière, 2000.

p. 211: Autograph of the poem "Les Olives" by Francis Ponge. Paris, Bibliothèque Nationale de France, Département des Manuscrits, NAF 17628, folios 6, 7, 8, 9. Photos: BNF.

p. 212: Top: René-Guy Cadou in 1949. Photo: collection Mme Cadou. Bottom: Cadou's house in Louisfert. Photo: Collection Mme Cadou.

p. 213: Autograph of the poem "Celui qui entre par hasard" by Louis-Guy Cadou. Collection Mme Cadou.

p. 214: Top: Max Ernst, *Portrait of Paul Éluard*, with a double dedication by Ernst and Éluard to Louis Aragon. Private collection. Photo: © ADAGP, Paris 2000. Bottom: *"Liberté," poème d'Éluard*, tapestry by Fernand Léger. Biot, Musée Fernand-Léger. Photo: RMN - Gérard Blot. Photo: © ADAGP, Pars 2000.

p. 215: Autograph of the poem "Ailleurs, ici, partout" by Paul Éluard, published in *Poésie Ininterrompue II* (1953). Paris, Bibliothèque Littéraire Jacques-Doucet, epsilon II 34, fol. 3. Photo: J.-L. Charmet.

p. 216: Top: Michel Butor. Photo: Louis Monier/Gamma. Bottom: Max Ernst: *The Hat Makes the Man*, 1920. Photo: © ADAGP, Paris 2000.

p. 217: First sheet of autograph draft of *Passage de Milan* by Michel Butor. The novel was considerably revised prior to publication. Paris, Bibliothèque Nationale de France, Département des Manuscrits, fonds Grenier. Photo: BNF.

p. 218: Top: Fernand Desnos, *Portrait of Georges Schehadé*, c. 1960. Photo: © ADAGP, Paris 2000. Upper right: Poster for the first production of *Le Voyage* by Georges Schehadé. Bottom left: Drawing of a steamer by Georges Schehadé in the margin of the autograph of *Le Voyage*. Photo: Fonds Schehadé-IMEC. Bottom right: Jean-Denis Malclès, set design for the first scene of *Le Voyage*. Photo: ADAGP, Paris 2000.

p. 219: Page from the autograph of *Le Voyage* by Georges Schehadé. Photo: Fonds Schehadé-IMEC.

p. 220: Top: Marcel Pagnol with his daughter Estelle in 1952. Archives Jacqueline Pagnol. Photo: Art-Go. Bottom left: Inkwell and pen of Marcel Pagnol. Archives Jacqueline Pagnol. Photo: Art-Go. Bottom right: Page from the autograph of *Manon des Sources* by Marcel Pagnol. Archives Jacqueline Pagnol. Photo: Art-Go.

p. 221: Page from the autograph of *Manon des Sources* by Marcel Pagnol. Archives Jacqueline Pagnol. Photo: Art-Go.

p. 222: Top: Marguerite Yourcenar in 1954 (detail). Anonymous photograph in the collection of Houghton Library, Harvard University. Bottom: Pieter Bruegel the Elder, *Hunters in the Snow (January)* (detail), oil on panel, 1565. Vienna, Kunsthistorisches Museum. Photo: museum.

p. 223: Page from the typed manuscript of *L'Oeuvre au Noir* by Marguerite Yourcenar with autograph revisions. Paris, Bibliothèque Nationale de France, Département des Manuscrits, fonds Grenier. Photo: BNF.

p. 224: Top: Georges Perec. Photograph Louis Monier/Gamma. Bottom: Two pages from the "Cahier des charges" of *La Vie: mode d'emploi* by Georges Perec. Paris, Bibliothèque de l'Arsenal, fonds Perec. Photos: Art-Go.

p. 225: Autograph draft of the opening of *La Vie: Mode d'Emploi* by Georges Perec. Paris, Bibliothèque de l'Arsenal, fonds Perec. Photo: Art-Go.

p. 226: Top: Marguerite Duras in October 1984. Photo: Louis Monier/Gamma. Bottom: "*The Lover*," watercolors by Maxime Rebière, 2000.

p. 227: Page from autograph working drafts that evolved into *L'Amant* by Marguerite Duras. Photo: © Fonds M. Duras/IMEC.

p. 228: Top: Andrée Chedid. Photo: Flammarion. Right: Autograph of the poem "Toi - Moi" by Andrée Chedid. Photo: © IMEC/fonds Andrée Chedid. Bottom: Detail, mythological papyrus of Neskapsouty, third intermediary period. Paris, Musée du Louvre, Département des Antiquités Egyptiennes. Photo: RMN - Chuzeville.

p. 229: Typed manuscript of "La Balade des siècles" by Andrée Chedid with autograph corrections in inks of various colors. Photo: © IMEC/fonds Andrée Chedid.

INDEX